CHINESE COOKING SECRETS

CHINESE COOKING SECRETS

KAREN LEE

Written with Alaxandra Branyon

Doubleday & Company, Inc., Garden City, New York
1984

52172

ACKNOWLEDGMENTS

The willingness of the author to share her "secrets" with anyone who has an interest in preparing special meals for family and friends is the first step in the making of a good cookbook. There must also be great recipes, or "show stoppers," the kind that win you friends for life. For this, I must thank my experimental class who faithfully met every Thursday night for two years to test virtually all the recipes in this book. Some nights we ate like royalty, and sometimes we went home hungry. Among this group, Stephanie Franklin deserves special thanks.

The person who pulled this whole project together is my writing collaborator, Alaxandra Branyon. Without her endless hours of research, concern, encouragement, and expertise, I could never have completed this challenging work.

I was fortunate to be assigned Karen Van Westering, a well-seasoned editor, with her invaluable suggestions and guidance, and I would also like to thank Shaye Areheart.

KAREN LEE

DESIGNED BY LAURENCE ALEXANDER

Photographs by Ken Korsh

Map by Judy Nemec

Library of Congress Cataloging in Publication Data

Lee, Karen.
Chinese cooking secrets.

1. Cookery, Chinese.   I. Branyon, Alaxandra.
II. Title.
TX724.5.C5L454   1983   641.5951

ISBN 0-385-15514-80-X
Library of Congress Catalog Card Number 80-1724
Copyright © 1984 by Karen Lee

*I dedicate this book to
my son Todd Hartman
for his unflagging patience.*

List of Photographs

PREPARATIONS AND TECHNIQUES ILLUSTRATED IN THIS BOOK

	PAGES
Preparing Bok Choy	59
Peeling, Shredding, and Mincing Ginger Root	62–63
Shredding Leeks	65
Stringing Snow Peas	65
Shredding Snow Peas	66
Triangle-Cutting Red or Green Peppers	67
Shredding Hairy Melon	67
Peeling and Slicing Fresh Water Chestnuts	69
Roll-Oblique-Cutting Carrots	70
Slicing and Shredding Bamboo Shoots	75
Slicing Lotus Root	79
Dicing Chinese Dried Mushrooms	80–81
Shaping Shrimp Balls in Rice Paper	98–99
Filling and Pleating Shao Mai	100–1
Filling and Pleating Jao-Tze	102–3
Filling and Shaping Steamed Roast Pork Buns	108–10
Filling and Rolling Tricolor Shrimp Roll	116–17
Filling Vegetable Rolls with Sesame Seed Sauce	128–29
Butterflying Shrimp: Method I and Method II	178–79
Splitting Shrimp	183
Boning a Whole Chicken	193–97
Dicing, Slicing, and Shredding Boneless Chicken	198–99
Cutting and Reassembling Whole Cooked Poultry	200–2
Removing Fat from Duck	234–35
Preparing a CT Butt for Barbecued Roast Pork	256–57
Slicing and Shredding Flank Steak	278–79
Making an Egg Pancake	315
Flipping a Chinese Omelet	318
Flipping Noodles for Lo Mein	324

Contents

HOW TO USE THIS BOOK   *1*

Chapter 1   **HISTORY OF THE CUISINE**   *3*

Chapter 2   **REGIONAL DISTINCTIONS**   *9*

Chapter 3   **EATING IN CHINA TODAY**   *23*

Chapter 4   **THE CHINESE MEAL**   *29*

Chapter 5   **SPECIAL COOKING TECHNIQUES**   *37*

Chapter 6   **EQUIPMENT**   *51*

Chapter 7   **FRESH VEGETABLES AND CUTTING TECHNIQUES**   *57*

Chapter 8   **SPECIAL INGREDIENTS**   *71*

Chapter 9   **APPETIZERS AND DIM SUM**   *89*

Chapter 10   **SOUPS**   *133*

Chapter 11   **FISH AND SHELLFISH**   *147*

Chapter 12   **CHICKEN**   *191*

Chapter 13   **DUCK AND SQUAB**   *231*

Chapter 14   **PORK**   *253*

Chapter 15   **BEEF**   *275*

Chapter 16   **VEGETABLES**   *289*

Chapter 17   **EGGS, RICE, AND STARCHY PREPARATIONS**   *313*

Chapter 18   **DIPS AND SAUCES**   *333*

Chapter 19   **DESSERTS**   *345*

Bibliography and Mail Order Sources   *357*

Index   *359*

CHINESE COOKING SECRETS

HOW TO USE THIS BOOK

Groupings of ingredients within a recipe mean that these ingredients can go into the same bowl or cup and will be added to the wok at the same time. This will help the reader organize the trays on which all the ingredients for any given dish are placed before cooking.

Next to certain ingredients there appears either one or two asterisks: one asterisk (*) means that this is a separate recipe and it is listed in the index. When the * sign refers the reader to a sauce for which there is a recipe, the reader may prefer to buy the sauce instead of making it. This of course is always an alternative; however, I believe the difference between good and great Chinese cooking is in the making of one's own sauces.

Two asterisks (**) mean that this is an ingredient requiring some special treatment before it is used within the recipe and it is listed in Chapter 8, "Special Ingredients." An example is *Chinese mushrooms, soaked.*** As a reminder to the cook, *reconstituting mushrooms, tree ears, and tiger lily buds* is mentioned as a first step in the recipe under *Preparation*.

It is crucial that the reader read Chapter 5, "Special Cooking Techniques," and Chapter 7, "Fresh Vegetables and Cutting Techniques," before trying one recipe, as well as the special boning and cutting techniques explained before the meat, fish and poultry chapters. With these techniques, a beginner can use and have wonderful results with this book, as I am in effect introducing in most cases intermediate and advanced recipes with nothing left to the imagination. Even advanced cooks, looking only to increase their repertoire, will benefit. To avoid repetition, I have not given lengthy explanations as to how you prepare various vegetables. This information is described and illustrated in Chapter 7, "Fresh Vegetables and Cutting Techniques."

In recipes that call for sliced or shredded meat, the first instruction under *Preparation* is to "partially freeze," as partially frozen meat is infinitely easier to cut. All poultry, pork, and beef that is to be sliced or shredded should be placed in the freezer for 1 to 1 1/2 hours, depending on the thickness of the meat and the temperature of the freezer. If the meat is already frozen, then let it partially defrost until the desired consistency is achieved.

I have called for small, medium, or large shrimp, and also have given the number of shrimp per pound in order to avoid confusion, as one person's idea of small is not necessarily another person's idea of small.

Unless otherwise specified, the flour called for in a recipe is all-purpose flour. The flour measurements for batters and doughs are based on the *light* measurement of unsifted flour. To obtain a light measurement, some air must be incorporated into the flour. This is done by taking a scoop of flour and placing it in the measuring cup, then leveling it off with the square end of a chopstick or the blunt edge of a knife. This will yield a lighter measurement than placing the measuring cup itself directly into the flour bin. When sifted flour is called for, sift the flour before measuring.

Unless otherwise specified, all measurements are level.

All temperatures are in degrees Fahrenheit.

In recipe ingredients, oil is always listed last (except for any garnish).

The yield at the end of each recipe varies because it is relative to the number of dishes being served. If you are serving only one dish, the number of servings it will yield will be the minimum number. If you are serving other dishes along with it, it will go farther and will yield up to the maximum number of servings. The Chinese prefer to serve several dishes, sampling a small portion of each. Americans frequently plan a main dish for the entire meal; in this case, a larger portion would be required.

Whenever possible, I have identified the origin of each recipe with both the Wade-Giles and the Pinyin system of Chinese spelling. For example, *Peking/Beijing*. As Pinyin means phonetic pronunciation, the Pinyin spelling is closer to the spoken language. Throughout the text, however, I have used only the Wade-Giles spelling, which is more familiar to Americans.

Chapter 1

HISTORY OF
THE CUISINE

In the summer of 1979, I went to China with a group of food writers and editors, people profoundly interested in food and its origins. I personally wanted several things: to have a more authentic frame of reference, to fulfill fantasies about the kind of cooking done there today, to see what the people were like, the culture, the country, a land of one billion people where the daily greeting is *"Ch'ih fan la mei yu?"*—"Have you eaten?" or, literally, "Have you had rice?"

The Chinese preoccupation with food has long pervaded all segments of society, from the ancient scholars, emperors, and poets who wrote volumes on the subject to the peasants I saw at the Golden Well Commune, sixty-five miles from Changsha, Hunan, tending their small piece of land where they raised and sold their own vegetables. Food is as precious to the Chinese as the fine arts are to the Westerner.

Possibly the Chinese reverence for food is rooted in a lingering memory of famine. Because of the scarcity of food, the Chinese have over the centuries learned to utilize with respect and care all edible materials. Grounded in truth is the jest that no dinosaurs have been found in China because they ate them all. They make use of every resource available to them, including duck's web, ox's penis, fish heads, dried fish lips, numerous varieties of fungus, and chicken blood (which is used not only to thicken Hot and Sour Soup but also for ink to cancel postage stamps).

The resourceful Chinese have added further variety to their cuisine by taking one product and creating numerous byproducts from it. The classic example of this is the soybean, from which the Chinese make soy sauce, over a dozen fermented bean sauces, bean curd, soybean milk, bean curd sheets, and so on.

Many classic Chinese dishes make deliberate use of contrasting flavors. Various blends of the spicy, mild, mellow, bland, pungent, salty, sweet, and sour are used along with contrasting textures to mix the chewy with the smooth, the juicy with the resilient, and to combine in various ways the gelatinous, spongy, and light. Glutinous shark's fin, crisp bean sprouts, cloud ears, and birds' nests add little taste but they absorb the seasonings and play an important textural role. These dishes attain a harmonious balance in flavor and texture, mixing what the Chinese refer to as hot (that is, having a stimulating effect) with the cold (having a quieting effect). In a classic banquet, there are contrasts not only in tastes and textures, but also in colors, aromas, and methods of cooking, which include stir-frying, red-cooking (slow stewing in soy sauce), braising, steaming, Lu cooking in a master sauce, multiple cooking, smoking, roasting, poaching or deep-frying. A further balance is achieved by the cutting, because when the principal ingredient is diced, all the subordinate ingredients are diced; when sliced, all is sliced; thick pieces are matched with thick pieces, slivers with slivers. The ultimate success of the presentation of the dish relies on the chef's precision cutting.

The Chinese have created one of the great cuisines of the world, an inventively refined, sophisticated cuisine with over five thousand individual classic dishes, each having its own distinguishing flavor, texture, fragrance, and color.

A classic cuisine does not develop overnight. China has a recorded history of over five thousand years. Four thousand years ago the Chinese were using butter. By the first millennium B.C. they were steaming, grilling, deep-frying, roasting, and using prominent seasonings such as ginger, scallions, and garlic. Imperial palaces employed thousands of people, more than half of whom were involved with the food and wine served to the royalty: 335 specialists in grains, fruits, and vegetables, 62 pickle and sauce specialists, 24 specialists in turtle and shellfish, hundreds of specialists for meat, game, and fish, 162 dietitians, and so on. Chopsticks were introduced in the third century.

Classic Chinese cooking, like Chinese history, began in the North along the Yellow River and slowly moved east and west along the Yangtze River. By the time of Confucius (551–479 B.C.), a standard had been set for the evolving classic cuisine, specifically formulated in his *Analects*. For Confucius, the rice could never be white enough nor the meat minced too finely. When the meat was not cut correctly he would not eat because, as he said, "The way you cut your meat reflects the way you live." Food had to be served with its proper sauce, and could not be discolored nor of a bad flavor. Anything that was ill-cooked or not in season was discarded. His ideals, concerning food and also of a humanistic culture, had an enormous effect on the Chinese way of life.

China was unified in the third century B.C. and had achieved an identity through its common culture, standardizing its currency, measurement, and language. The sophisticated Han Dynasty of 202 B.C. to A.D. 220 was the first to make its mark on the cuisine, blending the five flavors—bitter, sour, sweet, salty, and hot—in much of their cooking. The art of cutting, cooking methods that expanded to include pickling, stewing, and baking, and the use of lacquerware and earthenware distinguished this cooking style. After the Han Empire fell, the people fled south and established their court in Nanking, bringing a sophistication in cooking and culture to eastern and southern China. To this day, many Chinese still refer to themselves as the Han people.

China reverted during the next four hundred years to its feudal past. However, the T'ang (618–907) and Sung (960–1279) dynasties brought back the glories of the classic cuisine, and further developed it, partially due to innovations in agriculture that brought about changes in supply and distribution. The Chinese Empire was restored and elaborate palaces were built. The Grand Canal was constructed, which meant that rice could now be transported from the Yangtze Valley to other areas of China. The diverse elements of the Chinese cuisine blossomed during this period.

By the tenth or eleventh century the cuisine had attained an identity of its own, with the simplicity of home-style meals and the sophistication of refined, extravagant banquet dishes stressing exotic components and texture foods. China incorporated into its cuisine various crops introduced from foreign lands: spinach and celery from Nepal, pistachio nuts from Persia, kohlrabi from Europe. From the Indians, the Chinese learned how to make sugar out of sugarcane and wine out of grapes. China, in turn, exported its art objects, tea, and silk to the West.

In 1234 Genghis Khan breached China's northern border, which was protected by the 2,500-mile Great Wall. These Mongolians, who lived in tents and dressed in furs, brought with them a diet quite foreign to the Chinese, consisting primarily of milk, butter, and lamb. This is a period of Chinese history which included everything from bound feet to long fingernails (a status symbol, as also was being overweight, for it meant one was a scholar rather than a laborer) to that strange breed of bird called the cormorant, which was trained to fish for its master. Chinese inventions during this time included paper, printing, paper money, playing cards, and gunpowder.

Although the Mongols ruled for a century, the Chinese were less affected by them than the Mongols were by the Chinese, especially in food and dress. The greatest gastronomic legacy from these nomads was the Mongolian Hot Pot.

During the Ming Dynasty (1368–1644) and, later, the Manchu Dynasty (1644–1912), the cuisine was further refined and expanded, in part due to the vast amount of international trade. Portuguese ships sailed into Canton beginning in 1516, bringing with them not only potatoes and tobacco, but also the capsicum (chili) pepper which eventually became an important ingredient in the Chinese cuisine. The Portuguese were followed by other Europeans and the Americans. With this trade came significant new imports, including pineapples, papayas, tomatoes, peanuts, and maize. By the 1700s the Chinese cuisine had achieved its identity, and classic dishes we enjoy today reflect this evolution more so than any modern contribution.

From the fall of the Manchu Dynasty in 1911 until the Communist takeover in 1949 there was continual civil unrest, war, and increasingly frequent famines, during which time the emphasis was on feeding the people, not on refining and creating new dishes. There are further reasons for this momentary break in the evolution of the Chinese cuisine, not the least of which was Mao Tse-tung's well-intentioned idea of switching professions around during the Cultural Revolution, at which time the scientists were working in the fields and the chefs were anywhere but in the kitchens. Therefore the serious chefs fled to Taiwan and Hong Kong. It is for this reason that one finds excellent classic cooking today not in Mainland China but rather in these two places, where serious attention is given to seasonings, and expert treatment is employed for the wonderful fresh produce, seafood, and generally superior-quality ingredients.

The dishes in this book are variations on the classics, both banquet and home-style. The cooking techniques employed have been handed down from generations of Chinese chefs. It is no wonder that the Tai See Foo (master chefs) of China, who were instrumental in the evolution of China's classic cuisine, are held in high esteem in China and given respect usually reserved only for scholars.

Chapter 2

REGIONAL DISTINCTIONS

I have divided the Chinese cuisine primarily into four sections, North, South, East, and West, with a short look at the Fukienese school of cooking. In a general sense, these four regions are represented by Peking in the North; Canton in the South; Shanghai, Yangchow, and other large cities in the East; and Szechwan, Hunan, and Yünnan provinces in the West. Regional distinctions do exist and, because of the vastness of the continent, will probably tend to remain. They are distinguished by the ingredients used, the various combinations of spices and sauces, the cooking techniques employed, and the condiments served.

These distinctive regional characteristics evolved for various reasons, including a lack of refrigeration, which meant that each region had only certain foods available. If a province had exposure to foreign influence, as Peking did with the Mongols and as the eastern and southern port cities did from trade with faraway places, then these outside components became incorporated into that region's cuisine. The availability of fuel created its own regional differences, as did the history of those who lived there.

I would like to add, however, that the cuisine is still evolving and, with modern communication and transport systems, with Mandarin being made the universal spoken language of China, with the greater availability of food from province to province, regional characteristics tend to merge into a national cuisine. Popular Pekingese dishes are readily adopted in Canton, eastern dishes are found in Szechwan, and so forth. Some divide China's schools of cooking into three categories: northern, Yangtze Valley, and southern; some say there are four, five, maybe two dozen schools. Regardless of the number of categories and schools, when a dish is adopted from another region, each province still adds its local touch.

Northern Region

Known as the ancient heartland of China, the northern region, and especially its Eternal City, Peking (laid out by Kublai Khan in the thirteenth century), is noted for imaginative, elegant, classic dishes. After all, the North was the birthplace of China's civilization, and was for centuries inhabited by her emperors, aristocrats, great families, and philosophers, including Confucius and Mencius. The first great camel caravans connected the North with Europe and India as early as the Han Dynasty (202 B.C.–A.D. 220). Cultural and culinary exchanges occurred when these caravans journeyed along the renowned Silk Road. It was through the Silk Road that India's chairs were introduced to China; the Chinese adopted chairs, whereas the Japanese still enjoy dining while seated at floor level. The eclectic quality of the northern cuisine was brought about by many outside influences, not the least of which were the Mongolians and later the Manchus.

The Mongols, who ruled for a century, did leave one great culinary legacy: the Mongolian Hot Pot, which has remained a classic northern specialty. This ceremonial dish begins when the server places on the table a small round charcoal-burning brass stove wedged into the center of a ring-shaped pot that contains a boiling broth. The server then adds to the broth various ingredients such as cooked wheat noodles, soaked cellophane noodles, sliced pressed bean curd, raw cabbage or other vegetables. These are cooked briefly and ladled out onto the plates. Each diner, using chopsticks approximately two feet long, cooks thin slices of lamb to his liking, then dips the slices into various condiments, such as a dip of sesame seed paste and light soy sauce, and several garnishes, possibly sugared garlic or chopped scallion with minced coriander. The Hot Pot is traditionally served with sesame seed rolls (sometimes with a pumpernickel-like yeast dough). The broth itself is the final soup course.

Lamb, rarely eaten in any other region, is a Pekingese specialty. In fact, Peking has been called the mutton city of China. Both lamb and beef are used more extensively in the North than elsewhere in China. The northern provinces are famous for their roast and barbecued dishes, such as barbecued beef or lamb or whole-roasted chicken. Shantung, with its ample supply of chickens, was noted for its deep-fried birds being sold through train windows at the various stations. Classic northern dishes featuring chicken include Chicken Velvet* and Mo Shu Ro*, a specialty which has tree ears and golden needles for texture, with either chicken or pork being the primary ingredient. This classic dish is served with Peking Doilies*, also referred to as Mandarin Pancakes. Another classic northern dish featuring pork is Red-Cooked Shoulder of Pork*, the North being known for their red-cooked simmering of large whole pieces of meat.

Because fresh fish and seafoods are not available in the North, most of the fish is salted. The only fresh fish commonly eaten in this region are the plump fish of the Yellow River and prawns. Because of their ability to thrive in fresh or salt water, prawns are available throughout the year. These prawns have a taste reminiscent of lobster and are sometimes as large as five inches in length. The Chinese hold a prawn to their mouth with chopsticks and shell it in a most dexterous fashion with their teeth. In the North, prawns are often deep-fried or prepared with a highly garlicked tomato sauce (Charred Shrimp in Barbecue Sauce*).

The North's most famous culinary creation is the universally admired Peking Duck, a variation of which is Sliced Roast Duck with Scallions*. Peking, as the capital of China, has seen the development of some of the most refined, sophisticated, distinguished Chinese dishes. Peking Duck is a prime example. The original recipe was over fifteen thousand words, most of which were directions concerned with making the duck's skin as crisp as possible by utilizing procedures such as separating the skin from the flesh by a pumping technique, tightening the skin by submerging the duck in boiling water, air-drying the duck for a day by hanging it in a cool place with a breeze, and searing it in a large oven that has been preheated for almost an hour (which ensures that the duck will be roasted both from the fire below and from the walls of the oven). Peking's duck restaurants have dozens of ducks hanging by the neck on poles, which are rotated while the birds are roasting in ovens the size of small rooms. The ovens are fired by charcoal or compressed coal. The chefs in charge of this dish have had three months of study dedicated to the fattening, slaughtering, and cleaning of the duck, and nine months of study to master the preparation, roasting, carving, and final presentation of the dish.

As they represent marital fidelity, mandarin ducks are dear to the hearts of the Chinese. When the pair is separated, it is said that they never recover; rather, they mourn themselves into an early death. It is for this reason that pharmacologists as far back as the T'ang Dynasty prescribed duck soup for ailing marriages.

Peking ducks are slaughtered before they are seventy days old. During the last two and a half weeks of their lives, they are fed artificially. As one of the objectives is for the meat not to become sinewy, ducks are allowed little exercise.

Traditionally, Peking Duck is served in a multicourse fashion, beginning with the classic presentation of the whole roasted duck. Once the Peking Duck is formally presented—golden brown, and lacquered in appearance—it is carved at the table by the server. When Peking Duck is properly prepared, the layer of fat that exists between the skin and the meat is nonexistent. The first course—the crisp, golden skin— is then served with beautiful, utilitarian brushes made from scallions, which are used for painting the delicate, thin flour doilies with the Peking Duck dipping sauce (which consists of hoisin sauce, sherry, and sesame seed oil).

The second course is either the sliced duck meat folded by the diner into doilies, or duck meat stir-fried with bean sprouts (or any combination of vegetables). The classic format for the remaining courses utilizes other duck parts. Cold appetizers could include jellied crunchy duck web, gelatinous duck wing, fried duck liver and gizzards, or slivered duck breast with Shantung cabbage, bean curd, hot peppers, and cellophane noodles. Hot courses might consist of Duck Velvet or split duck heads containing cooked brains. Traditionally, the last course is a rich duck soup, making use of the duck's carcass, which is simmered with added ingredients of pureed bean curd, cabbage, and bean threads until it becomes thick and white from the marrow of the bones.

The Peking Doilies* (made with water and flour and steamed just before serving) and the Mongolian Hot Pot sesame seed rolls are an indication of the northern reliance on grain products other than rice. Northern China is wheat-growing country because the high plains are not suitable for rice cultivation. Daily meals are wheat-flour noodle dishes with pork, beef, chicken, duck, fish, and vegetables in various combinations; dumplings that are steamed, boiled, fried, or baked; wheat-flour buns made into simple or elaborate shapes, and wheat-flour pancakes, breads, and cakes (some of the crisp fried cakes are wrapped around scallions and garlic, and are traditionally served at breakfast).

Elsewhere in China, rice is the staple and several bowls are consumed with each meal. Except in the North, the average person in China eats a pound of rice a day. Children are taught not to leave a single grain of rice in the bowl, as each grain represents the sweat of the workers in the field.

A typical breakfast in Peking in a workmen's restaurant (where the people eat) would be various fried breads, dumplings, or steamed buns filled with pork, accompanied by a bowl of rice porridge called congee. Jao-tze* (the Chinese word for dumplings) originated in the North and their dumplings (and buns) are often stuffed with lamb or pork and seasoned with chives and garlic. Northern restaurants have been reputed to reek with the controversial aroma of garlic and mutton. The bowl of congee that accompanies breakfast is typical of every region of China. Made with short-grain river rice, it has a special significance to the Chinese as it has been the lifeblood of the poor during times of drought and flood, hardship and famine. The people were warmed during the harsh winters as they stood by the steaming kettles of congee, waiting for their bowls to be filled.

The northern Chinese were eating breads, noodles, and cakes as early as the Han Dynasty, although some of the cooking techniques were borrowed from foreign lands. Ultimately breads became significant aspects of certain Chinese holidays, and were even offered to deities.

An excellent northern specialty in this genre is Peking Rolls*—finely shredded vegetables encased in an egg pancake, which is dipped in a batter and deep-fried.

Originating in the province of Honan is the northern classic sweet-sour sauce, made primarily with sugar and vinegar. The sweet-and-sour dishes of Honan were adopted by Canton, and the Cantonese added fruit or tomato sauce to the northern version. An example of a sweet-and-sour dish is Sweet and Pungent Sea Bass*.

The variations in food and its preparation from one area to another are often distinguished by the use of seasonings. Northerners commonly use vinegar as a seasoning, frequently mixing it with soy sauce and adding the typical northern ingredients of onions, chives, scallions, leeks, and/or garlic. Northern use of garlic cannot be overemphasized. These same ingredients are often combined with a fermented bean sauce. Although bean sauce is used in other regions as well, northerners are known for their fermented bean pastes. They also characteristically use a thick form of soy sauce, known as soya paste, to thicken sauces and preserve meats. Other traditional seasonings in the North are wine stocks, dark soy sauce (used exclusively), Fermented Wine Rice* (which the eastern and western regions also use), ginger root, and star anise (the latter two are used throughout China). Northern cooking is generally less spicy and less oily than that of the western provinces. Dishes are more often light and mild, with restrained flavoring, an example of which is Fillet of Bass with Wine Sauce*.

The most commonly eaten vegetable in the North is Tientsin white cabbage, which is either white-cooked (blanched in water) or red-cooked (simmered in soy sauce). When it is preserved in salt and garlic it is called Tientsin Preserved Vegetable, and is sold in crocks as a seasoning for various stir-fried dishes. Today in Peking the markets have long lines of Chinese waiting for produce which varies in quality, including tomatoes, string beans, black-eyed peas, corn, potatoes, wonderful chili peppers, garlic, many varieties of chives, excellent eggplant, cabbage, and fresh lotus root. There are beautiful cucumbers, several varieties of fresh mushrooms, and spinach. Fruits include peaches, apples, plums, apricots, and melons. In the winter, the North is known for its pears and persimmons. Strawberries are sometimes available in the summer and grapes are widely produced.

A classic northern dessert featuring fruit is Peking Glazed Apples, which actually originated in Shantung. This exquisite specialty has a crispy, still-warm slice of apple (yucca is also traditionally used) within its hard-candy glazed encasement.

Southern Region

The name Cantonese has become virtually synonymous with the southern regional cuisine. The gateway into and out of China,

Canton has had a significant influence on the development of Chinese dishes and restaurants in the United States, which is why most Americans in the past who had a Chinese meal in fact had a Cantonese meal. The Cantonese first emigrated to Japan and southeast Asia, then in the mid-1800s to Hawaii, Australia, England, France, Indonesia, Thailand, Burma, Central America, South America, and North America. The Cantonese arrived in North America, "Land of the Golden Mountains," in time for the 1849 California gold rush. When they worked as laborers on the railroads they supplemented their income doing menial tasks such as cooking and washing. This circumstance gave rise to the numerous Chinese laundries and Cantonese restaurants in the United States. Most Chinese communities in this country are still primarily Cantonese.

Recently many Americans have developed a decided preference for Szechwan and Hunan cooking, because of the numerous Chinese restaurants that have bastardized the Cantonese classic cuisine and have bored their patrons repeatedly by serving bland dishes with cornstarch and chicken stock sauces accompanied by soggy vegetables. But it should be remembered that a true Cantonese chef is highly esteemed even in China, and is considered by many on a par with French chefs.

A great testimony to Cantonese cooking, with its more than fourteen hundred dishes, is represented in such culinary creations as Lemon Squab*, Roast Duck Lo Mein*, Steamed Sea Bass with Fermented Black Beans*, Beef Chow Fun*, Barbecued Roast Pork*, and the numerous varieties of dim sum served in tea houses, including Steamed Roast Pork Buns* and Shao Mai*. The Cantonese have proved that Chinese food can be tasty without the influence of chili peppers.

The Cantonese are a people with a difference, different even from other Chinese, shorter and darker with a great curiosity about life. They are given credit for being adventuresome eaters, going so far as eating live monkey brains. Their inherent adaptability is seen in the fact that most innovations in China begin in Canton, whether it be new dishes or communism. Possibly because of the abundance and wealth of the province, they are devoted to luxury and pleasure. They have a sizable middle class which indulges in Canton's tea houses and restaurants, the largest in China.

There is an old saying, "If you like good food, go to Canton." Another adage is even more potent: "To be born in Soochow (known for its beauty), to eat in Kwangchow (i.e., Canton, which is known for its food), to dress in Hangchow (known for its silk), and to die in Leouchow (from where the wood for coffins derives)."

Canton's gates have always been open to foreign traders, although before 1842 foreigners were either led to specific warehouses or forced to transact business from their ships. When any of these ships brought in new food products, such as Africa's okra, India's eggplant, and the New World's tomatoes, chili and sweet peppers, squash, corn, white and sweet potatoes, and peanuts, the Cantonese were quick to adopt and cultivate them, always adding to their already incredible diversity of crops. The province's semitropical southern climate with its warmth and abundant rainfall indeed encourages agriculture. Thanks to the bounty of nature and the determination of the peasants, fresh food of great diversity is available in Canton throughout the year. The Cantonese can choose from a large selection of herbs, and wild and cultivated plants and animals. Not only do they have abundant rice, they have a vast variety of quality fruits, vegetables, and grains, including tangerines, lemons, oranges, plums, lichees, longans, loquats, bananas, sugarcane, soybeans, mung beans, fava, cabbages, winter melon, taro, water chestnuts, lotus root, onions, garlic, chives, and mushrooms. Like the people of other regions of China, but more so, the Cantonese are fond of dishes combining vegetables with meats, as well as fruits with meats. One favorite pairing is duck with pineapple, plums, lichees, or oranges (Orange Spiced Duck*). Plums and lichees are used in many dishes. Vegetables and fruits are occasionally combined in sweet-and-sour dishes; however, generally speaking, the Cantonese do not favor sweet-and-sour dishes at all, except in the case of certain seasonal fish and pork. Incidentally, with the exception of Whole-Roasted Suckling Pig, pork rarely appears in Canton's banquet dishes.

Canton's cuisine reflects abundance also in the fish and seafood category. In addition to the East and West rivers (tributaries of the Pearl River) flowing into Canton, the province has a coastline of more than a thousand miles. Seafood is used in its fresh, dried, and salted form. The availability of countless species of fish and shellfish from the sea, as well as pond-raised crayfish, prawns, and carp, has made the Cantonese proficient in seafood and fish dishes, which are renowned throughout the world. Many of the fish are steamed to preserve their natural flavor. Seafood sauces such as fish sauce, shrimp paste, and oyster sauce are specialties characteristic of the region. Oyster sauce, used in many Cantonese dishes, is made by boiling oysters in giant vats until the liquid becomes thick and robust. Shrimp paste, rich in protein and calcium, is made from small dried shrimp.

Ginger is popular among the seasonings the Cantonese typically use for fish and seafoods, as it counteracts the fishiness. Soy sauce with chili is a favorite dip for prawns (Steamed Shrimp*); salted black beans season many seafood dishes (Clams in Black Bean Sauce*); and vinegar is used specifically for crab.

In general, Cantonese spices are interesting because they consist of a wide range of not only native spices, but also foreign ones. Like the western region, Canton has made use of Southeast Asia's and India's curries, as well as America's ketchup and England's Worcestershire sauce (which is made of typical Chinese ingredients—vinegar and soy sauce). A master sauce, composed of soy sauce, water, rice wine, star anise, sugar, and Five Spice Powder*, is used to simmer whole birds.

Being adventuresome, the Cantonese specialize in many exotic dishes. Some of the components of these dishes include shark's fin, fish maw, snakes, snails, eels, frogs, turtles, sparrows, and birds' nests. Often these ingredients are favored mainly for their texture, which is of prime importance to the Cantonese. The flavorful stock of Cantonese soups is often made with such ingredients as pigs' trotters, lungs, pork sweetbreads, snake, frogs' legs, shark's fin, large fish heads, and turtle.

There is no province in China that does not use stir-frying as a method of cooking; however, it is the Cantonese who are given credit for perfecting the art. They are famous for their delicate stir-fry dishes, which allow the flavor of the simplest ingredients to come through. An example of such a Cantonese classic is Stir-Fried Lobster with Shredded Leeks*.

The Cantonese favor quick stir-frying and quick boiling, as well as the quick dipping of vegetables and seafoods (a process much like blanching) and quick roasting, as with Barbecued Roast Pork*, a regional specialty. This Cha Shao roasting involves lengthy marinating of strips of meat, followed by a short roasting time. By American standards, the Cantonese like their foods undercooked. For instance, when they cook chicken they like the juices to run red. They prefer steaming to other cooking processes because it is quick and it leaves the food in a natural state. "Well done" to the Cantonese means not over-cooked.

Cantonese dim sum is universally renowned. The tea-house world of Canton is indeed an endless procession of dim sum. Waiters in the tea houses circulate in ballroom-sized rooms with trays, carts, or heated trolleys of dim sum, serving elaborate, delicate buns, pastries, dumplings, noodles, and breads. There are no menus; rather the diner chooses plates of these del-

icacies, and the final bill is calculated by the number of plates on the table.

Although the South has its share of poultry and meat fillings (including chicken, roast pork, spareribs in black bean sauce, and a chicken skin wrapped in duck's web), the great diversity of Cantonese dim sum emphasizes fish and seafood fillings.

The South is famous for its egg noodles (with Roast Duck Lo Mein*), dried and fresh rice noodles (with Beef Chow Fun*), and noodles with ch'a siu (Barbecued Roast Pork*). Each variety of Italian pasta has a Chinese counterpart. Some scholars say that noodles were introduced into Europe by China via the Middle East as early as the eleventh century.

Incidentally, there is one food in this genre familiar to most Americans which is never served in restaurants in the southern region, nor in any region of China for that matter: fortune cookies. George Jung, a Chinese immigrant, founded a noodle company in Los Angeles in 1916 and produced fortune cookies, some say to amuse the clientele in American Chinese restaurants, others say to brighten the spirits of the weary survivors of World War I. The inspiration for his creation possibly came from the fact that the Chinese have sent messages inside cakes and cookies for centuries, sometimes as military intelligence, sometimes as a birth announcement. There were also parlor games in ancient times in which the players wrote witticisms and tidbits of wisdom on a piece of paper that was put into a twisted cake.

Eastern Region

Much of the eastern cuisine is typical of China as a whole, partially because those traveling through China, whether from north to south or east to west, have passed through the area via the Yangtze River. Unlike the North, with its culinary center of

Peking, the South, with its Canton, or the West, with its cuisine thought of primarily in terms of the Szechwan and Hunan provinces, the eastern region is represented by large urban centers. The city that is most representative of the eastern region, and indeed China, is Shanghai, a densely populated industrial cosmopolitan seaport. Another great port city of the East is Yangchow. Before it became the shadow of Shanghai, it was called the "Paris of China." Yangchow was famous for its dim sum, and the delicate quality of its cuisine was reflected in its sophisticated clothing and art. Three other important eastern cities are Ch'ang-shu, which has its share of industry and agriculture, beautiful Soochow, with its gardens, canals, and famous silk, and Ningpo, the great historic port and trading center.

Historically speaking, the first city of importance in the East was Nanking, which was the capital of China for two centuries beginning in the fourth century A.D. Nanking so often served as China's seat of government over the centuries that the city's cuisine developed along imperial lines. Nearby Hangchow, another eastern city which became China's capital, is renowned throughout the world for its Hangchow silk. Marco Polo was so overwhelmed by Hangchow that he called it paradise, the noblest city in the world. These latter two cities are famous for two eastern classic duck specialties: Nanking Pressed Duck and Hangchow Soya Duck.

It is logical that the East would have several outstanding classic duck dishes, as the region breeds so many ducks. Nanking alone produces forty million ducks a year. The East is a region with countless ponds, streams, lakes, and the famous Yangtze River, referred to as China's Main Street. Saltwater duck is another Chinese banquet dish, and it too originates in Nanking. The many shops in Nanking that specialize only in this one product first marinate the duck for one or two days in salt and spices which have been dry-cooked in a wok to release

their flavor. Before cooking, the duck is dried in the sun for several more days.

Ducks and other poultry are often steamed inside the large melons and squashes that the East grows, and are beautifully presented at the table with the bird still encased in the melon. Other visually appealing dishes on the same order feature steamed stuffed lotus roots, peppers, or mushrooms. Like the Cantonese, Easterners seem to favor stuffings more than Northerners and Westerners do. Stuffings for birds usually include rice, but lotus seeds, melon seeds, ginkgo nuts, chestnuts, mushrooms, and fresh bamboo shoots are also used.

The Yangtze River cuts China in half, from west to east, and as the Yangtze region in general is called the major rice-producing region of China, the East places an emphasis on rice and rice-based products such as Chinese rice wine, two famous ones being Shao Shing Wine and Yellow Wine. Certain eastern dishes are known for their liberal use of wine; however, generally speaking, whatever the seasoning it is usually restrained. Instead of adding a large quantity of salt or soy sauce to a stir-fried dish, a characteristic eastern idiosyncrasy would be to season with salted pickle, salt pork, or a preserved vegetable (Shredded Pork with Preserved Hot Turnip*). The eastern emphasis on mild, delicate seasonings is seen in the characteristic way main ingredients are used to flavor each other, the combination itself becoming the seasoning rather than any specific additions.

The vinegars used as seasoning are produced in the region; the most famous is Chinkiang, a sweetened black rice vinegar. Many of the dishes of this region, especially those featuring fish, are flavored with black rice vinegar, which is added to red-cooked simmered, stir-fried, and deep-fried fish (Pinecone Fish*).

Sugar is characteristically employed (Smoked Fish Fillets*) to counteract the saltiness of soy. There are many sweet sauces, especially with meat dishes, that use honey and/or unrefined crystal sugar. Like the Southerners, Easterners rely upon vegetable oil instead of lard. Salt is used in abundance, primarily in Ningpo. Home-style meals in Ningpo feature salty dishes, including pickled and salted greens. Other preserved foods include salted fish, seafoods, dried mushrooms, and bamboo shoots.

Because Easterners typically favor slow-cooked dishes, they evolved their classic cooking method called red-cooking, a technique in which fish, poultry, or meats are simmered for hours in a rich soy-sauce-based stock. Another slow-cooking method widely used in the East is steaming (they also do quick steaming). Easterners, especially from Shanghai, steam their stuffed boneless chicken. They are also known for their robust casserole dishes, which are slowly simmered in a stock.

Whether one is thinking of the small towns along the Yangtze River, or Hang-chow on the beautiful West Lake, or Shanghai, China's largest seaport, one associates eastern cooking with great seafood and fish dishes, a classic example being Fried Blue Crabs*. Freshwater fish and shellfish, including shrimp, crab, carp, mullet, bream, perch, sturgeon, and shad, are readily available. Shad is steamed whole for a lengthy cooking period, rendering the bones soft enough to eat.

Another product of eastern fresh waters is lotus leaves, which are used for wrapping foods to be steamed or roasted (Beggar's Chicken*). When meat, poultry, seafood, or fish is marinated in wine, soy sauce, and sugar, with sauce and seasonings added, then wrapped in noninflammable paper and folded into little envelopes to be deep-fried, you can bet the dish originated in the eastern region, as paper-wrapped foods are an eastern specialty that has been adopted throughout China.

Like the other regions of China, the East has a wide variety of dim sum, which Easterners refer to as *tien hsin,* literally "to dot the heart." They sometimes use the unique method of placing dumplings and buns in bamboo steamers with linings made of pine needles soaked in sesame oil. The East is also famous for delicate noodles and cold tossed noodles. Yangchow noodles, an eastern specialty, are renowned throughout China.

"Delicate" is a key word regarding eastern cooking, as the cuisine emphasizes fine, delicate cutting, decoratively delicate preparation, and a stress on the natural, delicate flavor of the ingredients themselves.

Western Region

To those even vaguely aware of China's western cuisine, especially in Szechwan and Hunan, the words "hot" and "spicy" come to mind because of the frequent use of hot chili peppers, whether red or green, fresh or dried. There is much conjecture as to why this region developed such incredibly hot dishes. Both Szechwan and Hunan are hot, tropical inlands where chili peppers are grown in abundance. Some are eaten raw, thereby causing perspiration, which in turn has a cooling effect on the body. Some say, therefore, that the use of chili peppers in the western region was a direct result of the clammy, humid climate. Another theory as to the extensive use of chili peppers in Szechwan in particular is that much of the province is so mountainous that only one crop per year can be grown. In order to preserve their foods, they utilized dried chili peppers in the form of a chili paste. Others theorize that before salt was mined in the area (the Chinese were dependent upon salt from the evaporation of seawater, and its transportation to the West was an impossibility) Westerners compensated for the lack of salt with the liberal use of spices. A gastronomic theory as to the hot and spicy cuisine of the West is that the hot peppers stimulate the palate, causing a sensitivity that brings an awareness of the spectrum of flavors to follow: after the hot and spicy, the mild, mellow, sour, salty, sweet, aromatic, bland, bitter, and pungent flavors linger in the aftertaste.

The difference between Szechwan and Hunan in seasoning with chili peppers is that Szechwan cooking primarily uses chili paste, while Hunan dishes more commonly employ raw chili peppers (although chili paste is also used in some dishes). When the seeds and membranes are not removed from the chili peppers, Hunanese food becomes even hotter and spicier than the Szechwanese counterpart.

Szechwan peppercorns also create a slight numbing effect, followed by the wonderful taste sensation of this most aromatic, exotic seasoning. It is used as a dry dip for appetizers and to flavor many dishes, for instance Szechwan Diced Chicken*. These peppercorns are grown in Szechwan Province and are extensively used; whereas black peppercorns, which are actually much hotter, are used in the northern provinces and white peppercorns in the other parts of China. More aromatic than spicy, Szechwan peppercorns are dry-cooked in order to bring out their flavor. This is done by dry-roasting the peppercorns in a wok over medium heat until their reddish brown color turns darker, then pulverizing them to produce Szechwan Peppercorn Powder*.

Because of the emphasis on the harmonious blending of pungent flavors, Szechwan is famous for such dishes as Chun-Pi (orange peel) Chicken*, Sesame Seed Beef*, and Tea Smoked Duck*, which is traditionally marinated, steamed, then smoked above a combination of tea and camphorwood leaves over a charcoal fire. The West is renowned for their smoked dishes, especially smoked poultry.

Dishes emphasizing texture are the satinlike Slippery Chicken* and Dry Sautéed Shredded Beef*. Beef is often shredded and dry-fried here, resulting in the chewy texture that Westerners prefer. Possibly their preference for chewy rather than tender beef came out of necessity, as cows are not bred for eating but for their haulage function in the salt mines, which results in

tough meat. Westerners therefore not only shred and fry beef, but also often cook it for long periods of time.

Being so far from the sea, Szechwan created their renowned "in-the-style-of-fish" dishes utilizing not fish, but rather ingredients normally employed in the cooking of fish, such as wine, vinegar, ginger, garlic, onion, chili pepper, and dried salted black beans. Because of its scarcity, seafood is considered a delicacy in the region. Most of it comes from the South Seas, and is usually dried. Certain freshwater fish such as carp, perch, pike, and eel are available and are highly treasured.

Westerners have several wonderful freshwater fish specialties, one of the more famous banquet dishes being Lake Tungting Shrimp*, featuring the freshwater shrimp of Lake Tungting. Stir-fried frogs' legs and turtle soup are summertime specialties. Hunan's Yellow River carp is renowned throughout China, and a unique regional dish is Steamed Carp with Purple Basil*.

The Szechwanese often employ multiple cooking processes, as in the case of Szechwan Crispy Duck*, in which the duck is steamed and then deep-fried, producing an extraordinary texture. Another multiple-cooking technique indigenous to this province is "passing through," in which meat is fried in two or more cups of oil as a preliminary to stir-frying. Because the Szechwanese enjoy smoked flavor and crunchy texture, vegetables are often dry-cooked or deep-fried before being stir-fried. They sometimes "fry" with water instead of oil (water "frying"), and, as in passing through, the meat is then drained and stir-fried with various seasonings and/or vegetables (Double-Cooked Pork*.)

A multiplicity of flavors, as in Pon Pon Chicken*, is typical of Szechwan dishes. Also referred to as Hacked Chicken, Pon Pon Chicken has a sesame seed sauce (utilizing sesame seed paste) accented by chili oil and Szechwan Peppercorn Powder*. Sesame seed paste is the predominant flavor of many Szechwan dishes, including also Cold

Noodles with Spicy Sesame Sauce* and Vegetable Rolls with Sesame Sauce*. Another classic Szechwan chicken specialty is Kung Pao Chicken with its garlic and chili paste, a variation of which is Kung Pao Shrimp*.

Chefs strive for both tastes and aftertastes, using such seasonings as sesame seed paste, chili paste with garlic, and aromatic vinegar (vinegar and sugar are frequently added to seasoning sauces in small quantities). The aromatic vinegar is often combined with chili. Chili is also mixed with toasted ground rice, sesame seeds, peanuts, and other nutty products. Westerners coat meat with aromatic ground rice and sesame seeds, highlight dishes with aromatic dried tangerine or orange peel, and characteristically season with various combinations of onions, garlic, ginger, star anise, peppers, and cinnamon. An example of one of these dishes is Szechwan Crispy Duck*, which combines scallions, ginger, star anise, Szechwan Peppercorn Powder*, and cinnamon. China's various salty soybean products are used with numerous combinations of the above seasonings.

The Szechwanese use a large quantity of sesame oil; however, the Hunanese use even more. In the same manner as the French would use butter to enrich sauces at the end of the cooking period, the Hunanese use sesame oil.

I have mentioned the mountainous areas of Szechwan that have difficulty in crop output; however, the Red Basin of Szechwan, with its rich, red soil, is a vast fertile plain with foothills that have been terraced to as many as fifty levels. Although it is the most populous province in China, Szechwan sustains its people because almost anything can grow there. The green hillsides are covered with bamboo, both wild and cultivated. The intensive cultivation of its agriculture is aided by massive irrigation and by Szechwan's climate, with its abundant rainfall, humid summers, and winters that are never below freezing. Szechwan's rice is shipped throughout the world. The Szechwanese are known for their Fermented Wine Rice * and their Shrimp with Wine Rice, a variation of which is Steamed Whole Snapper with Fermented Wine Rice*. Most of the people are peasants who make their living from the land, cultivating sugarcane, citrus fruits, wheat, corn, potatoes, and tea. Walnuts, wood ears, and various tree fungi are abundant, as are wild and cultivated mushrooms. They grow kohlrabi, and one of their specialties is Szechwan preserved vegetable (which is kohlrabi preserved with chili and salt). They extensively use salted cabbage in their cooking. Szechwan is a major producer of silk, satin (Chungking), and brocade (Chengtu).

"South of the clouds" of Szechwan is Yünnan, one of the last provinces to be assimilated into China. To this day, the Chinese are a minority in Yünnan. Except for Szechwan to the north, the region is isolated from the rest of China by a uniquely un-Chinese mountain range that runs from north to south (most mountain ranges run from west to east in China). To the south of Yünnan is Burma, and to the west are Tibet and India. The Yünnanese cuisine has been influenced by its proximity to these places, and has assimilated a Szechwanese preference for the hot and spicy, a Burmese penchant for curry, and a Tibetan/Indian inclination toward dairy products. Generally speaking, the Chinese are not consumers of dairy products; however, Yünnan specializes in goat cheeses, yogurt, and fried milk curd. This Yünnanese interest in dairy products further increased in the thirteenth century with the intrusion of Kublai Khan and his army.

The most famous culinary product of Yünnan is its ham, which the Chinese prefer to all other hams. Pork is plentiful, and Yünnan's headcheese is the best in China.

Throughout the western region, much pork is eaten, as is chicken, substituting for beef, duck, lamb, and seafood, which the region lacks. As lard is the primary cooking oil in the West, pigs are bred with an emphasis on keeping the fat separated from

REGIONAL DISTINCTIONS

the lean meat. Because the Yünnanese eat a large quantity of salty ham, and as their famous sour pickles that they use in their cooking are quite salty, they have counteracted the saltiness with their sweet sauces, which typically use a large amount of both honey and sugar.

Although Yünnan, like Szechwan and Hunan, is inland, Yünnan has numerous lakes that produce a vast amount of fish. In fact, like the boat people of Fukien and Hong Kong who live on the sea, Yünnan's boat people live on these lakes. Yünnan's mountains support venison, bears (bear's paw is an exotic ingredient here), sparrows, and other game, herbs, and fungi. Both poultry and fish are often cooked with Yünnan's walnuts, chestnuts, pine nuts, and peanuts.

Hunan Province, in the mid-Yangtze Valley, is adjacent to Szechwan. Hunan has hills from which its famous black teas come (particularly renowned is Hunan's smoky Lapsang souchong) and it also has lowlands which produce its wonderful glutinous rice. Hunan, in fact, is called the rice province of China. Like Yünnan, it has excellent pork in many forms, including preserved pork, bacon, and smoked pork. There is a preponderance of smoked meats here—not only pork, ham, and bacon but also smoked duck, which is a Hunan as well as a Szechwan specialty.

When in Changsha, the capital of Hunan, the food editors and I discussed the region's method of smoking poultry in an interview with four chefs of the Xiang River Hotel. The chefs first fatten Peking ducks, then slaughter and clean them in a washing liquid. To help preserve the ducks, they marinate them for seven to ten days in a brine of sugar and wine, after which the ducks are smoked in a smoking room over rice husks or peanut shells (sometimes camphorwood is added). After hanging in the smoking room, the ducks are dried outside.

A preference for smoked flavor in meats is extended to sauces. Sugar is melted until it actually goes beyond the caramel stage; when it starts to burn, water is added, causing the characteristic smoky flavor of their sauces (Cured Pork Belly with Chili Peppers*).

The produce is wonderful in Hunan. The markets in Changsha have incredible variety and quality, and are many times superior to those of Peking. Three unusual vegetables I had there were onions that were similar in shape to shallots, but much whiter (they pickle these with sugar and vinegar), sword beans, and also a vegetable resembling jicama, but less sweet. Freshwater chestnuts are available after October. They make complete use of their peanuts: the nut is added to stir-fried dishes, and the shell is used in smoking poultry.

In the bread category, Changsha's crullers are excellent. Standing by his cart on the streets of Changsha, the cook folds the dark wheat flour dough, cuts two strips, places one on top of the other and then, with the dull side of the cleaver, presses down and quickly twists it, after which he fries it in very hot oil for less than a minute. Also famous are Yünnanese "across-the-bridge" noodles, so-called because the final cooking process takes place when the noodles are poured from the cooking vessel into the diner's bowl.

Fukien

Most Westerners are not aware of the respect the Chinese have for the Fukienese cuisine, regarded by many as one of China's five classic schools of cooking.

Fukien is the province directly north of Kwangtung, which gives its cooking some Cantonese influence. Although the Yangtze River plain lies to the north, Fukien's land is mountainous and often impassable. Because of its rocky cliffs, forests, and rugged coastline, Fukien has always been a very isolated area, not only cut off from the rest of China but also segmented within itself, and having more than one hundred different languages and dialects. Even the coastline has a minimum of flatland, with the result that Fukien has a large boat population. Many families spend their entire lives on the water, with no home on land. Because the difficult terrain leads to poor communication, certain specialties can be identified specifically with this region. The most famous of these are the soups, with their clear, delicate, highly refined broths, a classic example of which is Stuffed Clams in Broth*. The clear broth the Fukienese use as a base has a taste that is not only fresh, but also charmingly unfamiliar. It is made with a finely chopped, fresh-killed chicken, lean pork, ham, knuckle of pork, fresh shrimp heads, and a small portion of dried shrimp, with optional additions of turtle meat, fungi, small clams, and fish balls. These solids are then strained, resulting in an excellent, clear broth. A Fukien dinner will often include, between its eight courses, at least four outstanding soups.

The most distinctive, fascinating flavor in this province is red wine sediment paste, made from the lees of rice wine. It is used primarily in duck, chicken (Chicken with Fermented Red Wine Rice*), and pork dishes (Fukienese Fried Pork Chops*). Foochow, the capital of Fukien, is especially known for its extensive use of red wine sediment paste (Fermented Red Wine Rice*).

Below Foochow is the seaport Amoy, reputed to have the best soy sauce in China. Although famous for its excellent soy sauce, Fukienese cuisine uses it sparingly. This coastal city has an abundance of saltwater fish, and as the Fukienese in general rely on the sea for their livelihood, their seafood and fish dishes are noteworthy, including plump flatfish, fresh squid (usually dried), preserved fish, fried oysters, and dried cuttlefish. A classic dish in this genre is Fukienese Flatfish*.

Another specialty of Amoy is popia, a thin pancake that diners use to wrap the cooked filling that is placed on the table along with various side dishes and sauces. Also characteristic of this region is the making of dumpling skins out of meat. Ground pork and cornstarch are often kneaded together until a dough is formed. Called swallow skin, this thin dough skin, with its high meat content, is used as a wrapping for foods that are to be steamed or cooked in soups.

Bean curd, dried bean curd, and bean curd skins (or sheets) are used extensively here, especially in vegetable dishes. Sometimes the ingredients are shaped into replicas of fish, ducks, or chicken. Two fish dishes for which bean curd sheets are used as a wrapping are Crispy Fish Rolls* and Stuffed Shrimp in Bean Curd Sheets*.

Fukien is famous also for pork dishes, and one Fukienese specialty is to prepare 108 dishes from one pig. Other specialties include crystallized melon, salty-sour-sweet dried plums, longan (a sweet fruit similar to lichee), and green teas. Fukien was for centuries the center of the world tea market, as its mountainous, well-drained elevations encouraged the growth of excellent tender tea leaves. Traditionally the plucking of tea leaves from these small pruned trees has been done by both women and Buddhist-trained monkeys!

Chapter 3

EATING IN
CHINA TODAY

Under the state of affairs current in Mainland China today, Chinese classic cuisine has become somewhat dissipated. Nevertheless, there is nothing quite like the adventure of authentic dining in the workmen's restaurants, the communes, the sampans, the provincial inns, the tea houses, the Buddhist monasteries, the duck restaurants, the Szechwan, Cantonese and other regional eating places.

Street Vendors

The most ubiquitous form of public snacking in China today is on street food. Walk down the streets of any Chinese city and you will see tables set up with bowls on them, containing various condiments: chopped garlic, chives, soy sauce, chili paste, and fresh chili peppers. Next to the tables, meat pots simmer over hot coals. After being served a bowl of soup with a few pieces of meat in it, customers then add different condiments from the table to their soup. Besides these sidewalk food stands there are little dumpling places, merely one-room affairs heated by a charcoal stove. The purchased buns and dumplings are taken outside to be eaten. Street vendors and street hawkers are everywhere, the vendors selling such items as hot dishes of wonton, fried crullers, steamed dumplings, cookies, and cakes. Hawkers offer both goods and services, including kerosene by the ounce, fishing tackle, and porcelain repair.

Communal Dining

The dishes served at the communes of China are simple but delicious, not refined but fresh, because they are prepared with ingredients that are grown right on the commune. This dining experience could be compared to a peasant's banquet. Communes are all over China. The only privately owned land (there is no word for privacy in the Chinese language) is in fact the small plots surrounding the individually owned homes in every commune. Each owner uses his little patch of land to grow his own vegetables, pigs, or chickens, which he either consumes or sells.

One of the gastronomic highlights of my trip to China was lunch at the Golden Well Commune, sixty-five miles from Changsha, Hunan. The guest dining hall overlooks green rice fields, beyond which are mountainous areas, nine hundred water ponds, river beds, ten thousand pigs, a rice-processing factory, sixty tractors, two secondary schools, and a medical center with its barefoot doctors.

With fans humming overhead, we sat on stools and were served a deliciously fresh home-style meal. Our host presented us with platters of Pork Liver with Chili Peppers (the pig having been slaughtered that morning), Meat Ball Soup with pork balls, pork liver, egg shreds, mushrooms and cloud ears, Stir-Fried Long Beans, Chicken Soup (which had a very rich stock with mushrooms, eggs, chives, and black fungus as added ingredients), Pressed Bean Curd, several dishes featuring eggs, and a superb Steamed Carp with Purple Basil*. The tea served at the end of the meal was grown and processed on the commune.

Waterborne Dining

Another unique dining experience for travelers to China, especially in Hong Kong, occurs on boats of various sizes. The small, flat-bottomed boats, called sampans, have charcoal-burning stoves billowing blazes into the sky. On short voyages, a matter of hours, the meals sometimes include a dozen courses; at other times merely noodles and two or three stir-fried dishes. When I was in Hong Kong, the sampan I was on had no facilities for cooking, but a small boat which did pulled up alongside ours and, with incredible dexterity, two young men prepared in less than five minutes Hard-Shell Crabs with Black Bean Sauce (a variation of which is Soft-Shell Crabs with Black Bean Sauce*) and a steamed live shrimp dish, cooked in the shell and served with a spicy dipping sauce (Steamed Shrimp*).

Waterborne dining in China is a tradition dating back to A.D 300. during the Three Kingdoms, at which time houseboat dinner parties were held on one of China's many beautiful lakes. These were extravagant affairs executed by renowned chefs who prepared numerous dishes to be served with China's finest rice wines.

Dining on water had its functional purpose, too, as the primary means of travel in China was through its waterways. The world's longest artificial waterway, the thousand-mile Grand Canal (construction began in the fifth century B.C. and was completed by the end of the thirteenth century A.D.), has provided the setting for a countless number of culinary excursions.

Later, during the Yuan (i.e., the Mongols, 1271–1368) and Ming (1369–1644) Dynasties, writers described the pleasure boats of the West Lake (Hangchow) rented by the wealthy, with their extravagant banquets served in dishes of gold and silver, and with singing and lanterns completing the scene.

Workmen's Restaurants

Another category on the hierarchy of eating establishment in China is the workmen's restaurant, sometimes referred to as the people's restaurant as this is where the peasants eat, very inexpensively. In Changsha, Hunan, a food editor and I enjoyed a memorable lunch at a workmen's restaurant.

We ordered our meal by pointing to the dishes the peasants were eating, which included a soup, a pork and chili pepper dish (Cured Pork Belly with Chili Peppers*), another dish composed of smoked bacon and

straw mushrooms, and a wonderful smoky-flavored bean curd dish. A bowl of cold rice accompanied the meal (throughout China, rice was served cold). The soup (Hunan Home-Style Soup*) was clear, with slices of unpeeled ginger root, slices of pork, thinly shredded egg pancake, local greens, and two varieties of fungus. The outstanding pork and chili pepper dish had taste and character. Although it was too spicy for the Western palate, as the chili peppers had been chopped without removing the seeds and membranes, it had an excellent flavor. The bacon and dried straw mushroom dish was also superb, distinguished by the smoky flavor of the bacon which permeated the sauce. The quality of the straw mushrooms was superior to that of those available in the West.

If this is the restaurant food of peasants, they're doing very well. Although the dishes were not refined by classic Chinese food standards, they had distinguishing regional characteristics (chili peppers, smoky flavor of the meats), ingredients of excellent quality, and interesting seasoning. And they were authentic, representing the food which the people themselves eat. Another positive aspect of eating in the workmen's restaurant was that it was the only place that we, as foreigners, were not separated from the Chinese.

I vividly remember walking late at night, dodging the bicycles, past these workmen's restaurants after they had closed, with their chairs piled on top of the tables. I can still picture the solitary figure outside computing the day's earnings with an abacus.

Hotel Dining

The dishes produced in the kitchens of the hotels in China are presently referred to as their national cuisine. Regrettably, too often these kitchens have taken classic Chinese dishes and redesigned them to accommodate the foreigner's palate. To experience the variety of China's regional cooking is a delight, but in hotel cuisine, little attempt is made at maintaining a regional character.

Hotel breakfasts are better than lunches and dinners, with both Western breakfasts and Chinese-style breakfasts available. Chinese-style hotel breakfasts vary somewhat from region to region: in Peking there are breads and dumplings with primarily pork fillings, congee, relishes (pickled green peppers, for example), egg custard made into a patty, sponge cake, sliced Chinese sausage, and unripened fruit (why the fruit was unripened remains a mystery to me and to the entire group). Coffee and tea are available. In Changsha, Hunan, local fresh vegetables, blanched and served cold, are included in the breakfast menu and the congee is more substantial, with added meat. One unusually varied hotel breakfast in Changsha included shredded chicken with chives, sautéed peanuts, sautéed chili peppers (Spicy Charcoal Peppers*), congee, paper-thin slices of roast pork (a variation on the classic Barbecued Roast Pork* of Canton), and Almond Cookies*. Generally speaking, Canton hotel breakfasts had more variety, primarily because of the trays of dim sum.

Restaurant Dining

In China, restaurants are often located in palatial architectural structures surrounded by interconnecting courtyards. With many different floors and numerous rooms, there is a sense of isolation because diners in one area are not visible to diners in another, and foreigners in particular are always separated from the Chinese.

Reservations are required in most cases, at which point one is given a choice of various dinners based on a series of ascending prices, anywhere from 15 to 80 yuan (one yuan is approximately 75 cents). The Chinese dine early, and reservations are not available after six or seven o'clock. If possible, avoid the banquet dinners, as the best dishes are found by ordering off the menu or by requesting specific dishes with ingredients that are in season, which is easily discovered by visiting the local markets. Special requests should be made when making the reservation. Unless one speaks Mandarin, it is advisable to be accompanied by a Chinese guide.

Different restaurants feature various regional specialties. For instance, the Sick Duck Restaurant, so named because it is on the same street as Peking's main hospital, specializes in Peking Duck; and the Min Zu Fan Zhuang Restaurant, also called Nationality House, is a comfortable, almost serene restaurant that features the classic northern Mongolian Hot Pot. There is also an excellent Szechwan restaurant in Peking called the Chengtu Restaurant, named after the capital of Szechwan Province. This restaurant, which resembles a Peking lacquered temple, is known for its smoked dishes, especially smoked poultry, one of the most renowned of which is Tea Smoked Duck*. They also serve Ma Po Tou Fu*, a classic western vegetable dish favored throughout China. Dry Sautéed Shredded Beef* is another recommended featured dish. The Horn of Plenty Restaurant (Feng Ze Yuan) in Peking serves delicious classic Pekingese Silver Thread Rolls, Peking Rolls*, and red-cooked carp topped with shredded mushrooms and bamboo shoots, with an extraordinarily rich sauce seasoned with sherry and soy.

A unique Hunan specialty is Stinking Bean Curd, a favorite dish of Mao Tse-tung. It is served with a pepper sauce consisting of sesame oil and ground chili. Shaped something like a charcoal briquette, Stinking Bean Curd is spongy on the inside and crisp on the outside, with a curious dark greenish-brown color. This classic western specialty is the featured dish at Changsha's Fire Palace Restaurant in Hunan, where Mao frequently dined as a student. Built during the Ching Dynasty, the restaurant is over a hundred years old, and has pictures of Chairmen Mao and Hua on the wall, ceramic doves on the ceiling, and red lacquered molded horizontal projections from the walls.

In Canton, the Sha Ho Restaurant is the city's foremost noodle restaurant, specializing in hundreds of noodle dishes. Their very thin rice noodles are outstanding, partially because they use the best spring water. Also excellent is their Crabs Sautéed with Scallions (a variation of which is Stir-Fried Lobster with Shredded Leeks*). This restaurant has a nice touch with simple stir-fried fish and seafood dishes, perfectly cooked, simply seasoned, such as Perch Fillets Sautéed with Leeks and also Sautéed Frogs' Legs. Of the many restaurants in Canton specializing in dim sum, the most famous is the beautiful Pan Hsi Restaurant, which is actually a series of rambling dining areas and tea houses on Lake Liwan. One is guided to the foreigners' modern air-conditioned dining hall through a series of gardens, bamboo groves, courtyards, and rooms connected by little bridges over quiet streams. The Pan Hsi is famous for fashioning dim sum delicacies into intricate shapes, including beehives, numerous small animals, and various flowers. The menu constantly changes, and the endless range of dim sum is implied in the fact that one could order dim sum every day for one hundred days and never have one duplication. I was more impressed with the variety and visual aspect of the dim sum than the culinary outcome of the finished product.

A seasonal Cantonese specialty, Rice Birds Stuffed with Liver Sausage, can be found at the Economy Restaurant in Canton, if you dine there in the autumn. These tiny birds, which are a tender, wonderful southern delicacy, are caught in the rice fields in nets. They are cooked and eaten whole, as the bones are softened during the cooking process.

Some of the best Chinese food in the world is available in Hong Kong. At the Yung Kee Restaurant in Hong Kong, there are many outstanding dishes, two of which are the Roast Goose with Plum Sauce and Steamed Bean Curd*. The Spring Deer Restaurant there serves an excellent Barbecued Lamb and also Baked Whole Shad. In the Mandarin Hotel in Hong Kong there is an elegant, beautiful, and extraordinary restaurant called Man Wah. Although there are many outstanding dishes, two of my favorites are Lobster Sautéed with Soybean Paste* and Steamed Crab with Asparagus.

Chapter 4

THE
CHINESE MEAL

The People's Diet

Students always ask me, "What does a typical Chinese meal consist of?" I used to answer, "One seafood, one poultry, one beef, one pork, and one stir-fried vegetable dish." This is a fantasy. The classic Chinese meal, consisting of seafood *and* poultry *and* meat, is relegated to special occasions. The everyday diet for the peasant (nine tenths of the population is composed of peasants) consists primarily of rice (in the North, bread substitutes for rice), vegetable dishes to which small quantities of pork have been added, eggs, bean curd dishes, relishes, and soups.

Chinese Banquets

Banquets are a way of life in China. Every man there is assured of three banquets in his life, at least one of which he can enjoy: one when he is born (a month after his birth), one when he marries, and one after his funeral. Banquets are also given for birthdays—not every year, but rather every decade—at which time noodles are always served, symbolizing long life (and therefore the noodles are never cut). For birthdays and weddings, the Chinese wear red; for funerals, white.

The banquet itself has a certain traditional format and specific customs. Guests are seated at round tables for ten. The actual seating arrangement is according to the status or rank of the individuals. Everyone has chopsticks and his own serving spoon for the various dishes, and is expected to help himself. The hostess sometimes selects a tasty morsel from a serving platter and with the unused end of her chopsticks places it on a guest's plate. In a home-style meal, the dishes are placed in the center of the table and everyone reaches with his chopsticks, taking a little at a time, placing the piece of food first on top of his rice bowl, then in his mouth. The Chinese would consider it impolite if someone interrupted their meal to ask them to pass a dish. If there is drinking, no one drinks except when making or responding to a toast. Condiments are never put on the table, with the exception of the dips for appetizers and dim sum, as the chef is given the responsibility for the seasoning (and the cutting). It would be a great insult if additional seasonings were requested.

There is very little emphasis on table setting, tablecloth, candles, and centerpieces, as there is in the West; rather the emphasis is placed on the food. Sometimes an entire meal is consumed in the United States without a mention of the food, whereas in China this would never happen.

Banquets require that the dishes arrive at the table one at a time. The opposite is true with home-style Chinese meals. And the choice of dishes for a banquet is a departure from those served every day. Rice is not prominent at banquets; rather it is served at the end of the meal, primarily as a gesture. And the absence of vegetables in a dish is generally an indication that it is a banquet dish, or at least the ratio of meat to vegetables is proportionately higher. The home-style soups, pork dishes, eggs, vegetables, bean curd dishes, are relegated to the home, as the banquet calls for the extraordinary, the extravagant, the elaborate, the exotic. The exception to the rule that home-style dishes are not served at banquets is that everyday dishes from another province or region may very well happily appear on the table. Also, there is a tendency to do the opposite of whatever are the regional distinctions. For instance, Szechwan banquets would avoid hot, spicy dishes.

The traditional banquet format begins with cold hors d'oeuvres. Frequently the food on the hors d'oeuvre platters is shaped in the form of an animal, such as a peacock or a dragon. The hors d'oeuvres usually consist of cold cooked meats, poultry, fish and seafood—such as roast pork, chicken and duck, sliced abalone, split shrimp. The platter is elaborately garnished with icicle radishes carved in the shape of flowers.

After this, ten to twelve dishes may follow, one at a time—dishes requiring elaborate preparation and special skills—then possibly several stir-fried dishes and/or whole-cooked meats, poultry, or fish. In between courses, soups are served to refresh the palate. As diners are never given napkins, waiters bring hot towels at intervals throughout the meal, at the same time removing and replacing used plates. Sometimes there is one special vegetable dish before the final sweet soup. (Sweet soups are not served at home-style meals.) Rice, noodles, or some starch is served at the end of the banquet, as is fresh fruit, and always a whole fish. This particular aspect of the banquet, the serving of a whole fish, is so important symbolically that inland provinces, where it was impossible to obtain a fish, have gone to the extreme of presenting a wooden fish. The fish, represents abundance, that there is more to follow, and in China this is a very heartwarming finale.

Beverages

While I have gone into great detail about the food of China, I have barely mentioned their beverages, because eating and drinking are separate occasions to the Chinese. Tea is drunk during the day and between meals, not with meals*. Of the various categories of tea, the Chinese prefer green tea, although semifermented teas such as Oolong are held in high esteem. They export a vast amount of black tea, but drink very little of it. They also use tea in their cooking, either incorporated into the dish like dried tea leaves sautéed with meat or fish, or employed in the smoking of the dish, such as Tea Smoked Duck*. Of the various legends concerning the origin of tea drinking, my favorite is the one Madame Grace Zia Chu describes in her book *The Pleasures of Chinese Cooking:* There was a cholera epidemic in China, at which time the emperor decreed that all water must be boiled before being consumed. One day, as he was sipping his cup of rather dull boiled water, a tea leaf from a not-so-far-away bush gently dropped into his cup. He liked what he tasted and the Chinese have been drinking tea ever since.

At restaurant banquets in China, I was usually served either beer or orange soda. Sodas became popular in the 1930s. The Chinese are not particularly fond of alcohol, and if there is drinking at all, it is usually on festive occasions or at banquets. There are no cocktail hours, and no mixed drinks. Those who want to drink usually drink whatever everyone else at the table is having, which in my experience in China was either warmed-up, sweet, grain-based wine, served in what we would consider espresso cups, or a strong alcoholic beverage, colorless like vodka but made from wheat, called Mao Tai, which is served in tiny, stemmed glasses. Mao Tai is a wicked beverage, and regrettably the custom is bottoms-up after every "Gom Bay" toast. Chinese vodka is served in the South. I imagine there have been a few Chinese under the influence, based on their "guessing fingers" drinking game, in which two potential inebriates both quickly hold up between zero to five fingers, and at the same time shout a number between zero to ten. Whoever yells the correct sum of fingers extended by both players is the winner; it is bottoms-up for the loser.

Planning a Chinese Meal

Planning a Chinese meal can be likened to a general's planning a battle. You must have a calculated written plan, starting with the dishes you would like to serve down to the measuring of the tea leaves in the pot. I have suggested twelve possible dinners from which to select until you begin planning your own.

The first things to consider are how much time you have or want to devote to the preparations, and any economical considerations that may be necessary. After these there are various other considerations, as there is not a main course served at a Chinese meal, but rather a blend of dishes; therefore it is necessary to select those that provide a contrast of colors, textures, and seasonings. This is done by choosing dishes that feature a variety of fish, poultry, meat, and vegetables. These dishes should employ different cooking techniques, not only because different textures will be produced, such as crunchy, crispy, and soft (braising, roasting, deep-fat frying, steaming, and stir-frying), but also because it is the combining of different cooking techniques that makes it possible for one person to produce a multicourse Chinese dinner with all the dishes turning out at the same time. If you wish, choose a soup and then one or more appetizers. Avoid a repetition of seasonings. If you are serving Barbecued Roast Pork*, in which hoisin sauce plays a major role, hoisin sauce should not appear again in the meal.

Choose only one dish that is shredded, and only one that is cooked whole—for instance, a whole-roasted duck or a steamed fish. A contrast of spicy and bland, heavy and light dishes, starting with the subtle and working up to the spiced, should be another consideration. Select one dish that can be prepared entirely in advance and served at room temperature.

After the meal is planned and the shopping is completed, the preparations should be done systematically. The following steps are the most efficient order for completing the preparations: 1. marinate; 2. soak the dried ingredients; 3. mix the batters; 4. wash the vegetables; and 5. combine the seasoning sauces. If there is a repetition of procedure, such as the mincing of ginger root or the chopping of scallions, do this all at once. Ideally the mincing of the garlic should be done at the last moment, but if you wish to complete all the preparations in advance, add the minced garlic to the seasoning sauce or place it in a bowl and moisten it with peanut oil. Try to complete all the preparations, including the cutting of the vegetables, as early in the day as possible. In most cases, all the preparations can be done the day ahead and the food refrigerated.

A written plan blocking out the entire orchestration of the dinner, including the order of cooking, should be posted on the refrigerator or somewhere near the stove. Go through a dry run early in the day. Choose all the serving dishes, set up cookie sheets lined with paper towels if you are deep-fat frying. These details make the dinner go smoothly.

About an hour before the guests arrive, set up as many trays as there are dishes to be cooked. The tray concept is very important, because when you are actually down to the cooking, everything happens quite fast, and having the ingredients for each dish organized on a separate tray minimizes room for error. All the ingredients should be set up on the tray in the order in which they will be added to the wok. While you are cooking, it is extremely helpful if someone can read the recipe to you. For the conclusion of a Chinese meal, fresh fruit is refreshing and, moreover, authentic.

When calculating proportions, in most cases allow one dish for every two to three people. If you are serving a large number of people and wish to make only a few dishes, use the following formula to calculate how much food to prepare:

Number of people × *1/2 pound per person* ÷ *number of dishes.*

EXAMPLE: *Number of people: 12*
Pounds of meat, fish, or fowl: 6
Number of dishes: 3
Pounds per dish: 2

The following table provides a quick reference for speedy recipes and recipes that can be coordinated easily into a multicourse Chinese dinner.

I. Fast Preparation, Easy Cooking Procedure
PEARL BALLS
BARBECUED TILEFISH
STEAMED SEA BASS WITH FERMENTED BLACK
  BEANS
STEAMED CANTONESE LOBSTER
STEAMED CARP WITH PURPLE BASIL
STEAMED SHRIMP
SOY-BRAISED CHICKEN

*II. Completed Several Hours or a Day or More
in Advance, Served at Room Temperature*
SESAME SEED BEEF
SMOKED FISH FILLETS
TANGY TURTLE CHICKEN
TRICOLOR SHRIMP ROLL
FIVE FLAVORS CHICKEN
PON PON CHICKEN
BARBECUED DUCK PORTIONS
BARBECUED WHOLE DUCK
SZECHWAN CRISPY DUCK
TEA SMOKED DUCK OR CHICKEN
BARBECUED ROAST PORK
FIVE STAR SPICY BEEF
BRAISED MUSHROOMS
EGGPLANT IN GARLIC SAUCE
SEASONAL STIR-FRIED VEGETABLES
SHREDDED VEGETABLES HUNAN STYLE
SPICY BRAISED EGGPLANT
SPICY CHARCOAL PEPPERS
STIR-FRIED VEGETABLES WITH BRAISED MUSH-
  ROOMS
SZCHEWAN SWEET AND SOUR CABBAGE
CHINESE OMELET I
COLD NOODLES WITH SPICY SESAME SAUCE

*III. Completed Several Hours or a Day or More
in Advance, and Reheated*
BRAISED CHICKEN WITH BLACK BEANS
BRAISED GINGERED CHICKEN
SOY-BRAISED CHICKEN
ORANGE SPICED DUCK
SQUABS IN CASSEROLE
BARBECUED ROAST PORK
RED-COOKED SHOULDER OF PORK

*IV. Almost Completed in Advance, with Mini-
mal Amount of Attention for Last-Minute Cooking Procedure*
BAKED ROAST PORK BUNS
ICICLE RADISH BALLS

SHAO MAI
STEAMED ROAST PORK BUNS
STUFFED CLAMS IN BROTH
BAKED STUFFED CLAMS
STUFFED PRAWNS

The following is an example of a multi-course Chinese dinner served family style, that is, with all the dishes turning out at the same time.

DINNER FOR 8 SERVED FAMILY STYLE

Menu
SZECHWAN STEAMED WHOLE FISH
BRAISED GINGERED CHICKEN
CHARRED SHRIMP IN BARBECUE SAUCE
SPICY CHARCOAL PEPPERS

Advance preparation
Make chicken the day ahead
Make peppers the day ahead
Complete all preparations for the shrimp
Complete all preparations for the fish

30 minutes before serving dinner
Preheat oven to 350 degrees F.

20 minutes before serving dinner
Place the chicken in the oven to reheat
Place the fish in the steamer

10 minutes before serving dinner
Stir-fry the shrimp and place it on a heated serving dish
Remove the fish from the steamer and finish making the sauce
Remove the chicken from the oven
Immediately serve the fish, chicken, shrimp, and peppers

COCKTAIL PARTY

PEARL BALLS
TRICOLOR SHRIMP ROLL
DEEP-FRIED WALNUT CHICKEN
STUFFED SNOW CRAB CLAWS
BAKED STUFFED CLAMS, A VARIATION ON
  STUFFED CLAMS IN BROTH
SPICY BRAISED EGGPLANT (SERVED ROOM
  TEMPERATURE)

COLD BUFFET

PON PON CHICKEN
EGGPLANT IN GARLIC SAUCE
FIVE STAR SPICY BEEF
BARBECUED ROAST PORK
SMOKED FISH FILLETS

DINNER MENUS

Family-Style Dinner
SZECHWAN STEAMED WHOLE FISH
BRAISED GINGERED CHICKEN
SHRIMP WITH PIQUANT SAUCE
SPICY CHARCOAL PEPPERS

Banquet for 12
DEEP-FRIED BUTTERFLY SHRIMP
SESAME SEED BEEF
STUFFED CLAMS IN BROTH
STIR-FRIED LOBSTER WITH SHREDDED LEEKS
CHUNKED CHICKEN HUNAN STYLE
ROAST DUCK LO MEIN
CRISPY BASS HUNAN STYLE

Economy Dinner for 8
SZECHWAN SWEET AND SOUR CABBAGE
POOR MAN'S PEKING DUCK
FRIED BLUE CRABS
SAUTÉED BEAN CURD WITH SHRIMP SAUCE
BRAISED CHICKEN WITH BLACK BEANS

Vegetarian Dinner for 8
VEGETABLE ROLLS WITH SESAME SEED SAUCE
HUNAN HOME-STYLE SOUP (OMIT PORK)
BARBECUED EGGPLANT
SZECHWAN VEGETARIAN'S BEAN CURD
STIR-FRIED VEGETABLES WITH BRAISED
  MUSHROOMS

Dinner for 8
SZECHWAN RICE STICK NOODLES
BARBECUED TILEFISH
CHUN-PI CHICKEN
DOUBLE-COOKED PORK

Dinner for 8
SHREDDED SMOKED CHICKEN
FUKIENESE FRIED PORK CHOPS
STEAMED SEA BASS WITH FERMENTED BLACK
  BEANS
FOUR-STYLE MUSHROOMS

Dinner for 8
DICED SPICY CHICKEN IN LETTUCE LEAVES
SNOW-WHITE CLOUD SOUP
ORANGE BEEF
LAKE TUNGTING SHRIMP
CURRIED RICE VERMICELLI (OMIT SHRIMP)

Dinner for 8
ICICLE RADISH BALLS
BARBECUED WHOLE DUCK
DRY SAUTÉED SHREDDED BEEF
CLAMS IN BLACK BEAN SAUCE

Dinner for 8
BEGGAR'S CHICKEN
FILLET OF BASS WITH WINE SAUCE
LOTUS BEEF
STEAMED SPARERIBS WITH FERMENTED BLACK
  BEANS

Dinner for 8
RED-COOKED SHOULDER OF PORK
SHRIMP AND CRAB MEAT SZECHWAN-STYLE
STIR-FRIED CHICKEN WITH WALNUTS
STIR-FRIED WATERCRESS WITH FERMENTED BEAN
  CURD

Chapter 5

SPECIAL COOKING TECHNIQUES

Stir-Frying

Stir-frying is a cooking technique which involves the continuous tossing and turning with a spatula of small pieces of food in a little oil over an intense heat for a short duration of time. Because it requires less cooking time less fuel is used, and it is for this economic reason that stir-frying became the most commonly used technique in Chinese cooking.

PROCEDURE

1. Place a dry wok over intense heat for about 1 minute. (Stir-frying can be done in a dutch oven or even in a skillet, but it is much easier in a wok. It's like the difference between tossing a salad on a plate or in a bowl.)

2. Add oil with a tablespoon in a circular motion, starting at the top of the sides of the wok and continuing around, so the oil coats the sides as well as the bottom of the wok. Another reason for always adding the oil around the sides of the wok is that the oil heats faster. Do *not* lift the wok away

Alternative method of stir-frying: Shake the wok, keeping the spatula stationary.

from the burner or turn it to circulate the oil, as you would a saucepan, because the wok should at no time be lifted away from the source of heat. You can slide some oil onto the spatula and distribute it around the sides of the wok. Do this for about 30 seconds, or until the oil is hot but not smoking. It is the heating of the wok before oil is added and of the oil before food is added that prevents the food from sticking.

3. Add any one type of ingredient—vegetables, meat, fish, or poultry—all at once. Meat and vegetables are always cooked separately for two reasons: first, they require different cooking times; second, the vegetables contain moisture that would hinder the browning of the meat and the sealing of flavorful juices. To keep splattering to a minimum, add the ingredient from no higher than 3 inches from the bottom of the wok, and be certain that vegetables are dry before adding them.

4. Start stir-frying immediately by moving the spatula all the way through the food in the wok, continually tossing the contents every few seconds, making certain to reach the bottom center as otherwise the food will stick. The most important part of the technique is to set up a steady rhythm for yourself. The movement is from the shoulder and involves the whole arm. Stir-frying is tiring at first, but when done on a regular basis it becomes quite normal, fast, and efficient. An alternative way of stir-frying is to reverse the process, and instead of moving the spatula with a steady, continuous rhythm and keeping the wok stationary, you hold the spatula stationary and shake the wok with sharp, abrupt motions alternately away from you and then toward you, continuously and rhythmically. No matter which method you use, it is necessary to have the highest flame possible at all times except when the recipe indicates to lower it. Watch carefully when you are stir-frying vegetables because they may begin to scorch, in which case you should turn the flame down immediately. Even

though the timing is indicated in the precise form of seconds or minutes in the recipes, it is at best only an indication. The neophyte tends to stand by the wok watching a clock's second hand; however, it is the visual aspect of the food which should be considered. The timing will be determined by the intensity of the flame and the amount of food that the wok contains. Although stir-frying may appear to be the simplest of the Chinese cooking techniques, it is actually the most difficult to master because split-second timing is critical.

5. After the contents of the wok have been emptied, wash the wok immediately with hot water and a vegetable brush. Use a copper scouring pad to remove any rusty particles that the brush does not remove. Do not use soap. Dry the wok over a high flame, and for the first few months rub a teaspoonful of oil into the wok, to season the metal and to prevent rusting.

ADDING STOCK

When making a stir-fried dish, always add not only the oil but also the stock around the sides of the wok, as this will enable the stock to act as a deglazing agent and return to a boil faster. (When adding a half cup or more of stock at once to the wok, first bring it to a simmer in a separate saucepan. It will return to a boil faster and will improve the quality of the dish.)

THE SAUCE

In the event that a sauce containing a half cup or more of stock is not thickening or is too plentiful, remove the vegetables, meat, fish, or poultry with a wire strainer. Let any extra sauce drip down from the strainer into the wok. Place the vegetables, meat, fish, or poultry on a serving dish. Stirring constantly, boil the sauce until it reduces and thickens. Pour the reduced sauce over the vegetables and meat. This emergency technique prevents the ingredients from being overcooked.

THE HEAT SOURCE

The sizzling you hear when you stir-fry is an important sound, because it lets you know the heat is intense, and the success of the dish, assuming that all the other techniques are done correctly, is determined by the intensity of the heat source. If you are using a gas stove, you should have the valve released so the maximum amount of flame will be available. If you are using an electric stove, it is impossible to adjust the heat rapidly; therefore it is necessary to preheat as many burners as there are temperature changes in the recipe. Preheat one, two, or three burners to low, medium, and high. If the recipe requires a high, then a medium heat, remove the wok from the high burner and place it on the medium burner. Except for some vegetables, the hottest possible heat should be used. Read through the cooking procedure to determine the total number of temperature changes.

ORGANIZATION

Mastering the art of stir-frying requires practice and concentration. However, the most important part of putting together a dish is organization, and therefore from the very beginning you should get in the habit of putting all the ingredients for a recipe on a tray, in the order in which they will be added to the wok. Read the recipe over several times before you start to stir-fry. If possible, post a copy of it on a wall or cabinet at eye level for easy reference, or have someone read it to you while you are cooking.

Rewarming

Chinese food is fast, fresh, and also fragile; therefore it is not recommended that any dish be reheated. When serving a Chinese meal, have your guests seated at the table before the food arrives. If you reheat stir-fried foods, the vegetables become soggy, the shrimp become rubbery, the poultry dries out, and the meat toughens. If you reheat deep-fat-fried foods, they lose their crisp quality, and roasted poultry and meat dry out. Texture is far more important than temperature in Chinese food. Leftover dishes should be refrigerated and served cold or at room temperature the following day. Deep-fried leftover appetizers can be rewarmed for 5 to 7 minutes in an oven preheated to 450 degrees. They will of course not be as good.

Passing Through

Passing through is a cooking technique in which marinated pieces of meat, poultry, or seafood are deep-fat fried in 2 cups of oil at a temperature of 325 degrees as a preliminary to stir-frying. It can be compared to the blanching of vegetables. Passing through has many advantages over merely stir-frying: it sears the food evenly and quickly, prevents it from sticking together, gives it a more velvety texture and produces a superior finished dish. Indigenous to the Szechwan Province in the western part of China, passing through is a technique that evolved out of practical considerations. Meat that is partially cooked does not require refrigeration, and most homes in China do not have refrigerators. For the American cook, passing through is a time-saving device, as it can be done before the guests arrive.

PROCEDURE

1. Marinate the raw meat, fish, or poultry in egg white, water chestnut powder, and sherry. This marinade serves three purposes: it acts as a tenderizing agent, gives the food a velvety texture, and prevents it from absorbing oil. The food must be refrigerated in the marinade for at least 1 hour and preferably more, up to 12 hours. Longer marinating would make the meat too soft.

2. Place the wok over high heat for about 1 minute. The purpose of heating the wok before the oil is poured in is to prevent the meat from sticking.

3. Add 2 cups of peanut oil, turn the flame to medium, and heat until the oil reaches 325 degrees. The reason for warming the oil over a medium as opposed to a high heat, which would be quicker, is to provide an even heat distribution. Even though 2 cups of oil are used, this technique does not produce a greasy dish if the oil temperature is properly maintained and the meat is well drained.

4. After restirring the food in the marinade, turn the heat to high and add the food and the marinade to the wok all at once. If the oil temperature is correct (325 degrees), the food will move freely in the oil when stirred. If the oil is too hot, the food will stick together. If the oil is too cool, the food will sink to the bottom of the wok and will absorb too much oil. The most accurate way of judging the oil temperature is to use a deep-fat-frying thermometer. Another way is to place several pieces of the marinated food in the oil. Never pass through more than 1 pound of the marinated food at a time, as the cooking oil would cool down too rapidly, causing the food to absorb too much oil.

5. While the food is cooking, it should be stirred with a pair of long "cooking chopsticks" in a circular motion for 1 to 2 minutes. Shrimp and scallops require less time than diced chicken. Each individual recipe will indicate approximately how long the food should cook. Because passing through is only a preliminary to stir-frying, the food should not be entirely cooked. Meat should lose its redness, shrimp should turn pink almost all the way through, and chicken should turn white or opaque.

6. To drain, grasp the handle of the wok in one hand and pour the oil and the ingredients into a colander set over a bowl. Shake the colander a few times to aid the draining, then place the colander over an empty bowl to drain further. This is to ensure that the food will not be sitting in the oil from which it was drained. The first pound is removed from the wok with a

wire strainer and set to drain in a colander over a bowl; the second pound is poured with the oil into the same colander set over another bowl to catch the draining oil.

7. Once the oil has cooled, pour it into a glass jar, leaving any juices from the food that have settled in the bottom of the bowl. Refrigerate the oil uncovered until it has solidified; then cover it. This oil may be used again several times for any type of meat, fish, or poultry. When the oil starts to turn brown, it should be discarded. When reheating the oil, if it starts to splatter that means some of the juices from the draining food were not left behind. Cover the wok while the oil is heating until the splattering stops. Occasionally a recipe will call for "cooked oil." This refers to oil that was previously used for passing through (or, in some cases, oil used for deep-fat frying). The advantage of using "cooked oil" is that it adds the flavor of the cooked meat.

8. Wipe the outside of the wok where the oil was poured out. This is to prevent a flash fire.

9. Return the wok to a high heat and in the oil that glazes it, stir-fry the remaining ingredients in the recipe.

DOUBLING RECIPES

When you are doubling a recipe for passing through, you remove the first pound of meat, poultry, or fish with a wire strainer and place it in a colander set over a bowl. Before the second pound is added, you reheat the oil to the original temperature, that is, 325 degrees. Then you add the second pound, and after the second pound is cooked you pour the oil and the food into the colander set over the bowl. Shake the colander to aid the draining and place it over a clean bowl. Always remember to reheat the oil to 325 degrees between additions. Never add more than one pound of meat at a time, as the end result would be greasy, for you would be frying in oil that has cooled.

Deep-Fat Frying

Deep-fat frying is a cooking technique in which coated food, such as meat, poultry, seafood, and sometimes vegetables, is cooked in a large quantity of hot oil. This technique occurs in Chinese cooking more frequently than in any other cuisine. One of the main differences between Japanese and Chinese cooking is that the Japanese use a base of stock while the Chinese prefer an oil base. Deep-fat frying produces interesting textures and also seals in flavor and juices.

PROCEDURE

1. In most cases you will first marinate the food, as the marination procedure helps to tenderize and also adds flavor.

2. Place a wok over high heat for about 1 minute. The best cooking vessel for deep-fat frying is a wok, because the high sides prevent the oil from splattering. The preferred wok is of heavy-gauge steel, which is an excellent conductor of heat; this helps maintain the oil temperature and aids the browning process. An added benefit from using your wok for deep-fat frying is that it speeds up the process of seasoning the wok, which prevents food from sticking.

3. The food is now, according to the recipe, either coated with lumpy water chestnut powder or dipped in a batter. The coating serves two purposes: it prevents the meat from absorbing oil and produces a crunchy exterior.

4. Pour in the required amount of oil. The quantities of oil specified in this book are based on the recommended 14-inch flat-bottomed wok. Less oil is required for a smaller wok, but as the capacity is smaller, less food can be added to the wok at a time. Turn the heat to medium until the oil reaches the desired temperature, which is usually 350 degrees Fahrenheit. The oil temperature is extremely important. The most accurate way of judging it is to use a deep-fat-frying thermometer. In time this will not be necessary, as you will recognize

the waves in the oil as a signal that the oil has reached 325 degrees, and you will be able to judge the temperature by how the food reacts in the oil. To test the oil temperature without a deep-fat-frying thermometer, put a few pieces of the ingredient to be cooked into the wok. If they sink to the bottom, the oil is not hot enough, and therefore the end result would be greasy, because too much oil would be absorbed. If the ingredient bounces to the surface of the oil immediately and the oil has very rapid bubbles, the oil temperature is too hot and the outside will brown before the inside is cooked. If the ingredient submerges for a few seconds, then quickly rises to the surface with rapid bubbles, the oil temperature is correct. At all times avoid heating the oil to the smoking point because at this point it becomes saturated.

5. Once the desired oil temperature is achieved, the heat is then turned to high in most cases and the coated meat is added by hand to the wok. The recipe will indicate the quantity to cook at one time. When frying more than one batch, always remember to reheat the oil to the original temperature before adding the second batch. Never crowd the ingredients you are deep-fat frying as this creates steam, cools down the oil temperature too rapidly, prevents the food from browning, and causes it to absorb too much oil. When cooking more than one batch of coated ingredients, leave the heat source on and skim the oil with a fine-mesh skimmer to remove the particles of batter, powder, or nuts before adding a new batch.

6. Once in the wok, deep-fat-fried foods are best turned over with long "cooking chopsticks." These chopsticks decrease the chances of being splattered. If the oil begins to splatter, cover it with a wok lid for a few seconds or until the splattering stops. Wipe the stove frequently while deep-fat frying. This precaution will prevent flash fires, for which the Chinese are notorious.

7. Use a wire strainer to remove the food from the oil. Hold the strainer over the wok and move it up and down for a few seconds, letting the oil drain from the food. However, when cooking a duck, you tie it with a string looped around the wings to facilitate the turning. You also use this string to remove it. Always have ready at least one cookie sheet or shallow roasting pan lined with several layers of paper towels to drain the food in a single layer.

8. Have an empty metal bowl or pot nearby to remove the oil from the wok if the wok is to be used immediately for stir-frying, as in the case of Orange Beef*. If the wok is not being used again immediately, allow the oil to cool. If the oil has not turned brown, it can be reused, in which case you pour it through a strainer or a fine-mesh sieve, both of which should be lined with cheesecloth that has been rinsed and wrung out. Refrigerate the oil uncovered until it has solidified, then cover it.

9. Deep-fat-fried foods should be served immediately and should never be kept warm. When deep-fat frying appetizers, have someone else do the serving while you fry them in batches; that way they will reach the guest hot and crispy. Leftover deep-fried appetizers can be reheated in an oven preheated to 450 degrees; however, they are never as good. Do not reheat poultry, fish, or meat dishes; serve them at room temperature.

Twice-Frying

Twice-frying is a cooking technique in which coated meat, poultry, seafood, and sometimes vegetables are deep-fat fried two separate times. The first frying is done between 325 and 350 degrees, which cooks the ingredients almost completely. The pieces of food are then removed from the wok, drained, and allowed to cool thoroughly. This step can be done early in the day. For the second frying, the oil is reheated, this time to 375 degrees, and the food is added to the wok in small batches and refried. The second frying produces a very crisp texture and actually makes the food less greasy.

Passing Through and Deep-Fat Frying Compared

Frequently the question arises: How does passing through differ from deep-fat frying? The similarities and differences can be seen in the following chart:

PASSING THROUGH	DEEP-FAT FRYING
1. Wok is heated before oil is added to prevent food from sticking.	same
2. Oil is heated before food is added.	same
3. Two or more cups of oil are used.	same
4. Foods are drained after being cooked.	same
5. Foods have a protective coating, that is, a marinade, to prevent the food from sticking.	same
6. This cooking technique seals in juices.	same
7. Has the same marinade every time, consisting of egg white, water chestnut powder, and sherry.	Marinade varies: sometimes egg white, water chestnut powder, and sherry; sometimes a batter; sometimes a marinade that seasons, like light soy sauce, sesame oil, and sherry, which is drained from the meat (then the food is coated in water chestnut powder).
8. Done at a relatively low temperature, 325°.	Done at a relatively high temperature, between 350° and 375°.
9. Food stays in the oil for a short time, from 45 seconds to 1½ minutes.	Food stays in oil for a longer time, up to five minutes (or even longer in the case of a whole fish).
10. Produces a soft, velvety texture.	Produces a crisp texture (because a higher oil temperature is used and the food stays in the oil a longer time).
11. Only partially cooked. It is a preliminary to stir-frying.	Completely cooked.

Wet Steaming

Wet steaming is a cooking technique frequently employed by the Chinese in which live steam rises from boiling water, circulates around the food, and cooks it by direct contact. It is an easy way of preparing food that is low in calories and cholesterol, and it creates a light, delicate, and moist texture. Once your steamer is set up, it takes care of itself. That fact allows you to stir-fry another dish at the same time, which is a step in the direction of preparing a multicourse Chinese dinner. The difference between steaming and poaching is that the poached food comes into direct contact with the seasoned liquid. For example, in poaching a fish, it is totally immersed in a court bouillon (a seasoned liquid) and simmered until done. In steaming, the fish never actually touches the boiling water; it is cooked by the steam created by the boiling water in the bottom of the steamer. As the fish releases juices when steamed, it must be placed on a plate that has a lip. The seasoning is then distributed on top of the fish, and the plate is placed in the steamer on a rack. You cannot use a French fish poacher, because the fish would touch the water, and if you tried to use a high rack in the poacher, it would elevate the fish, thereby not allowing the flat cover to fit on the poacher. You would need a dome-shaped cover, which is not made.

Many different foods are steamed either whole (such as a whole fish or duck) or in small pieces (such as Pearl Balls* or dumplings). When steaming whole fish, duck, or chicken, the best setup is to use a large dome-shaped turkey roaster. This method allows you to cook the fish whole. When making dim sum or other foods in small shapes, the best steamer to use is the classic Chinese bamboo steamer. It is also possible to steam in a wok with a dome-shaped cover, by placing a round rack in the bottom of the wok and then the plate containing the food on this rack. This is the least desirable selection of all for many reasons. A fish will have to be cut in half and then reassembled when ready to present (however, the sauce will conceal most of the cut). The capacity of the wok for steaming dumplings is very small because you cannot form levels. The depth of water can only be an inch or two and this will evaporate very quickly. And finally, if you are steaming in a seasoned steel wok, it will soon lose its seasoned finish; when stir-frying, food will stick, and before long the wok will begin to rust.

THE WET-STEAMING PROCEDURE IN A DOME-SHAPED TURKEY ROASTER

1. Fill a large metal or enamel dome-shaped turkey roaster with water to a depth of 3 inches.

2. Place a cylindrical rack, standing vertically, in the bottom of the roaster. The best rack to use is an empty can (approximately 3 inches high and 4 inches in diameter),

the top and bottom of which have been removed.

3. Bring the water to a boil.

4. In order not to get a steam burn, turn the heat off.

5. Put the plate with the ingredient that you are steaming on the opened top of the can in the roaster. The dish that you choose does not have to be ovenproof, as the moist heat created by the steam will not damage even good china. *The important factor is the size of the dish, not its composition.* It must be at least 1 inch smaller on all sides than the bottom part of the roasting pan, in order for the steam to circulate up and around the food. The dish must also have sides of at least 1/2 inch or sides that slope up; otherwise the juices that collect around the food being cooked will spill out. All whole fish and also several steamed dishes require being served in this dish.

6. Place the lid on the roasting pan. If there is a vent, close it.

7. Steam over a high heat.

8. The water level should be checked every half hour in the case of foods such as poultry or meat that require a long period of steaming. Keep resetting the timer and have boiling water ready in a separate kettle to add every time it is needed.

9. Refer to the recipe for the cooking time. A 1 1/2-pound fish usually takes 15 minutes, but the time will vary according to the intensity of the heat source and the thickness of the fish. A 2 1/2- to 3-pound fish will take 18 to 20 minutes. When the eye bulges, it is done. The accumulated liquid will be used to make a sauce. This type of setup works with ducks and chickens as well. When the legs move freely in the joints, the bird is done.

10. Serve the fish from the same platter in which it was steamed. This keeps the fish warm and also makes an attractive presentation. If it must be transferred to another serving dish, gently slide a large flat spat-

ula underneath the fish and then slide it onto the serving plate. If you are steaming a bird, remove the dish from the roasting pan and allow the bird to cool at least 30 minutes before attempting to remove it from the dish, as otherwise it will fall apart.

THE WET-STEAMING PROCEDURE IN A CHINESE BAMBOO STEAMER

1. Fill a 14-inch wok with water until the level is 3 inches from the top. This will be approximately 3 quarts of water. A stainless steel round- or flat-bottomed wok is your best choice as it will not rust.

2. Bring the water to a boil.

3. Place the food in one, two, or three levels (depending on the recipe) of a 12-inch bamboo steamer; place the steamer in the wok.

4. Place the bamboo cover on the steamer.

5. Steam over a high heat, replenishing the boiling water if necessary.

6. Serve the food in the steamer. It stays warm that way and is appealing to the eye.

7. Clean the bamboo steamer with a vegetable brush and soapy water. Unfortunately bamboo steamers do not last a long time, as they fall apart. An aluminum steamer will last longer, but a bamboo steamer imparts a better flavor.

Sautéing

Sautéing is a cooking technique in which a small quantity of food is cooked or browned in hot fat. The heat is less intense than in stir-frying, and the food is not kept in constant motion. Sautéing is commonly employed in Western cooking but only occasionally in Chinese cooking. In a few recipes in this book I have called for the sautéing of shallots, for example, over a low heat in butter. The use of butter in Chi-

nese cooking, although rare, dates back over four thousand years. Butter is rarely if ever used today, as there is and has always been a scarcity of dairy products in China, and also butter in many cases does not harmonize in Chinese dishes. In stir-frying over intense heat, butter, or even the combination of butter and oil, would burn in a matter of seconds.

Roasting

Roasting is a cooking technique in which meat or poultry is cooked by dry heat and a crisp skin is obtained without the use of oil. Although roasting is an important part of Chinese cooking, it is rarely done in Chinese homes simply because most Chinese families do not have ovens. Both in China and in Chinese communities all over the world, this problem has been overcome by the use of central ovens where roasted meats, birds, and innards are prepared and can be purchased by the pound or by the piece, such as a whole or part of a roasted duck or a portion of a roasted pig.

The American can accomplish Chinese-style roasting at home, whether the pieces to be roasted are small, as in Barbecued Roast Pork*, or are whole poultry and large pieces of meat.

PROCEDURE FOR ROASTING WHOLE POULTRY AND LARGE PIECES OF MEAT

1. Place one oven rack on the floor of the oven.

2. Place the second oven rack in the center of the oven.

3. Place a shallow roasting pan containing water to a depth of approximately 1 inch on the rack that is on the floor of the oven. The purpose of this is to catch the drippings and keep them from burning, and to provide moisture.

4. Preheat the oven to the required temperature.

5. Place the prepared bird or roast on the center rack. This way, the heat will circulate all around the food to be roasted, and will produce a far crisper bird or roast than the traditional method of placing the bird on a rack resting on a shallow roasting pan.

6. Replenish the water if necessary during the roasting period. If the water evaporates, the drippings will burn. Even if there is no sauce called for, you will want to save the drippings for use in another recipe, such as Roast Duck Lo Mein*.

7. When the roasting period has ended, remove the bird or roast from the oven to a rack resting on a plate to cool before it is sliced or chopped according to the recipe.

8. Remove the roasting pan which now contains water, drippings, and fat.

9. Pour the entire contents of the roasting pan into a heatproof measuring cup; remove the fat. This is most easily accomplished with a fat separator.

10. Return the defatted liquid to the roasting pan and reduce the liquid until a scant 1/2 cup remains. Pour in approximately 1/4 cup of sherry, and continue to reduce a few more minutes.

11. Serve the sauce separately or reserve it for another recipe. Refrigerated, it will last at least five days; frozen, it will last one year.

Because the results are superior, I use this method for all types of poultry and meat in both Eastern and Western cuisines.

PREPARATION FOR ROASTING A WHOLE DUCK

1. If available, choose a fresh Long Island duckling. If using a frozen duck, FCH and Maple Leaf are two excellent brands of Long Island ducks. Defrost the duck slowly in the refrigerator for a minimal loss of juices. Depending on the temperature of the refrigerator, complete defrosting will take approximately two days.

2. Remove the excess fat from both sides of the tail-end opening of the cavity.

3. Remove the giblets and neck from the cavity; then run cold water on the inside of the cavity and on the outside of the duck.

4. Remove the pockets of fat lodged between the thigh and the leg on both the left and right sides of the duck. This is done by creating a hole (from the inside) with the index finger and pulling the fat out. This will take about 10 minutes.

5. Turn the duck breast side down; lift the piece of skin that extends over the neck and remove the excess fat, glands, and membranes with a sharp boning knife. Do not cut and discard this piece of skin, because when the duck is roasted the skin shrinks, and this piece is needed to cover the breast.

6. Beginning at the neck end of the cavity with the bird lying breast side up, carefully separate the skin from the meat for about 5 inches, by pulling the skin back with one hand and cutting with a boning knife through the fat and membranes with the other hand. Turn the duck breast side down and do the same procedure along the top part of the back, separating the skin from the meat for about 1 inch. This will help the fat drain while the duck is being roasted and will help produce a perfectly roasted bird with no layer of fat existing between the skin and meat.

7. Turn the duck breast side up. Put your hand against the outside of the skin and carefully shave off with the boning knife more excess fat from the inside of the skin.

8. Secure each wing tip underneath the shoulder.

9. Submerge the duck in a large pot of boiling water for about 1 minute. This is done by tying butcher's twine around the wings.

10. Air-dry the duck by hanging it for at least 12 hours, or until the skin is taut. Perfect duck weather is between 35 and 50 degrees Fahrenheit.

(a) You can hang the duck outside on a terrace or in the backyard. If the temperature is below 32 degrees or above 60, hang it outside only 1 hour, then refrigerate it for at least 24 hours or up to 36 hours on a roasting rack. Turn every 12 hours.

(b) You can hang the duck inside over the rod of your bathroom shower with the window open.

(c) You can hang the duck inside anywhere near an air conditioner or in front of a fan.

It is the blanching and air drying of the skin that produces a crispness that will last even after the duck has been allowed to cool. The blanching and air-drying procedure can be done with all types of poultry.

11. After the air-drying period, if the recipe calls for marinating, massage the duck with the marinade and either hang it once again or refrigerate it on a rack resting in a roasting pan.

Red-Cook Simmering

Red-cook simmering is a Chinese cooking technique in which whole pieces of meat, fish, or poultry are slowly simmered in liquid containing large amounts of soy sauce, water, stock, and sherry. Because of the large quantity of soy sauce used, the finished dish assumes a dark brown color, which is referred to as "red." Red rice is sometimes added to give a further reddish cast to the finished dish. The rather misleading name of this technique can be attributed to the Chinese preference for the color red over the color black. Examples of this type of cooking are Red-Cooked Shoulder of Pork* and also Orange Spiced Duck*.

THE RED-COOK SIMMERING PROCEDURE

In a heavy cooking vessel, combine soy sauce, water, stock, and sherry. (If red rice is called for, it is sometimes added early in the cooking procedure in order for it to dissolve.) Various spices are added, such as star anise, Five Spice Powder*, dried orange peel, scallions, and ginger.

Place the whole piece of meat, fish, or poultry in the vessel and cover. The cooking vessel remains covered throughout the cooking process. Slowly simmer. For even coloring as well as seasoning, turn the food several times during the simmering.

The time required for red-cook simmering varies, depending on the weight of the whole piece of meat, fish, or poultry. It should always be cooked until it is so tender that it can be carved easily with chopsticks at the table.

Red-cooked simmered dishes can be made several days in advance and rewarmed, which actually improves the flavor. Rewarming can be done in an oven preheated to 350 degrees or on top of the stove over a low heat.

Braising

In this manner of cooking, the meat, fish, poultry, or sometimes vegetables are first browned in hot oil, which seals in the juices, after which the liquid ingredients and seasonings are added. The cooking vessel is then covered and simmered over a low or medium heat, according to the recipe, until tender. An example of this technique is Braised Gingered Chicken*.

Deglazing

Although this is a French cooking term and technique (faire un déglaçage), it can be applied to Chinese cooking, as for Double-Cooked Pork*. When the food has been cooked and removed from the cooking vessel, flavorful juices that have coagulated during the cooking process remain. If a small quantity of liquid (mushroom or chicken stock, sherry or white wine) is added to this, and is reduced over a medium heat while constantly being stirred, it results in a thick syrupy glaze. This liquid is then poured over the food that was cooked, giving the finished dish a superior flavor.

Reducing

To reduce means to make less, and the reducing of stocks and sauces produces a more intense flavor. To reduce a stock or sauce, you simmer it, uncovered, over low heat until much of the liquid has evaporated. (The low heat prevents the stock from becoming cloudy.) In the final stages of reducing a stock or sauce, it should be stirred continuously.

Defatting

Here are several ways to remove the fat from stock or a sauce:

1. Place the liquid in a Pyrex measuring cup and refrigerate without a cover until the fat is congealed. This is the easiest method; however, since this procedure will take as long as 24 hours, it is not always the most practical.

2. Use a fat separator, which is made of heat-resistant plastic in the form of a Pyrex measuring cup with a fitted strainer on top. The New Colony Cup is the brand name.

3. Skim a spoon over the surface of the stock or sauce. This will remove most of the fat. To absorb the last few tablespoons of fat, float a piece of paper towel over the top of the liquid.

Deglazing, reducing, and defatting of stocks and sauces, which are techniques I have borrowed from the French, give Chinese cooking an extra refinement that produces superior dishes.

Blanching

Blanching means plunging into boiling water. It comes from the French verb *blanchir*, which means to soften. If a vegetable is too hard, stringy, or strong-flavored, it must be blanched first as a preliminary to stir-frying. Examples include Chinese broccoli, carrots, and string beans. Unfortunately vegetables lose 50 percent of their vitamins when blanched.

THE BLANCHING PROCEDURE

1. Submerge the vegetables in a large pot of rapidly boiling water for 30 to 60 seconds.

2. Remove them with a wire strainer.

3. To stop the cooking and hold the color, immerse the vegetables in a large bowl of ice water.

4. Before stir-frying, drain and dry them well. Vegetables can be blanched a day in advance and refrigerated. Allow them to become room temperature before stir-frying.

5. Use the water in which the vegetables were blanched to cook rice, to boil noodles, as a base for stock, or whenever a recipe calls for water, as in the case of Red-Cooked Shoulder of Pork* or Sesame Seed Beef*.

Marinades

The most common marinade called for in this book is a textural marinade consisting of egg white, water chestnut powder, and sherry. This marinade is for any type of raw meat, poultry, or fish. To use this marinade for passing through, the proportions are 1 egg white, 1 tablespoon of water chestnut powder, and 1 tablespoon of sherry for every 1 pound of meat. For stir-frying, use half the amount of marinade to avoid excessive sticking in the wok. When you are starting your preparations for a Chinese dinner and there are so many things to do and you don't know what to do first—marinate! The longer the better, *up to 12 hours.* Marinating longer than 12 hours will make the meat too soft. It is imperative to measure the ingredients for the marinade accurately. When measuring the water chestnut powder, level off the measuring spoon with the square end of a chopstick, as if you were measuring baking powder for a cake. When measuring the sherry, be certain to hold the measuring spoon level. If the recipe requires half of an egg white, it should be beaten with a pair of chopsticks before measuring. In this way the egg white will become thinner and will be easy to divide in half. All recipes in this book are based on large eggs. Any other marinade in this book is meant to season the meat.

Seasoning Sauces

Seasoning sauces can be prepared well in advance, if desired, even several days in advance and refrigerated. The measurements should be taken seriously. If, after trying the dish according to the recipe, you would like to alter the seasoning by adding your own personal touch, that of course is entirely up to you. Increasing the Hot Sauce* will make the dish more spicy; increasing the soy sauce or the various prepared sauces suggested (such as bean, hoisin, or oyster) give the dish a stronger as well as saltier taste. When a reduced mushroom stock is required in a recipe, you must let it cool thoroughly, otherwise the water chestnut powder will take action, thicken, and then later on, when added to the wok, will not take action again and the sauce will not thicken. If necessary you may substitute a salt-free poultry or vegetable stock for the reduced mushroom stock. Always restir the seasoning sauce very well before adding it to the wok. The sugar and the water chestnut powder will settle to the bottom in a matter of seconds. As a time-saving device, I have instructed that the water chestnut powder be dissolved into the sherry before it is added to the remaining ingredients in the seasoning sauce. If it is dissolved into a large quantity of liquid, it will take a longer stirring time for it to dissolve.

Stirring

When stirring sauces and soups, always stir with chopsticks or a wooden spoon in a fig-ure-eight motion, in order to cross the center of the saucepan.

Mixing

When mixing doughs and fillings, hold a bunch of chopsticks in one hand (approximately 10). I call this a Chinese wooden whisk.

Light Measurement of Flour

When measuring flour or cornstarch for doughs and batters, fill the measuring cup by spoonfuls, then level off any excess flour from the rim of the measuring cup with the square end of a chopstick or with a blunt knife.

Binder

A binder consists of water chestnut powder or cornstarch dissolved in room-temperature or cold liquid (mushroom or chicken stock, sherry, or water). It has several purposes: to thicken soups or sauces, to thicken any natural liquid released by fresh ingredients, and to create a luminous quality. It is very important to measure the water chestnut powder or cornstarch accurately. It is measured the same way you would measure baking powder when making a cake: insert the measuring spoon into the water chestnut powder or cornstarch, then level it off with the square end of a chopstick. In order to avoid cleaning the spoon, measure the dry ingredient first. Remember to restir the binder with a pair of chopsticks before adding it, because the starch separates quickly from the liquid.

Emergency Binder and Stock

Always keep an emergency binder and some extra stock near the stove in case a sauce does not thicken properly or becomes too thick.

Chapter 6

EQUIPMENT

Equipment

Two 14-inch carbon steel woks with flat bottoms and single wooden handles, Atlas Metal Spinning Company

One 12-inch carbon steel wok with flat bottom and single wooden handle, Atlas Metal Spinning Company

One 14-inch stainless steel wok with round bottom

One 13-inch dome-shaped aluminum wok cover

One heavy-weight carbon steel cleaver

Two light- or medium-weight carbon steel cleavers

One 5-inch carbon steel or high carbon stainless flexible boning knife

Butcher's steel and Carborundum stone

Bamboo chopsticks (40 pairs)

Cooking chopsticks (2 pairs)

A rubber mallet

A wooden chopping block

Two wire strainers, approximately 7 inches in diameter

Two steel spatulas for stir-frying

Deep-fat-frying thermometer (mercury), Taylor

An earthenware or sand pot with cover

A shallow roasting pan

A heavy-duty metal rack with 1½-inch legs that will fit into the roasting pan

Metal turkey roaster with a dome-shaped cover or enamel roaster with a dome-shaped cover

Metal cookie sheets

Trays

Lots of bowls of all sizes

Metal colander with handle

A large stockpot, preferably stainless steel

A fine-mesh metal skimmer

A fine-mesh metal sieve

A large vegetable brush

Copper scouring pads

Plastic fat separator (the New Colony Cup)

An electric coffee mill for crushing orange peel, water chestnut powder, Szechwan peppercorns, etc.

A bamboo steamer

Metal measuring spoons

Stainless steel graduated measuring cups

4-cup Pyrex measuring cup

Numerous glass jars for storing (plastic adds an undesired flavor and is not considered healthful as it can have a carcinogenic effect, especially with oily foods and long-term storage)

Bamboo steamer set in a 14-inch round-bottomed stainless steel wok.

Turkey roaster with dome-shaped cover and cylindrical rack standing vertically in the bottom of the roaster.

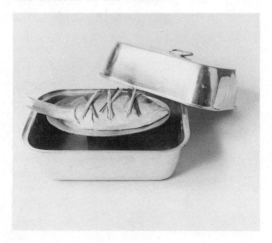

Metal strainers used for making Taro Nests*.

Clockwise from the bottom: cooking chopsticks, wok brush for cleaning, metal spatula for stir-frying, fine-mesh strainer and fine-mesh skimmer.

Earthenware pot or "sand pot" with cover.

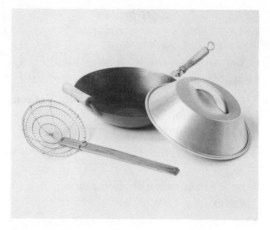

Wire strainer and 14-inch flat-bottomed steel wok with a single wooden handle. Dome-shaped aluminum wok cover.

Clockwise from top: rubber mallet, chopping cleaver (for cutting through raw fish and poultry bones), slicing cleaver.

Description of Equipment and Maintenance

I prefer to use a flat-bottomed carbon steel wok on a gas or an electric stove, as it comes in direct contact with the heat source. The single wooden handle allows you to hold the wok with one hand while stir-frying with the other. If the wok is filled with a large quantity of food and you need both hands for stir-frying, it will remain stationary. A heavy-gauge steel wok will last a lifetime if properly maintained.

SEASONING INSTRUCTIONS

1. Fill the wok with water and add two tablespoons of baking soda. Turn the heat to high and bring the mixture to a boil, stirring occasionally. Allow the mixture to boil for 5 minutes. Pour out the liquid.

2. Scrub the wok inside and out with a steel-wool soap pad. Rinse well and dry.

3. Place the wok over a low heat and rub several tablespoons of inexpensive oil over the inside surface of the wok with a clean rag or a paper towel for a few minutes.

4. With a vegetable brush and hot soapy water, wash out the wok. Rinse it with hot water. Return the wok to a low flame and repeat steps 3 and 4 two more times.

5. Run your finger over the inside of the wok to see if a grease film remains. If it does, repeat steps 3 and 4 again.

6. Fill the wok with at least 6 cups of oil and heat over a low heat for about 15 or 20 minutes. Leave the oil in the wok (you may cover it if you wish after the oil has cooled) for a few days, heating the oil two or three times a day. Discard the oil and wash the wok out with a vegetable brush and hot water; dry the wok over a high heat and wipe it with a paper towel.

Step 6 is an optional one but will aid the wok in performing well so that food will not stick when it is cooked in it for the first time. The best thing for a wok is deep-fat frying, which is what you are actually doing by heating up the 6 cups of oil. A beautifully seasoned wok is completely black. This will take a few months of regular use. If it doesn't turn evenly black in the beginning, don't be concerned.

MAINTENANCE OF THE WOK

The proper maintenance of a wok is to wash it with hot water (*never soap*) and a vegetable brush. If a few stubborn particles of food remain, use a copper scouring pad and more hot water. You should use soap and even a steel-wool soap pad on the outside of the wok to cut the grease, but if you use soap on the inside it will make food stick.

MAINTENANCE OF EQUIPMENT

The aluminum cover and the steel spatula can be washed with a steel soap pad and then dried well. The brush that is used to wash out the wok should be soaked in boiling-hot soapy water and then rinsed well. The wok brush can then be placed in the dishwasher. This procedure should be done at least once a week. The same procedure should be followed for the wire strainer, the fine-mesh skimmer, and the sieve after each use.

All carbon steel knives are guaranteed to stain, but they will not rust if they are washed with warm water and then dried well. In my opinion, the best cleaver is made by Dexter, which is located in Southbridge, Massachusetts. Since mincing is done with two cleavers, I recommend that you buy two. A third and heavier cleaver is necessary for cutting through fish bones, raw and cooked poultry, and so forth, as a lightweight cleaver will chip if given this task. The rubber mallet is to aid the cleaver in cutting through the bones. The lightweight cleaver will be used for other types of cutting. Clean your cleavers with warm water and a vegetable brush, as hot water and soap make them dull. Always use soap, however, after cutting raw chicken or pork, for health reasons.

There are at least two plastic heatproof fat separators on the market at this writing. The New Colony Cup, the one I prefer, looks like a measuring cup and has a perforated top. The bottom has an opening for the defatted liquid to drip through. It can be washed by hand or placed in the dishwasher.

Chopsticks should first be washed with soap and a copper scouring pad before being placed in a dishwasher.

The bamboo steamer can be washed with a vegetable brush and hot soapy water, then rinsed and allowed to drain until dry.

The stainless steel wok can be washed with a plastic sponge and water. Soap can be used if desired, although it is not necessary. Never use a steel-wool pad on any type of stainless equipment as it scratches the metal.

CHOPPING BLOCK
(without legs)

Buy as big a block as you have room for—at least two by three feet. Keep it out on a counter top so it is ready to be used at a moment's notice for any last-minute prepa-ration. A counter space near the stove is an ideal place to keep it. Proper home maintenance is important. A wooden chopping block accumulates and spreads germs; therefore it should be cleaned regularly and thoroughly. The block is best cleaned with water, soap, and a copper scouring pad. Always rinse and dry the board very well. A board left wet will warp. During the first year, rub it with cooking oil once a week, preferably left overnight, to prevent it from cracking. Once a month, pour a layer of salt over the entire surface of the board—make certain the board is dry—and let it remain overnight. In the morning, brush off the salt. This procedure eliminates germs and bleaches out the stains.

Chapter 7

FRESH VEGETABLES AND CUTTING TECHNIQUES

The Oriental vegetables used in this book are defined in the following list, which includes information on their season, how to select them, whether they store well beyond a few days or must be used immediately, and how to cut and cook them.

Amaranth In season from May to early February, amaranth is sold in bunches and is similar to spinach, except that it has a reddish cast and a more pungent flavor. The tough stems should be removed and discarded. The leafy portion is best stir-fried in oil, salt, garlic, and sugar. Serve with lemon wedges.

Bean Sprouts, Mung Available all year long, these sprouts of the mung bean should be purchased if possible from a market that does not store them in water. They should be very white and crisp. As they grow in water, washing them is not necessary. Stored wrapped in a towel in a plastic bag, they will last about three days in the refrigerator. They can be eaten raw in salads or used in stir-fried dishes. They acquire a smoky flavor if they are first dried well, then stir-fried for about two minutes or until they scorch in a hot wok without oil.

Bok Choy Available all year long, bok choy is best when purchased locally grown in the late spring, summer, and fall. It is in the cabbage family, and looks similar to swiss chard. The stems should be white and the leaves dark green with yellow flowers which are also edible. When possible, buy small young hearts of bok choy as they are sweeter. When cutting, it is a time-saving device to leave the bok choy tied in the bunch in which it was sold, remove a few inches of the stems with one slice, then slant-cut the remaining portion while the bunch is still whole and before it is washed. After cutting, separate the stems and leafy portions. Wash, drain, and dry. This technique can be applied to the entire choy family and also to mustard greens.

1. Bok choy. With one slice, remove a few inches of the stem.

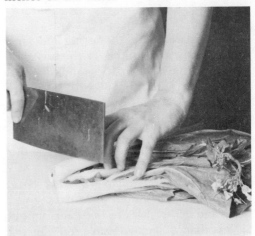

2. After cutting, separate the stems or leafy portions. Wash, drain, and dry.
3. Slant-cut the remaining portions while the bunch is still whole, before it is washed.

Yu choy.

Shantung cabbage.

Yu Choy Available in the spring and summer, yu choy is a member of the bok choy family, as is *Shanghai Bok Choy* and *Choy Sum* (*sum* meaning heart). Yu choy stems are thinner than those of bok choy, the color is pale green, and the leaves are a lighter green. The entire bok choy family is excellent stir-fried and in soups.

Broccoli, Chinese Available all year long, Chinese broccoli should have dark green stems and leaves. Ideally, the stems should be less than 1 inch in diameter. Cut off about 1 inch of the bottom of the stem. Pull off the outside leaves (which are tough) and stems (which are tough and pithy), leaving only the center stalk. The leaves and stems can be boiled in water for ten minutes. This water can be used as a base for vegetable soup or for cooking rice. Chinese broccoli has a slightly bitter taste, and blanching it is very important, otherwise it will be too tough and stringy. Blanch for 30 seconds.

Cabbage, Shantung Available all year round, Shantung cabbage should have light green leaves and crisp, solid, white stems. Sometimes there are brown specks which look like sand embedded in the stems. It is all right to eat this. Cut off ½ inch of the stems. Separate the stalks. Straight-cut or slant-cut the cabbage into 1

to 1½-inch pieces, separating the stems from the leafy parts, as the stems require longer cooking.

Chili Peppers *See* Peppers.

Chives Available all year long, chives are sold in large bunches and look like long blades of grass. They are very sandy. Remove about 2 inches of the bottom before washing. Stored in a plastic bag in the refrigerator, they will last one week at the most.

Duck Potatoes Also called arrowheads, duck potatoes are in season from October to February. This vegetable can be likened to an American new potato. Duck potatoes have a similar shape to fresh Chinese water chestnuts, but are slightly larger and have a lighter-color brown skin. Stored in the refrigerator, they will last two weeks. Peel, wash, and then slice into rounds. They can be sautéed in oil, butter, poultry fat, or with sliced preserved Chinese bacon. They can also be added whole, during the last 30 minutes of cooking, to slow-simmered red-cooked dishes, such as Red-Cooked Shoulder of Pork*

Eggplant Available all year long, western eggplant is purple and is more commonly used in the United States, but is also grown

Chinese chives.

Duck potatoes.

in China and can be used interchangeably with the several varieties used by the Chinese. The seasonal young Chinese white or lilac variety is long (about 8 inches) and thin (diameter of 2 or 3 inches). If eggplant is first cut (paring is not necessary in most cases), then salted and weighted for several hours, washed, drained, and dried, it will have no bitter taste and will require less oil when stir-fried.

Fava Beans Available from April to June, fava beans are similar in appearance to lima beans. Fava beans are rich, meaty green beans which come in a bumpy green shell. Shell, then remove the outer membrane that surrounds each bean. Once shelled, they should be left whole and stir-fried.

Fuzzy Melon *See* Squash.

Ginger Root Commonly grown in tropical climates, ginger root is obtained from the underground tuberous stem portion of a 2-to-4-foot-tall plant. It is an ancient Chinese spice used in many Chinese dishes. As it is available all year long, always use fresh ginger root. When selecting this irregularly shaped root, look for a smooth, tight skin that is very firm to the touch. Ginger root is a strong spice, and in order for the flavor to be distributed evenly, it should be finely minced when used in stir-fried dishes.

Chinese eggplant.

For long-term storage and convenience: Break off the outermost pieces, peel each piece with a vegetable peeler, then rinse under cold running water. Place the peeled ginger in a jar and cover with dry sherry; refrigerate in a covered jar, for up to one year. When ginger root and sherry are called for in a recipe, use the sherry in which the ginger is soaking ("ginger sherry"), then replenish it with more sherry so that the ginger is covered at all times. It is the replenishing of the sherry that acts as a cleansing agent and keeps the ginger fresh. If the ginger remains in the same sherry for over three months without being

Ginger root.

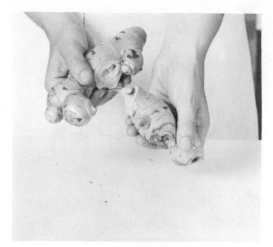

1. First break off the outermost pieces.

2. Peel with a vegetable peeler, then rinse under cold running water.

3. Make thin slices, always approaching the ginger from the angle that will yield the longest slice.

changed, it will begin to mold. If you are not preparing Chinese food regularly, empty the sherry from the jar and use it in a recipe that requires wine, then add new sherry to the ginger to preserve its freshness.

Another alternative and a great time-saving device for storing ginger is to cut the peeled ginger into small cubes. Turn on the food processor, and drop the cubes down the feeding tube. Turn the machine on and off until the ginger is finely minced. Place the minced ginger root in a glass jar and

add peanut oil to cover. Refrigerate, covered, for up to one month. Use both the minced ginger root and the oil it has been soaking in in the many recipes calling for minced ginger root.

Spring Ginger Also called *Young Ginger* or *Baby Ginger*, it is ginger that has been dug up when the leaves are still green and before the stalks begin to wither. Fresh spring ginger is similar in shape to winter ginger; however, it has a milder taste and thinner skin with a pinkish cast. Because it has a

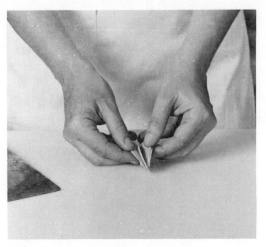

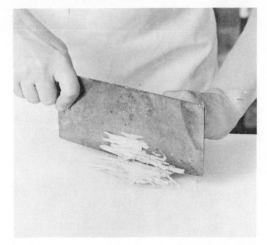

4. To shred, stack the slices.

5. Shred, keeping the long shape.

6. To mince, turn the shreds around.

7. Cross-cut to mince.
8. Mince more finely by holding a cleaver in either hand.

more delicate flavor, it can be used in generous quantities, generally speaking; specifically, when substituting spring ginger for winter, you can double the quantity. Shredded, or sliced for steamed and stir-fried dishes, it is used not only as a seasoning but also as a vegetable. It is best stored unpeeled in a plastic bag in the refrigerator, in which case it will keep for several weeks. As it is available only during late summer and in the fall, it is possible for long-term storage to pickle spring ginger (Pickled Spring Ginger*).

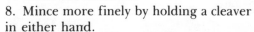

Icicle radish.

Young mustard greens.

Hairy Melon *See* Squash.

Icicle Radish (Chinese Turnip) Available all year long, this vegetable is referred to as daikon in Japanese markets. The many varieties differ in size, ranging in length from about 8 to 12 inches and in diameter, from 2 to 3 inches. Once pared, they can be shredded for soups and salads or minced for certain dishes such as shrimp toast or Icicle Radish Balls*. The best variety for soup is small with green on one end. For all other purposes, use the ones that are all white.

Leeks Available all year long, leeks look like very large scallions. The root end should be white with dark green stalks. They have a milder flavor and a tougher consistency and require longer cooking than scallions. Remove the root end, then split the remaining portion in half lengthwise. Wash well under warm running water to remove the sand, then drain. Stored in a plastic bag, they will last one week in the refrigerator.

Long Beans They are available all year but locally grown ones are best, as they deterio-

rate quickly. They are Chinese string beans, measuring about 16 inches in length and sold in bunches weighing approximately 1¼ pounds. They have a tougher consistency than American or French string beans, and should be blanched prior to stir-frying. It is a time-saving device to cut them, into approximately 3-inch lengths, while still tied in bundles before washing.

Mustard Greens They can be purchased all year long but are best when young, in the spring and summer. Because Chinese mustard greens are not as sharp as the Western variety, they are excellent for stir-frying and in soup. Refer to Bok Choy for cutting instructions.

Parsley, Chinese Available all year long, Chinese parsley is also called cilantro; it is actually fresh coriander. It is flat like Italian parsley, but the taste is totally dissimilar. Look for dark green leaves with no trace of yellow. Stored in a plastic bag in the refrigerator, it will last at least one week.

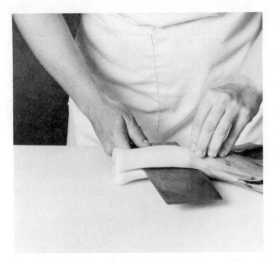

1. Fresh leeks. Remove the root end and split the leeks in half, lengthwise. Wash under warm running water to remove sand.

2. Cut the leeks into 3-inch lengths and shred.

PEAS

Snow Peas Available all year long, snow peas are small edible pods, which should be dark green with no trace of brown or yellow. Look for young snow peas—those with tiny, undeveloped peas inside the pod. Snow peas must be strung on the pea side before eating or cooking. When slant cutting is required, they should be cut in half once on the diagonal. For shredding, pile four on top of one another so that the pea side alternates with the flat side, to have a flatter stack. Snow peas are delicious when eaten raw in salads or with Spicy Dipping Sauce*. Cooking time should be less than a minute.

Sugar Snap Peas These are a new hybrid, similar to snow peas but shorter and fatter, with larger peas inside edible pods. They too must be strung before eating raw or cooking. Most plentiful in the spring, they are sweet and delicious, and can be used interchangeably with snow peas.

Snow peas.

1. String both ends of the pea side of the snow pea.

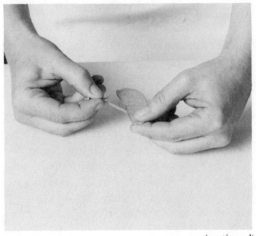

(continued)

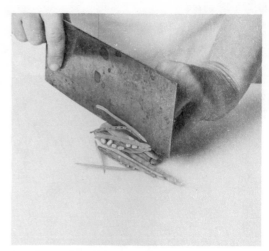

2. To shred snow peas, stack three at a time, alternating the pea side.

3. Then shred lengthwise.

PEPPERS

Sweet Red Peppers Although green peppers (sweet bell) are in season all year long, sweet red peppers are available most of the time and should be used whenever it is possible to buy them. Red peppers are green peppers that have been allowed to ripen on the vine. They are therefore prettier, sweeter, and contain six times the amount of vitamin C. Look for the ones that are crimson red, just before they rot. When preparing them, first make a cut all the way through (split in half). Carefully remove all the membranes and seeds (this is what is meant when recipes call for peppers to be "cleaned and seeded"). Dice, shred, mince, or triangle-cut according to the recipe.

Italian (Banana) Peppers Use these peppers interchangeably with sweet bell peppers.

Chili Peppers Fresh chili peppers are most plentiful in the fall, but they are available all year long. There are many different varieties. Generally speaking, the skinny chili peppers are the hottest. Which chili peppers you use is a matter of preference. Wear rubber gloves when removing the seeds and membranes: if you touch the

Hairy melon.

seeds with your hands and then touch your face, it will burn.

Scallions Also called spring onion, scallions are the onion most commonly used in Chinese cooking. Look for white ends with deep green stalks.

Shallots Available all year long, shallots are most plentiful in the spring and summer months. Shallots are considered the royalty of the onion family. In shape they are similar to garlic cloves, but they have a brown

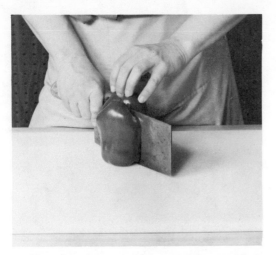

1. To triangle-cut red or green peppers, wash the pepper, cut it in half, and remove the seeds and membrane.

2. Cut each half lengthwise into even strips ¾ inch wide. Turn the strips and cut into triangles.

1. To shred: peel, then divide the hairy melon crosswise into 3-inch parts. Make about four slices on one side until you start to see the seeds, then turn the melon to the flat side.

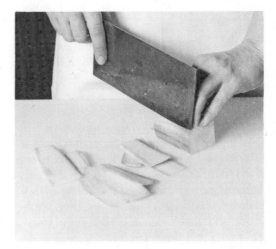

2. Depending on the diameter of the melon, slice approximately four times, then rotate it and slice approximately four more times. Do this on all sides. Discard the center section. Stack the slices and shred.

skin. Look for small ones. Do not buy them if roots are growing out at the end. Stored in the refrigerator, they will last at least six months. They can be sautéed whole or minced.

Sing Qua *See* Squash.

Snow Peas *See* Peas.

SQUASH

Hairy Melon (Fuzzy Melon) Available all year long, hairy melon is at its best during the spring and summer months. It is so called because it actually has a fuzz or hair on the outside of the skin. Choose young small ones, not larger than 2 inches in diameter, with deep green coloring. They

Sing qua.

Taro root.

should be firm and without flaws. The smaller ones are sweeter and contain fewer seeds. Peel and rinse under cold running water before cutting.

The procedure for shredding is as follows: divide the hairy melon crosswise into 3-inch sections. On one side make about four slices lengthwise until you start to see the seeds. Turn the melon to the flat side. Depending on the diameter of the melon, slice approximately four times, then rotate it and slice approximately four more times. Do this on all sides. Discard the center section. Stack the slices and shred.

The procedure for roll-oblique cutting is as follows: divide the melon lengthwise into four parts. With a lengthwise slice, remove the seeded section. Then roll-oblique cut. An excellent substitute for hairy melon is zucchini.

Sing Qua (Loofah or Sponge Melon) Available all year long, sing qua is best when purchased locally grown in the spring and summer months. It is a squash with ridges in its dark green, tough skin. Sing qua is also known as loofah or sponge melon because when it turns to seed, it is dried and used as an abrasive sponge. Once pur-

chased, sing qua should be used immediately, as it suffers with storing. At its best, it has a sweet but bland flavor. When cooked, its consistency is similar to that of okra. It is excellent stir-fried or added to soups.

Winter Melon Available all year long and sold by the pound, winter melon is a very large, bland squash. It will last for one week in the refrigerator. When preparing winter melon, remove both the rind and the seeds. The whole, uncut winter melon can be stored for several months in a cool dark place.

Sugar Snap Peas *See* Peas.

Taro Available all year long, taro is the very starchy root of a tropical plant. When possible, buy small young taro. Both the large and the small have a tough, dark brown skin.

Jicama.

Fresh water chestnuts.

Peel them and slice so that they keep their round shape.

Water Chestnuts In season all year long, water chestnuts are grown in the mud under several inches of water. When selecting them, feel each one to see if it is as hard as a potato. Once you have tasted a fresh water chestnut, you will never be able to eat the canned variety again. Many people have likened them to apples or coconut. Stored in a plastic bag in the refrigerator, they will last up to three weeks; however, do not peel and slice them until the day they are to be used. Slice to retain their round shape: first remove a thin slice from either end, pare the chestnut with a paring knife or vegetable peeler, then slice. They should be cooked only until they are heated through. Longer cooking will remove their naturally sweet flavor.

Jicama Available primarily on the West Coast, jicama is a Mexican radish. It can be substituted for water chestnuts if absolutely necessary. In some cases, Chinese icicle radish (Chinese turnip) can also be substituted, as for Shredded Pork with Garlic Sauce*.

Winter Melon *See* Squash.

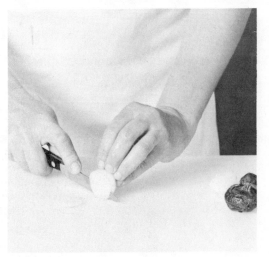

1. The carrots we are familiar with are the same as those in China. For roll-oblique cutting, start by making a slant cut at the thick end of the carrot.

2. Roll the carrot a quarter turn toward you, then make another slant cut so that the blade forms a triangle with the cut edge of the first slice.

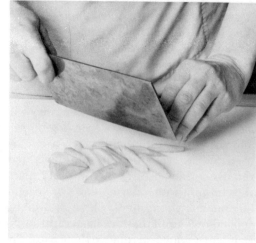

3. Now roll the carrot another quarter turn, forming a new triangle.

4. Continue cutting until you reach the end.

Chapter 8

SPECIAL
INGREDIENTS

Complete Staple List of Chinese Goods Used in this Book

CANNED
abalone
abalone (oyster) mushrooms
bamboo shoots (whole, spring)
bamboo shoots (whole, winter)
lichee
longan
loquat
straw mushrooms
sweetened white cucumber
water chestnuts, whole (if fresh are not available)

DRIED FRUITS
Chi-tzu berries
dates without stone
jujube (Chinese red dates)
pears
seedless plums

DRIED INGREDIENTS
Chinese mushrooms
dried orange peel
dried shrimp
straw mushrooms
tiger lily buds (golden needles)
tree ears
whole dried chili peppers

DRIED SPICES
five spice powder
star anise
Szechwan peppercorns
white peppercorns

**FERMENTED BEANS AND
FERMENTED BEAN SAUCES**
bean sauce
dark soy sauce
fermented bean curd
fermented black beans
hoisin sauce
hot bean sauce
light soy sauce
miso (dark; also called fermented soybean paste)
Peking broad bean paste
sweet bean sauce (also called sweet soybean paste)

FERMENTING AGENT
wine yeast

GINGER
ginger root, crystallized
ginger root, fresh
ginger root, pickled*
ginger root, spring

HAM
Smithfield ham

NUTS AND SEEDS
almonds
cashews
peanuts
pine nuts
sesame seeds, unhulled
walnuts

OILS
chili oil
peanut oil
sesame oil

PRESERVED VEGETABLES
preserved hot turnip (canned)
Szechwan preserved vegetable
Tientsin preserved vegetable (crock)

RICE
fermented red wine rice*
fermented wine rice*
long-grain white rice
red rice
rice flour
rice sticks for deep-fat frying
rice sticks for stir-frying
rice vermicelli
short-grain brown rice
sweet rice

SAUCES
curry sauce or paste
hot sauce* (chili paste)
oyster sauce
plum sauce
sesame seed paste or butter (tahini)

TEAS
black tea
Lapsang souchong tea

THICKENING AGENTS
cornstarch
water chestnut powder

VINEGARS
black rice vinegar
Chinese red vinegar
Japanese rice vinegar
red wine vinegar

WRAPPINGS
bean curd skins (sheets)
dried laver sheets
lotus leaves
rice paper

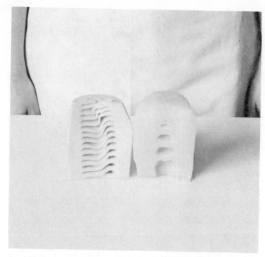

1. Two examples of bamboo shoots. On the left, a winter bamboo shoot. On the right, a spring bamboo shoot.

Abalone Distinctive and delicious, abalone is a type of mollusk available fresh only on the West Coast. In other places it is available dried and canned. Dried abalone is very expensive and has a strong flavor, as do all dried fish and crustaceans—the drying process intensifies the flavor. Its use is reserved for banquets. The best canned variety, in my opinion, is Calmex, because of its tenderness. However, it is expensive—at this writing it sells for $16.95 for a 15-ounce can. The juice from the can should be used in the recipe as well, but if there is leftover juice, freeze it and add it to soups later on.

The most important thing to remember about canned abalone is not to overcook it. Once heated, it is ready to eat; if overcooked it will toughen, so it should be added at the last possible moment of the cooking procedure, and cooked just enough for the heat to go through it. It can be kept refrigerated in water for one week if the water is changed every day, although canned abalone is better if used immediately. Abalone can be sliced and served cold as an hors d'oeuvre. It is frequently found on a cold platter as part of a first course at a banquet.

Anise, Star This spice is similar to anise seed, which Italians use in pastry. It has a licorice flavor and is used sparingly in red-cooked simmered and braised dishes. It is also one of the spices in Five Spice Powder*. Sold in cellophane packages, it should be transferred to a covered jar, where it will keep on a pantry shelf indefinitely. Star anise is an eight-pointed star.

Frequently most of the stars will be broken; therefore when a recipe indicates the use of 1 whole star anise, simply count 8 pods.

Bamboo Shoots These are young sproutings of the bamboo tree, which is an Oriental plant. (Bamboo wine is a specialty of Changsha, capital of Hunan Province.) Usually, only canned bamboo shoots are available in North America. The best are winter shoots, as they are crunchier and have a more distinguished flavor. However, if a recipe calls for the shredding of bamboo shoots, use the spring variety because their shape is more regular. The label for spring bamboo shoots will read "Selected bamboo shoots in water" or "Bamboo shoot tips." The winter variety will read "Winter bamboo shoots."

To store the winter or spring bamboo shoots, open the can when ready to use, rinse the shoots in cold water, then empty them into a jar or bowl of water. Do not save the liquid from the can, as it has preservatives. Refrigerate, and change the water every other day. They will last for a month. The same process is used for storing canned water chestnuts.

2. Slicing winter bamboo shoots.

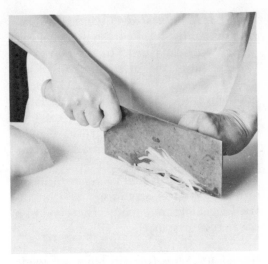

3. Shredding spring bamboo shoots.

Beans, Black (salted, fermented) These are black beans (like those the Spanish use in soup) which are steamed, spiced, and then dried. They are sold in plastic bags, and will last indefinitely. If they dry out, soak them in water before using. To retard their drying out, transfer them to a covered jar and store in the refrigerator. They are very inexpensive, and one package will last a long time. They are sometimes left whole and sometimes minced, depending on the recipe. Because they are extremely salty and have a strong flavor, they should be used sparingly.

Bean Curd or Fresh Bean Curd Cake It is made from soybean milk; the milk is extracted from soaked soybeans ground with water and strained through cheesecloth. When drained, the curd forms. In China the residue is given to animals. Bean curd is extremely high in protein, low in calories, and very inexpensive. The Chinese call it "meat without bones." Its consistency closely resembles custard. Although it has a bland taste, it has an interesting texture and limitless possibilities. Fresh bean curd is used not only in soups, but also in stir-fried, deep-fried, and steamed dishes. Ori-

ental food stores often keep bean curd cakes in a big container of water. There are two different types of fresh bean curd: Chinese and Japanese. The Chinese is a smaller square and more solid; the Japanese is larger (approximately double in weight), less solid, and falls apart very easily. They will both keep for one week in the refrigerator when placed in a bowl covered with water. The water must be changed every other day. After the drained bean curd is cut, liquid will still accumulate in the bowl. Drain the liquid off before adding the bean curd to the dish you are cooking. If you are using Japanese bean curd, remove it from the water in which it is soaking several hours before cooking, and allow it to drain on a terry-cloth towel, changing its position on the towel every half hour. This will make it more dense and will prevent it from falling apart when you cook it. If you live near a Chinese community, patronize a store that makes its own. The consistency and taste will be far superior.

Fresh bean curd is also available in a covered plastic container, and will last one month in the refrigerator, as preservatives have been added. Do not open until you are ready to use it. Buy the packaged bean curd only when the loose is not available.

Bean Curd, Fermented Purchased in glass jars, fermented bean curd has a label that reads "Wet Bean Curd." In addition to the soybean cubes, the jar contains rice wine, salt, red chili, and other spices. This brine liquid gives the bean curd a unique flavor, texture, color, and aroma. The 1-inch cubes of fermented bean curd have a soft consistency, and should be mashed or puréed before added to a dish. Stored in the refrigerator, fermented bean curd will last one year. It gives an unusual zest to stir-fried vegetables, and is especially good with watercress or spinach.

Bean Curd Skins (sheets) They are made from soybean milk; the milk is extracted from soaked soybeans ground with water and strained through cheesecloth. When the milk boils it forms a skin on top similar to the skin that occurs when cows' milk is boiled. The skin is removed with chopsticks and allowed to dry in the form of sheets. There are four layers of sheets. The fourth layer is the thinnest, and is the one used in the recipes in this book. The sheets are sold in packages, each package containing ten large half-moon shapes. They are used as wrappers in dishes such as Crispy Fish Rolls* and Stuffed Shrimp in Bean Curd Sheets*. Hang the package in the pantry, as the sheets are very fragile. They will last several months. As they are quite brittle in their dry form, they must be handled carefully. When preparing bean curd sheets for wrapping, it is important to allow them to soak between damp towels only until they are softened (about ten minutes). If you leave them longer, these fragile sheets will break when rolled. Before wrapping, trim off any hard edges.

Bean Curd, Pressed Made from fresh soybean cake, pressed bean curd cake is thinner and more dense because it has been weighted down and the moisture extracted. When it is shredded and used for stir-fried dishes, it will hold its shape.

Bean Curd, Spiced Pressed Made from fresh soybean cakes that have been weighted down and then simmered in a master sauce, spiced pressed bean curd has a prolonged freshness and an unusual smoky flavor. Commercially made or homemade, it will last for one week in the refrigerator.

BEAN SAUCES, FERMENTED

Bean Sauce This prepared sauce, sometimes referred to as yellow bean sauce, is purchased in a can. It contains soybeans (yellow beans), salt, flour, and vinegar. Always buy the whole bean sauce, never the ground bean sauce. Once the can is opened, the contents should be placed in a glass jar with a cover. Refrigerated, it will keep a year. It has a shelf life of one month.

As it is very salty, it should be used sparingly and measured accurately by leveling off a tablespoon with the square end of a chopstick. Bean sauce is used in many dishes, an example of which is Szechwan Steamed Whole Fish*.

Bean Sauce, Hot (Szechwan) This prepared sauce is sold in cans and is a spicy version of bean sauce. It contains soybeans, kidney beans, flour, chili, salt, sesame oil, sugar, and pepper. Stored in the refrigerator in a glass jar, it will last one year.

Bean Sauce, Sweet Also called sweet soybean paste, sweet bean sauce is made of wheat flour, soybeans, salt, sugar, and water. It comes in cans; after opening, store it in a glass jar with a tight lid in the refrigerator where it will last one year.

Hoisin Sauce This is one of the most popular of the Chinese prepared sauces. It is sold in a can; once opened, it must be transferred to a tightly covered jar. Its shelf life is approximately one month. Under refrigeration, it will keep for a year. It is made from yellow beans, sugar, flour, spices, and salt. Koon Chun is a good brand.

There are endless uses for hoisin sauce. It appears in various quantities in many stir-fried dishes as a minor or major ingredient which influences the flavor of the sauce and meat, poultry, or fish used in the recipe. There is no adequate substitute for hoisin sauce.

Miso (fermented soybean paste) Sold in plastic bags and containers, miso is made from fermented soybeans, salt, and rice. Miso ranges in color from light to dark brown. The dark miso has a richer flavor, as it has gone through a longer fermentation process, and is therefore a first choice. If only the light miso is available, mix one teaspoon of dark soy sauce with every tablespoon of light miso. Miso is high in protein and is used in red-cooked simmered dishes, seasoning sauces, and soups. Stored in a glass jar in the refrigerator, it will last six months. Miso was originally used by the Chinese but is now considered an important Japanese seasoning as well. An excellent brand is Skinshu Aka Miso.

Peking Broad Bean Paste It contains soybean paste, red chili peppers, chili oil, sugar, and salt. If this sauce is not available, you can substitute bean sauce or miso. For every tablespoon of broad bean paste called for in the seasoning sauce, use 1 tablespoon of miso and 1 teaspoon of hot sauce mixed together. Purchased in jars and stored in the refrigerator, it will last one year.

Chili Peppers, Dried (whole and crushed) Purchased in plastic bags, dried chili peppers should be transferred to a covered glass jar. Refrigerated, they will last indefinitely; if they are left stored on the shelf, bugs may form. They can be purchased crushed as well, but it is better to buy them whole and crush them, seeds and all, in a blender, electric coffee mill, or food processor. When chili peppers are used minced or shredded in a recipe, the stem end should be cut off and the seeds removed by shaking them out. Alert your guests that chili peppers provide spice to a dish and should not be eaten when they are served whole.

Chi-tzu These berries of the Chinese matrimony vine are sold dried. They have a similar shape to pine nuts but are red in color. Chi-tzu are very expensive but can be purchased by the ounce. They last indefinitely in a glass jar on the shelf. Chi-tzu have a high tonic value, especially for the eyes. They are used in slow-simmered soups, and as garnish for Snow-White Cloud Soup*.

Chow Fun See Noodles, Rice (fresh).

Cucumber, Sweetened White Sold in cans, sweetened white cucumber should be placed in a glass jar once a can is opened. It will keep refrigerated in the glass jar for about two months. Small quantities can be frozen with the syrup and will last for six months. These cucumbers have a similar texture and flavor to Kadota figs and are used in small amounts in sauces over fish, as in Sweet and Pungent Sea Bass* and Crispy Bass Hunan Style*. Do not buy the overly pungent variety that contains ginger. An excellent brand is Chun Tung.

Curry Sauce or Paste There are many different brands of curry sauce or paste. They will all last for at least six months in the refrigerator. Curry powder can be used as a substitute, but it is not as flavorful.

Date, Chinese (Jujube) Soak and remove the pit. Jujube is used in soups, and in desserts such as Water Chestnut Pudding*.

Dates, Without Stone The pit is removed from this fruit and it is more like the American dried date than jujube is. It can be eaten as a snack or used in Steamed Chinese Fruit Cake*.

Five Spice Powder* This is a marvelous as well as unusual spice which is composed of ground star anise, cinnamon, fennel, Szechwan peppercorns, and cloves. It can be made in the home or purchased. It is very aromatic and should be used sparingly.

The spice keeps for over a year if it is stored in the refrigerator in a tightly covered jar.

Ginger, Crystallized These dried and sugared slices of ginger can be eaten as dessert or used in desserts such as Steamed Chinese Fruit Cake*.

Ham, Smithfield Used in small amounts in soups and vegetable dishes, it is the American ham that most closely resembles, both in texture and its strong, salty taste, the ham used in China. It is possible to purchase it by the slice in Chinatown and a few department stores that have specialty food departments. If you buy it in the cured but uncooked state (which is the most common), prepare it as follows:

1. *Wash the whole 1-inch-thick slice of ham under cold running water with a vegetable brush.*

2. *Simmer in water to cover for 20 minutes.*

3. *After trimming the fat, cut the ham in about six pieces. It will keep in the freezer for several months if well wrapped in aluminum foil. The ham should be wrapped in individual pieces, as most recipes call for small quantities.*

When buying Smithfield ham, in order to get the maximum amount of meat and the minimum amount of fat and bones, request a center cut, 1 inch thick. Prosciutto or Westphalian ham can be substituted for Smithfield.

Hoisin Sauce *See* Bean Sauces, Fermented.

Hot Sauce Also referred to as *Chili Paste*, hot sauce is used in Szechwan and Hunan dishes. Many different hot sauces are available on the market. They are sold in glass jars and should be refrigerated as soon as purchased. It is, of course, preferable to make your own Hot Sauce*; this too must be refrigerated and will last from six months to one year. The amount used is according to taste. Generally, one teaspoon is enough to season a single recipe sufficiently. If a very spicy flavor is desired, up to one tablespoon can be used per single recipe. If you cannot tolerate spicy food, it is possible to omit the hot sauce entirely from the recipe.

Lard, Leaf Used when recipes call for rendered lard, leaf lard is from the chest of the pig. To render leaf lard, cut it into small pieces and place it in a heavy iron skillet or wok. Add 1/2 inch of water and simmer over a low heat until the fat has been rendered. Allow to cool. Refrigerated in a covered glass jar, it will last for one week, or several months in the freezer. It is used in pastries and dim sum.

Laver Sheets, Dried Purchased in plastic bags, laver sheets are square sheets of dried seaweed. They will last one year stored on the shelf. There are many different qualities, ranging in price from sixty cents to four dollars. The more expensive brands are well worth the price, as their flavor is far better. An excellent brand is Nagai's Dried Seaweed (Sagatami Yakisushi Nori). They can be used as a flavorful wrapper (Minced Shrimp in Laver Rolls*) or to provide color (dark green) and flavor to dishes (Tricolor Shrimp Roll*).

Lichee, Loquat, and Longan These Oriental fruits can be purchased fresh during the summer months, and when available fresh, they make a perfect ending to any meal. Lichees are also available dried and canned. Loquats and longans are available canned, as a substitute for fresh.

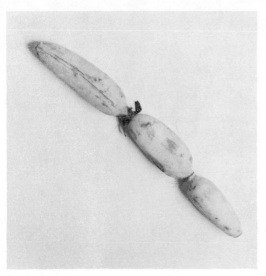

Lotus root.

Break apart attached pieces. Peel, then rinse under cold running water. Slice in rounds.

Lily Buds (Tiger), also called Golden Needles Originally for economic reasons, the Chinese have always tried to utilize a wide range of all edible growing things. The buds of the tiger lily flowers are just one example of a flower included in a recipe. Those buds shoot up straight and turn golden in the sun, hence the name "golden needles." Lily buds are sold dried in cellophane or plastic packages. Transferred to a tightly covered jar, they will keep indefinitely. Before use they must be soaked in warm water for a minimum of 20 minutes, then drained. (This, as well as the water in which tree ears have been soaked, should not be used in cooking, but has a salutary effect on plants.) If there are hard knots on the ends, cut them off. The lily buds are then sliced into two pieces widthwise or individually knotted. Tiger lily buds are used in soups, Mo Shu Ro*, and red-cooked simmered dishes. They have a slightly pungent taste and a chewy texture.

LOTUS

The lotus flower grows in the water like our water lily. The root is underneath the water. The root, seeds, and leaves are used in cooking.

Lotus Leaves Used fresh in China, lotus leaves are only available dried here. The leaves are inexpensive. They are not eaten but are used to flavor dishes like Beggar's Chicken*; the leaves are removed before serving. Pour boiling water over the leaves 15 minutes before using and allow to soak. Purchased in plastic bags, they will last one year.

Lotus Root Sold fresh, dried, and canned. The lotus root used in all recipes of this book is fresh, as the texture is far superior to that of the dried or canned. It is an expensive ingredient, available only in large Chinese markets. It is plentiful in the fall. The color of a light-skinned potato, lotus root is irregularly shaped like several sweet potatoes linked together. Not until it is pared and sliced can the beauty of the root

1. Dried mushrooms. Rinse the mushrooms under cold running water and allow to soak for two hours or until they become soft.

2. There are two ways of removing the mushroom stem: If mushrooms are to be shredded, diced, or minced, remove the stem from the whole mushroom.

be revealed. When sliced crosswise, each circle of lotus root reveals a lace-like pattern. Lotus root can be stored in the refrigerator in the vegetable compartment for two to three weeks. Lotus root is used in soups, desserts, and stir-fried dishes. Before stir-frying, blanching is required.

Lotus Seeds Available dried and canned in America, lotus seeds are used in soups and desserts.

Miso See Bean Sauces, Fermented.

Mushrooms, Chinese (dried) These black mushrooms have a wonderful flavor with a spongy, chewy texture, unlike American fresh cultivated mushrooms which have little flavor and a crisp texture. In Chinese markets they are sold in quarter-, half-, and one-pound quantities. The quality determines the price (from $20 to $40 per pound). The more expensive variety are called "flower" mushrooms. They are thicker and have a sculptured appearance on the outside of the cap. Used in small

quantities, they will enhance the flavor of many dishes. Once purchased, they should be stored in a covered glass jar, in which case they will last for years. Your hands must be dry when removing the mushrooms from the jar; if any moisture comes in contact with the mushrooms remaining in the jar, bugs will form and the mushrooms must be thrown out.

To prepare the mushrooms for cooking, you must reconstitute them. Measure the required amount of mushrooms. Rinse them under cold running water, then cover with cold water and allow to soak for approximately two hours or until they become soft. Soaked in hot water, they will soften in 20 to 30 minutes. Soaked in boiling water, they will soften in 10 to 15 minutes. Soaking them in cold water is best because they will retain the maximum amount of flavor. Once the mushrooms are soft, the stems must be removed. The remaining portion is then diced, shredded, minced, or left whole, according to the recipe. The mushroom stems are then returned to the mushroom "stock" (the water in which the mushrooms were soaking) and this is reduced until only a few tablespoons of liquid remain. Strain and cool the stock;

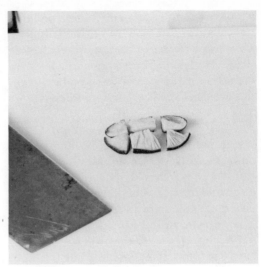

3. If mushrooms are to be quartered or cut into large, diced sections, cut them in half, then pull back two sides and remove the stem with a cleaver.

4. An example of large dicing.

use it in binders or add it to seasoning sauces or soups.

To prevent the water chestnut powder from taking action immediately rather than at the desired time, it is very important to allow the mushroom stock to cool before combining it with water chestnut powder. If you have no immediate use for the stock, it may be refrigerated for several days or frozen for one year. Mushroom stems may also be frozen and added to the stock pot at a later time. When a recipe calls for the dicing of mushrooms, each mushroom may be quartered or cut into as many as nine pieces according to its size. Save the larger mushrooms for shredding. If you have soaked too many, leftover soaked mushrooms may be removed from the water, squeezed dry, and stored in the refrigerator for several days. They will also keep frozen for one month.

Mushrooms, Straw Straw mushrooms are available canned or dried. The canned variety are beautiful and are used for aesthetic purposes in dishes such as Lake Tungting Shrimp*. If possible, the label should read "small and peeled." Unpeeled canned straw mushrooms are slightly less expen-

sive but require time to peel. Rowland is one of the brands I recommend. Drain and rinse the canned mushrooms, then drain again before using. Dried straw mushrooms are sold in quarter- or half-pound boxes ($5 for a quarter pound). To prepare them for cooking, you must first reconstitute them. Rinse under cold running water, then soak in cold water to cover for two hours or until they become soft. Remove the entire outer peeling, leaving them whole. They are not as pretty as the canned variety but have a strong smoky flavor that is unique. If you cannot easily obtain straw mushrooms, you can substitute dried black Chinese mushrooms; however, their appearance and taste are quite different. The water in which the mushrooms were soaking (the stock) is not used in cooking as the flavor is too strong and smoky, but the stock does have a salutary effect on plants.

Noodles, Egg Fresh Chinese egg noodles are made from cornstarch, flour, egg, and water. They are sold by the pound. If wrapped in aluminum foil and then placed in a plastic bag, they can be stored in the refrigerator up to five days, or in the freezer for a few months.

One substitute is dried Chinese or Japanese noodles; another substitute is Italian-style pasta (fettucine or linguine), freshly made or dried. They appear in lo mein dishes; lo mein means soft noodles, chow mein means shallow-fried noodles.

Noodles, Rice (fresh—Chow Fun) Often stores that make their own bean curd also make these fresh rice noodles called chow fun. When purchased, they are shaped in a large folded circle. On the day of purchase, you must cut them into half-inch widths. They can be stored for only a day before stir-frying, otherwise they will stick together in one lump. It is possible to stir-fry them and then return them to the refrigerator for one additional day before completing the dish in which they are used.

Noodles, Rice (dried—Rice Sticks) Sold in paper bags, rice sticks can be stored in a covered jar or canister for up to one year. They are excellent when deep-fried and used as a garnish. When deep-frying, do not soak them. Heat 2 cups of oil to 375 degrees. Break the rice sticks apart and deep-fry them for 1 to 2 seconds or until they puff up. Do not let them turn brown. Drain them well on several layers of paper towels. Deep-fry them early in the day and set aside. A good brand for rice sticks is Py Mei Fun.

Another variety of rice sticks are shaped like linguine, and must be soaked for 1 hour. They are used in stir-fried dishes such as Szechwan Rice Stick Noodles*. Two brand names for this are May Pride and Eagle.

Noodles, Rice (dried—Rice Vermicelli) These noodles are the same as rice sticks but thinner. Store them in a covered jar or canister for up to one year. Rice vermicelli are used in soups and stir-fried dishes. To prepare, soak them in warm water for 30 minutes, drain, and stir-fry them with meat or boil them in soup for a few minutes. A good brand for rice vermicelli is Double Swallow.

Nuts The Chinese often combine nuts with fish or poultry (never meat). The contrast in texture as well as taste has great appeal. Buy almonds, cashews, peanuts, or pine nuts in the raw state (blanched, with the outer shell and skin removed). Whether refrigerating or freezing, store them in glass jars. Frozen, they will last a year or more. To prepare: Preheat the oven to 325 degrees. Spread the desired amount of nuts evenly on a shallow roasting pan or cookie sheet. They should be golden brown before removing them from the oven. This will take from 7 to 20 minutes, depending on the type of nut. Pine nuts will have the shortest roasting time. This procedure will bring out the flavor of the nut and improve the taste considerably. Roast the nuts the same day you are going to use them. Walnuts and pecans do not require roasting, but certain recipes call for deep-frying as a preliminary to stir-frying. Stir-Fried Chicken with Walnuts* is an example of this.

Oil Many types of oil are used in China. Rapeseed oil and soybean oil are widely used; however, the preferred oil is peanut oil. It affects the taste of the food the least and it has the greatest resistance to becoming saturated. This is a very important point in Chinese cooking because so often the food is cooked over a very intense flame. Unless oil is to be used within one month's time, it should be stored in the refrigerator so that it won't become rancid. Remove the oil from the refrigerator about 30 minutes before using, to allow it to return to a liquid state.

Generally speaking, butter cannot be used in Chinese cooking, even in a clarified state, because it would burn when subjected to the high temperatures used in cooking most dishes. However, when a vegetable such as snow peas is shredded and sautéed over a low heat for a short period of time, butter can be substituted for the oil. This example is from the recipe for Lobster in Garlic Sauce*. Although butter is very rare in China today, the use of butter in Chinese cooking (primarily in desserts) dates back over four thousand years.

Oil, Sesame Used in Chinese cooking as a flavoring, sesame oil is added at the very end of preparing a dish. The oil imparts a nutty flavor. If it is added at the beginning, most of the aroma and wonderful flavor will be cooked out. The use of sesame oil can be likened to the use of butter in French cuisine: enriching a sauce by adding butter at the very end of the cooking. Do not buy sesame oil in a health food store—the flavor will not be the same. Chinese and Japanese sesame oil is made from white sesame seeds which have first been roasted and then pressed into oil. This is what gives it a good flavor and dark color. Some cheaper brands of Oriental sesame oil have food coloring added to them to make them look rich. The best test for choosing a good-quality sesame oil is smell. Stored in the refrigerator, it will last one year.

Orange Peel, Dried Although it is possible to dry your own orange peel, it is better to purchase the Chinese kind, as it has superior flavor. It can be stored indefinitely in a glass jar, and is said to improve with age. Dried orange peel and dried tangerine peel are interchangeable.

Oyster Sauce It is made from extract of oysters, water, salt, and two unfortunate ingredients, caramel coloring and preservative. For long periods of storing, it should be refrigerated. It appears frequently in Chinese cooking in fish, meat, vegetable, and noodle dishes. Hop Sing Lung is an excellent brand.

Peppercorns, Szechwan Grown and used in the western part of China in Szechwan Province, these peppercorns are actually more aromatic than they are spicy. They are sometimes referred to as brown peppercorns. Their flavor is best released when they are dry-roasted and then made into Szechwan Peppercorn Powder*. Szechwan peppercorns can be stored in a glass jar on the shelf. However, once they are made into a powder, this should be stored in a glass jar in the refrigerator.

Peppercorns, White These peppercorns come from the same seed as the black; they are a different color because the outermost husk has been removed, and their flavor, as a result, is more subtle and delicate than that of the black. The Chinese use white pepper in their cuisine for the same reason Europeans do: it is not visually conspicuous in light sauces, egg dishes, and clear soups. White peppercorns can be purchased in Chinese markets and most spice stores. It is a good idea to have two different pepper mills, one for black pepper and one for white.

Plum Sauce This prepared sauce is made from plums, chili, ginger, and other spices. It comes in a metal can; once opened, it should be transferred to a covered jar and stored in the refrigerator. Before measuring, remove the large chunks of ginger.

Poultry Fat, Rendered There are three ways to render poultry fat:

1. Poultry stock that has been cooled and refrigerated uncovered will form a thick coating of fat within twenty-four hours. This can be lifted off.

2. Remove the pockets of fat that are lodged in the cavity of the duck or chicken. Place this fat in a heavy iron skillet and cook over a low heat until the fat is rendered.

3. The best-tasting rendered poultry fat is that which is obtained from the roasting pan at the end of the roasting period. Remove the bird from the oven rack upon which it has been roasted, pour the contents of the roasting pan (which will include water, drippings, and fat), into a heatproof measuring cup. Allow it to cool. Place the measuring cup *uncovered* in the refrigerator overnight. When the fat has solidified, lift it off and place it in covered glass jars. Reduce the remaining liquid and use for deglazing and enriching sauces and soups. An example of deglazing is Double-Cooked Pork*.

In all three methods, the fat can be stored in covered glass jars in the refrigerator for up to two weeks. Frozen, it will last for one year.

PRESERVED VEGETABLES

Preserved Hot Turnip Purchased in cans, preserved hot turnip once opened should be stored in a glass jar, tightly covered. Refrigerated, it will last six months. A can contains shredded Chinese turnip (icicle radish), chili peppers, salt, oil, sugar, and pepper. This spicy condiment is used primarily as a seasoning. An example is its role in the stuffing of Beggar's Chicken*.

Szechwan Preserved Vegetable Kohlrabi, a member of the cabbage family, is a bulb with roots, preserved in chili and salt. It is sold in cans. In general, canned foods have a shelf life of six months, but once the kohlrabi is opened it may be stored in the refrigerator in a covered jar for up to six months. It adds an unusual, slightly spicy flavor when used in stir-fried dishes, such as Szechwan Pork and Pickled Cabbage Soup*. As it is preserved in fairly large pieces, kohlrabi must be minced or shredded before using in recipes.

Tientsin Preserved Vegetable Originating in the North, Tientsin Preserved Vegetable is prepared from Chinese celery cabbage. It is sold in earthenware crocks and should be stored in the refrigerator, in which case it will last six months. It is cut into small pieces, preserved, and seasoned with salt and garlic.

RICE

The Chinese are very resourceful in their use of rice. When I visited a rice commune in China, I saw all parts of the grain being used.

Rice husks are used three ways: 1. They are steamed and pressed into oil that is used for machinery. 2. Chefs in Szechwan and Hunan use rice husks as one of the ingredients for smoking poultry. 3. Husks are made into powder and used for pig fodder and fish food.

Imperfect grains of rice are soaked and boiled and used to make a sugar syrup that is an ingredient in cakes, pastries, and cookies.

Long-grain rice, steamed or boiled, is eaten with all meals. Rice forms 80 percent of the Chinese diet, except in the North, where wheat products are eaten instead. The average Chinese person eats a pound of rice a day. Use a good-quality long-grain rice in Chinese cooking, one that has not been precooked. When cooking rice, the Chinese use more water and cook the rice longer so that it will stick together and can be easily eaten with chopsticks.

Rice sticks (See Noodles, Rice) are made with rice that has been soaked in water, pressed into milk (the residue is given to cattle), kneaded, then put through a machine that makes rice sticks. The finished product is hung over racks to dry.

Rice liquor, made from rice, is much stronger than Japanese sake.

Rice Flour (Rice Powder) Made from both short-grain (Sweet Rice) and long-grain rice, rice flour is used primarily in desserts and should be stored in a glass jar on the shelf.

Rice, Glutinous It is also called two other names: (1) *Sweet Rice,* because its sweetness is released once it is fermented, as in Fermented Wine Rice*, and (2) *Sticky Rice,* because it is extremely sticky (glutinous) when steamed. This glutinous short-grain rice, rather than being eaten as a separate dish as you would eat long-grain rice, is used in stuffings, as a coating for Pearl Balls*, and to make Rice Patties* for Sizzling Rice Soup*. It is sold in 5-pound quantities and should be stored in a tightly sealed container to prevent bugs from forming. Glutinous rice is also ground into flour, which is used in some desserts.

Rice, Red Used to make Fermented Red Wine Rice*, red rice gives a reddish cast to red-cooked simmered dishes. It must be added early in the cooking to allow time for the color to penetrate the sauce.

Sesame Oil *See* Oil, Sesame.

Sherry Medium-dry sherry is the American substitute for Chinese rice wine. Never use cooking sherry that is sold in supermarkets because salt has been added. When purchasing sherry, bear in mind that if you wouldn't want to drink it, you wouldn't want to eat it either.

Shrimp, Dried Because of their very strong flavor, dried shrimp are used to season a dish. They can be rinsed under cold running water and then soaked in sherry for several hours before mincing, or soaked in boiling water until soft if a less intense flavor is desired. They are purchased in plastic bags in quarter-, half-, and one-pound quantities. Dried shrimp will last indefinitely if stored in a covered glass jar in the refrigerator.

SOY SAUCE

Dark Soy Sauce (Black) is made of fermented soybeans, molasses, water, and salt. It is thicker and sweeter than light soy sauce, not only because of the molasses but also because more solids have been added during the fermentation process. Koon Chun is a good brand. Dark soy sauce has a shelf life of a year or more and is the soy sauce most often used.

Light Soy Sauce contains fermented soybeans, water, and salt. Used primarily in salads and marinades, it is much saltier than dark soy sauce.

Low-Salt Soy Sauce There are currently two low-salt soy sauces on the market—Kikkoman and Tamari. They contain about 11 percent less salt than the Chinese soy sauce. For those who are restricted to low-salt diets, seasoning sauces can be adjusted by cutting down on soy sauce, any of the bean sauces, and also oyster sauce, all of which contain large quantities of salt.

Szechwan Peppercorns *See* Peppercorns, Szechwan.

Szechwan Preserved Kohlrabi *See* Preserved Vegetables.

TEA

The major beverage in China, tea that is superior requires a warm, damp climate. Of the 250 kinds of Chinese tea, the major classifications are as follows:

1. Scented tea, using flowers and fruits, such as jasmine, chrysanthemum, lichee, dried rosebuds, and narcissus.

2. Smoky tea, such as Lapsang souchong, a specialty of Hunan Province, which is not only drunk but is also used as an ingredient for smoking poultry, an example of which is Tea Smoked Duck*.

3. Unfermented (or, more specifically, incompletely fermented) tea, also called green tea, and known for its light color and natural bouquet.

4. Fermented tea, made from tea leaves that are picked then left to stand in the air until they are fully fermented before roasting. This black tea is grown in the Anhwei, Yünnan, Fukien, and Kwantung provinces.

5. Semifermented tea from Formosa, known as oolong tea, which looks like black tea but has the bouquet of green tea.

Buy only tea that is packaged in a tin. Boxed tea leaves may be spoiled as a result of damp weather during the voyage from China to the United States.

Tea can be brewed in three ways:

1. Rinse a porcelain teapot with boiling water. Add 1 teaspoon of tea leaves for every cup. Fill the pot with the measured boiling water. Cover and let steep for 5 minutes.

2. If you are brewing tea for more people than the capacity of your teapot, proceed as follows. Assume you want to make tea for 25 people in a pot that has a capacity of 2 to 6 cups. Measure 25 teaspoons of tea leaves into the pot. Cover the tea leaves by about 3 inches with freshly drawn cold tap water that has been brought to a full boil. Replace the lid and let the tea steep for 5 minutes. This liquid can now be called "tea concentrate." While the tea is steeping, bring a large kettle of water to a boil. Have all the cups ready. Add a little "tea concentrate" to each cup and then fill the rest of the cup with boiling water. When tea is made this way, the teacups are carried in from the kitchen. Another possibility, if you prefer to serve the tea in front of your guests, is to use porcelain or silver teapots. For every pot of the concentrate, you should have two of boiling water.

3. In China, guests consider it an honor if the tea is steeped in front of them, which assures them that it is fresh. Each teacup has its own lid and the tea is brewed individually as follows: one teaspoon of tea leaves is placed in each cup; boiling water is added, only enough to cover the leaves; the lid is then placed on the teacup, and the tea is allowed to steep for 5 minutes. The cup is then filled with boiling water. After the first cup has been drunk, the teacup is again filled with boiling water, and the tea leaves are allowed to steep another 5 minutes. The second cup of tea, made from once-used tea leaves, is considered the finest.

THICKENING AGENTS

Water Chestnut Powder For use in binders, marinades, and coating or dredging for deep-fat frying, water chestnut powder is the first choice. It is made by crushing water chestnuts into a powder or flour. It has a lighter, finer consistency (it is used the way the French would use arrowroot instead of flour), is less fattening than cornstarch, and gives a crunchier exterior to deep-fat fried foods, an example being Crispy Spareribs in Sweet Soybean Sauce*. It can also be used instead of flour to thicken sauces or deep-fry chicken in American cooking. There are many different brands available. I prefer the lumpier brands of water chestnut powder because they seem to be purer products and are whiter. Buy two boxes: keep one box as is for use in deep-fat frying and render the contents of the other box smooth in a blender, food processor, or electric coffee mill, for use in binders and marinades. One drawback: when water chestnut powder is used as a thickening agent, it breaks down if the dish is kept warm. If this ever happens, drain the liquid into a pot and rethicken the sauce with a new binder (sherry and water chestnut powder mixed to a smooth paste—$1/2$ tablespoon of water chestnut powder to 1 tablespoon of sherry for every $1/2$ cup of sauce). Heat the sauce over a high flame while stirring with chopsticks in one hand and adding the binder with the other hand. Pour the rethickened sauce over vegetables or meat.

Because water chestnuts are plentiful in China but not in the United States, the powder is more widely used there. It is rarely used here because of the expense. It sells for $1 to $1.69 per half pound. Most recipes use only a tablespoonful, so a half-pound box will last a long time unless you are using it for deep-fat frying, in which case it is worth the extra expense because of the incredibly crunchy exterior it produces. Stored on the shelf in a tightly sealed glass jar, it will last for over a year.

Cornstarch The thickening agent most widely used in Chinese cooking in America by professional as well as amateur cooks is cornstarch. Corn is plentiful in America and is therefore made into many products, such as oil and starch. In China there is not an abundance, and the corn that is grown is eaten in its natural state. If substituting cornstarch for water chestnut powder, use the same quantity. As with water chestnut powder, cornstarch will break down if heated too long; therefore it is added to thicken sauces during the last minute of cooking.

Tapioca Starch Also used to thicken sauces, tapioca starch contains the highest amount of carbohydrates of any of the thickening agents.

Tientsin Preserved Vegetable *See* Preserved Vegetables.

Tree Ears Also known or referred to as cloud ears, wood ears, or black fungus, tree ears are fungi that have been dried. They are sold in small cellophane packages, but stored in a glass jar they will keep indefinitely. They contain a good deal of calcium, and have recently been credited as a coronary preventative, a blood anticoagulant. Always measure tree ears from a dried state and sparingly, as they expand considerably while soaking. To be reconstituted, they must be soaked in warm water for twenty minutes. After they are soft, they must be rinsed thoroughly, as they can be very sandy. Tree ears are rubbery in consistency and have very little taste; however, they absorb the flavor of the other ingredients used in the same dish. I have found that the water in which the tree ears are soaked is excellent for plants, and has even revived sick ones. Tree ears are used in many stir-fried, braised, and red-cooked simmered dishes and soups.

VINEGAR

All vinegars can be stored on the shelf and will last for one year or more.

Black Rice Vinegar Made from rice, water, soy sauce, and salt, black rice vinegar is used in salads, soups, dips, and sweet-and-sour sauce.

Chinese Red Vinegar This vinegar is made from rice, water, and malt.

Japanese Rice Vinegar This vinegar is made from rice and water.

Red Wine Vinegar This vinegar is an important staple for Chinese cooking. For an excellent-tasting, full-bodied wine vinegar of a quality that far surpasses a commercial product, I replace the vinegar that I use with a little red wine occasionally. If you use a lot of vinegar, have several bottles going in order that the fermentation process can take place. Eventually a "mother" will develop. It should always remain in the bottom of the bottle, as it will help ferment the wine. Never pour it out.

Water Chestnut Powder *See* Thickening Agents.

Wine Yeast Sold in plastic packages, wine yeast comes in the shape of a round ball about the size of a Ping-Pong ball. It is used to make Fermented Wine Rice*. When stored in a covered jar in the refrigerator, it will last for four to six months.

Chapter 9

APPETIZERS AND DIM SUM

Since the tenth century the Chinese have been enjoying dim sum in their tea houses, and since the 1800s the Cantonese, who are especially noted for their dim sum, have been preparing dim sum brunches, lunches, snacks, and dinners in the Chinatowns of America. In the past few years these delicate buns, dumplings, pastries, noodles, and breads have become increasingly popular with Americans.

Dim sum is cooked in various ways, usually either steamed (as in Steamed Roast Pork Buns*), deep-fried (Peking Rolls*), or pan-fried (Jao-tze*). There is a practical reason why the Chinese have traditionally used these methods: very few Chinese homes have ovens, so baking is not usually an option. And because fuel has always been scarce in China, the Chinese formed the dough into small dumplings and buns rather than loaves, which would take longer to cook. Chinese breads differ from Western breads more in the cooking technique than in the type of dough, although when the dough is steamed, it goes through wonderful changes, sometimes even becoming translucent.

Bau or pao-tzu are steamed stuffed buns, a classic example of which is Steamed Roast Pork Buns*. Bau have sugar added to the dough. Eaten as snacks on festive occasions, they are often made with pork or chicken, sometimes with vegetables only, at other times stir-fried with vegetables. Sweet stuffings are also common, such as sweetened pureed black or red beans. When sweet and savory bau are served at the same time, a red dot on top of a bun indicates a sweet stuffing.

Man tou are steamed buns without the filling. The unstuffed man tou are commonly eaten at home meals, taking the place of rice because they are less sweet than bau and may accompany main dishes, often absorbing the sauce. Man tou are to the Chinese as breads are to the Westerner.

Dumplings, not to be confused with steamed stuffed buns, are often referred to as jao-tze but are also identified by other names, based on their filling (for instance, jiaoz is a pork dumpling) or their texture (chung-tzu are heavy dumplings). Then there are pet names, like the fried dumplings called kuo-t'ieh, or "pot stickers," in this book called simply Jao-tze*.

One difference between dumplings and buns is that the dough for dumplings has no leavening agent; dumplings are also usually smaller. Like buns, dumplings are not only a part of the daily diet, but are also a significant part of Chinese holiday meals, including the New Year and the Dragon Boat Festival. For centuries there have been dumpling food shops, vendors, and tea houses, recorded as early as the Sung Dynasty (tenth to thirteenth centuries).

DICED SPICY CHICKEN IN LETTUCE LEAVES   Hunan

¹/₂ pound boneless, skinless chicken breasts

MARINADE
¹/₂ egg white
1 teaspoon sherry
1 teaspoon water chestnut powder

¹/₄ cup Chinese mushrooms, soaked and diced**
¹/₄ cup diced carrot
³/₄ cup split, diced leeks (white part only)

¹/₄ cup cleaned, seeded, and diced fresh chili pepper
¹/₂ cup cleaned, seeded, and diced sweet red pepper

1 cup diced bok choy (white part only)

SEASONING SAUCE
2 teaspoons water chestnut powder dissolved in
2 tablespoons sherry
1¹/₂ tablespoons dark soy sauce
1 tablespoon dark miso
2 teaspoons Hot Sauce*
1 teaspoon sugar
1 tablespoon reduced mushroom stock**, cooled

1 head iceberg lettuce

3 tablespoons peanut oil

2 teaspoons sesame oil

PREPARATION

Partially freeze the chicken breasts, cut them into thick shreds, then dice. Place the chicken and the ingredients for the marinade in a bowl and stir in one direction vigorously with chopsticks. Place the mixture in the refrigerator for at least 1 hour or up to 12 hours.

Having reconstituted the mushrooms and done the necessary cutting, place the three groups of vegetables in separate bowls.

Combine the ingredients for the seasoning sauce.

Cut the lettuce in half, then core. Separate the large leaves; put these leaves on a plate.

COOKING PROCEDURE

Place the wok over high heat for about 1 minute. Add 1 tablespoon of the peanut oil and heat until hot but not smoking. Add the diced mushrooms, carrot, and leeks; stir-fry for 1 minute.

Add the chili and red peppers; stir-fry for 30 seconds.

Add the bok choy; stir-fry another 30 seconds. Empty the contents of the wok into a heated serving dish.

Add the remaining 2 tablespoons peanut oil to the wok. Restir the chicken in the marinade and add the contents of the bowl all at once to the wok; stir-fry the diced chicken until it turns opaque, or about 2 minutes.

Restir the seasoning sauce and add it to the wok along with the diced vegetables. Stir-fry until thoroughly mixed and heated.

Turn off heat and add the sesame oil. Mix briefly. Empty the contents of the wok onto a heated serving dish and serve immediately, along with the plate of lettuce leaves. Each person takes a lettuce leaf and wraps it around some of the diced chicken.

YIELD *4–8 servings*

NOTES

Substitutions For the dark miso, you can substitute either 1 tablespoon hoisin sauce, or 1 tablespoon light miso plus 1 teaspoon dark soy sauce.

¹/₄ cup Chinese mushrooms, soaked and diced**
3 dried shrimp
¹/₄ cup finely diced carrot

SEASONING SAUCE
1 teaspoon water chestnut powder dissolved in
1 tablespoon sherry
1 tablespoon hoisin sauce
1 tablespoon dark soy sauce
1 teaspoon Hot Sauce*
2 tablespoons reduced mushroom stock**, cooled

1 head iceberg lettuce

1 clove garlic, minced
1 teaspoon minced ginger root

1¹/₂ cakes Spiced Pressed Bean Curd*, diced
¹/₄ cup cleaned, seeded, and diced sweet red pepper
1 cup finely diced bok choy (white part only)
¹/₄ cup diced winter bamboo shoots

2 scallions (white and green parts), chopped

2 tablespoons peanut oil

1 teaspoon sesame oil

PREPARATION

Having reconstituted the mushrooms, set aside.

Rinse the shrimp, then soak in boiling water for 15 minutes. Drain, then mince.

Combine the ingredients for the seasoning sauce.

Cut the lettuce in half, then core. Wash, drain, dry, and separate the large leaves. Put these leaves on a plate.

COOKING PROCEDURE

Place the wok over high heat for about 1 minute. Add the peanut oil and heat until hot but not smoking. Add the garlic and ginger; stir-fry for a few seconds.

Add the dried shrimp, mushrooms, and carrot; stir-fry for 1 minute.

Add the pressed bean curd, red pepper, bok choy, and bamboo shoots; stir-fry for 1 minute.

Add the scallions; stir-fry for ¹/₂ minute.

Restir the seasoning sauce and add it all at once to the wok. Stir-fry another ¹/₂ minute.

Add the sesame oil. Mix for a few seconds. Empty the contents of the wok onto a heated serving dish and serve immediately, along with the plate of lettuce leaves. Each person takes a lettuce leaf and spoons some of the vegetable mixture in the leaf and rolls it up.

YIELD *3–6 servings*

DEEP-FRIED WALNUT CHICKEN   Peking/Beijing

2 whole chicken breasts (12–14 ounces each),
  boned and skinned

MARINADE
2 tablespoons light soy sauce
1 tablespoon sherry
1 teaspoon sesame oil
2 scallions (white and green parts), cut into
  1-inch pieces
Freshly ground white pepper

BATTER
2 egg whites
2 tablespoons water chestnut powder

1 cup ground walnuts

4 cups peanut oil

Szechwan Peppercorn Powder* (optional)

PREPARATION

Separate the chicken fillets from the cutlets. Remove the tendons from the fillets.

Combine the ingredients for the marinade. Place the chicken in the marinade and refrigerate for at least 1 hour or up to 12 hours, turning occasionally.

To make the batter, beat the egg whites until frothy, and then blend in the water chestnut powder.

Coat the chicken by dipping the pieces in the batter, then in the ground nuts. Refrigerate a second time for at least 1 hour or up to 24 hours.

COOKING PROCEDURE

Remove the chicken from refrigerator 30 minutes before frying.

Place the wok over high heat for about 1 minute. Pour in the peanut oil; turn the heat to medium until the oil reaches 350 degrees. Turn the heat to high. Lower the chicken pieces into the oil, one at a time. Do not overcrowd. Fry about half the chicken at a time if using a 14-inch wok. Fry the chicken pieces for about 4 minutes, turning once at midpoint. Drain well on paper towels. Allow to cool 5 minutes. Cut crosswise, against the grain, in ½-inch pieces. Serve immediately as is, or with Szechwan Peppercorn Powder.

YIELD *4–8 servings*

NOTES

Timing This recipe requires advance but not lengthy preparation.

Tips Never use larger chicken breasts for this recipe, as they will be too thick and the walnuts will burn before the chicken is cooked all the way through.

If the oil is too hot, the nuts will burn before the chicken is done. If the oil is too cool, the nuts will fall off.

If you dip the chicken in the batter with one hand and in the walnuts with the other, it prevents caking.

The purpose of cooling the chicken for five minutes is to prevent the nuts from falling off the chicken.

Substitutions For the walnuts, you can substitute unhulled sesame seeds.

TANGY TURTLE CHICKEN

1 whole chicken breast (about 1 pound)

GREEN SAUCE
1/3 cup minced scallions (white and green
    parts)
1 teaspoon Szechwan Peppercorn Powder*
2 tablespoons minced coriander leaves
1 tablespoon dark soy sauce
1 teaspoon sugar
1 tablespoon sesame oil
1/4 teaspoon Chili Oil*
2 cloves garlic, minced

PREPARATION AND COOKING PROCEDURE

Steam the chicken breast for 20 minutes. Allow it to cool.

During the following procedure, carefully retain the original shape of the chicken breast: skin it, then remove all the bones; with a sharp knife, cut along the center of the breast, halving it; reassemble the halves, then cut them at right angles to the first cut at 1/2-inch intervals; slide a cleaver underneath all the pieces of the chicken breast and transfer them to a flat serving plate.

In a food processor or blender, combine the ingredients for the green sauce. Pour the green sauce over the chicken breast, allowing it to seep into the crevices. Serve at room temperature.

YIELD 2–6 servings

NOTES

Timing The entire recipe can be prepared a day in advance, refrigerated, and served at room temperature.

ICICLE RADISH BALLS

Hunan

Delicious and easy to make, Icicle Radish Balls are similar to Shrimp Balls in Rice Paper*. The addition of the icicle radish (Chinese turnip) gives them a wonderful flavor.

ICICLE RADISH BALL MIXTURE
1/2 pound shrimp
4 ounces icicle radish (Chinese turnip), diced in 1/2-inch pieces
2/3 cup fatty ground pork
1 teaspoon finely minced Smithfield ham**
1 scallion (white and green parts), finely minced
1 egg white
1 1/2 teaspoons salt
1/4 teaspoon white pepper
1/2 teaspoon sugar
2 teaspoons sesame oil
2 tablespoons water chestnut powder dissolved in
1 tablespoon sherry

1/4 cup water chestnut powder for dredging

3 cups peanut oil

Spicy Dipping Sauce*

PREPARATION

Shell, wash, drain, and dry the shrimp well. Cut the shrimp in half.

Turn on the food processor and place the diced icicle radish through the feeding tube. Turn the processor on and off until the icicle radish is finely minced. Remove the minced icicle radish from the processor and place it in a strainer. Press down to remove any excess liquid.

Return the icicle radish to the processor bowl along with all the icicle radish ball mixture ingredients. Turn the processor on and off until the mixture forms a paste. Refrigerate the paste for at least 1 hour.

Form into Ping-Pong-sized balls. Roll each ball in water chestnut powder. Place the balls on a plate, put the plate in a steamer, and steam for 3 minutes. Remove the balls to another plate and allow them to cool.

COOKING PROCEDURE

Place the wok over high heat for about 1 minute. Pour in the oil; turn the heat to medium until the oil reaches 350 degrees. Turn the heat to high. Fry half of the balls at a time for about 2 minutes, or until they become light brown. Remove the balls with a wire strainer and place them on several layers of paper towel to drain.

Bring the oil temperature back to 350 degrees and repeat the frying process.

Serve immediately with Spicy Dipping Sauce.

YIELD *20 balls*

NOTES

Timing The entire preparation through the steaming procedure can be prepared a day in advance. Place the turnip balls on a greased cookie sheet in a single layer. Allow them to reach room temperature before frying. The first frying can be done several hours ahead.

Tips The alternate method of mincing the icicle radish, if you are not using a food processor, is with two cleavers which will create a similar paste. The shrimp and ham can also be minced with two cleavers to form a paste.

PEARL BALLS

Hunan

Pearl Balls are so called because of the opalescent quality the rice takes on when steamed. Because they are steamed, it's good to include Pearl Balls when you offer your guests a variety of appetizers, as so many Chinese appetizers are fried.

1/4 cup Chinese mushrooms, soaked and
 minced**
1 cup sweet rice
1/4 pound shrimp
3/4 pound ground pork
1 egg, beaten slightly
2 1/2 tablespoons dark soy sauce
2 scallions (white and green parts), chopped
1 teaspoon minced ginger root
1 teaspoon sugar
2 tablespoons water chestnut powder
 dissolved in
2 tablespoons sherry

Bok choy leaves, or kale

Spicy Dipping Sauce*

SPECIAL EQUIPMENT
Cheesecloth

PREPARATION

Having reconstituted the mushrooms, set aside. Soak the sweet rice in warm water to cover for 1/2 hour. Drain in a strainer.

Shell, wash, drain, and dry the shrimp well. Mince the shrimp with two cleavers.

Holding several chopsticks in one hand, combine the mushrooms, shrimp, pork, egg, soy sauce, scallions, ginger, sugar, water chestnut powder, and sherry. To keep the Pearl Balls from becoming too dense, do not overmix.

Refrigerate the mixture for at least 1 hour or the day ahead.

Keeping your hands wet, form the mixture into walnut-sized balls.

Spread the drained rice on a cookie sheet. Roll the Pearl Balls, one at a time, over the rice until each is well coated.

Line the various levels of the bamboo steamer with cheesecloth.

Arrange the Pearl Balls in the steamer with 1/2-inch space between them, to allow for the expansion of the rice.

COOKING PROCEDURE

Place 3 quarts water in a 14-inch round-bottomed wok. Set the bamboo steamer in the wok; cover, and steam for 25 minutes. Remove the Pearl Balls and cheesecloth, then cover the entire surface of each layer of the steamer with bok choy leaves. Rearrange the Pearl Balls and continue steaming for 5 more minutes.

Serve the Pearl Balls in the bamboo steamer with Spicy Dipping Sauce.

YIELD *approximately 30 balls*

NOTES

Timing Pearl Balls can be prepared a day in advance and refrigerated on a cookie sheet in a single layer.

Pearl Balls can be kept warm in the steamer for 5 to 10 minutes with the flame turned off.

Leftover Pearl Balls can be deep-fried in oil heated to 375 degrees. Fry 4 to 5 Pearl Balls at a time for about 30 seconds, turning once at midpoint. Drain well on paper towels.

APPETIZERS AND DIM SUM

97

SHRIMP BALLS IN RICE PAPER
Canton/Guangzhou

FILLING
1 pound shrimp
1 1/2 ounces ground raw pork fat
1 teaspoon salt
1/2 teaspoon freshly ground white pepper
2 tablespoons water chestnut powder
 dissolved in
3 tablespoons sherry
2 scallions (white and green parts), minced
2 teaspoons minced ginger root
1 egg white

27 sheets rice paper

3 cups peanut oil (approximately)

*Spicy Dipping Sauce**

1. Center the filling.

PREPARATION

Shell, wash, drain, and dry the shrimp.

With two cleavers, mince the shrimp and the pork fat together until they become a smooth paste. Add the salt, pepper, and the water chestnut powder dissolved in the sherry. Mix well.

Add the scallions and ginger to the shrimp mixture. Mix well in one direction with a pair of chopsticks.

In another bowl, beat the egg white until it becomes stiff, then add it to the shrimp mixture. Refrigerate for 1 hour or up to 24 hours.

COOKING PROCEDURE

Take a sheet of rice paper; hold it in one hand, with its smooth side down. Place about 1 teaspoon of the filling in the center. Draw all the edges of the paper together, forming a waist. You should have a round sack at the bottom with a thin column of extra paper on top.

Place a 12-inch iron skillet over high heat for about 1 minute. Pour in approximately 3 cups oil (to a depth of 1 1/2 to 1 3/4 inches), turn the heat to medium, and heat until the oil reaches 350 degrees. Turn the heat to high.

2. Form a waist with the filling in the bottom pouch.

3. Squeeze three packages together.

Divide the twenty-seven packages into nine sets of three packages each. Using chopsticks to hold them together, take three packages (one set) and submerge them in the oil. Add two more sets. The extra paper should be above the level of the oil; the ball should be completely submerged. Cook for about 2 minutes. Using a wire strainer, remove the three sets (nine shrimp balls) from the skillet. Drain well by placing them in a single layer on several sheets of paper towels. Repeat the procedure with the remaining six sets, cooking three sets at a time.

Serve immediately with Spicy Dipping Sauce.

YIELD *3–8 servings*

NOTES

Tips Ground raw pork fat can be purchased from a butcher.

The shrimp paste can be made in a food processor.

The oil for deep-fat frying should cover only the part of the rice paper containing the shrimp.

SHAO MAI (STEAMED DUMPLINGS IN WONTON SKIN)

FILLING
1/2 pound shrimp
1/2 pound ground pork
1 cup minced bok choy (white and green parts)
1/4 cup minced bamboo shoots
1/2 cup finely chopped scallions (white and green parts)
1 tablespoon water chestnut powder dissolved in
2 tablespoons dark soy sauce
1 tablespoon sherry
2 teaspoons sesame oil

24 square thin wonton skins (or round)

Bok choy leaves

*Spicy Dipping Sauce**

SPECIAL EQUIPMENT
Cheesecloth

PREPARATION

Shell, wash, drain, and dry the shrimp well; mince fine.

Place the shrimp and pork in a mixing bowl. Place the bok choy and bamboo shoots in a piece of cheesecloth that has been wrung out in cold water. Squeeze hard to extract the excess moisture. Place the bok choy and bamboo shoots in the bowl.

Add the scallions, water chestnut powder, soy sauce, sherry, and sesame oil to the bowl. Stir well in one direction with several chopsticks for about 2 minutes.

1. Place the filling in the center of the wonton skin.

Put a wonton skin in the palm of your hand. Place 1 full tablespoon of the filling in the center of the wonton skin. Shift the skin with the filling so that it is held securely in the fingers of one hand, and gather the four corners (two at a time) of the skin around the filling; squeeze the filling slightly upward. Let the corners pleat naturally and meet in the center, so that you have four loops. Then, using the thumb and index finger of the other hand, subdivide each large loop or pleat into three smaller pleats. Or you can just move around the filling, making small regular pleats. To pack the filling tightly, place the dumpling on the table and squeeze in the finished pouch slightly above the center, making a waist. Flatten out the bottom by tapping gently on the table. (This makes it stand upright.)

Canton/Guangzhou

2. Make four pleats, as you rotate the dumpling.

3. Subdivide the pleats.

COOKING PROCEDURE

Fill a 14-inch round-bottomed wok with water to 3 inches from the top (about 3 quarts). Line two levels of a bamboo steamer with cheesecloth. Place the dumplings on top of the cheesecloth and steam them for 10 to 12 minutes. Remove the dumplings and the cheesecloth, then cover the entire surface of each layer of the steamer with bok choy leaves. Rearrange the dumplings and continue steaming for 1 more minute. Serve the hot dumplings from the bamboo steamer; accompany with Spicy Dipping Sauce.

YIELD *24 dumplings*

NOTES

Timing The filling can be prepared a day in advance and refrigerated. The dumplings can be refrigerated for several hours before being steamed.

Tip The filling for these dumplings should be quite dense. Mix it very well.

Substitution For the bok choy leaves, you can substitute kale.

Storage The dumplings can be frozen on a greased cookie sheet. Once frozen, they should be placed in a plastic bag. Frozen, they will last one month. Steam frozen dumplings for ten extra minutes.

JAO-TZE (FRIED DUMPLINGS)   Peking/Beijing

1. Place the filling in the center; fold in half and pinch.

2. Pleat both ends.

These savory dumplings are a staple food in the northern wheat regions of China. Like other wheat products, such as noodles and bread, they make a delectable substitute for rice. Although they are time-consuming to prepare, dumplings are very popular in all the regions of China. In the southern and eastern regions, they are often served as a snack. Americans are also devoted to these dumplings, which can be steamed, boiled, or pan-fried (in which case they are called "Pot-Stickers," as the bottom of the dumpling does in fact stick to the skillet). In addition to the name Pot-Stickers, Jao-tze are sometimes referred to as "Fried Dumplings." Cooking them in a covered skillet that contains water produces two different textures: crisp on the bottom, and soft (as if steamed) on the top. Although they are a daily part of the Chinese diet, they are traditionally a New Year's food, when they are placed on trays and left outside to freeze, as a way of storing them.

FILLING

4 medium-sized Chinese mushrooms, soaked and minced**
1/4 pound shrimp
1 bunch watercress (about 4 ounces), stems removed
6 ounces ground pork
1/4 cup fresh water chestnuts, minced
2 scallions (white and green parts), chopped
1/2 teaspoon minced ginger root
2 tablespoons dark soy sauce
1 tablespoon sherry
1 teaspoon sesame oil
1/2 teaspoon sugar

DOUGH

2 cups flour, sifted, then measured
1/4 cup cold water
1/2 cup boiling water

5 tablespoons peanut oil

Spicy Dipping Sauce*

3. Tighten the seam.

4. Create a crescent shape.

PREPARATION

To make the filling Having reconstituted the mushrooms, set aside. Shell, wash, drain, dry, and coarsely mince the shrimp. Blanch the watercress for 30 seconds. Drain and squeeze it to remove any excess moisture. Chop it fine. Combine all the ingredients for the filling in a bowl. Stir well with several chopsticks in one direction.

To make the dough Put 1 cup of the flour in a bowl, and add a little cold water at a time. Mix it with several chopsticks (the dough will be crumbly and dry). Put the second cup of flour in a separate bowl. Add the boiling water gradually. Mix and knead it into a soft dough. Mix the hot and cold doughs together and knead them until blended (about 5 minutes). The dough should be elastic and not sticky. Add more flour if necessary. Place the dough in a bowl. Cover it with a damp towel, taking care not to let the cloth touch the dough. Let it rest for about 30 minutes.

After the dough has rested, place it on a lightly floured working surface and knead it again for a few moments. Separate the dough into two equal parts. Roll each piece of dough into a long, skinny sausage shape, thinning it until you have two pieces about a foot in length. Cut each sausage at ¾-inch intervals (in order to retain the round shape, rotate it toward you and make a cut, then rotate it away from you and make another cut). After lightly flouring each piece, round it out and flatten it with the palm of your hand. Before each circle is rolled out, it should be about 1½ to 2 inches in diameter. Lightly flour and flatten out each circle with a rolling pin, rotating the circle with one hand as you roll the dough with the other. Roll the circles as thin as possible; however, the center of each should be thicker than the edges. To avoid its drying out, cover the dough while you are not working with it.

(continued)

To fill the dumplings Hold a circle of dough in one hand; take about 1 rounded teaspoon of the filling and put it in the center of the circle. Fold the circle in half and press it together at the center. Gather the dough around the filling by making three or four pleats at each end. Place the dumpling on the board. To create a crescent shape, tighten the seam by squeezing it at the top. (The alternate method of filling the dumplings, sometimes used in Chinese restaurants as a time-saving device, is as follows: hold a circle of dough in one hand, take about 1 rounded teaspoon of the filling, and put it in the center of the circle. Make a half-moon; squeeze it together by holding it in the curve of your hand between the index finger and thumb.) To prevent the dumplings from drying out, cover them with a cloth until ready to cook. They can be refrigerated on a lightly floured cookie sheet early in the day.

COOKING PROCEDURE

Distribute 2 tablespoons of the peanut oil evenly over a 12-inch iron skillet. Line up the Jao-tze (dumplings) in the skillet. Pour in enough cold water to come halfway up the sides of the Jao-tze. Cover and cook for about 3 minutes over high heat. Remove the Jao-tze from the skillet with a wire strainer. Pour off the liquid from the skillet. The recipe can be prepared ahead up to this point.

Spread the remaining 3 tablespoons oil evenly in the skillet. Rearrange the Jao-tze in the pan. Cover and fry over medium-low heat until the bottoms are crisp and brown (about 5 minutes).

Serve with Spicy Dipping Sauce.

YIELD *18–20 dumplings*

NOTES

Timing The filling can be prepared a day in advance.

Storage If you are using freshly ground pork (as opposed to pork that has been defrosted), the dumplings can be frozen after being filled and before the cooking procedure. Place the dumplings on a greased cookie sheet in a single layer in the freezer. After they are frozen, put them in a plastic bag. Frozen, they will keep for one month. When cooking the dumplings from a frozen state, increase the first cooking procedure to six minutes.

STUFFED SNOW CRAB CLAWS

Canton/Guangzhou

2 pounds frozen crab claws (about 19 claws)

STUFFING
3/4 pound shrimp
1/3 cup ground raw pork fat
1/3 cup ground pork
1 1/2 teaspoons salt
1 tablespoon water chestnut powder
1 tablespoon sesame oil
1/4 teaspoon freshly ground black pepper
2 scallions (white and green parts), chopped

Lumpy water chestnut powder for dusting

4 cups peanut oil

Spicy Dipping Sauce*

PREPARATION

Defrost the crab claws in a colander set over a bowl. This will take about 3 hours. When completely defrosted, drain further on several layers of paper towels for 30 minutes. Change the paper towels and drain another 30 minutes.

Shell, wash, drain, dry, and mince the shrimp. Place the shrimp in a bowl along with the rest of the ingredients for the stuffing. Stir well in one direction with several chopsticks. A food processor can be used for preparing the stuffing.

With wet hands, mold about 2 tablespoons of the stuffing around that part of the claw which is not covered by the shell. Leave the shell exposed and retain the shape of the original crab claw. Dust each claw (but not the shell) with water chestnut powder.

COOKING PROCEDURE

Place the wok over high heat for about 1 minute. Pour in the peanut oil; turn the heat to medium until the oil reaches 325 degrees. Add one third of the claws to the wok and fry for 3 minutes, turning once at midpoint. Using a wire strainer, remove the claws from the wok. Drain well by placing the claws in a single layer on several sheets of paper towels. Return the oil temperature to 325 degrees and repeat the frying process with the remaining crab claws, one third at a time.

Allow the claws to cool for at least 1/2 hour.

Reheat the oil to 375 degrees and fry the claws in three separate batches for 1 minute, turning once at midpoint. Drain well on several layers of paper towels.

Serve immediately with Spicy Dipping Sauce.

YIELD *about 19 claws*

NOTES

Timing The entire preparation and the first frying can be done early in the day. Allow the crab claws to cool thoroughly, then refrigerate until 1/2 hour before the second frying.

Tips As the crab claws remain separated when frozen, this recipe can be cut in half.

Ground raw pork fat can be purchased from a butcher.

BAKED ROAST PORK BUNS

DOUGH

1/2 cake fresh yeast
1/4 cup lukewarm water
3 tablespoons sweet butter, melted
3/4 cup milk, at room temperature
1/4 teaspoon salt
1/2 cup sugar
4–4 1/2 cups sifted flour
1 egg, beaten

SEASONING SAUCE

1 1/2 tablespoons oyster sauce
1 tablespoon sugar
1 1/2 tablespoons light soy sauce
1 teaspoon plum sauce

BINDER

1 teaspoon flour
2 teaspoons cornstarch
1/3 cup chicken stock

FILLING

1/2 pound Barbecued Roast Pork*
1 1/2 cups chopped white American onions
2 cloves garlic, minced

1 tablespoon peanut oil

1 tablespoon sesame oil

1 egg, beaten, for glazing

PREPARATION

Dissolve the yeast and water in a cup. Melt the butter and allow it to cool. Combine the butter, milk, salt, and sugar in a large bowl. Add the dissolved yeast to the milk mixture, and stir briefly with chopsticks. Gradually add the flour. Add the beaten egg and continue to mix. If the dough is too soft, add up to 1/2 cup more flour. Knead the dough in the bowl for 15 to 20 minutes. Cover the bowl with a damp cloth, taking care not to let the cloth touch the dough. Let the dough rise until double in bulk (about 1 hour).

Knead the dough again for about 5 minutes and allow it to rise, covered, for another 1/2 hour.

Knead the dough a final time for about 5 minutes.

Separate the dough into two equal parts. Roll each part into a long sausage shape, 12 to 14 inches long. Lightly flour the working surface. Cut each sausage into nine pieces (in order to retain the round shape, rotate it toward you and make a cut, then rotate it away from you and make another cut). Lightly flour both sides of the cut rounds and slightly flatten them with the heel of your hand.

Combine the ingredients for the seasoning sauce.

Mix the binder.

COOKING PROCEDURE

To prepare the filling Dice the pork into small cubes, removing any of the fat that is not charred.

Place the wok over high heat for about 1 minute. Add the peanut oil and heat until hot but not smoking. Add the onions and garlic; stir-fry for about 1 minute.

Add the pork and mix briefly.

Restir the seasoning sauce and add it all at once to the wok; stir-fry another minute.

Restir the binder and add it to the wok with one hand while stir-frying with the other. Stir-fry the mixture for another 30 seconds, or until the sauce has thickened.

Add the sesame oil. Mix. Empty the contents of the wok onto a plate and allow it to cool thoroughly. Refrigerate until ready to fill the dough.

To fill the buns Hold a circle of dough in one hand; place 1 full tablespoon of the filling in the center of the dough round. Gently gather up the sides of the dough; wrap them over the filling, and tightly seal. Turn it over and pat it all around, making it very round.

Place buns on a greased cookie sheet, sealed side down. Cover them with a dry cloth; let them rise another 45 to 50 minutes.

Preheat the oven to 375 degrees. Remove the cloth. Brush each bun with the beaten egg glaze; bake them 15 to 20 minutes, or until the buns are golden brown. Remove the buns from the oven. Let them cool 5 to 10 minutes and serve.

YIELD *18 buns*

NOTES

Timing Leftover Baked Roast Pork Buns can be refrigerated and rewarmed the next day in a preheated 350-degree oven for 7 to 10 minutes.

The final rising period of the filled buns can take place in the refrigerator overnight. Remove the buns from the refrigerator 2 hours before baking.

STEAMED ROAST PORK BUNS

1. Cut by rotating the dough toward you, then away from you.

2. Rotate the dough while thinning it into 3¹/₂-inch circles.

DOUGH
¹/₂ cake fresh yeast
¹/₄ cup sugar
1 cup warm water
3¹/₂ cups sifted flour
1 tablespoon chilled sweet butter or lard
¹/₂ teaspoon white vinegar

FILLING
¹/₂ pound Barbecued Roast Pork*
1¹/₂ cups chopped Spanish onions
2 cloves garlic, minced

BINDER
1 teaspoon flour
2 teaspoons cornstarch
¹/₃ cup chicken stock

SEASONING SAUCE
1¹/₂ tablespoons oyster sauce
1 tablespoon sugar
1¹/₂ tablespoons light soy sauce
1 teaspoon plum sauce

2 tablespoons peanut oil

1 tablespoon sesame oil

SPECIAL EQUIPMENT
Cooking parchment

PREPARATION

To make the dough In a small bowl, combine the yeast with 2 tablespoons of the sugar and 6 tablespoons of the warm water, stirring to blend with a wooden spoon. Add ¹/₂ cup of the flour and stir to blend. Place the remaining 3 cups of flour in a large bowl and add the butter. Using the same technique as you would to make a piecrust, rub the flour and butter together rapidly with the tips of your fingers, blending them well. Blend in the remaining 2 tablespoons sugar.

Add the yeast mixture to the contents of the larger bowl. Work the dough with your hands while adding the rest of the warm water. When blended, the dough should be fairly stiff. Knead the dough for about 2 minutes. Add the white vinegar and continue to knead for another 3 minutes, until smooth.

Shape the dough into a ball and place it in a clean bowl. Cover with a damp cloth, taking care not to let the cloth touch the dough. Put it in a warm place for 1¹/₂ to 2 hours, or until the dough has doubled in volume.

3. Place the filling in the center of the circle.

4. Rotate the circle while pinching the edges.

5. Gather all the edges.

While the dough is rising, prepare the filling.

To make the filling Dice the pork into small cubes, removing any of the fat that is not charred. In a cup, blend the flour, cornstarch, and chicken stock. In a bowl, blend the oyster sauce, 1 tablespoon sugar, the light soy sauce, and plum sauce.

To cook the filling Place the wok over high heat for about 1 minute. Add the peanut oil and heat until hot but not smoking. Add the onions and garlic; stir-fry for about 1 minute.

Add the pork; stir-fry another 30 seconds.

Add the seasoning sauce all at once to the wok; stir-fry another minute.

Restir the binder and add it to the wok with one hand while stir-frying with the other. Stir-fry the mixture for another 30 seconds, or until the sauce has thickened.

Add the sesame oil. Mix. Empty the contents of the wok onto a plate and allow them to cool thoroughly. Refrigerate until ready to fill the dough.

6. Secure the top folds.

(continued)

7. Twist the top together.

8. Buns after steaming.

After the dough has risen for 2 hours, uncover it and knead it for 5 more minutes. Separate the dough into two equal parts.

Roll each piece of dough into a long sausage shape, about 9 inches long. Lightly flour the working surface. Cut each sausage into ten pieces (in order to retain the round shape, rotate it toward you and make a cut, then rotate it away from you and make another cut). With the heel of your hand, flatten each piece so it forms a thick circle. Flatten out each circle with a rolling pin, rotating the circle with one hand as you roll the dough with the other. The finished circles should be about 3½ inches in diameter. The center of each circle should be thicker than the edges. Cover the dough while you are not working with it to avoid its drying out.

To fill the buns Put 1½ tablespoons of the filling in the center of each circle of dough. Put the bun in the palm of one hand and rotate it with the other hand. To gather the edges, make an initial fold at the circumference, pinch it, and continue to make even pinches until you have gone all the way around. Push with the index finger of one hand as you pinch with the thumb and index finger of your other hand; secure the top folds by twisting the top together. Cover the buns with a dry cloth and let stand for 15 to 20 minutes.

COOKING PROCEDURE

Out of cooking parchment cut 2 large circles the size of the circumference of the bamboo steamer. Grease the circles with butter. Place a circle on each of the two layers of the steamer. Arrange the buns in the lined steamer at least 2 inches apart. Steam over boiling water for 10 to 12 minutes. Serve hot.

YIELD *20 buns*

NOTES

Timing The filling can be prepared a day ahead and refrigerated. The buns can be frozen after filling and the final rising period. Freeze them on a greased cookie sheet in a single layer, then place them in a plastic bag.

Substitution One teaspoon dried yeast can be substituted for the fresh yeast.

Storage Frozen, the buns will last one month. Steam them from a frozen state, adding 5 extra minutes to the steaming time.

APPETIZERS AND DIM SUM

CURRIED CHICKEN FILLING

¹/₂ pound boneless, skinless chicken

SEASONING SAUCE
2 tablespoons curry sauce
1 tablespoon dark soy sauce
1 tablespoon sugar
¹/₄ teaspoon freshly ground black pepper
¹/₄ teaspoon salt

BINDER
1 teaspoon flour
1 teaspoon water chestnut powder
*   dissolved in*
2 tablespoons sherry

1 cup diced Spanish onions

1 clove garlic, minced

2 tablespoons peanut oil

PREPARATION

Partially freeze the chicken; slice, then dice it into ¹/₄-inch pieces.

Combine the ingredients for the seasoning sauce.

Mix the binder.

COOKING PROCEDURE

Place the wok over high heat for about 1 minute. Add 1 tablespoon of the oil and heat until hot but not smoking. Add the onions; stir-fry for 1 minute. Remove the onions to a plate.

Return the wok to the high heat and add the remaining tablespoon of oil. Add the garlic; stir-fry for a few seconds.

Add the diced chicken; stir-fry for 1 minute.

Return the onions to the wok and mix briefly.

Restir the seasoning sauce and add it all at once to the wok; stir-fry for about 30 seconds.

Restir the binder and add it to the wok, stirring until the sauce thickens. Empty the contents of the wok onto a plate and allow the filling to cool.

NOTES

Tip Prepared curry sauce can be purchased at Chinese and Indian markets. If stored in the refrigerator, it will last one year.
    This is an excellent filling that can be used as a substitute for pork in the Steamed Roast Pork Buns* or in Chinese Omelet I*.

SHRIMP AND MINCED MEAT FILLING Canton/Guangzhou

2 Chinese mushrooms, soaked and minced**
1/4 pound shrimp, shelled, washed, drained,
   dried, and minced
1 duck liver, minced

1/4 pound ground pork
1/2 tablespoon dark soy sauce
1 teaspoon water chestnut powder

SEASONING SAUCE
1/2 tablespoon water chestnut powder
   dissolved in
1 tablespoon sherry
1/4 cup chicken stock
1 tablespoon dark soy sauce
1 teaspoon sugar
1 teaspoon salt
1/4 teaspoon freshly ground black pepper
1 teaspoon sesame oil

1 tablespoon peanut oil

PREPARATION

Having reconstituted the mushrooms and
done the necessary cutting, place the
mushrooms, shrimp, and duck liver in a
bowl.

Combine the ground pork, 1/2 tablespoon
dark soy sauce, and 1 teaspoon water chestnut powder in a bowl.

Combine the ingredients for the seasoning
sauce.

COOKING PROCEDURE

Place the wok over high heat for about 1
minute. Add 1 tablespoon of oil and heat
until hot but not smoking. Add the ground
pork and stir-fry for 2 minutes, or until the
pork turns white.

Add the mushrooms, shrimp, and duck liver; stir-fry for a few seconds.

Restir the seasoning sauce and add it all at
once to the wok; stir-fry for about 30 seconds. Empty the contents of the wok onto a
plate and allow to cool.

NOTES

Tip This is an excellent filling that can be
used as a substitute for Steamed Roast Pork
Buns* or Chinese Omelet I*.

If it is used in the omelet, add 1/4 cup
minced water chestnuts to the wok at the
same time as the seasoning sauce.

SHRIMP STUFFED MUSHROOMS

24 *medium-sized Chinese mushrooms, soaked and left whole***

MARINADE
*2 tablespoons reduced mushroom stock***
1 tablespoon dark soy sauce
1 tablespoon sherry
1/2 tablespoon sesame oil
1 teaspoon sugar
1/2 teaspoon salt
1 scallion (white and green parts), cut into 1-inch pieces
3 slices ginger root

SAUCE
*1/2 cup reduced mushroom stock***
1 tablespoon oyster sauce
1/2 tablespoon dark soy sauce

SHRIMP PASTE
3/4 pound shrimp
2 ounces ground raw pork fat
1/2 egg white
1/2 tablespoon water chestnut powder
1 tablespoon sherry
1 scallion (white and green parts), chopped
1 teaspoon sesame oil
1/2 teaspoon salt
1/4 teaspoon freshly ground white pepper

1 tablespoon (approximately) water chestnut powder for sprinkling

GARNISH
*2 tablespoons minced Smithfield ham***
A few sprigs Chinese parsley

BINDER
1 teaspoon water chestnut powder dissolved in
*1 tablespoon mushroom stock***

PREPARATION AND COOKING PROCEDURE

Having reconstituted the mushrooms, place the mushrooms and the ingredients for the marinade in a bowl and stir with chopsticks; marinate for 1/2 hour. Place the mushrooms and the marinade on a plate that will fit into a steamer; steam for 20 minutes. Pour the marinade with the mushroom liquid that has been released during the steaming into the sauce. Discard the scallion and ginger.

Shell, wash, drain, dry, and mince the shrimp.

Combine the ingredients for the shrimp paste. Stir well in one direction with several chopsticks.

Using a tea strainer, sprinkle the concave side of each mushroom with water chestnut powder. Spread a portion of the shrimp mixture over the dusted side of each mushroom; smooth the filling with the underside of the spoon.

Garnish each mushroom with some minced ham and a parsley leaf.

Place all the mushrooms on a plate that will fit in whatever steaming arrangement you are using, whether wok, roasting pan, or bamboo steamer. Steam the mushrooms for 8 to 10 minutes.

Mix the binder.

In a saucepan, bring the sauce to a simmer. Restir the binder and add it to the saucepan, stirring with a pair of chopsticks in a figure-8 motion until the sauce thickens. Pour the sauce over the mushrooms and serve immediately.

YIELD *4–8 servings*

NOTES

Timing The mushrooms can be stuffed and refrigerated early in the day.

5 chicken legs and 5 chicken thighs (yielding
   14 ounces skinless and boneless chicken)
³/₄ pound shrimp
¹/₃ cup minced Smithfield ham**
¹/₂ cup minced water chestnuts (about 12)
¹/₂ cup minced Spanish onion
1¹/₂ tablespoons sherry
2 tablespoons light soy sauce
1 teaspoon salt
¹/₂ teaspoon freshly ground black pepper
1 teaspoon sugar
1 tablespoon sesame oil
1 tablespoon water chestnut powder

**WATER CHESTNUT POWDER
MIXTURE**
1 egg
3 tablespoons water chestnut powder
1 teaspoon salt

1 pound caul fat

Flour for dredging

Extra water chestnut powder for dusting

4 cups peanut oil

GARNISH
4 cups shredded bok choy leaves (green part
   only)

Szechwan Peppercorn Powder*, for dipping

PREPARATION

Skin and bone the chicken legs and thighs.
Remove all the fibers and tendons. You
should have about 14 ounces chicken meat.
Dice the boneless chicken, then mince it
with two cleavers and place it in a mixing
bowl.

Place 10 raw chicken leg and thigh bones in
a kettle and add cold water to cover. Bring
to a boil, then turn the heat to low and
simmer for 30 minutes. Remove the bones
from the broth and rinse them well in cold
water. Clean the bones with your hands under the cold running water, drain, and let
dry.

Peel, wash, drain, and dry the shrimp well.
Mince the shrimp finely, and add them to
the bowl containing the minced chicken.
Add the minced ham, water chestnuts, and
onion to the bowl and stir well in one direction with several chopsticks.

To this mixture add the sherry, soy sauce, 1
teaspoon salt, pepper, sugar, sesame oil,
and 1 tablespoon water chestnut powder.
Mix well with several chopsticks.

Place the egg in a small mixing bowl and
beat well. Add the 3 tablespoons water
chestnut powder and 1 teaspoon salt. Beat
well again, until smooth.

Rinse the caul fat under cold running water
and squeeze it dry with your hands. Spread
it on a flat surface. With a cleaver, remove
the thick edges, then cut it into ten pieces
that measure about 6 × 7 inches each.

Place one piece at a time on a cookie sheet
and brush lightly with the water chestnut
powder mixture. (You will need two cookie
sheets or flat roasting pans.) Refrigerate
for 30 minutes.

Dredge the chicken bones in flour, leaving
the top third bare.

Divide the minced chicken mixture into ten
equal portions. Press the mixture tightly
around the floured end of each bone. Finished, it should resemble a plump chicken
leg.

Place each reshaped leg on a piece of the caul fat and bring up the edges so the leg is tightly sealed. Brush the outside of each leg with the water chestnut powder mixture, then dust lightly all over with water chestnut powder. Refrigerate for at least 1 hour.

The legs can be prepared 1 day ahead up to this point.

COOKING PROCEDURE

Place the wok over high heat for about 1 minute. Pour in the peanut oil; turn the heat to medium until the oil reaches 325 degrees. Turn the heat to high. Place five of the chicken legs in the wok; fry for 10 minutes, turning every 2 minutes. Using a wire strainer, remove the chicken legs from the wok. Drain well by placing them in a single layer on several sheets of paper towels. Repeat the process with the remaining five legs. Allow the legs to cool for at least 30 minutes.

Strain the oil; return it to the wok.

When ready to serve, heat the oil over medium heat until it reaches 350 degrees. Add the legs to the wok again, and fry for another 5 minutes, or until very brown. Drain well on fresh paper towels.

Heat the oil over high heat to 375 degrees. Add 2 cups of the shredded green bok choy leaves and fry until crisp, for about 2 minutes. Drain on paper towels. Repeat with the remaining 2 cups.

Place the fried bok choy leaves in the center of a heated flat round serving dish and arrange the legs so that they radiate out from the center, like the spokes of a wheel.

Serve with Szechwan Peppercorn Powder.

YIELD *10 servings*

NOTES

Timing The entire preparation and first frying can be done the day ahead. Allow the Phoenix and Dragon Legs to cool thoroughly after the first frying before refrigerating them.

Tips The mincing of the raw chicken can be done in a food processor.

Do not wash the bok choy leaves, as they will then not become crisp when fried.

TRICOLOR SHRIMP ROLL

1. Spread half the shrimp mixture on the pancake.

2. Center the laver sheet.

3 Chinese mushrooms, soaked and shredded**

SHRIMP PASTE
1/2 pound shrimp
1 1/2 ounces fatty pork, ground
2 scallions (white and green parts), chopped
2 teaspoons minced ginger root
1 tablespoon sherry
1/2 teaspoon salt
1/2 teaspoon pepper
1/2 egg white
1 tablespoon water chestnut powder

BATTER
1 1/2 eggs, beaten
1/2 teaspoon salt
1 teaspoon water chestnut powder
* dissolved in*
1 tablespoon reduced mushroom stock**,
* cooled*

1 dried laver sheet

Extra water chestnut powder

2 teaspoons peanut oil

PREPARATION

Having reconstituted the mushrooms, set aside.

Shell, wash, drain, dry, and mince the shrimp until it forms a paste. Mix the shrimp paste and ground pork in a bowl.

Put the scallions and ginger in a small bowl and add the sherry, salt, pepper, egg white, and water chestnut powder. Stir well in one direction with chopsticks until the mixture is smooth, then add it to the shrimp and pork.

Combine the batter ingredients.

Place a 12-inch sauté pan over high heat for about 1 minute, then add the oil. Heat until the oil is hot and evenly distributed. Pour in the batter and spread thinly. Rotate the pan above the heat, so the pancake cooks evenly. When set, remove it from the skillet.

Using a small strainer, dust water chestnut powder over the pancake. Spread half the shrimp mixture evenly over the pancake, then sprinkle more water chestnut powder over it.

3. Square the round pancake by trimming the edges. Spread the second layer of the shrimp mixture; arrange the mushroom rows.

Place the laver sheet over the shrimp mixture, then cover the laver sheet with the second half of the shrimp mixture, reserving 1 tablespoon. Spread the mixture evenly over the entire surface with a spatula. Cut off the edges to form a slightly larger square than the laver sheet.

Take the mushroom shreds and put two rows across the edge of the square pancake farthest from you and two rows across the edge nearest you. Roll the near end toward the center, away from you; roll the far end also toward the center, toward you. Stick the two rolls together in the center, using a little reserved shrimp paste. Sprinkle the top lightly with water chestnut powder. Turn the roll over so the seam is on the bottom.

COOKING PROCEDURE

Place the roll on a greased rectangular or oval plate and put it in the steamer for 10 minutes. Remove the roll from the steamer. Let it cool a few minutes, then slice across into 12 to 15 pieces, about ¹/₂ inch thick. Serve immediately.

YIELD *4–8 servings*

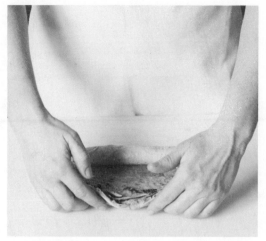

4. Roll both ends toward the center.

5. Straight-slice roll into ¹/₂-inch pieces.

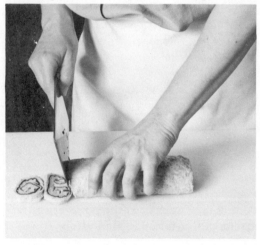

NOTES

Timing The entire preparation can be done a day in advance and the roll refrigerated. Remove the roll from the refrigerator a half hour before steaming.

Tip The shrimp paste can be made in a food processor. Place all the ingredients in the bowl of the processor and, using the on and off technique, process until they become a paste.

CRISPY FISH ROLLS

1 1/2 ounces raw pork fat
1 pound boneless firm fish fillet
  (yellow pike, sea bass or striped bass, red
  snapper, or tilefish)

FILLING

4 water chestnuts, chopped (if using canned,
  squeeze dry after chopping)
3 scallions (white and green parts), chopped
2 teaspoons minced ginger root
1/2 teaspoon salt
1 tablespoon light soy sauce
2 tablespoons water chestnut powder
  dissolved in
1 tablespoon sherry
1 teaspoon sesame oil
1/4 teaspoon freshly ground white pepper
1 egg white

7 half-moon bean curd sheets**

FLOUR PASTE FOR SEALING

2 tablespoons cold water
1 tablespoon flour

4 cups peanut oil

Szechwan Peppercorn Powder*, for dipping
  (optional)

PREPARATION

Slightly freeze the pork fat, then shred.
Pour boiling water over the pork fat and let
it stand for 2 minutes, then drain.

Cut the fish, first lengthwise into long thin
strips (about 3 inches in length), then into
1-inch pieces (about 1/4 inch wide and 1/4
inch thick).

Place the fish along with the pork fat and
the ingredients for the filling in a bowl and
gently stir in one direction with chopsticks.
Place the mixture in the refrigerator for at
least 1 hour or up to 12 hours.

Layer the bean curd sheets between damp
towels for 10 minutes. When soft, cut each
sheet in half, crosswise.

Place 1/4 cup of the fish mixture on the
edge of the rectangle nearest you. Fold this
edge tightly over the filling and continue
rolling the skin over the fish until all the
paper is used. Seal with flour paste along
the sides and the top.

COOKING PROCEDURE

Place the wok over high heat for about 1
minute. Pour in the peanut oil; turn the
heat to medium until the oil reaches 350
degrees. Turn the heat to high. Deep-fry 7
fish rolls at a time for 2 to 3 minutes, or
until well browned, turning once at midpoint. Using a wire strainer, remove the
fish rolls from the wok. Drain well by placing the fish rolls on several sheets of paper
towels. Repeat the procedure with the remaining fish rolls. Cut each fish roll into 3
pieces.

Serve immediately with Szechwan Peppercorn Powder, if desired.

YIELD *14 rolls*

NOTES

Timing The fish rolls can be refrigerated
on a flat plate in a single layer several hours
before frying.
  Fry them at room temperature.

Tip The pork fat called for in this recipe
can be obtained from the trimming of a
piece of raw pork such as a fresh ham, Boston butt, or loin chop.

APPETIZERS AND DIM SUM

MARINADE

1/2 teaspoon sugar
1/4 teaspoon freshly ground white pepper
1 teaspoon sherry
1 teaspoon sesame oil
1 egg yolk
1 tablespoon water chestnut powder
1 scallion (white and green parts), chopped
1 teaspoon minced ginger root

*1 pound pike or grouper fillet, cut into
 20 slices, about 2 1/4 × 1 1/2 × 1/4 inch*

*1 slice center-cut Smithfield ham (1 3/4 inches
 thick)*
4–5 slices stale white bread

Water chestnut powder for dredging

4 cups peanut oil

PREPARATION

Combine the ingredients for the marinade.
Place the fish slices in the marinade, stirring in one direction gently with a pair of
chopsticks until they are evenly coated. Refrigerate for 1/2 hour or up to 12 hours.

Simmer the ham in water to cover for 40
minutes. Remove the ham and place it on a
rack until cool. Slice the ham into 20 pieces,
approximately the same size as the fish
slices.

Cut the bread into pieces approximately
the same size as the fish, by placing the fish
on the bread and cutting around each
piece.

Make open-faced sandwiches with the marinated fish slices and the bread.

Lay thin slices of ham on top of each "sandwich." Brush the ham with any leftover
marinade. Dredge each sandwich with water chestnut powder.

COOKING PROCEDURE

Place the wok over high heat for about 1
minute. Pour in the peanut oil; turn the
heat to medium until the oil reaches 350
degrees. Turn the heat to high. Place half
of the slices in the oil, bread side down, and
fry for 2 minutes, turning once at midpoint. Using a wire strainer, remove the
slices from the wok. Drain them well by
placing them ham side up in a single layer
on several sheets of paper towels. Repeat
the procedure with the second batch. Serve
immediately.

YIELD *20 slices*

NOTES

Timing Ham and Fish Slices can be prepared the day ahead and refrigerated on a
cookie sheet in a single layer.

SMOKED FISH FILLETS   Shanghai

These fish fillets are not smoked but, in the traditional Chinese manner, have a "smoky" flavor acquired by the way in which they are cooked and seasoned. The Chinese serve Smoked Fish Fillets as part of a cold platter for a banquet. In addition to making an excellent, as well as unusual, cold appetizer, they can be served as part of a dinner.

1 pound tilefish fillet, sliced against the grain into 1/4-inch-thick pieces

MARINADE
1 1/2 tablespoons dark soy sauce
2 slices ginger root, shredded
2 scallions (white and green parts), shredded

SEASONING SAUCE
2 tablespoons chicken stock
2 tablespoons sugar
2 tablespoons sherry
1/4 teaspoon Five Spice Powder*

1 teaspoon minced ginger root
1 scallion (white and green parts), chopped

3 cups peanut oil

GARNISH
Coriander leaves

PREPARATION

Remove the center bone from the fish fillet. Slice the fish fillet against the grain by using the same technique as for slicing flank steak. Place the fish fillet slices in the marinade. Refrigerate for at least 2 hours or up to 24 hours.

Combine the ingredients for the seasoning sauce.

Remove the fish from the refrigerator 1 hour before frying.

COOKING PROCEDURE

Place the wok over high heat for about 1 minute. Pour in the oil; turn the heat to medium until the oil reaches 375 degrees. Turn the heat to high. Lower half the fish slices into the oil and deep-fry for 7 minutes, or until they become very crisp. Using a wire strainer, remove the fish from the wok. Drain well by placing the fish in a single layer on several sheets of paper towels. Repeat the frying procedure with the remaining pieces of fish. Turn off the heat and pour out the oil. Separate any fish fillet slices that have stuck together.

Return the wok to high heat. In the oil that glazes the wok, stir-fry the ginger and scallion for 30 seconds.

Restir the seasoning sauce and add it to the wok, stirring for a minute or two, or until the sauce has caramelized.

Return the fish fillet slices to the wok and stir-fry rapidly until the sauce has formed an even glaze around the fish.

Empty the contents of the wok onto a serving dish. Garnish with a cluster of coriander leaves. Smoked Fish Fillets may be served either hot or at room temperature.

YIELD *4–8 servings*

NOTES

Substitution Fresh sturgeon can be substituted for the tilefish.

Storage Smoked Fish Fillets can be made up to three days in advance and stored in the refrigerator with a *loose* cover (to avoid losing their crisp texture).

DEEP-FRIED BUTTERFLY SHRIMP Canton/Guangzhou

INGREDIENTS
1 pound medium shrimp (21–25 to the pound)

MARINADE
Juice from ³/₄-inch cube ginger root
1 teaspoon minced garlic
1 teaspoon sherry
¹/₂ tablespoon light soy sauce

BATTER
¹/₂ cup flour
¹/₃ cup cornstarch
1 tablespoon sesame oil
1 teaspoon dark soy sauce
²/₃ cup cold, flat beer (or more)
2 teaspoons double-acting baking powder

4 cups peanut oil

Spicy Dipping Sauce*
Duck Sauce*
Chinese Mustard Sauce*

PREPARATION

To butterfly shrimp (Method I can also be used: see Chapter 11.) As in Method II, shell the shrimp, leaving the last section and the tail intact. Cut the shrimp along the convex side, but do not let the knife go all the way through the meat. With the tip of the boning knife, make a slit about 1 inch long in the middle of the shrimp on the convex side. Push the tail of the shrimp through the slit and pull it out neatly. Carefully rinse the shrimp under cold running water. Drain and dry the shrimp very well with paper towels.

Place the cube of ginger in a garlic press and extract as much juice as possible. Combine the ingredients for the marinade on a flat plate.

Dip each shrimp in the marinade, on the split side. Place the shrimp on a plate and refrigerate. Marinate the shrimp for at least ¹/₂ hour or up to 12 hours.

To make the batter Place the flour and the cornstarch in a bowl. Mix with several chopsticks. Combine the sesame oil, soy sauce, and beer. Add this liquid all at once to the dry ingredients, mixing until the batter is almost smooth. Add the baking powder and mix again. Refrigerate, uncovered, for at least 4 hours or up to 12 hours. If it becomes too thick, add a little more beer.

COOKING PROCEDURE

Bring the shrimp to room temperature. Place the shrimp on paper towels in a single layer. Put another towel on top and pat them gently to remove excess marinade.

Place the wok over high heat for about 1 minute. Pour in the peanut oil; turn the heat to medium until the wok reaches 375 degrees. Turn the heat to high. Take each shrimp by the tail, dip it in the batter, then put it directly into the hot oil. The shrimp should puff up and float to the surface almost immediately. After about 1 minute, the shrimp should be golden brown. Turn it with chopsticks and fry another minute. Do not fry more than six shrimp at a time. Repeat until all the shrimp have been fried. Using a wire strainer, remove the shrimp from the wok. Drain well by placing the shrimp in a single layer on several sheets of paper towels. Serve immediately with Spicy Dipping Sauce or Duck Sauce and Chinese Mustard Sauce.

YIELD *7–10 servings*

(continued)

NOTES

Timing The batter is best made and refrigerated at least 4 hours ahead or up to 12 hours ahead.

The shrimp must be at room temperature before being fried, otherwise they will not be cooked through even though the batter is brown and crisp.

Never keep deep-fat-fried foods warm. They will lose their crisp texture.

Tips In order to decrease the beer's carbonization, either pour it from glass to glass a few times, then refrigerate, or pour it into a glass filled with ice cubes for a few seconds.

Reheat the oil before adding a new batch of battered shrimp. It is the contact of the cold batter with the hot oil that makes the batter crisp. Test one shrimp first.

A simple and attractive way to serve an appetizer, such as Deep-Fried Butterfly Shrimp, is to place a good-quality solid-color paper napkin on a bamboo tray. Lay one interesting flower (I use tiger lilies when in season) diagonally on top of the napkin. Place Spicy Dipping Sauce, Duck Sauce, and Chinese Mustard Sauce in small dishes on the tray. Place 6 or 8 shrimp on the tray and serve.

Substitutions For the shrimp, you can substitute scallops, any fish fillet, or boneless, skinless chicken. Vegetable substitutions are also a possibility, including triangle-cut sweet pepper, roll-oblique-cut zucchini, and thinly sliced slant-cut carrots, to name a few.

1 pound large shrimp (16–18 to a pound)

MARINADE
1/4 teaspoon salt
1 teaspoon sesame oil
1 teaspoon sherry
1 teaspoon minced garlic

BATTER
4 egg whites, at room temperature
1 tablespoon flour
1 teaspoon cornstarch

2 cups fresh bread crumbs

4 cups peanut oil for deep-frying

Spicy Dipping Sauce*

PREPARATION

To butterfly shrimp Using Method I, shell the shrimp, leaving the last section and the tail intact. Cut the shrimp from the underside, almost through to the back (but not all the way through). Turn the shrimp over and make a few vertical cuts across the back. Flatten each shrimp with the side of the cleaver. Carefully rinse the shrimp under cold running water. Drain and dry the shrimp very well with paper towels.

Combine the ingredients for the marinade in a flat dish. Place the cut side of each shrimp in the marinade and allow to marinate for at least 1/2 hour, or up to 12 hours (in which case refrigerate).

To make the batter Beat the egg whites to form soft peaks. Add the flour and cornstarch; continue to beat until the egg white mixture stands in stiff peaks.

Dip each shrimp in the egg white mixture to coat thickly; then dip in the bread crumbs. Refrigerate the shrimp for at least 1 hour or up to 12 hours in a single layer on a cookie sheet lined with waxed paper.

COOKING PROCEDURE

Place the wok over high heat for about 1 minute. Pour in the peanut oil; turn the heat to medium until the oil reaches 350 degrees. Turn the heat to high. Deep-fry the shrimp, four at a time, for 1 1/2 minutes, or until golden brown, turning once at midpoint. Using a wire strainer, remove the shrimp from the wok. Drain well by placing the shrimp on several layers of paper towels. Bring the oil temperature back to 350 degrees and repeat with four more shrimp. Continue until all the shrimp have been fried. Serve immediately with Spicy Dipping Sauce.

YIELD *6–10 servings*

MINCED SHRIMP IN LAVER ROLLS

FILLING

1/2 pound shrimp

3 ounces very fatty pork, ground

1 teaspoon minced ginger root

2 whole scallions (white and green parts), chopped

1 tablespoon sherry

1 tablespoon light soy sauce

1 tablespoon water chestnut powder

1/2 egg, beaten slightly

1/2 teaspoon salt

Freshly ground white pepper to taste

3 laver (dried seaweed) sheets (about 8 × 8 inches)

1/2 egg, beaten slightly

1 teaspoon salt

2 bunches watercress, stems removed

1 tablespoon peanut oil

3 cups peanut oil

Szechwan Peppercorn Powder*
    or
Spicy Dipping Sauce*

PREPARATION

Shell, wash, drain, and dry the shrimp well; mince and place in a bowl.

Add the pork, ginger, scallions, sherry, soy sauce, water chestnut powder, 1/2 egg, and salt and pepper to the shrimp. Stir well in one direction with several chopsticks. Refrigerate the mixture for at least 1 hour or up to 24 hours.

Take 3 sheets of dried laver and lay them on top of one another. Using scissors, cut them in half. Place one half on top of the other, and then cut in 3 sections at right angles to the first cut. There should be a total of 18 small rectangles.

Take one rectangle of laver, place it with a short side toward you, and put a tablespoon of shrimp filling on the edge closest

to you. Moisten the edge farthest from you with the beaten egg. Roll the laver paper away from you, until the paper completely surrounds the filling. Some filling should protrude slightly on both ends of the roll. If necessary, press the sides to make the roll even. Leave the seam (where the paper was sealed) touching the work surface.

COOKING PROCEDURE

Place the wok over high heat for about 1 minute. Pour in the 3 cups peanut oil; turn the heat to medium until the oil reaches 350 degrees. Turn the heat to high. With your hand, quickly lower one shrimp roll at a time into the oil, sliding each in from the side of the wok. You can fry them all at once in a 14-inch wok. Keep the heat on high and fry the rolls for 2 minutes. Using a wire strainer, remove the rolls from the wok. Drain well by placing the rolls in a single layer on several sheets of paper towels.

While the rolls are draining, place a second wok over high heat for about 1 minute. Add the 1 tablespoon peanut oil and heat until hot but not smoking. Add the salt and then the watercress; stir-fry for about 1 minute, or until the watercress wilts.

Place the watercress in the center of a serving dish and arrange the laver rolls in a wheel around it, radiating out. Serve as is with Szechwan Peppercorn Powder, or with Spicy Dipping Sauce.

YIELD *3–6 servings*

NOTES

Timing The filling can be prepared a day in advance.

The rolls can be made and refrigerated on a cookie sheet in a single layer early in the day. Remove them from the refrigerator 1/2 hour before deep-frying.

STUFFED SHRIMP IN BEAN CURD SHEETS Fukien/Fujian

10 ounces medium shrimp (21–25 to the
  pound)

MARINADE
1/2 tablespoon sherry
1/2 tablespoon light soy sauce

STUFFING
6 ounces shrimp
1/2 cup minced fresh water chestnuts
2 scallions (white and green parts), chopped
1 tablespoon light soy sauce
1 tablespoon sherry
1 tablespoon water chestnut powder
1/4 teaspoon freshly ground white pepper
1 teaspoon minced ginger root
1/2 teaspoon sugar

4 dried half-moon bean curd sheets**

PASTE
1/4 cup flour
    mixed with
1/4 cup water

4 cups peanut oil

Spicy Dipping Sauce*

PREPARATION

To butterfly shrimp Using Method I (see
Chapter 11), shell the 10 ounces shrimp,
leaving the last section and the tail intact.
Cut the shrimp from the underside, almost
through to the back (but not all the way
through). Turn the shrimp over and make
a few vertical cuts across the back. Flatten
each shrimp with the side of the cleaver.
Carefully rinse the shrimp under cold running water. Drain and dry the shrimp very
well with paper towels.

Pour the sherry and light soy sauce on a
plate. Dip each shrimp in the marinade on
the split side. Marinate the shrimp for 1/2
hour, or up to 12 hours (in which case, refrigerate).

To make the stuffing Shell, rinse, drain, dry,
and mince the 6 ounces shrimp. Combine
with the remaining ingredients for the
stuffing.

Layer the bean curd sheets between damp
tea towels for 10 minutes. Cut the bean
curd sheets into 3-inch-wide strips, lengthwise.

Place 1 heaping teaspoon of the stuffing on
the split side of each butterflied shrimp.
Place the shrimp at one end of the cut bean
curd strip and fold diagonally, American
flag style. Seal with paste.

COOKING PROCEDURE

Place the wok over high heat for about 1
minute. Pour in the oil; turn the heat to
medium until the oil reaches 350 degrees.
Turn the heat to high. Fry four shrimp at a
time for 2 minutes, turning once at midpoint. Using a wire strainer, remove the
shrimp from the wok. Drain well by placing
the shrimp on several sheets of paper towels. Repeat the frying process with the remaining shrimp. Serve immediately with
Spicy Dipping Sauce.

YIELD *6–10 servings*

NOTES

Timing The stuffing can be prepared and
refrigerated a day in advance.

The wrapped, stuffed shrimp can be
placed in a single layer in the refrigerator
several hours before frying. Fry them at
room temperature.

FILLING
1 whole chicken breast (12–14 ounces)

MARINADE
^{1}/$_2$ egg white
1 teaspoon water chestnut powder
1 teaspoon sherry

^{1}/$_3$ cup Chinese mushrooms, soaked and
    shredded**
1 cup split, shredded leeks (white part only)
^{1}/$_2$ cup shredded bamboo shoots

1 cup mung bean sprouts

2 tablespoons dark soy sauce
1 tablespoon oyster sauce

^{1}/$_2$ cup cleaned, seeded, and shredded sweet
    red pepper
1 fresh chili pepper, cleaned, seeded, and
    shredded

^{1}/$_4$ pound Barbecued Roast Pork*, shredded
1^1/$_4$ cups shredded bok choy

BINDER
1 tablespoon water chestnut powder
    dissolved in
2 tablespoons sherry

BATTER
1 cup flour
^{2}/$_3$ cup cornstarch
2 tablespoons sesame oil
2 teaspoons dark soy sauce
1^1/$_3$ cups cold, flat beer (or more)
1 tablespoon plus 1 teaspoon double-acting
    baking powder

EGG PANCAKES
9 eggs, beaten
^{1}/$_4$ teaspoon freshly ground white pepper
1^1/$_2$ tablespoons water chestnut powder
    dissolved in
4^1/$_2$ tablespoons reduced mushroom stock**,
    cooled
2 egg yolks
    beaten with
1 tablespoon water
4^1/$_2$ cups (approximately) peanut oil

Spicy Dipping Sauce*
Duck Sauce*
Chinese Mustard Sauce*

PREPARATION

Bone and skin the chicken breast. Partially freeze it flat on a cookie sheet; then shred. Place the chicken and the ingredients for the marinade in a bowl and stir in one direction vigorously with chopsticks. Place the mixture in the refrigerator for at least 1 hour or up to 12 hours.

Having reconstituted the mushrooms, set aside.

To make the batter Place the flour and the cornstarch in a bowl. Mix with several chopsticks. Combine the sesame oil, soy sauce, and beer. Add this liquid all at once to the dry ingredients, mixing until the batter is almost smooth. Add the baking powder and mix again. Refrigerate, uncovered, for at least 4 hours or up to 24 hours. If it becomes too thick, add a little more beer.

Mix the binder.

To cook the filling Place the wok over high heat for about 2 minutes. Add the bean sprouts and stir-fry without oil for about 2 minutes. Remove them from the wok. Return the wok to the high heat. Add 2 tablespoons of the peanut oil and heat until hot but not smoking. Add the chicken shreds; stir-fry for 1 minute. Remove the chicken from the wok.

Return the wok to the high heat and add a further 1 tablespoon peanut oil. Add the mushrooms, leeks, and bamboo shoots; stir-fry for 2 minutes.

Add the soy sauce and oyster sauce and the sweet red and chili peppers; stir-fry for 1 minute.

Add the roast pork, chicken, and bok choy; stir-fry for 30 seconds.

Add the bean sprouts and mix for a few seconds.

Restir the binder with one hand and add it to the wok while stir-frying with the other hand, continuing until all the juices have thickened.

Empty the contents of the wok into a colander set over a bowl and allow the filling to cool thoroughly.

To make the egg pancakes Combine the egg pancake ingredients. Place an 8-inch omelet pan over medium heat for 30 seconds. Add 2 tablespoons of the peanut oil, then pour out all the oil so that only a thin film remains. Place a scant 1/4 cup of the egg pancake mixture in the pan and rotate the pan above the heat until a thin circle forms. Remove the pancake when it is set. This takes only a few seconds. Repeat this procedure (oil the pan, add the egg mixture, etc.) until all the egg mixture is used up. This should yield twelve 8-inch egg pancakes.

To assemble Once the filling has cooled, place 2 tablespoons of the filling on the uncooked side of each egg pancake, a little to the side of the center nearest you. Take the nearest edge of the circle and fold it over the filling. Then take the two sides and fold them in toward the center at right angles to the bottom fold, covering the filling. The result should look like an envelope. Take the end with the enclosed filling and roll it over, away from you, toward the far side of the circle. After two rolls, the envelope should be complete. Seal it with beaten egg yolk.

(At this point the rolls can be refrigerated.)

COOKING PROCEDURE

Place the wok over high heat for about 1 minute. Pour in 4 cups of the peanut oil; turn the heat to medium until the oil reaches 375 degrees. Turn the heat to high. One at a time, dip each roll into the batter with your hands and then slide it down the side of the wok into the oil. Fry no more than four rolls at once. Fry for 1 1/2 minutes, or until they become golden brown, turning at midpoint with chopsticks. Remove the rolls from the oil with a wire strainer. Place on several layers of paper towels to drain.

Cut the Peking Rolls in half diagonally and place them on a flat serving dish.

Serve with Spicy Dipping Sauce, Duck Sauce, and Chinese Mustard Sauce.

YIELD *12 rolls*

NOTES

Timing The entire filling can be cooked, allowed to cool, and then refrigerated the day before.

The egg pancakes can be cooked, allowed to cool, stacked, then covered and refrigerated the day before.

The batter can be prepared and refrigerated, uncovered, early in the day.

Once the rolls have been made and sealed, but *not* dipped in the batter, they can be refrigerated early in the day.

Tips In order to decrease the beer's carbonization, either pour it from glass to glass a few times, then refrigerate, or pour it into a glass filled with ice cubes for a few seconds.

Remove the rolls from the refrigerator 1/2 hour before frying.

It is the hot oil and the cold batter that will make the coating crisp. Reheat the oil about 15 to 30 seconds before adding more rolls. Place a paper towel on the serving dish after the rolls have been cut to allow them to drain further. They will continue to release the oil in which they were fried.

Although Peking Rolls are an appetizer, they are best served at the table because they are large and difficult to handle.

The preparation of Peking Rolls is quite time-consuming, and as the dish is also very filling, a light dish such as Szechwan Steamed Whole Fish*, which requires little preparation, can complete the meal.

Substitution Peking Rolls can be made without pork or chicken, in which case the amount of vegetables in the recipe should be increased by 2 cups.

VEGETABLE ROLLS WITH SESAME SEED SAUCE

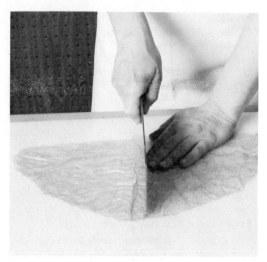

1. Cut the bean curd sheet in half cross-wise.

2. Turn the sheet with the right angle toward you; add one eighth of the filling.

FILLING

*1/3 cup Chinese mushrooms, soaked and
   shredded***
1 cup split, shredded leeks (white part only)
4 cups bean sprouts
1 tablespoon peanut oil

SAUCE

1 tablespoon Sesame Seed Butter*
1 tablespoon dark soy sauce
2 tablespoons sherry
2 teaspoons sugar
2 teaspoons wine vinegar
2 teaspoons Hot Sauce*
1/4 cup salt-free chicken stock

PASTE

1/4 cup flour
1/4 cup water

4 half-moon bean curd sheets**

*1/2 cup chopped scallions (white and green
   parts)*

4 cups peanut oil

2 teaspoons sesame oil

PREPARATION

Having reconstituted the mushrooms, set aside.

Spread the bean sprouts on several layers of paper towels for 1 hour.

Combine the ingredients for the sauce.

To cook the filling Place the wok over high heat for 2 minutes. Add the bean sprouts; stir-fry them without oil for 2 minutes. Remove them from the wok.

Return the wok to high heat; add the 1 tablespoon peanut oil. Add the mushrooms and leeks; stir-fry for 2 minutes.

Return the bean sprouts to the wok, continuing to stir-fry a few more seconds. Turn off the heat; empty the contents of the wok into a strainer set over a bowl. Allow them to cool thoroughly.

Make a paste for the bean curd sheets by combining flour and water.

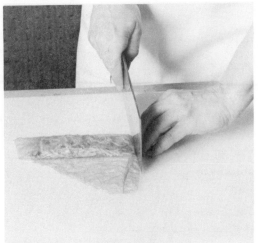

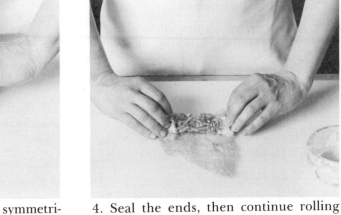

3. Make the left and right sides symmetrical.

4. Seal the ends, then continue rolling away from you.

5. The completed roll has the sealed side down.

Layer the bean curd sheets between damp tea towels for 10 minutes. When soft, cut each sheet in half. Cut off the hard ends.

Filling the vegetable rolls Place one eighth of the filling on a bean curd sheet across the end nearest you, a little way in from the edge. Lift the end nearest you and fold it over the filling. Rolling it away from you, make one complete roll, until the filling is covered by the sheet. If the left and right sides need to be trimmed to make the sheet more symmetrical, do this. Moisten each end piece (both left and right sides) with the paste. Fold in both ends to create an envelope shape; make a complete roll. With the paste, moisten the end farthest away from you. In order to keep it tight, tuck the sides in as you roll. Seal any ragged ends with some paste on your fingertips. Continue rolling away from you. Complete the roll, and seal. The sealed side goes down. Repeat until you have formed 8 vegetable rolls.

(continued)

COOKING PROCEDURE

Place the wok over high heat for about 1 minute. Pour in the 4 cups peanut oil; turn the heat to medium until the oil reaches 350 degrees. Turn the heat back to high. Fry the vegetable rolls four at a time for 2 minutes, turning once at midpoint. Using a wire strainer, remove them from the wok. Drain them well by placing them in a single layer on several sheets of paper towels.

Turn off the heat. Remove the oil from the wok. Turn the heat to high. In the oil that glazes the wok, stir-fry the scallions for 30 seconds.

Restir the sauce and add it all at once to the wok, stirring for about 1 minute.

Turn off the heat; add the sesame oil and mix briefly.

Cut each vegetable roll into four pieces and arrange them on a flat, heated serving dish. Pour the sauce over the rolls and serve immediately.

YIELD *4—8 servings*

NOTES

Timing The filling can be stir-fried several hours in advance. The vegetable rolls can be wrapped and refrigerated on a flat plate in a single layer early in the day. Fry them at room temperature.

Tip The purpose of stir-frying the bean sprouts in a dry wok is to produce a smoky flavor.

Substitution For the Sesame Seed Butter you can substitute tahini.

SESAME SEED BEEF

Sesame Seed Beef is traditionally served at banquets as a cold appetizer. Its appeal lies in the unusual combination of sweet, aromatic, and spicy seasonings and the crisp texture of the deep-fried beef slices. The unique spice is the orange peel; like a nut before and after roasting, orange peel releases a more intense flavor when fried. The secret and the ultimate success of this dish lie in the high temperature of the oil in which the beef is fried. After the fourth frying, the beef should be as crisp as a potato chip. Although the shin of beef is visually unappealing after it has been simmered in the seasoned stock, once the beef has been sliced, fried, and stirred in its seasoning sauce it becomes appealing both to the eye and to the palate. Shin of beef is as economical as it is authentically Chinese.

1 whole piece boneless shin of beef
(2 1/2 pounds)

Ingredients for 2 1/2 pounds of shin
1 teaspoon Szechwan Peppercorn Powder*
1 teaspoon Five Spice Powder*

2 tablespoons sugar
3 tablespoons dark soy sauce
2 slices ginger root
1 cup leeks (green part only), cut into 1-inch
pieces

Ingredients for 1/2 pound of the boiled
shin
1 tablespoon unhulled sesame seeds

SEASONING SAUCE
1 tablespoon sugar
1/2 tablespoon dark soy sauce
1/2 tablespoon light soy sauce
1 tablespoon sherry
1 tablespoon chicken stock
1/2 teaspoon Hot Sauce*

2 pieces (1 × 2 inches each) dried orange
peel

1 scallion (white and green parts), chopped
1 clove garlic, minced

4 cups peanut oil

1 teaspoon sesame oil

Coriander leaves for garnish

PREPARATION

Rub the shin of beef with the Szechwan Peppercorn Powder and Five Spice Powder. Wrap the beef in waxed paper and refrigerate for 24 hours.

Bring 4 quarts water to a rapid boil in a heavy saucepan. Add the beef and simmer for 5 minutes, removing any scum that accumulates. Add the sugar, soy sauce, ginger, and leeks. Turn the heat to low; cover, and simmer for 30 minutes. Remove the cover, turn the beef over, recover, and simmer for another 30 minutes. Remove the cover and continue to simmer the beef until it is tender, about 2 to 2 1/2 hours total. Pierce the beef from time to time with a poultry skewer to judge tenderness. Remove the beef with a wire strainer onto a rack resting on a plate and allow to cool. Refrigerate the beef until it is very cold (at least 6 hours or overnight).

Cut 1/2 pound of the meat into thin slices. Refrigerate or freeze the remaining meat.

Place the wok over low heat. Add the sesame seeds; stir until they turn brown. Remove them from the wok and allow to cool.

Combine the ingredients for the seasoning sauce.

Place the wok over high heat for about 1 minute. Pour in the peanut oil; turn the heat to medium until the oil reaches 350 degrees. Add the orange peel and fry for 15 seconds, or until it turns brown. Drain on paper towels. Once it is cool, break the orange peel into smaller pieces, then pulverize it in an electric coffee mill.

COOKING PROCEDURE

Reheat the oil to 375 degrees. Turn the heat to high. Place the beef in a Chinese metal strainer and lower it into the hot oil for 30 seconds. Remove, then reheat the oil to 375 degrees and repeat this process until the meat is very crisp—four times in all. Drain the meat on several layers of paper towels. Remove the oil from the wok.

Turn the heat to medium. In the oil that glazes the wok, stir-fry the scallion and garlic for 1 minute.

Turn the heat to high. Restir the seasoning sauce and add it all at once to the wok, stir-frying for about 15 seconds.

Return the beef and orange peel to the wok, continuing to stir-fry until the sauce has evenly glazed the meat.

Turn off the heat. Add the sesame oil and sesame seeds. Mix briefly. Empty the contents of the wok onto a flat serving dish, and let it cool. Before serving, garnish with coriander leaves.

YIELD *2–4 servings*

NOTES

Timing The entire dish can be cooked early in the day, as it should be served at room temperature.

Plan to start this dish at least one day in advance, so that the meat will be very cold and therefore easier to slice.

Refrigerated, the boiled beef will keep for four days; frozen, it will keep for one month. If using beef that has been cooked and frozen, slice the beef in a semi-defrosted state. After slicing, place it on paper towels for $1/2$ hour before frying.

Sesame Seed Beef will keep up to one week in the refrigerator. It should be served at room temperature and never rewarmed.

Tips Shin of beef has gristle running through it; however, because it will become crisp when fried four times in the hot oil, it is not necessary to trim the beef before or after boiling.

After the meat is simmered and sliced, $1/2$ pound is required. In order to allow for the initial shrinkage, you must begin with more than $1/2$ pound. I have called for $21/2$ pounds of shin because shin of beef is an unfamiliar cut of meat that in some cases must be specially ordered and therefore cannot be purchased in smaller quantities; and because when you make Sesame Seed Beef on another occasion, the remaining stored portion of the boiled shin will already have undergone the lengthy initial cooking procedure, thereby cutting the preparation in half.

A whole shin after boiling will make approximately three recipes of Sesame Seed Beef. If, instead of refrigerating or freezing the remaining portion of boiled shin, you wish to make a double or triple recipe of Sesame Seed Beef, you must increase the sesame seeds, seasoning sauce, orange peel, scallions, garlic, and sesame oil accordingly, as from the sesame seeds to the sesame oil, the recipe lists the correct seasoning for $1/2$ pound sliced and cooked shin.

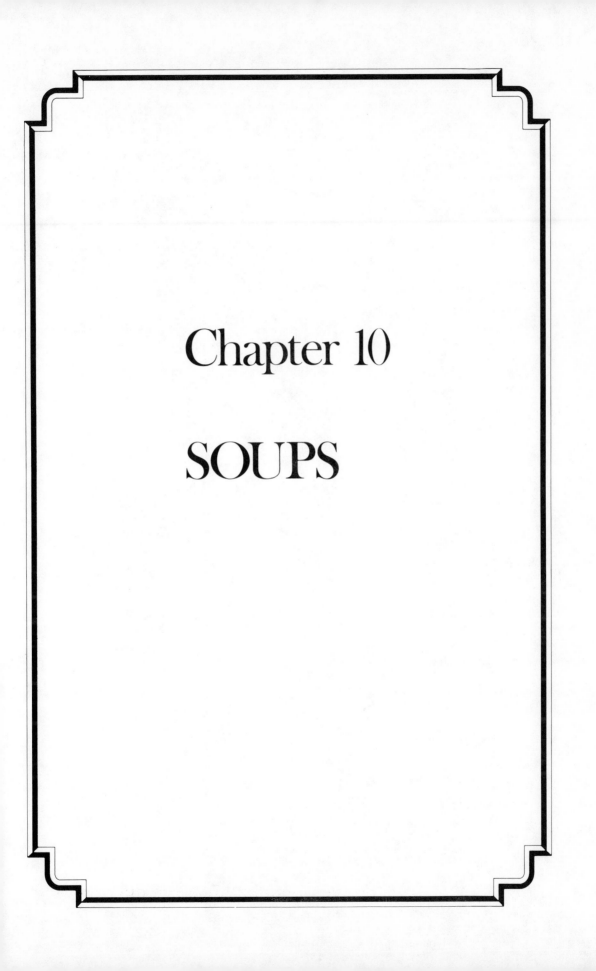

Chapter 10

SOUPS

Light, savory, or sweet soups are traditionally served between courses of a multi-course banquet, both to cleanse the palate and to denote the end of a series of courses. In a home-style meal, they are served simultaneously with other dishes, functioning as added nourishment and as a beverage. Basically there are three types of soups in the Chinese cuisine: clear (an example of which is Hunan Home-Style Soup*), long-simmered (Sparerib and Lotus Root Soup), and thickened (Chicken Velvet Soup with Shrimp Balls*).

The Chinese have had a large repertoire of soups for centuries. Soups in ancient times were even used as a treatment for tuberculosis. Chicken soup is to this day prescribed in China to mothers after child-bearing, a daily dose of it for one month, with sesame oil added in the eastern provinces and ginger root added in the South. Some soups have fanciful names, such as Wonton Soup, which literally means "swallowing the cloud," as the wontons with their skirtlike sides float in the soup like little trailing clouds.

Regional soups, utilizing the indigenous products of their respective provinces, further enhance the Chinese repertoire: the Cantonese, with their flavorful stocks and exotic ingredients such as pigs' trotters, lungs, pork sweetbreads, snake, frogs' legs, shark's fin, large fish heads, and turtle; the Easterners with their Preserved Mustard Green Soup and their fish and seafood soup garnishes; the refined soup of the West such as Pork Chop Noodle Soup*; the Hot and Sour Soup, the Bird's Nest Soup and the Minced Chicken and Abalone Soup* of the North. Of the general regions, Fukien is one particular province that is renowned for its soups, an example of which is Stuffed Clams in Broth*.

POULTRY STOCK

Poultry Stock can be substituted for chicken stock in all the recipes of this book. Rather than being made from chicken specifically, Poultry Stock is made from a combination of various birds. Frozen carcasses and giblets from chickens, ducks, and squabs, or even roasted birds can be used. Chicken feet are not crucial to making stock, but they will give the stock greater flavor as well as a more gelatinous consistency. Also enriching the flavor is the long simmering process of 8 to 12 hours. The recipe does not call for the addition of salt, as many recipes in this book use a salt-free chicken or poultry stock. Salt can always be added when making soup or any recipe that requires a salted stock.

1 chicken (4–5 pounds) in pieces or a combination of chicken, duck, and squab parts (skin included)
1/2 pound chicken feet, nails removed
4 cups leeks (green parts only), split and cut in 2-inch pieces
2 slices ginger root
6 whole black peppercorns

SPECIAL EQUIPMENT
Cheesecloth

PREPARATION

Rinse the poultry parts under cold running water.

(continued)

COOKING PROCEDURE

Place the poultry parts in a large stockpot and add enough water to cover the parts by 2 inches. Bring to a simmer over high heat. With a fine-mesh skimmer, remove the scum as it rises to the top. This process will take about 10 minutes.

Add the leeks, ginger, and peppercorns. Turn the heat to low and simmer the stock for 8 to 12 hours, stirring occasionally.

Strain the stock through a colander and then through a fine-mesh sieve (or line a strainer with cheesecloth that has been rinsed under cold running water and then wrung out).

Refrigerate the stock *uncovered* until it has thoroughly cooled and the fat has solidified.

NOTES

Tips It is very important to allow the stock to cool in the refrigerator without a cover to prevent it from becoming sour. Before using the stock, lift the layer of fat off the top. This fat can be used in recipes calling for rendered poultry fat, but it is not as flavorful as the rendered poultry fat that is obtained from the roasting of a bird (Poultry Fat**).

Substitutions It is possible to use a canned chicken stock, but the taste will of course not be the same.

Storage Homemade poultry stock will keep for about one week in the refrigerator (longer if it is brought to a simmer every day). Poultry stock can be frozen in small containers, preferably glass jars, allowing at least 2 inches of space for expansion. It can also be frozen in ice-cube trays, after which the frozen stock cubes can be placed in a glass jar or plastic bag.

VARIATIONS

Quantity Larger or smaller quantities of stock can be made than called for in this sample recipe. When using over 4 or 5 pounds of poultry parts, add enough water to cover the parts by 2 to 3 inches. When using less than 4 or 5 pounds of poultry parts, allow the water to cover the parts by at least 6 inches, as less liquid is involved and therefore it will evaporate more rapidly. In either case, if the level of water becomes too shallow, add more water as necessary.

Reduced Poultry Stock If you are making large quantities of stock, in order to conserve on space in the freezer return the stock to a clean pot after the final straining and reduce it by half. Reducing stock is done over a very low flame. Never boil the stock, as it will become cloudy. In recipes calling for "reduced chicken stock" in a seasoning sauce, this concentrate should be used as is. In recipes requiring regular chicken stock, add half water and half reduced poultry stock.

CHICKEN VELVET SOUP WITH SHRIMP BALLS

Peking/Beijing

1/3 cup Chinese mushrooms, soaked and
    diced**

SHRIMP BALLS
3/4 pound medium shrimp
1 egg white
1/4 pound ground pork
1 teaspoon minced ginger root
1 scallion (white and green parts), minced
1/4 teaspoon freshly ground white pepper
3/4 teaspoon salt
1 teaspoon sesame oil
1 teaspoon water chestnut powder
    dissolved in
1 tablespoon sherry

CHICKEN VELVET
2 egg whites
2 teaspoons water chestnut powder
    dissolved in
4 teaspoons reduced mushroom stock, cooled**
4 ounces minced boneless, skinless chicken
    breast

6 cups chicken stock

1 bunch watercress, stems removed

2 teaspoons sesame oil

1 tablespoon minced Smithfield ham**

PREPARATION

Having reconstituted the mushrooms, set aside.

To make the Shrimp Balls Shell, wash, drain, dry, and mince the shrimp. Place the shrimp in a bowl and combine it with the remaining shrimp ball ingredients. Refrigerate the mixture while continuing with the recipe.

To make the Chicken Velvet Beat the egg whites until foamy. Add the remaining chicken velvet ingredients and combine well.

COOKING PROCEDURE

Bring the chicken stock to a simmer in a saucepan. Add the mushrooms and cook 1 minute over low heat. Drop the shrimp ball mixture, 1 full teaspoon at a time, into the simmering chicken stock, working as quickly as possible. The Shrimp Balls will float when they are done.

Turn the heat to high. Add the chicken velvet mixture, stirring in a figure-8 motion with a pair of chopsticks. This should only take a few seconds.

Add the watercress and return the soup to a simmer.

Turn off the heat; add 2 teaspoons of sesame oil.

Pour the soup into a tureen; sprinkle with ham and serve immediately.

YIELD *6 servings*

NOTES

Timing The Shrimp Balls can be prepared and cooked the day ahead, removed from the soup, and refrigerated.

Substitutions Fillet of sole, flounder, or pike can be substituted for the shrimp.

MINCED CHICKEN AND ABALONE SOUP   Peking/Beijing

³/4 cup abalone

¹/3 cup minced boneless, skinless chicken
  breast
1 teaspoon sherry
¹/4 teaspoon salt
2 egg whites

2¹/2 cups chicken stock
1 cup abalone liquid (from can)

2¹/2 tablespoons sweet butter
2 tablespoons water chestnut powder

¹/4 teaspoon freshly ground white pepper
2 scallions (white and green parts), chopped

1 tablespoon minced Smithfield ham**

PREPARATION

Slice the abalone thin.

Combine the minced chicken with the sherry and salt. Add the egg whites one at a time, stirring vigorously with a pair of chopsticks in one direction.

COOKING PROCEDURE

Combine the chicken stock and abalone liquid in a saucepan and place over a low heat.

In a second, heavy saucepan, melt the butter over a low heat. Add the water chestnut powder and stir continuously with a wooden spoon for 3 minutes. Pour in the warmed stock all at once, continuing to stir constantly in a figure-8 motion until the stock comes to a simmer.

Add the chicken and egg white mixture, continuing to stir in a figure-8 motion for about 30 seconds.

Add the pepper and scallions; cook for a few more seconds.

When the soup returns to a simmer, add the abalone. Return it to a simmer again.

Pour the soup into a tureen; sprinkle with minced ham, and serve immediately.

YIELD 4 servings

STUFFED CLAMS IN BROTH

Fukien/Fujian

This is an unusually beautiful soup, which is traditionally served at banquets.

FILLING

3 Chinese mushrooms, soaked and minced**
1/4 pound shrimp
1/4 pound ground pork
4 fresh water chestnuts, peeled and minced
1 tablespoon minced Smithfield ham**
1 teaspoon salt
1 tablespoon sherry
1 teaspoon sesame oil
1/4 teaspoon freshly ground pepper
1 tablespoon water chestnut powder

24 littleneck clams
2 tablespoons cornmeal

2 cups salt-free chicken stock
White pepper
1 teaspoon sesame oil
2 tablespoons shredded spring ginger

PREPARATION

Having reconstituted the mushrooms, set aside.

Scrub, rinse, then soak the clams for at least 1 hour in water to which the cornmeal has been added. After soaking, scrub the clams a second time.

Place the clams in 5 cups of fresh boiling water and cook until they open slightly. Remove the clams from the broth. Reduce the broth over low heat to 4 cups, strain, and reserve.

Remove the meat from the clams and mince it in a food processor or with two cleavers. Keep 24 shells and discard the rest.

Shell, wash, and drain the shrimp. Mince.

Combine the clam meat with the ingredients for the filling. Stir well in one direction with several chopsticks.

Place 1 teaspoon of the combined filling in each of the 24 clam shells, smoothing the top with the bottom of a spoon. If preparing the stuffed clams ahead, refrigerate.

COOKING PROCEDURE

Place the stuffed clams on a dish in a steamer and steam for 7 minutes.

While the clams are steaming, heat the strained clam broth with the chicken stock until it simmers; then add freshly ground pepper to taste, sesame oil, and shredded ginger.

Place the clams in a serving bowl and pour the broth over the clams. Serve immediately.

YIELD *6 servings*

NOTES

Timing The clams can be stuffed and refrigerated early in the day.

Tips The stuffed clams can be run under the broiler and served as an appetizer. Preheat the broiler for 15 minutes. Place the clams 3 inches from the source of heat and broil for 5 minutes. Serve immediately.

Substitutions For the spring ginger, you can substitute Pickled Spring Ginger*. Winter ginger can also be substituted for spring ginger, but use half the amount.

HUNAN HOME-STYLE SOUP

Hunan

One day while walking along the streets of Changsha, the capital of Hunan, a food editor and I discovered a workmen's restaurant. At first we weren't quite certain that it was a restaurant. The walls were bare, the doorway was merely an open space, and the décor consisted of stools and tables. Through the opening, we could see many Chinese men sitting inside, smoking with one hand while eating with the other.

Inside, a wall separated the kitchen from the dining area. A woman sat behind a desk near a small blackboard that had the daily specials written in Chinese characters. There were no empty tables, but as soon as we gestured that we wanted to eat, several men got up from their table to offer us seats. They also offered food from their plates. They were drinking a warmed local rice wine, which was a bit too strong but hot and soothing. The meal, more interesting than most banquets we had eaten so far on the China trip, was composed of soup, several pork dishes, and bean curd. The bill came to less than 75 cents. The warmth of the patrons, who treated us like important guests, remains a vivid memory. Upon finishing our meal, we stepped into the kitchen to watch the chef stir-frying over a huge flame. The heat source was compressed charcoal. Ginger, garlic, smoked and fresh pork, a local green vegetable, and many more ingredients were placed in straw baskets, ready to be tossed in the three woks and bamboo steamer that were set up in the kitchen area. We saw the chef using a ladle to skim the scum off some pork slices he was blanching in water. I wanted to give him a skimmer. When I go back to China, I will definitely bring dozens with me.

1/2 cup Chinese mushrooms, soaked and shredded**
2 tablespoons tree ears, soaked and shredded**
1/4 pound boneless pork
1 tablespoon shredded ginger root
1 tablespoon dark soy sauce

4 cups chicken stock
2 tablespoons reduced mushroom stock**

6 cups spinach leaves, shredded
2 scallions (white and green parts), chopped

1 egg pancake, shredded*
1/4 teaspoon freshly ground black pepper

1 teaspoon sesame oil

PREPARATION

Having reconstituted and shredded the mushrooms and tree ears, set aside.

Partially freeze the pork; then shred.

COOKING PROCEDURE

Combine the stocks and bring to a simmer.

Add the mushrooms, tree ears, pork, ginger, and soy sauce; simmer for 3 minutes, stirring occasionally.

Add spinach and scallions; simmer 1 minute.

Add the egg shreds and pepper; stir briefly.

Turn off the heat. Add sesame oil. Mix briefly and serve.

YIELD *4 servings*

NOTES

Tips This soup is typically prepared with a base of water, but is more flavorful when a good chicken stock is used.

SZECHWAN PORK AND PICKLED CABBAGE SOUP

Szechwan/Sichuan

$^1/_4$ cup Chinese mushrooms, soaked and shredded**
$^1/_4$ cup preserved Szechwan vegetable, rinsed and shredded**
1 tablespoon shredded spring ginger root
$^1/_4$ cup shredded bamboo shoots

$^1/_4$ pound boneless pork

4 cups chicken stock
2 tablespoons reduced mushroom stock**

1 scallion (white and green parts), shredded

PREPARATION

Having reconstituted the mushrooms and done the necessary cutting, place the first four ingredients in a bowl.

Partially freeze the pork; slice it thin, then shred.

COOKING PROCEDURE

Combine the stocks in a saucepan; bring to a simmer.

Add the pork shreds and simmer 1 minute.

Add the mushrooms, preserved vegetable, ginger, and bamboo shoots; simmer for 3 minutes, stirring occasionally.

Add the scallions and simmer another 30 seconds.

Pour the soup into a tureen and serve immediately.

YIELD *4 servings*

NOTES

Substitutions Pickled Spring Ginger* can be substituted for spring ginger, using the same amount; however, if winter ginger is substituted, use half the amount.

PORK CHOP NOODLE SOUP　　　　Szechwan/Sichuan

8 center-cut pork chops (4 ounces each)

MARINADE
2 teaspoons sugar
1 teaspoon salt
2 tablespoons light soy sauce
2 teaspoons sherry
1 teaspoon black vinegar
1 teaspoon Hot Sauce*
2 cloves garlic, minced
2 egg whites, beaten
1/4 teaspoon freshly ground white pepper

5 cups chicken stock
1 tablespoon dark soy sauce
1 teaspoon Hot Sauce*

1 pound fresh egg noodles (lo mein)
1 teaspoon salt

4 cups peanut oil

1 teaspoon sesame oil

GARNISH
2 scallions (white and green parts), chopped
24 coriander leaves

PREPARATION

Trim the fat from the pork chops.

Combine the ingredients for the marinade and pour it over the pork chops. Allow the pork chops to marinate for 1 hour, turning them once in the marinade at midpoint.

COOKING PROCEDURE

Place the 5 cups of chicken stock in a saucepan and bring to a simmer over very low heat.

To cook the noodles Bring 4 quarts of water to a boil in a large kettle and add 1 teaspoon salt.

While the water is coming to a boil, place a wok over high heat for about 1 minute. Pour in the peanut oil; turn the heat to medium until the oil reaches 350 degrees. Turn the heat to high. Deep-fry the pork chops, 4 at a time, for 5 minutes, turning once at midpoint. Using a wire strainer, remove them from the wok. Drain well by placing the pork chops in a single layer on several sheets of paper towels. Any excess marinade from the pork chops should be added to the chicken stock.

Add the dark soy sauce and Hot Sauce to the simmering stock. Turn off the heat.

Add the noodles to the boiling water and boil over high heat for about 3 minutes, stirring and lifting with a pair of chopsticks the entire time. Drain the noodles and divide them up among 8 large soup bowls.

Return the soup stock to a simmer; add sesame oil and remove the soup from the heat.

Place one pork chop in each soup bowl on top of the noodles. Ladle the soup into the soup bowls and sprinkle a little chopped scallion on each pork chop. Garnish with coriander leaves and serve immediately.

YIELD *8 servings*

¹/₃ cup Chinese mushrooms, soaked, stemmed, and diced**

¹/₂ cup split and finely diced leeks (white part only)

¹/₄ teaspoon freshly ground white pepper

1 tablespoon Chi-tzu berries

¹/₄ cup reduced mushroom stock**
2 cups chicken stock
2 cups smoked chicken or duck stock*

1 cup cooked and diced fresh lobster or crab meat
2 tablespoons minced Smithfield ham**
¹/₂ cup peeled and sliced water chestnuts

3 egg whites, stiffly beaten

PREPARATION

Having reconstituted the mushrooms, set aside.

Rinse, then soak the Chi-tzu berries in ¹/₄ cup warm water for 15 minutes.

Strain the liquid into the stock and reserve the berries.

If using crab meat, remove any shell or cartilage.

COOKING PROCEDURE

Combine the stocks and bring to a simmer in a saucepan.

Add mushrooms, leeks, and pepper; simmer 2 minutes.

Add lobster or crab, ham, and water chestnuts; stir well. Return to a simmer, then remove the soup from the heat.

Pour the contents of the saucepan into a soup tureen that will fit into a steamer.

Distribute the stiffly beaten egg whites evenly on top of the soup.

Sprinkle the Chi-tzu berries on top of the egg whites.

Place the soup tureen in the steamer; cover (making sure the cover does not touch the egg whites) and steam for 1 minute.

Remove the tureen from the steamer and serve immediately.

YIELD *4 servings*

NOTES

Tips It is possible in some fish stores to buy fresh cooked lobster meat. If you are cooking the lobster, steam it 4 minutes, then allow it to cool slightly before removing the meat. A 1¹/₄-pound lobster will yield 1 cup of meat. If steaming your own lobster, use the juice from the lobster, and any roe and tomalley (the liver) in the stock. Also use the liquid that is released while the lobster is steaming as part of the 4 cups of stock.

This is an excellent opportunity to use any leftover smoked chicken stock or smoked duck stock (Tea Smoked Duck*); however, this soup is also wonderful if a good homemade poultry stock is used.

Have the egg whites at room temperature so they will beat to a greater volume. If they are steamed for longer than 1 minute, they will deflate.

You can use your best china soup tureen, as it will not crack with the moist heat of the steam.

Substitutions Jujube, soaked overnight and diced, can be substituted for the Chi-tzu berries.

Shrimp can be substituted for the lobster. If using shrimp, dice them and simmer the soup an extra 30 seconds.

SIZZLING RICE SOUP

1/2 cup Chinese mushrooms, soaked and diced**

1/4 pound pork fillet

1/4 pound boneless, skinless chicken breast
1/2 egg white

1/4 pound small shrimp (35 to the pound)

5 cups chicken stock
1 cup reduced mushroom stock**

1 cup snow peas, strung and triangle-cut
1/2 cup peeled and sliced fresh water chestnuts
2 scallions (white and green parts), chopped
1 tablespoon light soy sauce
1/4 teaspoon freshly ground white pepper

1/2 recipe Rice Patties*

4 cups peanut oil

1 tablespoon sesame oil

PREPARATION

Having reconstituted the mushrooms, set aside.

Partially freeze the pork; slice, then triangle-cut.

Partially freeze the chicken; slice, then triangle-cut. Mix the chicken with the egg white.

Shell the shrimp; wash, drain, dry, and leave them whole.

COOKING PROCEDURE

Preheat the oven to 375 degrees. Place a heatproof soup tureen uncovered in the oven.

While preparing the soup, place a wok over high heat for about 1 minute. Pour in the 4 cups of oil; turn the heat to medium until the oil reaches 375 degrees.

In a saucepan, bring the chicken and mushroom stock to a simmer. Add the pork; simmer for 1 minute. Add mushrooms; simmer for 1 minute. Add chicken, shrimp, snow peas, water chestnuts, scallions, soy sauce, and pepper. Continue to simmer for 1 more minute, stirring with chopsticks in a figure-8 motion. Turn off the heat; add sesame oil, and mix briefly.

Fry the Rice Patties in the peanut oil for 2 minutes over a high heat, turning once at midpoint, until they puff up. Remove them from the wok with a wire strainer and drain on paper towels.

Return the soup to a simmer. Transfer the Rice Patties to the heated soup tureen.

PRESENTATION

Immediately bring the soup tureen to the table and pour the simmering soup over the Rice Patties in order to achieve a sizzling effect.

YIELD *6 servings*

RICE PATTIES

1 cup sweet rice
1 1/4 cups cold water
2 cups peanut oil

Rinse the rice in cold running water. Place the rice in a greased square aluminum or stainless steel pan, 8 × 8 inches, and add the 1 1/4 cups cold water. Spread evenly over the bottom of the pan. Cover with foil.

COOKING PROCEDURE

Preheat the oven to 375 degrees, and bake the rice for 30 minutes.

Remove the foil and bake at 300 degrees for 1 1/4 hours, or until the rice is dry enough to remove from the pan with a spatula.

With your hands, break the rice into 1 1/2 × 1 1/2-inch squares.

Deep-fry the rice squares in oil at 375 degrees over high flame for 1 minute, turning once, until light brown and crisp.

Drain on paper towels and place the Rice Patties in an uncovered serving dish. Keep warm in a 300-degree oven.

Chapter 11

FISH AND SHELLFISH

STEAMED SEA BASS
WITH FERMENTED BLACK BEANS Canton/Guangzhou

1 whole 1 1/2-pound sea bass

SEASONING SAUCE
1 tablespoon sherry
1 tablespoon dark soy sauce
1 tablespoon sesame oil
1 tablespoon oyster sauce

1 tablespoon shredded ginger root
2 scallions (white and green parts), shredded
2 teaspoons fermented black beans, coarsely chopped

BINDER
2 teaspoons water chestnut powder dissolved in
1 tablespoon sherry

PREPARATION

Wash and clean the fish, leaving it whole. Place the fish in front of you horizontally and make three deep (not quite to the bone) crescent-shaped incisions vertically along the fish about 2 inches apart on both sides. Place it on a plate small enough to fit into a steamer. Combine the ingredients for the seasoning sauce and spoon it over the fish. Refrigerate, if time permits, for two hours.

Baste the fish, then place the ginger and scallions on top of the fish in a crisscross pattern. Place any remaining ginger and scallion in the cavity of the fish. Sprinkle the black beans on top of the fish.

Mix the binder.

COOKING PROCEDURE

Put the plate with the fish and seasoning sauce in the steamer and steam for 15 minutes. Remove the plate from the steamer.

Pour into a saucepan all the liquid that has accumulated. (The fish releases juices when steamed.) Bring to a boil.

Restir the binder and add it to the sauce, stirring until the sauce thickens. Pour it over the fish and serve immediately.

YIELD *2–6 servings*

NOTES

Tips If a spicier sauce is desired, 1 fresh chili pepper (cleaned, seeded, and shredded) can be placed on top of the fish as part of the crisscross pattern before steaming. A tablespoon of shredded Smithfield ham is another optional flavoring to add before steaming.

SZECHWAN STEAMED WHOLE FISH   Szechwan/Sichuan

The Chinese frequently cook and present fish whole, with head and tail intact. It is most often served at the end of a banquet as a spectacular finale, symbolizing abundance. When fish is cooked with the bones, it has more flavor, as well as a higher calcium content, because the calcium in the bones penetrates the meat of the fish. The cheeks are considered the most savory portion, and are given to the guest of honor; however, portions near the back of the head are equally as good. In fact, a fish head is sometimes steamed and served as a separate dish unto itself.

Once, an assassination was attempted on an emperor and the weapon was concealed in the stomach of the fish. It is for this reason that the stomach of the fish is always turned toward the guest of honor to show that nothing is concealed.

1 whole 1 1/2-pound red snapper

1 tablespoon sherry

1 clove garlic, minced
1 teaspoon minced ginger root
1 tablespoon bean sauce
1 teaspoon Hot Sauce*

1 tablespoon light soy sauce
1 tablespoon sherry
1 teaspoon sugar

BINDER
2 teaspoons water chestnut powder
    dissolved in
1 tablespoon sherry

1 tablespoon sesame oil

1/2 teaspoon peanut oil

1 scallion (white and green parts), chopped

PREPARATION

Rinse the fish under cold running water and dry it with paper towels. Place the fish in front of you horizontally, make three deep (not quite to the bone) crescent-shaped incisions vertically along the fish about 2 inches apart on both sides. Place on a plate small enough to fit into a steamer. Pour sherry over the fish.

Combine the garlic, ginger, bean sauce, and Hot Sauce.

In a small saucepan, combine the light soy sauce, sherry, and sugar.

Mix the binder.

COOKING PROCEDURE

Put the plate with the fish on it in the steamer and steam for 15 minutes. Pour all the fish stock into the saucepan containing light soy sauce, sherry, and sugar. (The fish releases juices when steamed.)

Heat the sesame oil in a small wok until very hot (about 1 minute). Pour the sesame oil over the steamed fish.

Heat the 1/2 tablespoon peanut oil in the same small wok or iron skillet; when it is hot, add the bean sauce mixture and stir for 1 minute.

Add scallions and mix briefly.

Add the fish stock and the soy sauce mixture to the wok. Bring to a boil; let simmer 1 more minute, stirring constantly.

Restir the binder and add it to the wok, stirring until the sauce thickens.

Pour the sauce over the fish and serve immediately.

YIELD *2–6 servings*

NOTES

Timing All the preparations can be done early in the day. Allow the fish to become room temperature before placing it in the steamer.

Tips This is an easy dish to coordinate when planning a multicourse Chinese dinner. While the fish is steaming, another dish can be stir-fried at the same time. Because the recipe contains no vegetables, which normally require cutting, and because the fish is whole, the entire preparation should take less than 10 minutes.

Substitutions For the red snapper, you can substitute sea bass, striped bass, tilefish, carp, sea trout (weakfish), yellow snapper, or pompano.

Although any kind of fish can be steamed, it is preferable to choose a thick, firm-fleshed fish.

The same ingredients used for the snapper also make a delicious sauce for shrimp, scallops, or diced chicken which have been marinated in egg white, water chestnut powder, and sherry and passed through (see Chapter 5).

Once the oil has been removed from the wok, add the bean sauce mixture (garlic, ginger, bean sauce, and Hot Sauce); stir-fry for 1 minute. Add the scallions and mix briefly. Add the light soy sauce, sherry, and sugar, along with $1/3$ cup salt-free chicken stock, then the binder, followed by the sesame oil. Return the shrimp, scallops, or chicken to the wok, stir-frying a few more seconds.

STEAMED CARP WITH PURPLE BASIL   Hunan

While traveling in China, I had the good fortune to visit a fish commune about seventy-five miles outside of Changsha, the capital of Hunan. I saw carp of all sizes fly out of the water; some were caught for the noon meal. Although carp is not popular in America, it is the most common fish raised in China. It is a very bony fish; however, when it is cooked within minutes of being caught it is light, delicate, and quite tasty. This fish was part of one of the best meals served to me in China. The meal was eaten at a commune where all the food was raised and grown.

1 whole 2-pound carp, with head and
   tail intact
1¹/₂ tablespoons dark soy sauce
2 tablespoons sherry
3 tablespoons rendered poultry fat**
¹/₂ cup chopped fresh purple basil leaves
2 scallions (white and green parts), shredded
2¹/₂ tablespoons shredded spring ginger

BINDER
1 tablespoon water chestnut powder
   dissolved in
2 tablespoons sherry

PREPARATION

Have the fish cleaned and scaled, then rinse it under cold running water and dry with paper towels. Place the fish in front of you horizontally, make three deep (not quite to the bone) crescent-shaped incisions vertically along the fish about 2 inches apart on both sides. Place the fish on a plate small enough to fit into a steamer.

Pour soy sauce, sherry, and poultry fat over the fish. Sprinkle chopped basil over it. Arrange the shredded scallion and ginger in a crisscross pattern on top of the fish.

Mix the binder.

COOKING PROCEDURE

Put the plate with the fish in the steamer; steam for 18 minutes. Remove the plate from the steamer.

Pour all the liquid that has accumulated into a saucepan. (The fish releases juices when steamed.) Bring to a boil.

Restir the binder and add it to the sauce, stirring until the sauce thickens. Pour it over the fish and serve immediately.

YIELD *2–6 servings*

NOTES

Timing The timing will vary according to the thickness of the fish. A 1¼-pound red snapper will be done in 15 minutes. A 2- to 2½-pound bass will take about 30 minutes. The fish is done when the eyes bulge.

Tips This dish can be prepared in the oven. Wrap the fish and all the ingredients in cooking parchment paper and place in a preheated 350-degree oven for 30 minutes.

Substitutions Use one portion of the frozen purple basil mixture, which follows this recipe, to substitute for the fresh purple basil leaves and rendered poultry fat. If you are unable to find purple basil in your area, the seeds are available; also, Italian (sweet) basil can be substituted for the purple basil.

Winter ginger can be substituted for spring ginger, but the quantity used must be reduced by half.

For the carp, you can substitute sea bass, striped bass, red snapper, yellow snapper, pompano, sea trout (weakfish), brook trout, whiting, or tilefish.

FROZEN PURPLE BASIL BASE

4 cups purple basil leaves, tightly packed
9 tablespoons rendered poultry fat

PREPARATION

Wash and dry the basil leaves very well and place in the container of a food processor or blender. Add the poultry fat and blend until the basil leaves are finely chopped. Divide into three separate portions.

Storage This mixture may be covered and refrigerated for up to one week, or frozen for up to one year.

STEAMED WHOLE SNAPPER
WITH FERMENTED WINE RICE   Szechwan/Sichuan

*1 whole 1 1/2-pound red snapper, with head
    and tail intact*
1 tablespoon sherry

SEASONING SAUCE
6 tablespoons Fermented Wine Rice,
    measured with liquid*
2 tablespoons Tomato Sauce*
2 teaspoons Hot Sauce*
1 1/2 teaspoons dark soy sauce
2 teaspoons hoisin sauce

BINDER
*1 tablespoon water chestnut powder
    dissolved in*
2 tablespoons sherry

1 teaspoon minced garlic
2 teaspoons minced ginger root
*1/3 cup chopped scallions (white and
    green parts)*

1 tablespoon sesame oil

PREPARATION

Rinse fish under cold running water and
dry with paper towels. Place the fish in
front of you horizontally, make three deep
(not quite to the bone) crescent-shaped incisions vertically along the fish about 2
inches apart on both sides. Place the fish on
a plate small enough to fit into a steamer.
Pour 1 tablespoon of sherry over the fish.

Combine the ingredients for the seasoning
sauce.

Mix the binder.

COOKING PROCEDURE

Put the plate with the fish in the steamer;
steam for 15 minutes.

Pour the liquid that has accumulated on the
bottom of the fish plate into the bowl containing the seasoning sauce. (The fish releases juices when steamed.)

Place the wok over high heat; add the tablespoon of sesame oil and heat for 30 seconds.

Add garlic, ginger, and scallions; stir-fry 1
minute.

Add the seasoning sauce to the wok all at
once; bring to a boil.

Restir the binder and add it to the wok,
stirring until the sauce thickens. Pour the
sauce over the fish and serve immediately.

YIELD *2–6 servings*

NOTES

Tips This unique, delicious sauce can be
used on shrimp, whole bay scallops (or
sliced sea scallops), or boneless, skinless
chicken (diced or sliced). Marinate one of
these selections in egg white, water chestnut powder, and sherry; pass through,
then remove from the wok. In the oil that
glazes the wok, stir-fry the garlic, ginger,
and scallions for 1 minute. Restir the seasoning sauce and add it all at once to the
wok; stir-fry about 30 seconds. Restir the
binder and add it to the wok, stirring until
sauce thickens. Return either the shrimp,
scallops, or chicken to the wok and continue to stir-fry a few more seconds.

CRISPY BASS HUNAN STYLE

Hunan

2 Chinese mushrooms, soaked and minced**
2 tablespoons cleaned, seeded, minced sweet
  red peppers
1 tablespoon minced sweet white cucumber

1 scallion (white and green parts), chopped
1 teaspoon minced ginger root
1 clove garlic, minced

1 whole 1½-pound sea bass

SEASONING SAUCE
2 tablespoons hoisin sauce
1 tablespoon dark soy sauce
1 teaspoon Hot Sauce*
1 tablespoon sugar
1 teaspoon Chinese red vinegar

½ cup chicken stock

BINDER
1 teaspoon water chestnut powder
  dissolved in
2 tablespoons sherry

BATTER
4 tablespoons cornstarch
4 tablespoons flour
¼ cup sherry
1 tablespoon dark soy sauce

6 cups peanut oil for deep-frying

PREPARATION

Having reconstituted the mushrooms and done the necessary cutting, place the two groups of ingredients in separate bowls.

Wash and clean the fish, leaving it whole. After draining, pat it dry inside and out with paper towels. Place the fish in front of you horizontally, make three deep (not quite to the bone) crescent-shaped incisions vertically along the fish about 2 inches apart, on both sides.

Combine the ingredients for the seasoning sauce.

Mix the binder.

Stir the batter ingredients into a smooth paste and rub all over the fish, inside and out.

COOKING PROCEDURE

Place the wok over high heat for about 1 minute, then pour in the oil and turn the heat to medium until the oil reaches 375 degrees. Turn the heat to high and place the fish in the oil, using a wire strainer. Deep-fry for about 8 minutes, turning once at midpoint. Using a ladle, baste constantly with oil. Remove the fish from the oil with the wire strainer, and drain on several layers of paper towels. Pour the oil out of the wok.

Over a low heat, stir-fry the scallion, ginger, and garlic for 30 seconds in the oil that glazes the wok.

Add the mushrooms, red peppers, and cucumber; stir-fry another 30 seconds.

Restir the seasoning sauce, add it to the wok, and stir for another 30 seconds.

Add the stock, continuing to stir until the liquid comes to a boil.

Restir the binder and add it to the wok, stirring until the sauce thickens.

PRESENTATION

Slightly open the underside of the fish to use as a base, then place the fish in an upright, swimming position on a platter. Pour the sauce over the fish and serve immediately.

YIELD 2–6 servings

SWEET AND PUNGENT SEA BASS Peking/Beijing

$^1/_4$ cup Chinese mushrooms, soaked and
    shredded**
$^1/_4$ cup shredded carrots

$^1/_4$ cup snow peas, shredded
2 scallions (white and green parts), shredded
$^1/_4$ cup shredded bamboo shoots
2 tablespoons shredded sweetened Chinese
    white cucumber

SWEET AND PUNGENT SAUCE
3 tablespoons sweetened Chinese white
    cucumber juice (taken from can)
2–3 tablespoons honey
4 tablespoons wine vinegar
1 tablespoon dark soy sauce
1 tablespoon American chili sauce
$^3/_4$ cup chicken stock
$^1/_4$ cup mushroom stock**

1 whole 2-pound sea bass

BATTER
3 tablespoons cornstarch
3 tablespoons flour
4–5 tablespoons sherry
1 teaspoon salt
1 tablespoon dark soy sauce

BINDER
$1^1/_2$ tablespoons water chestnut powder
    dissolved in
4 tablespoons reduced mushroom stock**,
    cooled

6 cups peanut oil for deep-frying

$^1/_4$ cup pine nuts, roasted**

PREPARATION

Having reconstituted the mushrooms and
done the necessary cutting, place the first
two groups of ingredients in separate
bowls.

Combine the liquid ingredients for the
Sweet and Pungent Sauce.

Wash and clean the fish, leaving it whole.
After draining, pat it dry inside and out
with paper towels. Place the fish in front of
you horizontally, make three deep (not
quite to the bone) crescent-shaped incisions
vertically along the fish about 2 inches
apart, on both sides.

Mix the batter ingredients into a smooth
paste and rub this mixture all over the fish,
inside and out.

Mix the binder and set aside.

COOKING PROCEDURE

Place the wok over high heat for about 1
minute. Pour in the oil; turn the heat to
medium until the oil reaches 375 degrees.
Turn the heat to high. With a wire strainer,
place the fish in the oil and deep-fry for
about 8 minutes, turning once at midpoint.
Using a ladle, baste it constantly with the
oil. Drain the fish on paper towels.

In a separate saucepan, heat the liquid portion of the Sweet and Pungent Sauce; restir
the binder and add it to the sauce, stirring
until it thickens.

(continued)

Add the mushrooms and carrots and cook for 1 minute.

Add the snow peas, scallions, bamboo shoots, and cucumber and bring the sauce with the vegetables to a simmer. Remove from heat.

PRESENTATION

Slightly opening the underside of the fish to use as a base, place the fish in an upright, swimming position on a platter. With a perforated spoon, place some of the vegetables over the fish and arrange the rest around it. Pour about ¼ cup of the sauce over the fish. The remaining sauce may be served separately.

Sprinkle with roasted pine nuts and serve immediately.

YIELD *2–6 servings*

NOTES

Timing The entire preparation can be done early in the day and refrigerated. The batter should be placed in an uncovered jar (to allow it to breathe) and refrigerated.

Substitution Kadota figs, in syrup, may be substituted for the sweetened Chinese white cucumber.

BARBECUED TILEFISH

Barbecued Tilefish is a dish for all seasons, and is especially outstanding when cooked on an outdoor barbecue. The marinade is excellent for any thick fish fillet, such as salmon or swordfish. This simple recipe for broiled fish, which only requires about five minutes of preparation, has the further advantage of using one dish in which to marinate, broil, and serve.

1 pound tilefish fillet, about 1¹/₄ inches thick

MARINADE
1 tablespoon unhulled sesame seeds
3 tablespoons sherry
1 tablespoon dark soy sauce
1 tablespoon sesame oil
2 teaspoons minced ginger root
2 scallions (white and green parts), chopped
1 clove garlic, minced

PREPARATION

Rinse the tilefish under cold running water and dry well with paper towels.

Combine the ingredients for the marinade. Rub the marinade over both sides of the tilefish. Allow to marinate in the refrigerator 2 hours.

COOKING PROCEDURE

Preheat the broiler for 20 minutes. Place the tilefish in the marinade on a heatproof platter. Broil for 10 minutes 3 inches from the heat source. Do not turn. Serve immediately.

YIELD *3–8 servings*

FUKIENESE FLATFISH

Fukien/Fujian

When a flatfish such as flounder or fluke is cooked in this manner, it becomes so crisp that the fins and all the bones, with the exception of the backbone, can be eaten.

1 whole 1¹/2–2-pound flounder or fluke with fins attached

SEASONING SAUCE
¹/2 cup salt-free poultry stock
2 tablespoons light soy sauce
2 tablespoons sugar
1¹/2 tablespoons black rice vinegar
1 teaspoon Hot Sauce*
¹/2 teaspoon Five Spice Powder*

BINDER
1 teaspoon water chestnut powder dissolved in
1 tablespoon sherry

2 teaspoons minced ginger root
1 clove garlic, minced
2 scallions (white and green parts), chopped
¹/4 cup cleaned, seeded, and diced sweet red peppers

Peanut oil for frying

PREPARATION

Wash and clean the fish, leaving it whole. Dry the fish well and place it on several layers of paper towels for at least 1 hour, changing the towels if necessary.

Turn the fish after 30 minutes. Make three crescent-shaped incisions on each side of the fish, cutting within ¹/4 inch of the bone. Put the fish on paper towels on a plate and refrigerate.

Combine the ingredients for the seasoning sauce.

Mix the binder.

Remove the fish from the refrigerator and allow it to return to room temperature.

COOKING PROCEDURE

Place a heavy skillet over high heat for about 1 minute. Pour in 1 inch of oil; turn the heat to medium until the oil reaches 375 degrees. Turn the heat to high. Lower the fish into the oil. Shallow-fry on each side for 4 to 5 minutes, basting constantly with a ladle. Slipping two spatulas under the fish, remove it and drain on paper towels.

Pour out the oil from the skillet.

Place the skillet over medium heat. Add the ginger, garlic, scallions, and red pepper; stir-fry 1 minute.

Add the sauce and bring to a boil.

Restir the binder and add it to the skillet, stirring until the sauce thickens slightly.

Place the fish on a flat serving platter and pour the sauce over the fish. Serve immediately.

YIELD *2–6 servings*

NOTES

Tips In order for the fish to be crisp, it is very important that the skillet in which the fish is fried be at least 2 inches larger than the fish.

The seasoning for this fish is a departure from the more common, heavier sauces frequently used on fish in the Peking area. It makes a simple and delicate dish that relies on a fresh fish fillet, which must be carefully poached in warm oil, rather than the hot oil used for the deep-fried or stir-fried technique.

1-pound fillet striped bass or sea bass

MARINADE
1 egg white
1 tablespoon water chestnut powder
1 tablespoon sherry

SEASONING SAUCE
1 teaspoon water chestnut powder
    dissolved in
2 tablespoons sherry
1/4 cup sherry
1 teaspoon sugar
1 teaspoon salt

2 scallions (white and green parts), chopped
2 cloves garlic, minced

1 cup snow peas, slant-cut
1/2 cup sliced fresh water chestnuts

2 cups peanut oil

1 teaspoon sesame oil

PREPARATION

Rinse the fish under cold running water; drain, and dry well with paper towels. Slice against the grain into 3 × 2-inch pieces 1/2 inch thick.

Place the ingredients for the marinade in a bowl and mix well. Add the fish slices and mix gently. Refrigerate at least 1 hour or up to 12 hours.

Combine the ingredients for the seasoning sauce.

COOKING PROCEDURE

Place the wok over high heat for about 1 minute. Pour in the 2 cups of peanut oil; turn the heat to medium until the oil reaches 300 degrees. Restir the fish in the marinade.

Turn the heat to high and add the contents of the bowl all at once to the wok, stirring in a circular motion with a pair of chopsticks for about 1 minute, or until the fillets turn white. Turn off the heat and pour out the oil and the fish into a colander set over a bowl. Shake the colander gently to aid the draining, then place the fish over a clean bowl.

Place the wok over high heat for a few seconds. Add the scallions and garlic; stir-fry about 30 seconds.

Add the snow peas and water chestnuts, stir-frying another 15 seconds.

Return the fish fillets to the wok and mix a few seconds.

Restir the seasoning sauce and add it all at once to the wok; stir-fry about 30 seconds.

Turn off the heat; add sesame oil and mix. Empty the contents of the wok onto a heated serving dish and serve immediately.

YIELD *3–8 servings*

NOTES

Substitutions For the bass, you can substitute red snapper, flounder, fluke, or sole.

For the 1/4 cup sherry in the seasoning sauce, you can substitute 1/4 cup Fermented Wine Rice*.

PINECONE FISH

In China, chefs use mild-flavored, firm-textured yellowfish for the pinecone presentation. Red snapper is a more than adequate substitute. Once the fish has been deep-fried, it curls around, and it is the diamond-shaped, deep scoring of the fish's flesh that gives the fish the appearance of a pinecone.

1 whole 2-pound snapper

MARINADE
1 tablespoon sherry
1/2 teaspoon salt
1/4 teaspoon freshly ground white pepper

SWEET-AND-SOUR SAUCE
3/4 cup chicken stock
3 tablespoons brown sugar
3 tablespoons wine vinegar
1 tablespoon Chinese red vinegar
1 tablespoon black rice vinegar
1 tablespoon dark soy sauce
1 tablespoon American chili sauce

BINDER
1/4 cup pineapple juice
1 1/2 tablespoons water chestnut powder

1/4 cup water chestnut powder for dredging

1 clove garlic, minced

1/4 cup snow peas, strung and diced
1/4 cup cleaned, seeded, and diced sweet red
  peppers
2 scallions (white and green parts), chopped
1/4 cup diced water chestnuts

6 cups peanut oil

1/4 cup pine nuts, roasted**

Fresh coriander for garnish (optional)

PREPARATION

Rinse the fish under cold running water and dry with paper towels. Lay it on its side and with a boning knife placed behind the collar bone, cut along the backbone. Turning the knife flat, cut to 2 inches above the tail. Turn the fish over and repeat on the other side. Cut off the backbone at the base of the tail. Remove the head. Wash, drain, and dry the fish. The tail and skin should be intact and the fish should be separated into 2 fillets joined at the tail. Lay the fish skin side down. Score the flesh with deep, opposing diagonal cuts 1 inch apart. Rub the flesh with the marinade and allow the fish to marinate while proceeding with the recipe.

Combine the ingredients for Sweet-and-Sour Sauce.

Mix the binder.

Dredge the fish in water chestnut powder on both skin and flesh sides. Shake off the excess.

COOKING PROCEDURE

Place the wok over high heat for about 1 minute. Pour in the 6 cups of oil; turn the heat to medium until the oil reaches 375 degrees. Turn the heat to high. Turn the fillets so the skin sides touch and the scored flesh is exposed. Grasp both ends while lowering the fish into the oil. Deep-fry the fish for 5 minutes, constantly ladling oil over it while it is cooking. Using a wire strainer, remove the fish from the oil; drain on several layers of paper towels.

Place a saucepan over medium heat. Add 1 tablespoon of the cooked oil. Add garlic; stir a few seconds.

Add the Sweet-and-Sour Sauce, stir briefly, then bring to a boil.

Restir the binder and add it to the sauce; stir constantly until the sauce thickens.

Add snow peas, red peppers, scallions, and water chestnuts, continuing to cook for another 15 seconds.

Place the fish on a heated platter. Pour Sweet-and-Sour Sauce over the fish. Sprinkle with pine nuts and garnish with coriander leaves if desired.

YIELD *2–6 servings*

2 whole brook trout (1¹/₄–1¹/₂ pounds total)

SEASONING
1 teaspoon salt
1 teaspoon Szechwan Peppercorn Powder*
1 tablespoon minced ginger root
1 scallion (white and green parts), shredded

¹/₂ cup sugar
¹/₂ cup Lapsang souchong tea leaves
1 cup raw short-grain brown rice

¹/₄ cup water chestnut powder for dredging

4 cups peanut oil

PREPARATION

Place the wok over medium heat and add the salt. Dry-roast for a few minutes, then rub the salt and the Szechwan Peppercorn Powder on the inside and outside of the fish. Place the ginger and scallions on top and inside the cavity of the fish. Cover and refrigerate for 24 hours.

COOKING PROCEDURE

Line a wok with heavy-duty aluminum foil. Mix together in a bowl the sugar, tea leaves, and rice. Place this mixture in the wok. Set a greased 8-inch cake rack in the wok, with 4 chopsticks in a tic-tac-toe arrangement on top of the rack. Lay the fish on top of the chopsticks along with the seasoning ingredients. Line a wok cover with aluminum foil, extending the foil a few inches beyond the rim. Put the cover on the wok. It should fit tightly.

Place the wok over medium heat and smoke the fish for 8 minutes.

Turn off the heat but do not remove the cover. Let stand for 30 minutes.

Using an oven mitt or a spatula, carefully remove the rack with the fish from the wok. Allow the fish to cool.

The smoked fish may be eaten at this point (at any temperature).

FINAL COOKING PROCEDURE

Sprinkle the fish with water chestnut powder inside and out. Place the wok over high heat for about 1 minute. Pour in the 4 cups of oil; turn the heat to medium until the oil reaches 375 degrees. Turn the heat to high. Lower the fish into the oil and fry for 2 minutes, turning once at midpoint. Using a wire strainer, remove the fish from the wok. Drain well by placing on several sheets of paper towels. Serve immediately.

YIELD *2–6 servings*

NOTES

Substitution Any unscented Chinese black tea can be substituted for Lapsang souchong tea leaves.

FRIED BLUE CRABS

Shanghai

4 large, live hard-shell blue she-crabs
2 tablespoons cornmeal

SEASONING SAUCE
1 tablespoon dark soy sauce
1/2 tablespoon light soy sauce
3 tablespoons sherry
1 teaspoon sugar

BATTER
1 cup flour
1 cup water

*2 scallions (white and green parts),
slant-cut in 1/2-inch pieces*
1 clove garlic, minced
2 teaspoons minced ginger root

2 tablespoons Amoy hoisin sauce

2 cups peanut oil

1 teaspoon sesame oil

PREPARATION

Soak the crabs in a large basin of water to which 2 tablespoons of cornmeal have been added.

Lay crab on its back on a chopping block; place heavy cleaver along crab's midline and hit hard with a rubber mallet to kill the crab instantly. Pull off the large claws by holding the crab in one hand with an oven mitt while twisting the claw off with the other hand. Rinse each crab under cold running water, scrubbing with a vegetable brush to remove the sand. Holding the crab in one hand, push it down hard on a chopping block; pry off the carapace (shell) with the other hand. Hold onto the carapace by grasping it by the central point. Once the carapace has been pulled away from the body, remove and discard the spongy, feathery lungs on either side. Save any yellow or orange matter inside; this is the roe. Using your fingers, remove the "apron" on the underside of the crab. Cut the crab into quarters on a wooden chopping block, using a heavy cleaver and rubber mallet. Twist off all the legs except one on each quarter. Put all these quarters into a bowl.

Repeat procedure for rest of crabs. Before the next step, pour 3 tablespoons of the accumulated crab juices into the bowl for the seasoning sauce. Save the claws for another use (see Tips). Transfer the crab quarters onto paper towels and dry well.

Combine the ingredients for the seasoning sauce.

To prepare the batter Put the flour into a bowl and add the water all at once. Stir rapidly with a wire whisk until there are no lumps.

COOKING PROCEDURE

Place the wok over high heat for about 1 minute. Pour in the peanut oil; turn the heat to medium until the oil reaches 375 degrees, then turn the heat to high. Working quickly, hold each crab quarter by its remaining leg and dip the cut edges into the batter, then immediately drop it into the hot oil. Deep-fry the crab pieces in two batches for 2 minutes or until they turn light golden brown. Using a wire strainer, remove the crab pieces from the wok. Drain well by placing them on several layers of paper towels.

Pour off all the oil from the wok. Place the wok over high heat. Add the scallions, garlic, and ginger; stir-fry for a few seconds.

Add the hoisin sauce and stir a few more seconds.

Restir the seasoning sauce and add it all at once to the wok; stir-fry about 5 seconds.

Return the crab pieces to the wok, stir-frying quickly until they are evenly coated with sauce. This should take no longer than 30 seconds.

Turn off the heat; add sesame oil and stir briefly. Empty the contents of the wok onto a heated serving dish and serve immediately.

YIELD *2–6 servings*

(continued)

FISH AND SHELLFISH

NOTES

Timing The crabs can be purchased the day before and refrigerated. Once they have been cut, they should be cooked immediately.

The batter can be made early in the day and refrigerated, uncovered.

Tips This dish requires an adept stir-fryer. There is very little sauce and for the dish to turn out properly, each crab piece should be evenly coated during the final 30 seconds of stir-frying.

She-crabs are more desirable because of the roe; however, male crabs are also satisfactory if they are large enough.

The reserved crab claws can be placed over steaming rice during the last few minutes of the cooking period.

Substitution Koon Chun hoisin sauce can be substituted for the Amoy.

CHILI CRABS   Szechwan/Sichuan

4 large, live hard-shell blue she-crabs
2 tablespoons cornmeal

SEASONING SAUCE
1 tablespoon dark soy sauce
1 1/2 tablespoons sugar
3 tablespoons sherry
1 teaspoon wine vinegar
3 tablespoons crab juice

1/2 cup flour for dredging

2 scallions (white and green parts), chopped
2 teaspoons minced ginger root
1 clove garlic, minced
2 seeded and shredded dried chili peppers

2 cups peanut oil

PREPARATION

Follow the Preparation instructions in recipe for Fried Blue Crabs.

Save the claws for another use (see Tips for Fried Blue Crabs*). Transfer the crab quarters onto paper towels and dry well.

Combine the ingredients for the seasoning sauce.

COOKING PROCEDURE

Place the wok over high heat for about 1 minute. Pour in the oil; turn the heat to medium until the oil reaches 375 degrees, then turn the heat to high. Working quickly, hold each crab quarter by its remaining leg and dip the cut edges into the flour, then immediately place half the crab quarters in a wire strainer and lower them into the oil. Deep-fry the crabs for 2 minutes, turning once at midpoint. Remove the crabs with the wire strainer and drain on several layers of paper towels. Reheat the oil to 375 degrees and repeat the process with the second batch of crab quarters.

Pour off all the oil from the wok.

Place the wok over high heat. Add the scallions, ginger, garlic, and chili peppers; stir-fry for a few seconds.

Restir the seasoning sauce and add it to the wok, continuing to stir for about 30 seconds.

Return the crab quarters to the wok, stir-frying quickly until they are evenly coated with sauce. This should take no longer than 30 seconds.

Turn off the heat and empty the contents of the wok onto a heated serving dish. Serve immediately.

YIELD *2–6 servings*

SHRIMP AND CRAB MEAT SZECHWAN-STYLE

Szechwan/Sichuan

When I developed this recipe with my experimental class, it took eight students half an hour to remove one-quarter pound of meat and one-quarter pound of roe and tomalley from 12 hard-shell Atlantic Blue she-crabs. Obviously it is not practical to spend 4 hours removing the meat from small crabs for a dish that yields 3 portions. However, if you live in an area where large crabs are available (such as the Dungeness crab of the Pacific Northwest), this dish is superior-tasting when fresh, raw crab meat is used, in which case you must steam the crabs just long enough to loosen the meat from the shell.

¹/₂ pound medium shrimp (21–25 per pound)

MARINADE
¹/₂ egg white
1 teaspoon water chestnut powder
1 teaspoon sherry

¹/₂ pound fresh lump crab meat

SEASONING SAUCE
2 teaspoons water chestnut powder
  dissolved in
2 tablespoons sherry
3 tablespoons chicken stock
1 tablespoon dark soy sauce
*2 teaspoons Hot Sauce**
1 teaspoon sugar

GARNISH
2 ounces rice stick noodles, broken

2 teaspoons minced garlic
2 scallions (white and green parts), chopped
2 teaspoons minced ginger root
¹/₂ cup cleaned, seeded, shredded sweet red
  peppers

2 cups peanut oil

PREPARATION

Wash, drain, dry, and split the shrimp. Place the shrimp and the ingredients for the marinade in a bowl and stir in one direction vigorously with chopsticks.

Place the mixture in the refrigerator for at least 1 hour or up to 12 hours.

Pick over the crab meat to remove any cartilage and shell.

Combine the ingredients for the seasoning sauce.

Heat the 2 cups of oil in a wok to 375 degrees. Drop the broken rice stick noodles into the oil and fry for 2 seconds, or until they puff (but before they turn brown). Using a wire strainer, remove the rice stick noodles from the wok. Drain well by placing the noodles in a single layer on several sheets of paper towels. Remove the oil from the wok; reserve for next step.

COOKING PROCEDURE

Place the wok over high heat for about 1 minute. Pour in the 2 cups of oil; turn the heat to medium until the oil reaches 325 degrees. Restir the shrimp in the marinade. Turn the heat to high and add the shrimp and marinade all at once to the wok, stirring with a pair of chopsticks in a circular motion for about 1 minute. Turn off the heat and pour out the oil and the shrimp into a colander set over a bowl. Shake the colander gently a few times to aid the draining, then place it over a clean bowl.

Return the wok to high heat. Add garlic, scallions, ginger, and peppers; stir-fry for 1 minute in the oil that glazes the wok.

Restir the seasoning sauce and add it all at once to the wok; stir-fry a few seconds. Return the cooked shrimp along with the crab meat to the wok; stir-fry another 30 seconds. Empty the contents of the wok onto a heated serving dish. Surround the shrimp and crab meat with the rice stick noodles and serve immediately.

YIELD *3–8 servings*

SOFT-SHELL CRABS WITH GINGER SAUCE

Canton/Guangzhou

I have adapted the following two recipes for soft-shell crabs from dishes I had in China that featured fresh Chinese hard-shell crab claws. Soft-shell crabs, not indigenous to Chinese waters, are a favorite among many Americans. They are common from Texas to Delaware, on the Atlantic and Gulf coasts. In the eastern United States they are in season May through early October, especially in the Chesapeake Bay area. In fact, Chesapeake Bay has produced more crabs than any other body of water in the world. Soft-shell crabs are merely hard-shell crabs that have molted (shed their shell) as they grow bigger. Molting occurs three times during the season. Each time the crab grows a new shell it is thicker and tougher; therefore, when possible, it is preferable to choose small ones. Not only are soft-shell crabs easier to clean than hard-shell crabs, but also the yield of meat is greater, because the entire crab is edible—the shell as well as the legs and meat.

1 pound live soft-shell crabs (small, 8 or 9 to the pound)

1/2 cup flour for dredging

SEASONING SAUCE
2 teaspoons water chestnut powder dissolved in
2 tablespoons sherry
1 tablespoon dark soy sauce

3 tablespoons minced shallots
2 tablespoons shredded spring ginger root

1/2 cup chicken stock

4 tablespoons peanut oil

PREPARATION

For minimal loss of juices and maximum flavor, it is best to clean the crabs immediately before cooking; however, if you prefer for the fish store to do it, it can be done several hours ahead of time.

To clean the crabs In order not to lose the juices, rinse the crab under cold running water before cleaning. Cut off the head with scissors or poultry shears. Using your fingers, take out the sac lodged behind the eyes. Turn the crab over and twist off the apron that folds under the rear of the body. Lift the soft carapace (shell) and remove the feathery lungs. Leave the crabs whole. Place them on several layers of paper towels; then place more paper towels on top of the crabs. After 10 minutes, flip them over to dry the other side. If the crabs are still wet, repeat the drying procedure.

Dredge each crab in flour and shake off the excess.

Combine the ingredients for the seasoning sauce.

COOKING PROCEDURE

Place the wok over high heat for about 1 minute. Add 3 tablespoons of the oil and heat until hot but not smoking. Place the crabs in the wok in a single layer, shell side down. Fry the crabs over medium heat for about 2 minutes on each side. Shake the wok occasionally. Remove the crabs from the wok to a heated serving dish.

Add the remaining 1 tablespoon of oil. Sauté the shallots and ginger over low heat for 1 minute.

Pour in the stock. Turn the heat to high, bring the stock to a boil, then simmer for 1 minute.

Restir the seasoning sauce and add it all at once to the wok, stirring until sauce thickens slightly.

Pour the sauce over the crabs. Empty the contents of the wok onto a heated serving dish and serve immediately.

YIELD *3–8 servings*

SOFT-SHELL CRABS WITH BLACK BEAN SAUCE
Canton/Guangzhou

See introduction to previous recipe.

*1 pound live soft-shell crabs (7–8 to
 the pound)*

¹/2 cup flour for dredging

BINDER
*2 teaspoons water chestnut powder
    dissolved in*
2 tablespoons sherry
2 teaspoons dark soy sauce

1¹/2 tablespoons minced fermented black beans
1 teaspoon minced ginger root
1 clove garlic, minced

2 scallions (white and green parts), chopped

²/3 cup salt-free chicken stock

3 tablespoons peanut oil

PREPARATION

Clean, dry, and flour the crabs (see Preparation instructions in preceding recipe for Soft-Shell Crabs with Ginger Sauce*).

Mix the binder.

COOKING PROCEDURE

Place the wok over high heat for about 1 minute. Add the oil and heat until hot but not smoking. Place the crabs in the wok in a single layer, shell side down. Fry the crabs over medium heat for 2 minutes on each side.

Add the black beans, ginger, and garlic.

Turn the crabs over again. Continue to cook the crabs over medium heat for about 30 seconds, shaking the wok continuously.

Add the scallions on top of the crabs.

Pour in the stock around the sides of the wok; bring to a boil over high heat.

Turn the heat to medium and cover the wok. Shaking it occasionally, cook for another 2 minutes.

Uncover the wok, then restir the binder and add it, stirring until the sauce thickens. Empty the contents of the wok onto a heated serving dish and serve immediately.

YIELD *3–8 servings*

NOTES

Timing If using larger soft-shell crabs, increase the sautéing time to 3 minutes on either side.

Tip Since knives and forks are never used, it is considered proper Chinese etiquette to lift a morsel of food to the mouth, bite it, and then place it on the plate again.

Substitutions If spring ginger is not available, use Pickled Spring Ginger* or 1 tablespoon of winter ginger.

SPINACH WITH CRAB MEAT SAUCE   Canton/Guangzhou

1 pound spinach leaves

GARNISH
1/4 cup carrots, pureed
*1 tablespoon minced Smithfield ham***
1 tablespoon minced coriander (optional)

BINDER
*1 tablespoon water chestnut powder
    dissolved in*
1 tablespoon sherry

1 teaspoon salt
1/4 teaspoon white pepper
1/2 teaspoon sugar

SAUCE
1 clove garlic, minced
1 scallion (white and green parts), chopped
1 teaspoon minced ginger root

1 cup lobster or chicken stock

1/2 teaspoon salt
1/4 teaspoon white pepper

*1 cup fresh crab meat, shell and cartilage
    removed*

2 egg whites, slightly beaten

2 tablespoons rendered chicken fat

PREPARATION

Wash the spinach, drain, and dry well.

Having minced the ham and coriander, prepare the carrot puree: Peel, then slice the carrot thin. Blanch the slices in boiling water for 5 minutes. Drain, then pass through a food mill or puree in a food processor or blender.

Mix the binder.

COOKING PROCEDURE

Place the wok over high heat for 30 seconds. Add only 1 tablespoon of the chicken fat and heat for a few more seconds. Add the spinach all at once; stir-fry a few seconds.

Add the salt, pepper, and sugar; continue to stir-fry for another minute, or until the spinach begins to wilt. Remove the wok from the heat. While making the sauce, leave the spinach in the wok to keep it warm.

Place the remaining tablespoon of chicken fat in a saucepan and heat for a few seconds. Add the garlic, scallions, and ginger, then sauté for 1 minute.

Add the lobster or chicken stock and bring it to a boil.

Add the salt and pepper; stir.

Restir the binder and add it to the saucepan with one hand while stirring with a pair of chopsticks in the other hand until the sauce thickens.

Add the crab meat and stir briefly.

Add the egg whites, turn off the heat, and stir the sauce until the egg whites are set.

Place the spinach on a platter and pour the sauce over the spinach.

Garnish with the carrot puree, minced ham, and coriander, and serve immediately.

YIELD *2–6 servings*

NOTES

Tip Use lobster stock from another recipe such as Lobster in Garlic Sauce*.

Substitutions For the spinach you can substitute broccoli (separate florets and blanch) or asparagus tips (roll-oblique-cut).

LOBSTER IN GARLIC SAUCE   Szechwan/Sichuan

1 live female lobster (1 1/2 pounds) or 1 cup
    cooked lobster meat

2 cloves garlic, minced
2 scallions (white and green parts), chopped
1 teaspoon minced ginger root

1/4 cup cleaned, seeded, and shredded sweet
    red peppers
2 tablespoons tree ears, soaked and diced**

1/4 cup quartered water chestnuts

SEASONING SAUCE
1 teaspoon water chestnut powder
    dissolved in
1 tablespoon sherry
1 tablespoon salt-free chicken stock
1 tablespoon dark soy sauce
2 teaspoons sugar
2 teaspoons wine vinegar
1/2 teaspoon Hot Sauce*

2 tablespoons peanut oil

1 teaspoon sesame oil

GARNISH
1/2 tablespoon sweet butter
1 cup snow peas, strung and shredded
1/4 teaspoon salt
1/4 teaspoon sugar

PREPARATION

Steam the lobster for 3 minutes. Remove it
from the steamer and let it cool for 10 minutes. Remove the lobster meat from the
shell and cut it into 1 1/2-inch pieces. Leave
the head and tail of the lobster intact to use
for garnish. Add the lobster roe and tomalley (the liver) to the water left in the steamer and reserve this stock for use in another
recipe, specifically Spinach with Crab Meat
Sauce*, or Snow-White Cloud Soup*.

Having reconstituted the tree ears and
done the necessary cutting, place the three
groups of ingredients in separate bowls.

Combine the ingredients for the seasoning
sauce.

COOKING PROCEDURE

Place the wok over high heat for about 1
minute. Add the peanut oil; heat until it is
hot but not smoking. Add the garlic, scallions and ginger; stir-fry for 30 seconds.

Add the peppers and tree ears; stir-fry for
30 seconds.

Add the lobster meat; stir-fry for 1 minute.

Add the water chestnuts and mix for a few
seconds. Empty the contents of the wok onto a heated dish, preferably a white oval
one.

Restir the seasoning sauce and add it all at
once to the wok; stir-fry about 30 seconds.

Return the lobster and vegetables to the
wok and stir-fry 1 more minute. Turn off
the heat and add sesame oil; mix well.

Empty the contents of the wok into the center of the heated serving dish.

In a separate wok, heat the tablespoon of
butter over a low heat until the foam subsides. Turn the heat to medium and add
shredded snow peas, salt, and sugar; stir-
fry 1 minute.

Place the ingredients on the serving dish in
the following order: the lobster's head, the
lobster meat, the shredded snow peas, and
finally the lobster's tail.

YIELD 2-6 servings

LOBSTER SAUTÉED WITH SOYBEAN PASTE
Canton/Guangzhou

1 live female lobster (2–2¹/₂ pounds)

SEASONING SAUCE
1 tablespoon dark miso (soybean paste)
¹/₂ tablespoon dark soy sauce
2 tablespoons sherry
¹/₂ teaspoon sugar
¹/₄ cup salt-free chicken stock

BINDER
2 teaspoons water chestnut powder
    dissolved in
2 tablespoons sherry

GARNISH
Fried rice noodles**

1 clove garlic, minced
2 scallions (white and green parts), shredded
1 teaspoon minced ginger root

¹/₂ cup cleaned, seeded, triangle-cut sweet red
    peppers

2 tablespoons peanut oil

PREPARATION

Steam the lobster for 5 minutes; remove it from the steamer and allow it to cool for 10 minutes. Remove the lobster meat from the shell and cut it into 1¹/₂-inch pieces. Reserve the lobster roe, tomalley (the liver), and juices to add to the seasoning sauce.

Combine the ingredients for the seasoning sauce.

Mix the binder.

Fry the rice noodles.

COOKING PROCEDURE

Place the wok over high heat for about 1 minute. Add the oil and heat until it is hot but not smoking. Add garlic, scallions, and ginger; stir-fry for 30 seconds.

Add peppers; stir-fry for 30 seconds.

Add the lobster meat; stir-fry for 1 minute.

Restir the seasoning sauce and add it all at once to the wok; stir-fry about 30 seconds.

Restir the binder and add it to the wok, stirring until the sauce thickens. Empty the contents of the wok onto a heated serving dish, surround with fried rice noodles, and serve immediately.

YIELD *2–6 servings*

NOTES

Tip The purpose of steaming the lobster is to remove the meat easily from the shell.

Substitution For the live lobster, you can substitute 2 cups of diced, cooked lobster meat, in which case the steaming procedure would be eliminated. As there will be no lobster juices, increase the chicken stock to ¹/₂ cup.

LOBSTER CANTONESE

Canton/Guangzhou

1 live female lobster (1¹/₄–1¹/₂ pounds)

¹/₂ cup chicken stock

1 whole egg, plus 1 egg white

BINDER
*¹/₂ tablespoon water chestnut powder
    dissolved in*
2 tablespoons sherry

1 tablespoon sherry
1 teaspoon dark soy sauce
¹/₂ teaspoon sugar

2 teaspoons minced fermented black beans
2 cloves garlic, minced
1 teaspoon minced ginger root

¹/₂ cup (¹/₄ pound) ground pork

*2 scallions (white and green parts), slant-cut
    in 1-inch pieces*

2 tablespoons peanut oil

PREPARATION

Using a heavy cleaver and rubber mallet, chop the body of the lobster into 2-inch sections and crack the claws.

Add the lobster roe and tomalley (the liver) to the chicken stock.

Place the lobster meat in a strainer set over a bowl; collect the drained juices to add to the stock.

Beat the egg and the egg white slightly.

Mix the binder.

Combine the 1 tablespoon sherry with the soy sauce and sugar.

COOKING PROCEDURE

Place the wok over high heat for about 1 minute. Add the oil and heat for 20 seconds or until it is hot but not smoking. Add the black beans, garlic, and ginger; stir-fry 10 seconds.

Add the pork and stir-fry until it turns white, about 3 minutes.

Add the lobster pieces; stir-fry 2 minutes.

Add the mixture of sherry, soy sauce, and sugar. Mix well.

Add the scallions and mix again.

Add ¹/₂ cup of the stock. Bring to a boil. Cover and cook over medium heat for 2 to 3 minutes.

Restir the binder and add it to the wok, stirring until the sauce thickens.

Stir in the eggs and immediately turn off the heat. Empty the contents of the wok onto a heated serving dish and serve immediately.

YIELD *2–6 servings*

170

FISH AND SHELLFISH

STEAMED CANTONESE LOBSTER   Canton/Guangzhou

1 *live female lobster (3 pounds)*

MARINADE
1 *tablespoon dark soy sauce*
2 *tablespoons sherry*
2 *tablespoons sesame oil*
1 *scallion (white and green parts), shredded*
1 *tablespoon minced ginger root*

1 *scallion (white and green parts), shredded*

PREPARATION

Using a heavy cleaver and rubber mallet, chop the body of the lobster into 2-inch sections. Crack the claws. Leave the lobster roe and tomalley (the liver) intact. Place the lobster pieces on a plate that will fit into a steamer and arrange them to resemble the shape of a lobster, flesh side up.

Combine the ingredients for the marinade. Spoon it over the entire lobster and allow it to marinate for 30 minutes.

COOKING PROCEDURE

Place the plate containing the lobster in a steamer. Cover and steam for 12 minutes.

Remove the plate from the steamer, scatter the shredded scallion over the lobster, and serve immediately.

YIELD *2–6 servings*

STIR-FRIED LOBSTER WITH SHREDDED LEEKS

Canton/Guangzhou

1 1/2 cups water
1/2 cup salt-free chicken stock
2 cups leeks (green part only), split and
  chopped
1/4 cup coriander leaves

BINDER
1 tablespoon plus 1 teaspoon water chestnut
  powder
    dissolved in
2 tablespoons sherry

1 live female 2 1/2–3-pound lobster

2 tablespoons shredded spring ginger root
2 cups leeks (green part only), split and
  shredded
1 clove garlic, minced

1/4 cup peanut oil

PREPARATION

Place the water, chicken stock, 2 cups chopped leeks, and coriander leaves in a saucepan and simmer over a low heat until the liquid is reduced to 1/2 cup. Strain the stock; discard the leeks and coriander, which have served their purpose of flavoring and coloring the stock green.

Mix the binder.

Using a heavy cleaver and rubber mallet, chop the body of the lobster into 2-inch sections. Chop the claws in half. Add the lobster roe and tomalley (the liver) to the 1/2 cup of reduced green chicken stock. Place the lobster pieces in a strainer set over a bowl; collect the drained juices to add to the stock.

COOKING PROCEDURE

Place the wok over high heat for about 1 minute. Add the oil and heat until hot but not smoking. Add the ginger, shredded leeks, and garlic; turn the heat to medium and sauté for 3 minutes.

Turn the heat to high. Add the lobster pieces to the wok and stir-fry for 2 minutes.

Pour in the green chicken stock to which the roe and tomalley have been added. Bring to a boil; cover for 2 to 3 minutes, cooking over a medium heat.

Uncover, then restir the binder and add it to the wok, stirring until the sauce thickens slightly. Empty the contents of the wok onto a heated serving dish and serve immediately.

YIELD *3–8 servings*

NOTES

Timing The cooking time varies according to the size of the lobster. If it is not possible to buy a large lobster, you may use two lobsters weighing 1 1/4 to 1 1/2 pounds each.

Tip Add the binder slowly. The amount of binder needed in this recipe may vary. You will probably need the entire amount if you chop the body of the lobster yourself and reserve all the juices. If the fish store has chopped the lobster for you, the sauce may require only half the binder. In either case, add it slowly and use your own judgment.

CLAMS IN BLACK BEAN SAUCE

18 littleneck clams
2 tablespoons cornmeal

1 tablespoon black beans

1 seeded, cleaned, and finely diced fresh chili
  pepper
1 teaspoon grated lemon rind
1 teaspoon minced ginger root
2 cloves garlic, minced
1 scallion (white and green parts), chopped

1 tablespoon sherry
3/4 tablespoon oyster sauce
1/2 tablespoon dark soy sauce
1 teaspoon sugar

BINDER
1/2 tablespoon water chestnut powder
  dissolved in
2 tablespoons water or salt-free chicken stock

1 tablespoon peanut oil

SPECIAL EQUIPMENT
Cheesecloth

PREPARATION

Scrub, rinse, then soak the clams for at least
1 hour in water to cover, to which 2 tablespoons of cornmeal have been added. After soaking, scrub the clams a second time.

Place the clams in a dish with a lip and
steam until they open. As they all will not
open at the same time, remove them individually by every so often opening the lid of
the steamer. Line a sieve with cheesecloth
and pour the clam stock through it into a 4-
cup heatproof glass container. You should
have about 3/4 cup clam broth. Set this liquid aside.

Soak the black beans in water to cover for
10 minutes, then drain.

Combine the peppers, lemon, ginger, garlic, and scallions.

Combine the sherry, oyster sauce, soy
sauce, sugar, and the 3/4 cup clam liquid.

Mix the binder.

COOKING PROCEDURE

Place the wok or heavy skillet over high
heat for about 1 minute. Add the 1 tablespoon of oil and heat until hot but not
smoking. Add the black beans and the pepper mixture. Stir-fry 1 minute.

Pour in the seasoned clam liquid and bring
to a boil.

Restir the binder and add it to the wok,
stirring until the sauce thickens.

Add the whole clams in their shells and
cook until they are heated through (1 minute or less).

Empty the contents of the wok onto a heated serving dish and serve immediately.

YIELD 2–6 servings

SCALLOPS IN GARLIC SAUCE

1 pound bay scallops

MARINADE
1 egg white
1 tablespoon sherry
1 tablespoon water chestnut powder

1 tablespoon minced garlic
1 teaspoon minced ginger root
2 scallions (white and green parts), chopped

*2 tablespoons tree ears, soaked and diced***

1/2 cup sliced water chestnuts

SEASONING SAUCE
2 teaspoons water chestnut powder
dissolved in
2 tablespoons sherry
1 tablespoon dark soy sauce
1 tablespoon light soy sauce
2 teaspoons sugar
2 teaspoons wine vinegar
*2 teaspoons Hot Sauce**

2 cups peanut oil

1 teaspoon sesame oil

PREPARATION

Wash, drain, and dry the scallops, then spread them on several layers of paper towels for 30 minutes. Place the scallops and the ingredients for the marinade in a bowl and stir with chopsticks vigorously in one direction. Place the mixture in the refrigerator for at least 1 hour or up to 12 hours.

Having reconstituted the tree ears and done the necessary cutting, place the three groups of ingredients in separate bowls.

Combine the ingredients for the seasoning sauce.

COOKING PROCEDURE

Place the wok over high heat for about 1 minute. Pour in the peanut oil; turn the heat to medium until the oil reaches 325 degrees. Restir the scallops in the marinade. Turn the heat to high and add the contents of the bowl all at once to the wok, stirring with a pair of chopsticks in a circular motion for about 1 minute. Turn off the heat and pour the oil and the scallops into a colander set over a bowl. Shake the colander gently to aid the draining, then place over a clean bowl.

Return the wok to high heat and add the garlic, ginger, and scallions. In the oil that glazes the wok, stir-fry about 30 seconds.

Add the tree ears and stir-fry a few seconds longer.

Return the scallops to the wok and mix briefly.

Restir the seasoning sauce and add it to the wok all at once; quickly add the water chestnuts and continue to stir-fry until the sauce thickens, about 1 minute.

Turn off the heat. Add sesame oil and mix briefly. Empty the contents of the wok onto a heated serving dish and serve immediately.

YIELD *3–8 servings*

NOTES

Substitution For the scallops, you can substitute shrimp.

¹/₄ pound boneless pork
¹/₂ pound scallops

MARINADE
1 egg white
³/₄ tablespoon water chestnut powder
2 teaspoons sherry

SEASONING SAUCE
1 teaspoon water chestnut powder
*   dissolved in*
2 tablespoons sherry
1¹/₂ tablespoons dark soy sauce
2 teaspoons Hot Sauce*
¹/₂ teaspoon sugar
1 teaspoon Chinese red vinegar
2 tablespoons salt-free chicken stock
¹/₄ teaspoon freshly ground black pepper

2 teaspoons minced garlic
2 teaspoons minced ginger root
2 scallions (white and green parts), chopped

1 cup snow peas, strung and slant-cut

2 cups peanut oil

1 teaspoon sesame oil

PREPARATION

Place the pork in the freezer for about 1 hour or until it is partially frozen, then slice thin and shred very fine.

Wash and drain the scallops. Leave whole if using bay scallops; cut in circles ¹/₄ inch thick if using sea scallops. Dry them very well on paper towels.

Place the scallops, pork, and ingredients for the marinade in a bowl and stir with chopsticks vigorously in one direction. Place the mixture in the refrigerator for at least 1 hour or up to 12 hours.

In another small bowl, combine all the ingredients for the seasoning sauce.

COOKING PROCEDURE

Place the wok over high heat for about 1 minute. Pour in the peanut oil and turn the heat to medium until the oil reaches 325 degrees. Restir the scallops and pork in the marinade. Turn the heat to high and add the contents of the bowl all at once to the wok, stirring with a pair of chopsticks in a circular motion for about 1 minute. Turn off the heat; pour the oil, scallops, and pork into a colander set over a bowl. Shake the colander gently to aid the draining, then place it over a clean bowl.

Place the wok over high heat for a few seconds. Add the garlic, ginger, and scallions; stir-fry 30 seconds.

Add the snow peas and stir-fry for another 30 seconds.

Return the scallop mixture to the wok and immediately add the seasoning sauce; stir-fry about 1 minute.

Turn off the heat. Pour in the sesame oil and mix briefly. Empty the contents of the wok onto a heated serving dish and serve immediately.

YIELD *2–6 servings*

STIR-FRIED SCALLOPS WITH PORK TENDERLOIN
Canton/Guangzhou

Pork and scallops blend well together in appearance, texture, and taste. Pork tenderloin is the required cut of meat for this dish because its shape is similar to that of a sea scallop.

1/2 pound pork tenderloin
1/2 pound sea scallops

MARINADE
1 egg white
1 tablespoon water chestnut powder
1 tablespoon sherry

3/4 pound yu choy

2 scallions (white and green parts), slant-cut in 1-inch pieces
1 clove garlic, minced
1 tablespoon minced spring ginger root

SEASONING SAUCE
2 teaspoons water chestnut powder dissolved in
2 tablespoons sherry
1 tablespoon dark soy sauce
1 tablespoon oyster sauce

1/2 cup chicken stock

2 cups peanut oil

1 teaspoon sesame oil

PREPARATION

Place the pork in the freezer for about 1 hour until it is partially frozen, then slice in circles 1/8 inch thick.

Wash, drain, and dry the scallops thoroughly; slice in circles 1/2 inch thick.

Place the scallops, the pork, and the ingredients for the marinade in a bowl and stir in one direction vigorously with chopsticks. Place the mixture in the refrigerator for at least 1 hour or up to 12 hours.

Remove 1 inch of the yu choy stems with a slant cut and discard. Slant-cut the remaining stems and leafy portions of the yu choy into 1½-inch pieces. Separate the stems from the leafy portions. Wash, drain, and dry.

Combine the ingredients for the seasoning sauce.

COOKING PROCEDURE

Place the wok over high heat for about 1 minute. Pour in the peanut oil and turn the heat to medium until the oil reaches 325 degrees. Restir the scallops and pork in the marinade. Turn the heat to high and add the contents of the bowl all at once to the wok, stirring in a circular motion with a pair of chopsticks for about 1 minute. Turn off the heat and pour the oil, scallops, and pork into a colander set over a bowl. Shake the colander gently to aid the draining, then place it over a clean bowl.

Place the wok over high heat for a few seconds. Add 1 tablespoon of the cooked oil. Add the scallions, garlic, ginger, and yu choy stems; stir-fry 30 seconds.

Add the leafy parts of the yu choy; stir-fry another 15 seconds.

Pour in the chicken stock around the sides of the wok and bring it to a boil; continue to stir-fry for another 30 seconds.

Restir the seasoning sauce and add it all at once to the wok along with the scallops and pork; stir-fry about 30 seconds.

Turn off the heat, add the sesame oil, and mix briefly. Empty the contents of the wok onto a heated serving dish and serve immediately.

YIELD *3–8 servings*

(continued)

NOTES

Tip It is important that the pork be sliced thin and the scallops sliced thick so they will cook in the same amount of time.

Substitutions For the yu choy, you can substitute a variety of fresh green vegetables such as broccoli, asparagus, string beans (all of which should be blanched prior to stir-frying), or snow peas or bok choy (which do not require blanching).

SHRIMP WITH PIQUANT SAUCE

Szechwan/Sichuan

1 pound medium shrimp (21–25 to the pound)

MARINADE
1 egg white
1 tablespoon sherry
1 tablespoon water chesinut powder

SEASONING SAUCE
1 tablespoon Tomato Sauce*
1 tablespoon dark soy sauce
2 tablespoons salt-free chicken stock
2 teaspoons hoisin sauce
2 teaspoons Hot Sauce*

BINDER
2 teaspoons water chestnut powder
    dissolved in
2 tablespoons sherry

2 teaspoons minced garlic
2 teaspoons minced ginger root
1/3 cup chopped scallions (white and green parts)

2 cups peanut oil

PREPARATION

Shell, split, wash, drain, and dry the shrimp.

Place the shrimp and the ingredients for the marinade in a bowl and stir in one direction vigorously with chopsticks. Place the mixture in the refrigerator for at least 1 hour or up to 12 hours.

Combine the ingredients for the seasoning sauce.

Mix the binder.

COOKING PROCEDURE

Place the wok over high heat for about 1 minute. Pour in the oil; turn the heat to medium until the oil reaches 325 degrees. Restir the shrimp in the marinade.

Turn the heat to high and add the contents of the bowl all at once to the wok stirring in a circular motion with a pair of chopsticks for about 1 minute. Turn off the heat and pour the oil and shrimp into a colander set over a bowl. Shake the colander gently to aid the draining, then place it over a clean bowl.

Return the wok to high heat and add the garlic, ginger, and scallions. Stir-fry for about 30 seconds.

Restir the seasoning sauce and add it all at once to the wok; stir-fry for a few seconds.

Restir the binder and add it to the wok along with the shrimp; stir-fry until the sauce has thickened and has evenly coated the shrimp. Empty the contents of the wok onto a heated serving dish and serve immediately.

YIELD *3–8 servings*

STUFFED PRAWNS

Canton/Guangzhou

STUFFING
2 Chinese mushrooms, soaked and minced**
1/4 pound ground pork
1/4 pound fresh crab meat, finely chopped
1/4 cup minced water chestnuts
1 scallion (white and green parts), minced
1 teaspoon minced ginger root
1 tablespoon soy sauce
1/2 tablespoon water chestnut powder
    dissolved in
1 tablespoon sherry
1 egg white

1 pound large shrimp (approximately 16 to
    the pound)

1 egg yolk, beaten

PREPARATION

Having reconstituted the mushrooms,
combine all the ingredients for the stuffing
and mix well.

To butterfly shrimp Shell the shrimp, leaving the last section and the tail intact. Cut
the shrimp from the underside almost
through to the back, but not all the way
through. Turn the shrimp over and make a
few cuts across the back. Flatten each
shrimp with the side of the cleaver and
carefully rinse them under cold running
water. Drain and dry the shrimp very well
with paper towels.

Brush the split side of each shrimp with the
egg yolk.

Place about 1 tablespoon of stuffing on the
split side of each shrimp. Arrange the
shrimp, stuffing side up, in a single layer
on a flat, heatproof, greased serving dish.

COOKING PROCEDURE

Preheat the oven to broil. Broil the shrimp
for 8 minutes, 3 inches from the heat
source, and serve immediately.

YIELD *3–8 servings*

METHOD I
1. Cut along the underside of the shrimp,
leaving the last section and the tail intact on
the partially shelled shrimp.

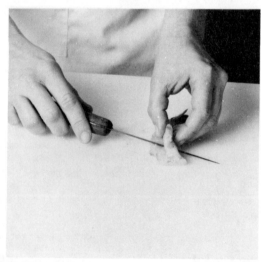

METHOD II
1. Cut the shrimp along the convex side
but do not let the knife go all the way
through the meat. With the tip of the boning knife, make a slit about 1 inch long in
the middle of the shrimp on the convex
side.

FISH AND SHELLFISH

Butterflying Shrimp

2. Cut as deep as possible without splitting the shrimp in half.

3. Turn the shrimp horizontally and make vertical cuts along the back, then flatten with the side of a cleaver.

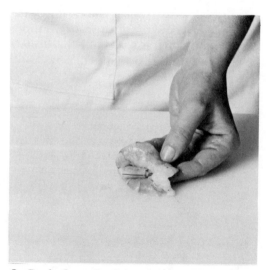

2. Push the tail of the shrimp through the slit.

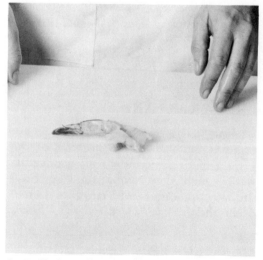

3. Pull the tail out neatly.

NOTES

Tip The purpose of butterflying shrimp is to prevent the shrimp from curling up when cooked. There are two different methods which will accomplish this task.

CHARRED SHRIMP IN BARBECUE SAUCE   Peking/Beijing

In China, shrimp are frequently cooked in the shell, an excellent way of preserving their flavor. When the shrimp are stir-fried in their shells, they become scorched and thereby take on a smoky flavor.

The seasoning sauce is one that I developed especially for shrimp, but it is also excellent as a barbecue sauce on poultry and meat.

1 pound medium shrimp (21–25 per pound)

SEASONING SAUCE
1 teaspoon water chestnut powder
   dissolved in
2 tablespoons sherry
3 tablespoons Tomato Sauce*
2 tablespoons salt-free chicken stock
2 tablespoons dark brown sugar
1 tablespoon plus 1 teaspoon dark soy sauce
2 teaspoons wine vinegar
1 teaspoon Hot Sauce*

2 teaspoons minced garlic
1/2 cup shredded scallions (white and green
   parts)

3 tablespoons peanut oil

PREPARATION

Using a pair of scissors, cut (but do not remove) the shell along the back of the shrimp, cutting into the shrimp about halfway through; then remove the legs. Rinse the shrimp under cold running water; drain, then dry very well.

Combine the ingredients for the seasoning sauce.

COOKING PROCEDURE

Place the wok over high heat for about 1 minute. Add 2 1/2 tablespoons of the peanut oil and heat until hot but not smoking. Add the shrimp and stir-fry for 4 to 5 minutes or until the shrimp are almost cooked through. They should be charred. Empty the contents of the wok onto a heated serving dish.

Return the wok to high heat and add the remaining 1/2 tablespoon of oil. Add the garlic and scallions; stir-fry 30 seconds.

Restir the seasoning sauce and add it all at once to the wok, stirring until the sauce thickens.

Return the shrimp to the wok and stir-fry another 30 seconds, until the shrimp have been evenly coated with the sauce. Empty the contents of the wok onto the heated serving dish and serve immediately.

YIELD *3–8 servings*

NOTES

Tip If desired, the shrimp can be stir-fried several hours in advance.

KUNG PAO SHRIMP

By Chinese standards, a dish is considered more prestigious if it is named after a general. Kung Pao was a general who lived in Szechwan Province and served during the Ching Dynasty. Obviously he had excellent taste.

1 pound medium shrimp (21–25 per pound)

MARINADE
1 egg white
1 tablespoon water chestnut powder
1 tablespoon sherry

SEASONING SAUCE
2 tablespoons dark soy sauce
1 tablespoon sherry
1 1/2 teaspoons sugar
1 1/2 teaspoons wine vinegar
1 1/2 teaspoons Hot Sauce*

BINDER
1 teaspoon water chestnut powder
    dissolved in
1 tablespoon chicken stock

4 scallions (white and green parts), chopped
2 teaspoons minced ginger root
1 clove garlic, minced

1/2 cup sliced fresh water chestnuts

1/4 cup pine nuts, roasted**

2 cups peanut oil

PREPARATION

Shell, split, wash, drain, and dry the shrimp. Place the shrimp and the ingredients for the marinade in a bowl and stir in one direction vigorously with chopsticks. Place the mixture in the refrigerator for at least 1 hour or up to 12 hours.

Combine the ingredients for the seasoning sauce.

Mix the binder.

COOKING PROCEDURE

Place the wok over high heat for about 1 minute. Pour in the 2 cups of oil; lower the heat to medium until the oil reaches 325 degrees. Restir the shrimp in the marinade. Turn the heat to high and add the contents of the bowl all at once to the wok, stirring with a pair of chopsticks in a circular motion for about 1 minute. Turn off the heat and pour out the oil and the shrimp into a colander set over a bowl. Shake the colander gently to aid the draining, then place it over a clean bowl.

Place the wok over high heat for a few seconds. In the oil that glazes the wok, stir-fry the scallions, ginger, and garlic for 30 seconds.

Add the water chestnuts and pine nuts; mix briefly.

Restir the seasoning sauce and add along with the shrimp, continuing to stir-fry for a few seconds.

Restir the binder and add it to the wok, stirring until the sauce has evenly glazed the shrimp. Empty the contents of the wok onto a heated serving dish and serve immediately.

YIELD *3–8 servings*

NOTES

Substitutions Bay scallops, left whole, or sea scallops, sliced in circles 1/4 inch thick, can be substituted for the shrimp. After the scallops have been washed, drained, and dried, they should be spread out on several layers of paper towels for at least 30 minutes to remove any excess moisture before placing them in the marinade.

Boneless, skinless chicken meat, diced, is another excellent choice for this dish. If you use chicken, cook it an additional minute when passing through.

LAKE TUNGTING SHRIMP   Hunan

This famous dish from Hunan Province, where Lake Tungting (Dongtinghu) is located, is ideally composed of freshwater shrimp, which have an excellent flavor that has been likened to lobster. Because the use of fresh chili peppers would mask the taste of the shrimp, they are not employed in this dish. Lake Tungting Shrimp is served at banquets in Hunan as its pure flavor is a departure from their characteristic hot and spicy seasoning.

3/4 pound medium shrimp (21–25 to the pound)

MARINADE
1 egg white
3/4 tablespoon water chestnut powder
2 teaspoons sherry
1/2 teaspoon salt

2 cups broccoli florets
2 scallions (white and green parts), slant-cut in 1-inch pieces
1/2 cup canned straw mushrooms, drained
1 teaspoon minced ginger root

5 egg whites
2 teaspoons water chestnut powder
1 tablespoon chicken stock

SAUCE
2 teaspoons water chestnut powder
1/3 cup chicken stock
1/4 cup sherry
1/2 teaspoon salt

1 cup warm chicken stock

2 cups peanut oil

2 tablespoons minced Smithfield ham**
1 teaspoon sesame oil

PREPARATION

Shell, split, wash, drain, and dry the shrimp well. Place the shrimp and the ingredients for the marinade in a bowl and stir in one direction vigorously with chopsticks. Place the mixture in the refrigerator for at least 1 hour or up to 12 hours.

Separate the broccoli florets into small pieces. Blanch them for 1 minute, then remove the florets from the boiling water and plunge them into ice water for 1 minute to stop the cooking and retain the color. Drain and dry well.

Beat the egg whites until they foam slightly. Mix together the 2 teaspoons of water chestnut powder with the 1 tablespoon of chicken stock and gently but thoroughly beat the mixture into the egg whites.

To make the sauce, dissolve the 2 teaspoons of water chestnut powder in 1 tablespoon of the chicken stock. Stir in the remainder of the 1/3 cup chicken stock, the sherry, and the salt.

COOKING PROCEDURE

Place the wok over high heat for about 1 minute. Pour in the 2 cups of oil; turn the heat to medium until the oil reaches 280 degrees. Pour in the egg white mixture, stirring in a circular motion with a pair of chopsticks until the egg whites are set (about 15 seconds).

Pour the egg whites from the wok into a colander set over a bowl, collecting the oil for immediate use. Shake the colander gently a few times to aid the draining process.

Holding the colander over the sink, pour the 1 cup of warm chicken stock over the set egg whites. The stock serves to wash off as much oil as possible. Place the egg whites on the serving dish.

Splitting Shrimp

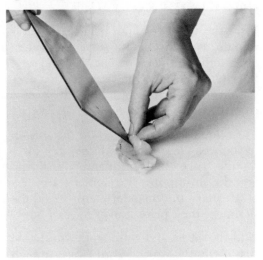

1. Shell, split, wash, drain, and dry the shrimp. Cut along the convex side of the shrimp but do not go all the way through.

2. Flatten each shrimp with the side of a cleaver.

The recipe up to this point can be prepared several hours ahead.

Place the wok over high heat for about 1 minute. Pour in the 2 cups of cooked oil and turn the heat to medium until the oil reaches 325 degrees. Restir the shrimp in the marinade. Turn the heat to high and add the contents of the bowl all at once to the wok, stirring in a circular motion with a pair of chopsticks for about 1 minute.

Turn off the heat and pour out the oil and the shrimp into a colander set over a bowl. Shake the colander gently to aid the draining, then place it over a clean bowl.

Place the wok over high heat for a few seconds. Add the broccoli, scallions, mushrooms and ginger; stir-fry for 1 minute.

Return the shrimp to the wok and mix briefly.

Restir the sauce and add it to the wok, mixing for a few seconds.

Add the set egg whites to the contents of the wok, gently stir-frying for a few seconds over high heat. Empty the contents of the wok onto a heated serving dish. Sprinkle the minced ham on top, and then drizzle 1 teaspoon of sesame oil over the entire surface. Serve immediately.

YIELD *2–6 servings*

SALT AND PEPPERY SHRIMP

1 pound medium shrimp (21–25 to the
  pound)

MARINADE
1/2 teaspoon salt
1 teaspoon sherry

2 teaspoons water chestnut powder

1 teaspoon minced garlic
1 cleaned, seeded, and minced fresh chili
  pepper

1/2 teaspoon salt
2 tablespoons sherry

2 scallions (white and green parts), shredded

2 cups peanut oil

PREPARATION

Using a pair of scissors, cut (but do not
remove) the shell along the back of the
shrimp, cutting about halfway through the
shrimp; remove the legs. Rinse the shrimp
under cold running water; drain, then dry
very well.

Place the shrimp in a bowl and mix in the
marinade; allow to stand for 15 minutes.

COOKING PROCEDURE

Place the wok over high heat for about 1
minute. Pour in the oil; turn the heat to
medium until the oil reaches 375 degrees.
Sprinkle the water chestnut powder over
the shrimp; toss them until they are evenly
coated.

Turn the heat to high and add the shrimp
to the wok all at once and deep-fry for 1
minute. Turn off the heat and pour the oil
and the shrimp into a colander set over a
bowl. Shake the colander gently to aid the
draining, then place it over a clean bowl.

Add the garlic and chili pepper to the oil
that glazes the wok. Turn the heat to high
and stir-fry about 30 seconds.

Return the shrimp to the wok, add the 1/2
teaspoon salt and 2 tablespoons sherry, and
stir-fry a few seconds.

Place the shredded scallions on top of the
shrimp, cover the wok with the lid, and
continue to cook about 15 seconds. Shake
the wok a few times. Remove the cover.
Turn off the heat and slide the shrimp onto
a heated serving dish so the scallions remain on top. Serve immediately.

YIELD 3–8 servings

SHRIMP WITH SNOW PEAS

1 pound medium shrimp (21–25 to the
   pound)

MARINADE
1 egg white
1 tablespoon water chestnut powder
1 tablespoon sherry
1 teaspoon salt

BINDER
1 teaspoon water chestnut powder
   dissolved in
2 tablespoons sherry
2 teaspoons Hot Sauce*

4 scallions (white and green parts), chopped
2 cloves garlic, minced
2 teaspoons minced ginger root
1/2 teaspoon salt

3 cups snow peas, strung and slant-cut

1/3 cup chicken stock

2 cups peanut oil

1 teaspoon sesame oil

1/4 cup almonds, roasted**

PREPARATION

Shell, split, wash, drain, and dry the
shrimp. Place the shrimp and the ingredients for the marinade in a bowl and stir in
one direction vigorously with chopsticks.
Place the mixture in the refrigerator for at
least 1 hour or up to 12 hours.

Mix the binder.

COOKING PROCEDURE

Place the wok over high heat for about 1
minute. Pour in the 2 cups of oil and turn
the heat to medium until the oil reaches
325 degrees. Restir the shrimp in the marinade. Turn the heat to high and add the
contents of the bowl all at once to the wok,
stirring in a circular motion with a pair of
chopsticks for about 1 minute.

Turn off the heat and pour the oil and the
shrimp into a colander set over a bowl.
Shake the colander gently to aid the draining, then place over a clean bowl.

Return the wok to high heat. Add the scallions, garlic, ginger, and salt; stir-fry for 1
minute.

Add the snow peas; stir-fry about 30 seconds.

Return the shrimp to the wok and stir-fry a
few seconds.

Add the stock around the sides of the wok
and allow it to come to a boil.

Restir the binder and add it to the wok,
continuing to stir-fry until the sauce thickens and the shrimp turn pink. This should
take no longer than 30 seconds.

Turn off the heat. Add the sesame oil, stir-
frying briefly. Empty the contents of the
wok onto a heated serving dish, sprinkle
with almonds, and serve immediately.

YIELD *3–8 servings*

NOTES

Substitutions Boneless, skinless chicken,
scallops, or boneless leg of veal can be substituted for the shrimp.

   Roll-oblique-cut zucchini or asparagus
can be substituted for the snow peas.
Blanched, slant-cut broccoli or string beans
are another possibility. In fact, any fresh
green vegetable can be substituted, as it
provides a pleasing contrast to the pink
shrimp.

SHRIMP WITH TWO FLAVORS   Szechwan/Sichuan

1 pound small shrimp (30–35 to the pound)

MARINADE
1 egg white
1 tablespoon water chestnut powder
1 tablespoon sherry

1/4 cup Chinese mushrooms, soaked and
    quartered**
1/2 cup slant-cut scallions (white and green
    parts)
1 teaspoon minced garlic
1 teaspoon minced ginger root

1 cup snow peas, strung and slant-cut
1/2 cup peeled and sliced fresh water chestnuts

SEASONING SAUCE
1 teaspoon water chestnut powder
    dissolved in
1 tablespoon sherry
1 tablespoon dark soy sauce
1 teaspoon Hot Sauce*
1 teaspoon sugar
1 teaspoon wine vinegar
2 tablespoons, reduced mushroom stock,**
    cooled

SEASONING SAUCE
FOR WATERCRESS
1/2 teaspoon water chestnut powder
    dissolved in
1 tablespoon sherry
1/2 teaspoon sugar
1/2 teaspoon salt

1/4 teaspoon salt

2 bunches watercress, stems removed

2 cups peanut oil

PREPARATION

Shell, split, wash, drain, and dry the
shrimp. Place the shrimp and the ingredients for the marinade in a bowl and stir in
one direction vigorously with chopsticks.
Place the mixture in the refrigerator for at
least 1 hour or up to 12 hours.

Having reconstituted the mushrooms and
done the necessary cutting, place the two
groups of ingredients in separate bowls.

Combine the ingredients for the seasoning
sauce.

Combine the ingredients for the watercress
seasoning sauce.

COOKING PROCEDURE

Place the wok over high heat for about 1
minute. Pour in the 2 cups of oil; turn the
heat to medium until the oil reaches 325
degrees. Restir the shrimp in the marinade.
Turn the heat to high and add the contents
of the bowl all at once to the wok, stirring
with a pair of chopsticks in a circular motion for about 1 minute. Turn off the heat
and pour the oil and shrimp into a colander
set over a bowl. Shake the colander gently
to aid the draining, then place over a clean
bowl.

Return the wok to high heat. Add the
mushrooms, scallions, garlic, and ginger;
stir-fry 30 seconds.

Add the snow peas and water chestnuts;
mix well.

(continued)

Return the shrimp to the wok and stir-fry a few seconds, then remove half of the shrimp and vegetable mixture to one side of a heated serving dish. Sprinkle with ¼ teaspoon salt.

Restir the seasoning sauce and add it to the shrimp that remain in the wok. Stir-fry a few more seconds or until the sauce has evenly coated the shrimp and vegetables. Place the shrimp mixture on the opposite side of the serving dish.

Place a second wok over high heat and add 1 tablespoon of the cooked oil; heat until hot but not smoking. Add the watercress; stir-fry about 30 seconds.

Restir the seasoning sauce for the watercress and add it, stir-frying for another 30 seconds.

Place the watercress in the center of the serving dish, dividing the shrimp with two flavors. Serve immediately.

YIELD *3—8 servings*

STEAMED SHRIMP

Canton/Guangzhou

1 pound shrimp (live, if possible)

PREPARATION

Wash the shrimp, leaving all parts (head, tail, shell) intact.

COOKING PROCEDURE

Place the shrimp on a serving plate that will fit into a bamboo steamer.

Bring 6 cups of water to a rapid boil in a 14-inch round-bottom wok. Place the bamboo steamer with the shrimp in the wok; cover and steam for about 3 minutes or until the shrimp turn pink.

Remove the plate from the steamer. Serve immediately with Spicy Dipping Sauce*.

Each guest peels his own shrimp.

YIELD *3—8 servings*

SPICY SHRIMP WITH PORK FLAVOR   Szechwan/Sichuan

³/₄ pound medium shrimp (21–25 to the pound)

MARINADE
1 egg white
³/₄ tablespoon water chestnut powder
³/₄ tablespoon sherry

SEASONING SAUCE
1 teaspoon water chestnut powder dissolved in
1 tablespoon chicken stock
1 tablespoon dark soy sauce
1 tablespoon miso
2 teaspoons Hot Sauce*
1 tablespoon sherry
¹/₂ teaspoon wine vinegar
¹/₂ teaspoon sugar

2 cloves garlic, minced
2 teaspoons minced ginger root
3 scallions (white and green parts), chopped

¹/₄ pound ground pork

2 cups peanut oil

1 teaspoon sesame oil

PREPARATION

Shell, split, wash, drain, and dry the shrimp. Place the shrimp and the ingredients for the marinade in a bowl and stir in one direction vigorously with chopsticks. Place the mixture in the refrigerator for at least 1 hour or up to 12 hours.

Combine the ingredients for the seasoning sauce.

COOKING PROCEDURE

Place the wok over high heat for about 1 minute. Pour in the 2 cups of oil; turn the heat to medium until the oil reaches 325 degrees. Restir the shrimp in the marinade. Turn the heat to high and add the contents of the bowl all at once to the wok, stirring in a circular motion with a pair of chopsticks for about 1 minute. Turn off the heat and pour the oil and the shrimp into a colander set over a bowl. Shake the colander gently to aid the draining, then place it over a clean bowl.

Return the wok to high heat; add the garlic, ginger, and scallions; stir-fry 30 seconds.

Add the ground pork; stir-fry a few minutes or until it turns white. Empty the contents of the wok onto a heated serving dish.

Return the wok to high heat. Restir the seasoning sauce and add it all at once to the wok, stirring about 30 seconds.

Return the shrimp and pork mixture to the wok; stir-fry another 30 seconds.

Turn off the heat. Add the sesame oil and mix briefly. Empty the contents of the wok onto the heated serving dish and serve immediately.

YIELD *3–8 servings*

TARO SEAFOOD NEST

This is an exciting banquet dish, both appealing and unusual. The taro nest is similar to French potato baskets but even more interesting because of the three starches used: taro, potato, and rice sticks.

1/3 pound bay scallops
1/3 pound small shrimp (30–35 to the pound)
1/3 pound fresh cooked lobster meat, diced

MARINADE
1 egg white
2 teaspoons water chestnut powder
2 teaspoons sherry

1/4 cup Chinese mushrooms, soaked and
  quartered**
2 cloves garlic, minced
2 scallions (white and green parts), chopped
1 teaspoon minced ginger root

1/4 cup sliced water chestnuts

SEASONING SAUCE
1 teaspoon water chestnut powder
  dissolved in
1 tablespoon sherry
1 tablespoon dark soy sauce
1 tablespoon light soy sauce
2 teaspoons Hot Sauce*
2 teaspoons sugar
2 teaspoons wine vinegar
1 tablespoon chicken stock

1 Taro Nest* (see Preparation)

2 cups peanut oil

1 teaspoon sesame oil

PREPARATION

Wash, drain, and dry the scallops.

Shell, split, wash, drain, and dry the shrimp.

Place the scallops and shrimp and the ingredients for the marinade in a bowl; stir in one direction vigorously with chopsticks. Place the mixture in the refrigerator for at least 1 hour or up to 12 hours.

Having reconstituted the mushrooms and done the necessary cutting, place the two groups of ingredients in separate bowls.

Combine the ingredients for the seasoning sauce.

Follow Taro Nest* recipe through first frying.

COOKING PROCEDURE

Preheat the oven to 350 degrees.

Place the fried Taro Nest on a flat, heatproof serving dish in the oven while preparing the seafood filling.

Place the wok over high heat for about 1 minute. Pour in the peanut oil and turn the heat to medium until it reaches 325 degrees. Turn the heat to high.

Restir the scallops and shrimp in the marinade and add the contents of the bowl all at once to the wok, stirring with a pair of chopsticks in a circular motion for about 1 minute.

Turn off the heat, pour out the oil, scallops, and shrimp into a colander set over a bowl. Shake the colander gently to aid the draining, then place it over a clean bowl.

Return the wok to high heat. Add the mushrooms, garlic, scallions, and ginger. Stir-fry 1 minute.

Add the water chestnuts; mix briefly.

Restir the seasoning sauce and add it all at once to the wok; stir-fry about 30 seconds.

Return the scallops and shrimp to the wok, add the lobster meat, and continue to stir-fry for another 30 seconds.

Turn off the heat. Add sesame oil; mix briefly.

Remove the Taro Nest from the oven and pour the contents of the wok into the nest. Serve immediately.

YIELD *3–8 servings*

TARO NEST

2 cups peeled and shredded taro root
2 cups peeled and shredded potato
2 cups broken and separated rice noodles

6 cups peanut oil

COOKING PROCEDURE

Toss the shredded taro and potato together. Place the mixture on a plate and put it into a bamboo steamer and steam for 5 minutes. Remove the taro and potato shreds from the steamer and allow them to cool slightly. Place the shreds on paper towels and dry them very well.

Place the wok over high heat for about 1 minute. Pour in the oil and turn the heat to medium until the oil reaches 375 degrees.

Combine the rice noodles with the taro and potato shreds.

Turn the heat to high. Immerse two 7-inch wire strainers in the oil for a few seconds. Remove.

Line one metal strainer with half of the taro mixture and press down on it with the second metal strainer. Lower the nest into the oil; deep-fry until lightly brown and set. Remove the nest from the oil; dislodge it from the strainer and drain it well on several sheets of paper towels. Return the oil to 375 degrees. Fry the second nest; then remove.

Return the oil to 375 degrees. Sandwiched between the strainers as before, return the first nest to the oil; continue to fry until golden brown and crispy. Remove the nest from the oil and allow it to drain on paper towels. Refry the second nest; then remove. These nests are used as the base for Taro Seafood Nest. Alternative fillings for the Taro Nest could be any spicy boneless chicken dish or a seafood dish such as Scallops in Garlic Sauce*.

NOTES

Timing The entire recipe can be prepared several hours ahead through the first frying. The completed Taro Nest can be kept warm in a preheated 350-degree oven for no more than 10 minutes. Do not cover the nest. The purpose of keeping it warm is to allow time for preparing the seafood filling.

Tip If only one nest is desired, this recipe can be halved. It is advisable not to halve the recipe, however, as the nests are very fragile and it's always good to have one in reserve. In the event that two come out perfectly, one can be snacked on in the kitchen while passing through.

YIELD *2 nests*

Chapter 12

CHICKEN

Whenever possible, poultry should be purchased fresh-killed, as it has better flavor and texture. Several recipes in this chapter call for a whole fresh-killed chicken, with the legs and wings to be reserved for another use. The legs and wings can be used in the following recipes:

Braised Gingered Chicken
Soy-Braised Chicken
Five Flavors Chicken
Fried Chicken with Scallion Sauce
Chicken Wings with Oyster Sauce
Barbecued Duck Portions
    (substitute chicken)
Barbecued Roast Pork
    (substitute chicken)

When recipes in this chapter call for boneless, skinless chicken, it is a matter of preference whether you use light or dark meat. If using all dark meat, cook the chicken one minute longer in the passing-through procedure. If using a combination of dark and light meat, cut the dark meat in smaller pieces so that they will both require the same amount of cooking time.

It is common practice for the Chinese to cut and cook chicken with the skin and bone, as they add more flavor. This is usually an indication of a home-style dish rather than a banquet dish, in which case the chicken would be skinned and boned before being marinated and cooked.

Boning a Whole Chicken (or any other poultry) for Recipes Requiring Boneless, Skinless Chicken Meat, Dark or Light

The purpose of this procedure is to remove the meat from the skin and bone in order to use the white meat from the breasts and the dark meat from the thighs. Reserve the wings and legs for other recipes. The meat from the breasts and thighs can then be sliced, diced, shredded, or minced. Except for dicing, the meat should be partially frozen before cutting.

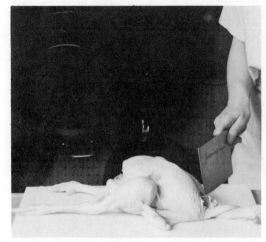

1. Place the bird on a chopping block, breast side up.

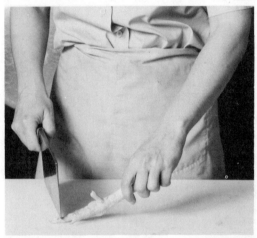

2. Remove the feet and trim the toenails.

3. Feel for the joint between the thigh and the leg. It should feel like the space between two knuckles on your hand.

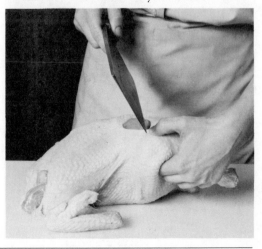

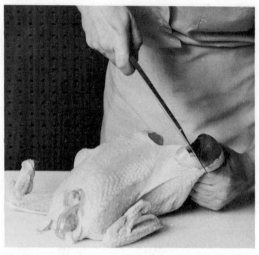

4. Cut all the way through the joint; detach the leg from the thigh.

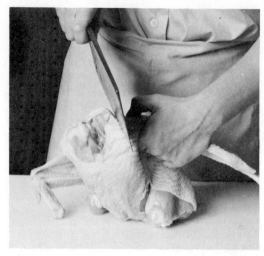

5. Repeat this procedure with the wings, first feeling for the separation at the joint, then cutting through.

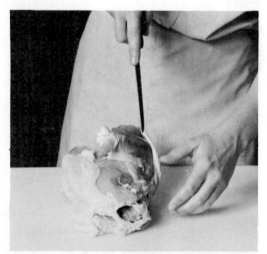

8. Remove the skin from the thighs, back, and neck using the same nicking and pulling technique.

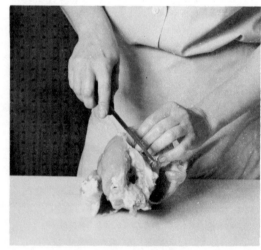

9. To remove the meat from the breast, begin at the shoulder (wishbone), making one long cut; follow the upper ridge or contour of the breastbone.

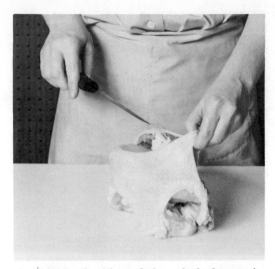

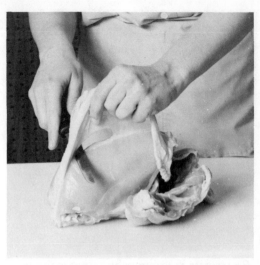

6. Skin both sides of the whole breast in the following manner: insert the knife between the skin and the meat where the breast meets the thigh, and cut through until the skin is separated from the meat. Do this on both sides.

7. Pull the skin with one hand while nicking with the other, taking care not to cut the underlying meat. Remove the membrane at the same time. Repeat this procedure with the other breast half.

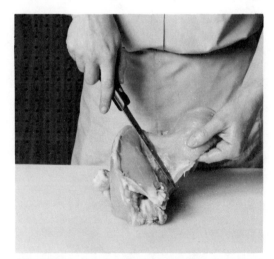

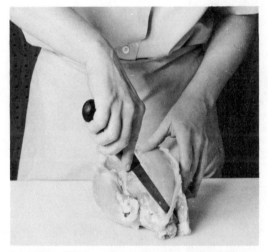

10. There is a natural separation between the cutlet and the fillet. Remove the cutlet first, by holding it with one hand and pressing in toward the carcass with the knife in the other hand. Repeat the procedure with the other cutlet, starting at the shoulder again, but this time drawing the boning knife away from you, again following the upper ridge or contour of the breastbone.

11. The fillets are removed in the following manner: sever the tendon attached to the shoulder by making two incisions with the point of the boning knife; pull the cutlet away from the carcass while making nicks with the point of the boning knife with the other hand; continue this pulling, with a minimum amount of nicking; pull off the last few inches; do the same procedure on the other side.

(continued)

12. In order to remove the long white tendon that runs through the fillet, hold the exposed end of the tendon in place with a small piece of paper towel at the edge of the work surface.

13. Using your other hand, put the dull edge of the boning knife perpendicular to the exposed tendon; keep the blade stationary while pulling the tendon slowly and steadily toward you. In order not to break the tendon, do not press down too heavily on the blade; the tendon will slide out in one entire piece. This procedure is done with both hands off the board.

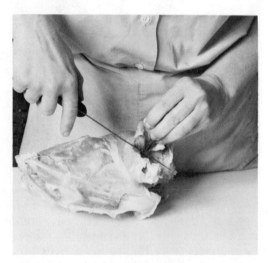

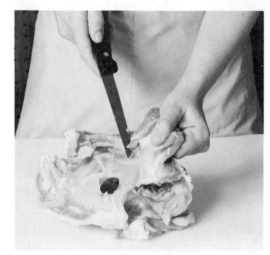

16. . . . continuing along the bone, cutting close to the bone to save all the meat.

17. Turn the thigh around and do the same procedure on the other side; twist the thighbone in the socket until it separates. Remove the two small oyster-shaped pieces of meat located along the back on either side.

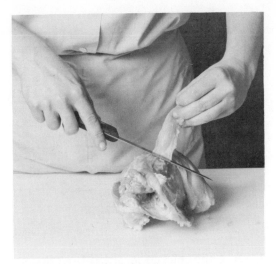

14. Remove the small piece of white meat near the shoulder.

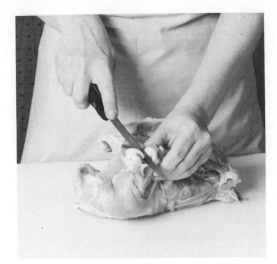

15. To remove the thigh meat, hold part of the thigh with one hand, feel for the bone with the other, and cut down a few inches into the meat . . .

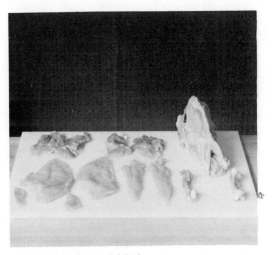

18. The deboned bird.

Dicing Boneless Chicken

Boneless, skinless chicken should always be perfectly trimmed. The fat that you stir-fry is the fat that you eat.

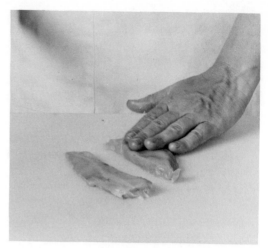

1. Once the chicken meat has been boned and the fat removed, it is necessary to cut the two cutlets in half lengthwise. Adding these four strips to the two fillet strips yields six strips.

Slicing and Shredding Boneless Chicken Breasts

Partially freeze the boned chicken breast (2 cutlets and 2 fillets) flat. (To facilitate the slicing and shredding of meat, fish, or poultry, it is necessary to freeze it partially.)

1. Place the partially frozen chicken breast on a cutting board. Put one hand on top of the chicken breast, leaving about 1 inch of chicken exposed beyond your fingertips. Slice the chicken at this angle. The purpose of this angling (rather than slicing straight down) is to get a wider slice.

2. To dice the cutlet strips, do not make the cuts straight across as you would when cutting the fillet strips, because the cutlet is too wide and too thick; rather, angle the cleaver. Dice in ¾-inch pieces. Depending on the size of the bird, the procedure sometimes becomes triangle cutting. The exception to this is the thinner end, which is straight-cut.

3. To dice the thighs, cut along the muscle separations, rather than cutting the thigh into strips. If there is a longer strip without muscle separations, dice it with the cleaver at the same angle as for the breast. Remove any excess membrane, cartilage, and tendon. If both white and dark meat are required in the same recipe, the dark meat should be cut into smaller pieces, as it requires a longer cooking time.

2. Keep moving your hand back while slicing the meat. When you get to the very end, turn the end piece around, place two or three fingers on top of the chicken, and slice through its thickness. If shredding is not required, continue this procedure until both breasts are sliced.

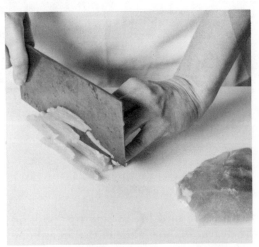

3. If you are going to shred the chicken, slice only four pieces at a time and then shred those four pieces immediately, because if you slice all the chicken at once the slices will defrost, making it harder to shred. Stack four pieces of sliced chicken and shred.

Cutting and Reassembling Whole Cooked Poultry

In most cases, whole cooked poultry is not carved at the table in China, but rather cut through the skin and bone into bite-size pieces (in order to be eaten with chopsticks) and presented on a serving platter reassembled to look like a whole bird flattened out. The equipment required for cutting whole cooked poultry is a boning knife, which is used to remove the legs and wings at the joint, and a heavy cleaver and rubber mallet, which are used to cut through the bone and skin.

Cut off any extending portion of the neck. Cut the neck into bite-size pieces. Place it, reassembled, on a large flat serving platter.

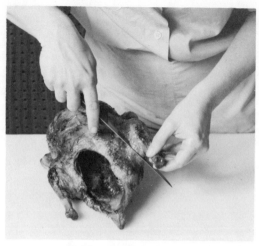

1. Remove the leg by pulling with one hand while cutting through the joint with the other hand. After removing both legs, cross-cut each one into 1½-inch pieces. Place both legs, reassembled, on the serving platter at the opposite end from the neck.

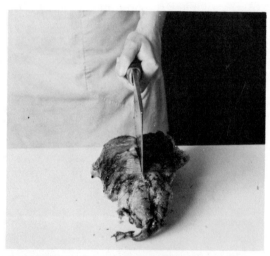

4. Place the bird breast side up; position the cleaver in the middle of the breastbone and split the breast in half. When the cleaver reaches the back, place it on one side of the neck (do not split the neck in half) and continue cutting until the bird is divided in half. Take the upper half of the bird and, starting at the neck, cut along the length of the backbone. Cut this long piece into 1½-inch pieces. Reassemble the pieces in the center of the serving platter between the neck and the tail.

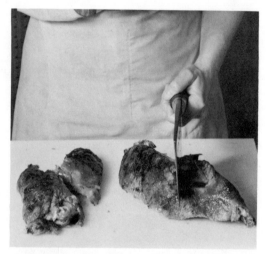

5. Separate the breast from the thigh.

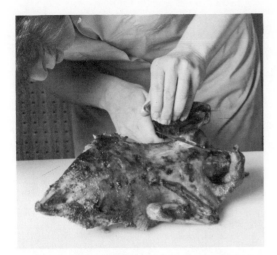

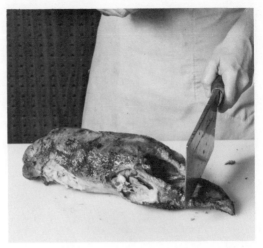

2. Remove the wing by cutting through the joint at the shoulder with one hand and pulling it away with the other hand. After removing both wings, separate the three parts of each wing by cutting through the two joints. Place both wings, reassembled, on the serving platter on either side of the neck.

3. Remove the tail and place it on the serving platter between the two legs.

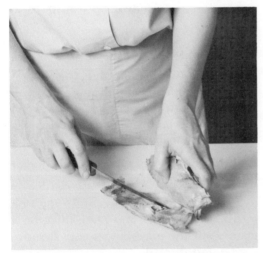

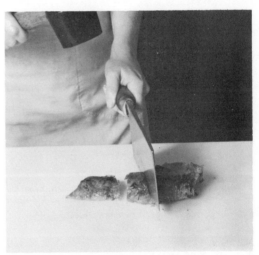

6. Separate the skin from the breast and the thigh. Scrape away any fat that has not been rendered out during the cooking process and replace the skin. Cut the breast crosswise into 1-inch pieces. Reassemble the pieces on the serving platter on one side of the neck, touching the backbone.

7. Cross-cut the thigh into 1-inch pieces, then reassemble the pieces on the serving platter above the leg and below the breast.

(continued)

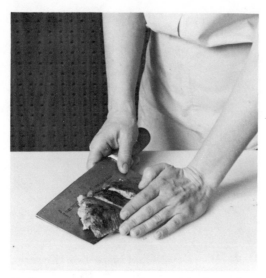

8. Repeat this procedure with the other breast and thigh.

9. The whole bird reshaped.

CHICKEN WINGS WITH OYSTER SAUCE

Canton/Guangzhou

8 chicken wings

MARINADE
2 teaspoons water chestnut powder
1 tablespoon sesame oil
1 tablespoon dark soy sauce
1 teaspoon honey
1 clove garlic, minced
2 teaspoons minced ginger root
4 scallions (white and green parts), chopped

3 tablespoons salt-free chicken stock

1 tablespoon oyster sauce
2 tablespoons sherry

2 tablespoons peanut oil

PREPARATION

Cut off the tips of the chicken wings and reserve them for stock. Cut the main wing bone from the second joint, making 16 pieces. Place the chicken pieces and the ingredients for the marinade in a bowl; toss with your hands. Marinate for 1 hour.

COOKING PROCEDURE

Place the wok over high heat for about 1 minute. Add the oil and heat until hot but not smoking. Add the chicken mixture and sauté for 5 minutes, turning the chicken pieces occasionally.

Add the chicken stock, cover, and simmer for 10 more minutes.

Remove the chicken pieces from the wok with a wire strainer and place them on a plate. Pour the juices into a cup. Remove the fat and discard.

Return the chicken pieces and the sauce to the wok. Turn the heat to high. Add the oyster sauce and sherry; stir-fry for another minute. Empty the contents of the wok onto a heated serving dish and serve immediately.

YIELD *2–6 servings*

FIVE FLAVORS CHICKEN

This is considered a home-style dish because the chicken is cooked without removing the skin and bones; this makes it very flavorful. Since Five Flavors Chicken is delicious at any temperature, it is recommended for buffets and picnics.

2 pounds chicken, whole or parts

MARINADE
1¹/2 teaspoons ground Szechwan Peppercorn Powder*
1 teaspoon Five Spice Powder*
1 tablespoon light soy sauce
1 tablespoon sherry
1 tablespoon hoisin sauce

1 cup leeks (white and lighter green parts only), split and cut in 1-inch pieces
3 slices ginger root, minced

DEGLAZING LIQUID
¹/4 cup sherry
¹/4 cup salt-free chicken stock

3 tablespoons peanut oil

PREPARATION

Have the butcher chop the chicken into 1¹/2-inch pieces, with skin and bone intact. Rinse and dry the chicken well. Remove the skin from each piece except for the wings.

Combine the ingredients for the marinade. Pour the marinade over the chicken and toss with your hands until the chicken is well coated. Refrigerate for ¹/2 hour or up to 24 hours.

COOKING PROCEDURE

Place the wok over high heat for about 1 minute. Add the oil and heat until hot but not smoking. Add the chicken; stir-fry 5 minutes. If the chicken is browning too quickly, lower the heat.

Add the leeks and ginger; continue to stir-fry another 5 minutes.

Using a spatula, place the chicken, leeks, and ginger in a wire strainer. Let it drain a minute over the wok, then empty the contents of the strainer into a colander set over a bowl and drain well. Transfer to a heated serving dish.

Pour off the remaining fat from the wok. Deglaze the wok with the sherry and chicken stock. Pour the sauce over the chicken and serve immediately.

YIELD *2–6 servings*

NOTES

Tip Deglazing means incorporating into the sauce all the coagulated juices left in the bottom of the cooking vessel by cooking briefly while stirring.

FRIED CHICKEN WITH SCALLION SAUCE

Canton/Guangzhou

1 whole 3-pound chicken

SEASONING SAUCE
1 tablespoon dark soy sauce
2 tablespoons sherry
2 tablespoons chicken stock

$1/2$ cup chopped scallions (white and green parts)

6 cups peanut oil

PREPARATION

Have the butcher chop the chicken into $1 1/2$-inch pieces with the skin and bone intact. Rinse and dry the chicken well. Separate the dark meat from the white meat.

Combine the ingredients for the seasoning sauce.

COOKING PROCEDURE

Place the wok over high heat for about 1 minute. Pour in the oil; turn the heat to medium until the oil reaches 375 degrees. Turn the heat to high. Fry the dark-meat chicken pieces for 5 minutes. Using a strainer, remove the chicken from the wok. Drain well by placing the pieces in a single layer on several sheets of paper towels.

Reheat the oil to 375 degrees; fry the white-meat chicken pieces for 4 minutes. Using a wire strainer, remove the chicken pieces; drain separately on paper towels.

Reheat the oil to 375 degrees; refry the dark-meat chicken pieces for 30 seconds. Remove them with the wire strainer and drain.

Reheat the oil to 375 degrees; refry the white-meat chicken pieces for 30 seconds. Remove them with the wire strainer and drain.

Pour off all the oil in the wok through a fine-mesh sieve. Return the browned drippings to the wok.

Immediately add scallions; stir-fry over medium heat until slightly charred.

Restir the seasoning sauce; add it all at once to the wok and stir 1 minute.

Turn the heat to high. Return the chicken pieces to the wok; mix well, evenly coating the chicken with sauce. Empty the contents of the wok onto a heated serving dish and serve immediately.

YIELD 3–8 servings

BRAISED GINGERED CHICKEN Peking/Beijing

1 whole 3–3¹/₂-pound chicken

MARINADE
1 clove garlic, minced
2 teaspoons light soy sauce
1 teaspoon sugar

¹/₃ cup sherry
³/₄ cup salt-free chicken stock
2¹/₂ tablespoons dark miso

1 cup leeks (white and green parts), split and
  cut in 1-inch pieces
2 slices ginger root

2 tablespoons peanut oil

PREPARATION

Have the butcher chop the chicken into 1¹/₂-inch pieces with the skin and bone intact. Rinse and dry the chicken well. Remove the skin from each piece except for the wings. Mix the marinade and toss the chicken pieces in it. Refrigerate for 4 hours or up to 24 hours.

Combine the sherry, stock, and miso.

COOKING PROCEDURE

Place the wok over high heat for about 1 minute. Add the oil and heat until it is hot but not smoking. Add half the amount of the chicken and stir-fry slowly, allowing the pieces to brown. Cook the chicken for about 2 minutes. Holding a wire strainer in one hand and a spatula in the other, transfer the chicken from the wok to the wire strainer, allowing the chicken to drain over the wok. Place the chicken pieces on a plate.

In the oil that remains in the wok, repeat the entire process with the second half of the chicken.

Add the leeks and ginger slices to the wok; stir-fry a few seconds.

Return the browned chicken pieces to the wok; stir-fry a few seconds.

Add the sherry, stock, and miso to the wok. Bring to a boil, stir well, then cover and cook at a fast simmer over medium-low heat for 20 to 25 minutes, checking every 10 minutes (see Tip). At the end of the cooking period, no sauce should remain in the wok—only a dark, rich glaze coating the chicken.

Remove the chicken pieces from the wok with a wire strainer, leaving behind any fat residue. Serve immediately.

YIELD *3–8 servings*

NOTES

Timing Braised Gingered Chicken can be prepared a day ahead and reheated in a heatproof serving dish with a loose cover. Allow approximately 15 minutes in a preheated 350-degree oven.

Tip If the stock evaporates before the chicken has finished cooking, pour in ¹/₂ cup of water around the sides of the wok. If too much liquid remains at the end of the cooking time, remove the cover, turn the heat to high, and stir the chicken slowly until the sauce is reduced and glazes the chicken.

Substitution Instead of chicken, this recipe can be made with 2 pounds of spareribs cut in 1-inch pieces. Cook the spareribs 45 minutes. Just before serving, place the spareribs in a heatproof serving dish and run them under the broiler for 5 to 7 minutes. Tilt the dish to remove the fat before serving.

BRAISED CHICKEN WITH BLACK BEANS   Peking/Beijing

Earthenware (clay) pots are exotic-looking, practical, and decorative enough to bring to the table. Braised Chicken with Black Beans is traditionally served in an earthenware cooking vessel, which is literally translated from the Chinese as "sand pot." It is the best way to produce the rich, concentrated flavor of the braised dishes enjoyed by the northern Chinese in wintertime.

1 whole 3–3 1/2-pound chicken

SEASONING SAUCE
1/2 cup salt-free chicken stock
1 tablespoon oyster sauce
1 tablespoon dark soy sauce
1/4 cup sherry

BINDER
1 tablespoon water chestnut powder
   dissolved in
2 tablespoons sherry

2 tablespoons fermented black beans
1 clove garlic, minced
2 teaspoons minced ginger root

1/2 cup roll-oblique-cut winter bamboo shoots
2 fresh chili peppers, cleaned, seeded, and
   triangle-cut
3 scallions (white and green parts), slant-cut
   in 2-inch pieces

2 tablespoons peanut oil

SPECIAL EQUIPMENT
1-quart earthenware casserole with cover

PREPARATION

Remove the wings and legs and reserve them for use in another recipe. Skin and bone the chicken. The breast and thigh meat combined should yield 1 pound.

As the white meat cooks faster than the dark, cut the white meat into 1 1/2-inch cubes, the dark meat into 1-inch cubes.

Combine the ingredients for the seasoning sauce.

Mix the binder.

COOKING PROCEDURE

Place the wok over high heat for about 1 minute. Add the oil and heat until hot but not smoking. Add the chicken cubes; stir-fry for 2 minutes. Turn off the heat. Remove the chicken cubes from the wok with a spatula and a wire strainer, allowing the fat to drip through and remain in the wok. Place the chicken in an earthenware casserole.

Return the wok to high heat. Add the black beans, garlic, and ginger; stir-fry 1 minute.

Add the bamboo shoots, chili peppers, and scallions; continue to stir-fry 1 more minute.

Restir the seasoning sauce and add it all at once to the wok. Bring it to a boil and stir the contents of the wok for about 1 minute.

Pour the contents of the wok into the earthenware casserole. Cover and simmer over a medium-low heat for 10 to 15 minutes.

Remove cover. Restir binder and add it to the casserole, stirring until the sauce thickens. Serve immediately in the earthenware casserole.

YIELD *3–8 servings*

(continued)

NOTES

Timing The entire preparation and cooking can be done a day ahead. Remove the contents of the clay casserole to a bowl and refrigerate. Before reheating the Braised Chicken with Black Beans, allow it to return to room temperature. To reheat, cover the earthenware pot and heat for 15 minutes in a preheated 350-degree oven, or for 5 minutes over low heat on top of the stove.

Tip When cooking this dish ahead, do not thicken the sauce until ready to serve.

Substitutions For the earthenware pot, a heavy-lidded saucepan of enamel, copper, or iron can be used.

SOY-BRAISED CHICKEN   Canton/Guangzhou

This is a home-style dish which is both simple and delicious.

1 whole chicken, or chicken parts (2¹/₂ pounds total)

MARINADE
3 scallions (white and green parts), cut in 1-inch pieces
¹/₄ cup sherry
2 tablespoons wine vinegar
1 tablespoon sugar
1 tablespoon light soy sauce
2 tablespoons dark soy sauce
5 tablespoons salt-free chicken stock

PREPARATION

With a heavy cleaver and rubber mallet, cut the chicken or chicken parts into serving pieces about 1¹/₂ inches long. Place the chicken pieces and the ingredients for the marinade in a bowl; mix well. Marinate for 30 minutes.

COOKING PROCEDURE

Place the wok over high heat for about 1 minute. Add the chicken and all the marinade; bring to a boil over high heat. Cover, turn the heat to medium low, and simmer 15 to 20 minutes. Remove the cover; turn the heat to medium high. Stirring with a wooden spoon, turn the chicken until the sauce reduces into a thick, syrupy glaze. Empty the contents onto a heated serving dish and serve immediately.

YIELD *2–6 servings*

CHICKEN CHENGDU STYLE   Szechwan/Sichuan

Chengdu is the capital of Szechwan, a hot, tropical inland province where they grow and eat a large quantity of not only peanuts, but also chili peppers and spices. Many of the chili peppers are dried and made into a chili paste, which is added to seasoning sauces in varying quantities. The principal ingredient that makes this dish spicy is the chili paste. In America, the closest prepared sauce we have to the hot soya paste of Szechwan is Peking broad bean paste.

1 pound boneless, skinless chicken

MARINADE
1 egg white
1 tablespoon water chestnut powder
1 tablespoon sherry

SEASONING SAUCE
2 teaspoons water chestnut powder
  dissolved in
1 tablespoon chicken stock
1 tablespoon Peking broad bean paste
1 tablespoon dark soy sauce
1 teaspoon Hot Sauce*
2 teaspoons black rice vinegar
1 teaspoon sugar
2 tablespoons sherry

1 tablespoon minced garlic
1 tablespoon minced ginger root
2 scallions (white and green parts), slant-cut
  in 1-inch pieces

¹/₄ cup peanuts, roasted**

2 cups peanut oil

2 tablespoons sesame oil

PREPARATION

Partially freeze the chicken, then cut it in 1¹/₂ by 2¹/₂-inch slices ¹/₄ inch thick. Place the chicken slices and the ingredients for the marinade in a bowl and stir in one direction vigorously with chopsticks. Place the mixture in the refrigerator for at least 1 hour or up to 12 hours.

Combine the ingredients for seasoning sauce.

COOKING PROCEDURE

Place the wok over high heat for about 1 minute. Pour in the peanut oil; turn the heat to medium until the oil reaches 325 degrees. Restir the chicken in the marinade. Turn the heat to high and add the contents of the bowl to the wok all at once, stirring in a circular motion with a pair of chopsticks for 1¹/₂ to 2 minutes, or until the chicken becomes opaque. Turn off the heat and pour the oil and the chicken into a colander set over a bowl. Shake the colander gently to aid the draining, then place it over a clean bowl.

Turn the heat to high. Add the garlic, ginger, and scallions to the wok; stir-fry 30 seconds.

Restir the seasoning sauce and add it all at once to the wok; stir-fry 30 seconds.

Return the chicken to the wok, along with the peanuts; stir-fry a few more seconds, or until the sauce has evenly coated the chicken.

Turn off the heat; add sesame oil and mix briefly. Empty the contents of the wok onto a heated serving dish and serve immediately.

YIELD *3–8 servings*

NOTES

Substitutions For the Peking broad bean paste, you can substitute 1 tablespoon of bean sauce or dark miso plus an additional 1 teaspoon of Hot Sauce.

CHUNKED CHICKEN HUNAN STYLE   **Hunan**

I have enjoyed many outstanding dishes at Chinese restaurants in New York City, one of which was Chunked Chicken Hunan Style, the creation of Mr. Chou and Chef Ho who were kind enough to show me how this dish is prepared.

6 to 7 chicken thighs (³/4 pound yield when boned and skinned)

MARINADE
¹/2 egg white
¹/2 tablespoon sherry
1 tablespoon water chestnut powder

SEASONING SAUCE
1 teaspoon water chestnut powder dissolved in
1 tablespoon sherry
1 tablespoon dark soy sauce
1 tablespoon light soy sauce
1 tablespoon sherry
2 tablespoons chicken stock
1 teaspoon sugar
1 teaspoon Chinese red vinegar

12 whole dried chili peppers

1 clove garlic, minced
1 teaspoon minced ginger
2 scallions (white and green parts), chopped

2 cups peanut oil

2 teaspoons sesame oil

PREPARATION

Bone and skin the chicken thighs, then dice them into 1¹/4-inch pieces. Place the chicken and the ingredients for the marinade in a bowl and stir in one direction vigorously with chopsticks. Place the mixture in the refrigerator for at least 1 hour or up to 12 hours.

Combine the ingredients for the seasoning sauce.

COOKING PROCEDURE

Place the wok over high heat for about 1 minute. Pour in the peanut oil; turn the heat to medium until the oil reaches 350 degrees. Restir the chicken in the marinade; turn the heat to high and add the contents of the bowl to the wok all at once, stirring with a pair of chopsticks and separating the chicken pieces if they stick together. Fry the chicken for about 2 minutes. Turn off the heat and pour the oil and the chicken into a colander set over a bowl. Shake the colander gently to aid the draining, then place it over a clean bowl.

Return the wok to medium heat and add the chili peppers; stir-fry about 1 minute or until they turn much darker, almost black.

Add the garlic, ginger, and scallions; turn the heat to high and continue to stir-fry another minute.

Return the cooked chicken to the wok and mix briefly.

Restir the seasoning sauce and add it all at once to the wok; stir-fry about 30 seconds.

Turn off the heat and add the sesame oil. Mix briefly. Empty the contents of the wok onto a heated serving dish and serve immediately.

YIELD *2–6 servings*

This is a variation on Mo Shu Ro, using chicken instead of pork. Because the egg pancake covers the chicken-vegetable mixture, it is given this rather whimsical title. This dish is usually served as part of a Chinese meal, but because of the eggs and accompanying light chicken and vegetable mixture, it makes an excellent brunch.

1/3 pound boneless, skinless chicken breast

MARINADE
1/2 egg white
1 teaspoon sherry
1 teaspoon water chestnut powder
1/4 teaspoon salt

1 cup bean sprouts

1/4 cup Chinese mushrooms, soaked and shredded**
1 cup leeks (white part only), split and shredded

2 tablespoons tree ears, soaked and shredded**
1/2 cup shredded bamboo shoots

1 cake Spiced Pressed Bean Curd*, shredded

SEASONING SAUCE
2 teaspoons water chestnut powder dissolved in
1 tablespoon sherry
2 tablespoons dark soy sauce
1 tablespoon reduced mushroom stock**, cooled
1/2 teaspoon sugar

DIPPING SAUCE
2 tablespoons hoisin sauce
1/2 tablespoon sherry
1 teaspoon sesame oil

6 Peking Doilies*

2 eggs, beaten

1 scallion (white and green parts), shredded

4 tablespoons peanut oil

PREPARATION

Partially freeze the chicken; slice, then shred. Place the chicken and the ingredients for the marinade in a bowl and stir in one direction vigorously with chopsticks. Place the mixture in the refrigerator for at least 1 hour or up to 12 hours.

Having reconstituted the mushrooms and tree ears and done the necessary cutting, place the various groups of ingredients in separate bowls.

Combine the ingredients for the seasoning sauce.

Combine the ingredients for the dipping sauce.

COOKING PROCEDURE

Place 2 quarts of water in a 14-inch round-bottom stainless steel wok. Stack the doilies, then wrap them in a cloth napkin and place them in a bamboo steamer. Bring the water in the wok to a boil; place the bamboo steamer on top of the wok and allow the doilies to steam while stir-frying the filling.

Place a second wok over high heat for about 2 minutes. Dry-cook the bean sprouts without oil for 2 minutes or until they scorch. Remove the bean sprouts from the wok.

Return the wok to high heat; add 2 tablespoons of peanut oil, and heat until hot but not smoking.

Restir the chicken shreds in the marinade and add the contents of the bowl to the wok all at once; stir-fry until the chicken shreds turn white (opaque). Remove the chicken from the wok.

Return the wok to high heat and add 1 tablespoon of peanut oil. Add the mushrooms and leeks; stir-fry 2 minutes.

Add the tree ears and bamboo shoots; stir-fry 1 minute.

Add the bean curd; stir-fry 1 more minute.

Restir the seasoning sauce and add it all at once to the wok along with the cooked chicken shreds; stir-fry another 30 seconds.

Add the bean sprouts and mix briefly. Empty the contents of the wok onto a heated serving dish.

Place a 10-inch iron skillet over high heat for 30 seconds. Add 1 tablespoon oil, tilting the skillet to distribute the oil evenly. Add the beaten eggs, rotating the skillet so the eggs cover the entire surface. When the eggs are set into a pancake, remove it from the skillet and place it over the filling mixture.

Remove the doilies from the steamer.

PRESENTATION

Each person takes a doily, spreads it with about 1 teaspoon of the dipping sauce, adds a few shreds of scallion, then places a few tablespoons of the filling in the doily. The doily is then rolled and eaten.

YIELD *2–6 servings*

NOTES

Tip An alternative as well as easier way of serving this dish would be to make an egg pancake, shred it and add it along with the bean sprouts at the end.

CHUN-PI CHICKEN

Chun-Pi, meaning orange peel, is only one of the many interesting flavors in this dish. The unique combination of seasonings makes Chun-Pi Chicken one of my favorite recipes. In order to appreciate the subtlety of tastes, serve this dish as a separate course.

1 pound boneless, skinless chicken

MARINADE
1 egg white
1 tablespoon water chestnut powder
1 tablespoon sherry

2 pieces (1 × 2 inches) dried orange peel
10 whole dried chili peppers
1 whole star anise
1 teaspoon Szechwan Peppercorn Powder*

SEASONING SAUCE
2 teaspoons water chestnut powder dissolved in
2 tablespoons sherry
2 tablespoons dark soy sauce
1 tablespoon black rice vinegar
2 teaspoons sugar
3 tablespoons Fermented Wine Rice* (measured with the liquid)

10 shallots, peeled, left whole

1 tablespoon sweet butter

2 cups peanut oil

1 tablespoon sesame oil

PREPARATION

Partially freeze the chicken, then cut it in 1½ × 2½-inch slices ¼ inch thick. Place the chicken and the ingredients for the marinade in a bowl and stir in one direction vigorously with chopsticks. Place the mixture in the refrigerator for at least 1 hour or up to 12 hours.

Break the orange peel into small pieces.

Combine the ingredients for the seasoning sauce.

Sauté the shallots in the 1 tablespoon butter for 2 to 3 minutes over a low heat. Remove them from the wok and reserve.

COOKING PROCEDURE

Place the wok over high heat for about 1 minute. Pour in the peanut oil; turn the heat to medium until the oil reaches 325 degrees. Restir the chicken in the marinade; turn the heat to high and add the contents of the bowl to the wok all at once, stirring with a pair of chopsticks in a circular motion for about 1 minute, or until the chicken turns opaque. Turn off the heat and pour out the oil and the chicken into a colander set over a bowl. Shake the colander gently to aid the draining, then place it over a clean bowl.

Return the wok to medium heat. Add the sesame oil. Add the orange peel, chili peppers, star anise, and Szechwan Peppercorn Powder. Stir-fry for about 1 minute or until the orange peel has turned a darker brown.

Return the heat to high. Restir the seasoning sauce and add it all at once to the wok; stir-fry about 30 seconds.

Return the cooked chicken and the shallots to the wok, continuing to stir-fry 1 more minute.

Turn off the heat. Remove the star anise. Empty the contents of the wok onto a heated serving dish and serve immediately.

YIELD *3–8 servings*

NOTES

Tip The purpose of slicing the chicken is so that the seasoning sauce is better absorbed.

Substitutions Depending upon personal preference, either all white-meat chicken or both light- and dark-meat chicken can be used.

SZECHWAN DICED CHICKEN

Szechwan/Sichuan

1 whole 3¹/₂-pound chicken, or
³/₄ pound boneless chicken

MARINADE
1 egg white
2 teaspoons sherry
¹/₂ tablespoon water chestnut powder

2 teaspoons minced garlic
2 teaspoons minced ginger
2 scallions (white and green parts), chopped

¹/₄ cup Chinese mushrooms, soaked and
    diced**
¹/₂ cup cleaned, seeded, triangle-cut sweet red
    peppers

¹/₂ cup snow peas, strung and slant-cut

SEASONING SAUCE
2 teaspoons water chestnut powder
    dissolved in
1 tablespoon sherry
1¹/₂ tablespoons dark soy sauce
1 tablespoon sherry
2 teaspoons Hot Sauce*
¹/₂ teaspoon sugar
1 teaspoon Chinese red vinegar
2 tablespoons reduced mushroom stock**,
    cooled

2 cups peanut oil

1 teaspoon sesame oil

¹/₂ teaspoon Szechwan Peppercorn Powder*

PREPARATION

Remove the wings and legs and reserve for another recipe, then skin and bone the chicken. Dice the breast into 1-inch pieces. Dice the thighs into ³/₄-inch pieces. Place the chicken and the ingredients for the marinade in a bowl and stir vigorously in one direction with chopsticks. Place the mixture in the refrigerator for at least 1 hour or up to 12 hours.

Having reconstituted the mushrooms and done the necessary cutting, place the two groups of ingredients in separate bowls.

Combine the ingredients for the seasoning sauce.

COOKING PROCEDURE

Place the wok over high heat for about 1 minute. Pour in the peanut oil; turn the heat to medium until the oil reaches 325 degrees. Restir the chicken in the marinade; turn the heat to high and add the contents of the bowl to the wok all at once, stirring with a pair of chopsticks in a circular motion for about 2 minutes. Turn off the heat and pour out the oil and the chicken into a colander set over a bowl. Shake the colander gently to aid the draining, then place it over a clean bowl.

Return the wok to high heat; stir-fry the garlic, ginger, and scallions for 30 seconds.

Add mushrooms and peppers; stir-fry 1 minute.

Add the snow peas; stir-fry 30 seconds.

Restir the seasoning sauce and add it all at once to the wok along with the chicken; stir-fry about 30 seconds. Turn off the flame. Add sesame oil; mix briefly. Empty the contents of the wok onto a heated serving dish. Sprinkle with Szechwan Peppercorn Powder. Serve immediately.

YIELD 2–6 servings

SHREDDED CHICKEN WITH GARLIC SAUCE

Szechwan/Sichuan

³/₄ pound boneless, skinless chicken

MARINADE
1 egg white
2 teaspoons water chestnut powder
2 teaspoons sherry

¹/₂ cup shredded scallions (white and green parts)
2 cleaned, seeded, shredded fresh chili peppers
1 tablespoon minced garlic
2 teaspoons minced ginger root

2 tablespoons tree ears, soaked and shredded**
¹/₂ cup shredded bamboo shoots

SEASONING SAUCE
1 teaspoon water chestnut powder dissolved in
2 tablespoons sherry
2 tablespoons dark soy sauce
2 tablespoons chicken stock
2 teaspoons sugar
2 teaspoons wine vinegar
1 teaspoon Hot Sauce*

2 cups peanut oil

1 tablespoon sesame oil

PREPARATION

Partially freeze the chicken; slice thin, then shred.

Place the chicken shreds and the ingredients for the marinade in a bowl and stir in one direction vigorously with chopsticks. Place the mixture in the refrigerator for at least 1 hour or up to 12 hours.

Having reconstituted the tree ears and done the necessary cutting, place the two groups of ingredients in separate bowls.

Combine the ingredients for the seasoning sauce.

COOKING PROCEDURE

Place the wok over high heat for about 1 minute. Pour in the peanut oil; turn the heat to medium until the oil reaches 325 degrees. Restir the chicken in the marinade. Turn the heat to high and add the contents of the bowl to the wok all at once, stirring in a circular motion with a pair of chopsticks for about 1 minute or until the chicken turns white (opaque). Turn off the heat and pour out the oil and the chicken into a colander set over a bowl. Shake the colander gently to aid the draining, then place it over a clean bowl.

Return the wok to high heat and add the scallions, chili peppers, garlic, and ginger; stir-fry 1 minute.

Add the tree ears and bamboo shoots; continue to stir-fry another 30 seconds.

Restir the seasoning sauce and add it all at once to the wok; stir-fry about 30 seconds.

Return the chicken to the wok; stir-fry another 15 seconds, or until the sauce has evenly coated the chicken shreds.

Add the sesame oil; turn off heat. Mix a few seconds. Empty the contents of the wok onto a heated serving dish and serve immediately.

YIELD *2–6 servings*

CHICKEN VELVET

Chicken Velvet is appealing for its texture—silky, delicate, and soft. It is served at banquets in northern China.

1 whole chicken breast (14–16 ounces), skinned and boned

1¹/₂ tablespoons water chestnut powder
1 cup chicken stock
¹/₂ teaspoon salt
¹/₂ teaspoon sugar
2 tablespoons sherry

8 egg whites

BINDER
1 teaspoon water chestnut powder dissolved in
1 tablespoon sherry
¹/₃ cup chicken stock

1 cup chicken stock

1 cup snow peas, strung and slant-cut

2 cups peanut oil

*¹/₄ cup minced Smithfield ham***

PREPARATION

Cut the chicken into small pieces and puree in a blender or food processor.

Place the water chestnut powder in a bowl and gradually add the 1 cup of chicken stock; then add the salt, sugar, and sherry and mix well. Combine with the chicken puree.

In a separate bowl, beat the egg whites with a wire whisk until foamy. Fold the chicken mixture into the beaten egg whites. This will take 4 to 5 minutes.

Mix the binder.

COOKING PROCEDURE

Place the wok over high heat for about 1 minute, then turn the heat to medium. Pour in the oil and heat until the oil reaches 325 degrees. Add the chicken mixture to the wok all at once, stirring gently in a circular motion with a pair of chopsticks until the mixture has set. Turn off the heat and pour out the oil and the chicken mixture into a colander set over a bowl. Shake the colander gently to aid the draining, then place it over a clean bowl.

Heat the remaining cup of chicken stock until it is warm. Holding the colander over the sink, pour the warm chicken stock over the chicken mixture to help rinse off some of the oil. The entire dish can be prepared several hours ahead up to this point.

Return the wok to high heat. Stir-fry the snow peas for 30 seconds.

Return the chicken mixture to the wok.

Restir the binder and add it to the wok, stirring until the sauce thickens. Empty the contents of the wok onto a heated serving dish. Sprinkle with minced ham and serve immediately.

YIELD *2–6 servings*

ORANGE CHICKEN

This is a recipe I created combining the texture of Cantonese Lemon Chicken and the seasoning of Szechwan's Orange Beef*.

2 whole chicken breasts, 14 ounces each

MARINADE
2 tablespoons light soy sauce
1 teaspoon sesame oil
1 tablespoon sherry

SEASONING SAUCE
1 teaspoon water chestnut powder
    dissolved in
2 tablespoons sherry
2 tablespoons Kikkoman soy sauce
2 tablespoons sugar
2 tablespoons salt-free chicken stock
*1 teaspoon Hot Sauce**
1/2 teaspoon wine vinegar
1 teaspoon sesame oil

2 pieces dried orange peel, 1 × 2 inches

3 egg whites, slightly beaten

3/4 cup lumpy water chestnut powder

2 scallions (white and green parts), chopped
2 teaspoons minced ginger root
1 clove garlic, minced
1 cleaned, seeded, chopped fresh red chili
    pepper

3 cups peanut oil

PREPARATION

Skin and bone the chicken breasts. Separate the fillet from the cutlet of each, yielding 8 pieces.

Combine the ingredients for the marinade. Dip the chicken pieces in the marinade and let stand for 30 minutes. If marinating longer, refrigerate.

Combine the ingredients for the seasoning sauce.

COOKING PROCEDURE

Place the wok over high heat for about 1 minute. Pour in the oil; turn the heat to medium and allow the oil to reach 350 degrees. Add the orange peel; fry for about 15 seconds or until it turns darker brown. Drain on paper towels. Allow to cool, then crush the orange peel by hand or in an electric coffee mill; set aside.

Dip the chicken in beaten egg whites, one piece at a time. Coat the chicken in water chestnut powder; shake off excess. Turn heat to high, until the oil reaches 350 degrees. Fry half the amount of chicken for 4 minutes, turning once at midpoint. The chicken should fry in the oil at a temperature of 325 degrees. Using a wire strainer, remove the chicken from the wok. Drain well by placing the chicken in a single layer on several sheets of paper towels. Reheat the oil to 350 degrees and repeat the frying and draining process with the second batch of chicken. The chicken breasts must cool at least 30 minutes before they are fried a second time. Strain the oil through a sieve lined with cheesecloth. Return the strained oil to the wok.

Reheat the oil to 375 degrees. Refry the chicken breasts over high heat, a few pieces at a time, for about 30 seconds, turning once at midpoint. Drain on several sheets of paper towels. Remove the oil from the wok.

When all the chicken has been fried a second time, slice the chicken breasts crosswise into 1/2-inch pieces; place them on a flat, heated serving dish.

Place the wok over high heat and heat for 30 seconds. Add 1 tablespoon of the cooked oil and heat until hot but not smoking. Add the scallions, ginger, garlic, and chili pepper. Stir-fry about 30 seconds.

Add the crushed orange peel and mix briefly.

Restir the seasoning sauce and add it all at once to the wok; stir well until the sauce thickens, about 30 seconds. Pour the sauce over the sliced chicken breasts and serve immediately.

YIELD *3–8 servings*

NOTES

Timing All the preparations, as well as the first frying of the chicken, can be done early in the day.

After the chicken has completely cooled, refrigerate it in a single layer. Allow the chicken to return to room temperature before the second frying.

Substitution You can substitute ¼ cup chopped red pepper for the chili pepper, in which case add an additional 1 teaspoon of Hot Sauce.

Hacked Chicken is another name for this dish where chicken is "hacked" into serving pieces prior to poaching. I prefer to poach the chicken whole to retain the maximum amount of juices. As it holds up well, it is an excellent luncheon choice for a cold buffet on a hot summer's day.

1 whole 3-pound chicken
2 cups leeks (green part only), cut into 1-inch pieces

SAUCE
3 tablespoons Sesame Seed Butter*
1^1/$_2$ tablespoons brewed black tea
^{1}/$_2$ tablespoon Chili Oil*, strained
1 teaspoon sugar
^{1}/$_2$ cup chopped scallions (white and green parts)
1^1/$_2$ tablespoons dark soy sauce
1 tablespoon Tientsin preserved vegetable, minced
2 tablespoons sesame oil
^{1}/$_2$ tablespoon minced garlic
2 tablespoons red wine vinegar
^{1}/$_2$ tablespoon Szechwan Peppercorn Powder*
2 tablespoons peanut oil

GARNISH
Watercress or stir-fried asparagus

COOKING PROCEDURE

Bring 2 cups of water to a boil in a saucepan. Add the chicken and leeks; turn the heat to high and return to a boil. Turn the heat to low, cover, and simmer for 30 minutes. Remove the chicken from the broth with a wire strainer and let it cool on a rack set over a plate. When the chicken is cool, shred it with your fingers.

Put the Sesame Seed Butter in a bowl; gradually stir in the tea until smooth. Add the Chili Oil, sugar, scallions, soy sauce, Tientsin preserved vegetable, sesame oil, garlic, vinegar, Szechwan Peppercorn Powder, and peanut oil and stir well to blend.

Several hours before serving, mix the chicken with the sauce. Transfer to a serving platter. Use the watercress to form a ring around the chicken, or garnish with roll-oblique-cut, stir-fried asparagus.

YIELD 3–8 servings

NOTES

Timing Both the sauce and the chicken (poached, cooled, and shredded) can be made the day ahead and refrigerated.

Tip The entire sauce, with the exception of the chopped scallions, can be made in a food processor.

Substitution For the Sesame Seed Butter, you can substitute tahini.

CHICKEN WITH FERMENTED RED WINE RICE

Fukien/Fujian

Fermented red wine rice is a specialty of Fukien Province. It adds an unusual flavor and appealing color to this subtle but savory dish.

2 whole chicken breasts, 14 ounces each

MARINADE
3 tablespoons Fermented Red Wine Rice*
1 tablespoon sherry
1/2 egg white
1 tablespoon water chestnut powder
2 teaspoons sugar
1 teaspoon salt

BINDER
1 teaspoon water chestnut powder
dissolved in
1 tablespoon sherry

1 pound fresh spinach leaves
1 clove garlic, minced

2 scallions (white and green parts), shredded

2 tablespoons Fermented Red Wine Rice

1/4 cup pine nuts, roasted**

2 cups peanut oil

PREPARATION

Bone and skin the chicken breasts, then partially freeze. Slice thin, then shred. Place the shredded chicken and the ingredients for the marinade in a bowl and stir in one direction vigorously with chopsticks. Place the mixture in the refrigerator for at least 1 hour or up to 12 hours.

Mix the binder.

COOKING PROCEDURE

Place the wok over high heat for about 1 minute. Pour in the oil; turn the heat to medium until the oil reaches 325 degrees. Restir the chicken in the marinade; turn the heat to high and add the contents of the bowl to the wok all at once, stirring with a pair of chopsticks in a circular motion for about 1 minute. Turn off the heat and pour out the oil and the chicken into a colander set over a bowl. Shake the colander gently to aid the draining process, then place over a clean bowl.

In another wok, stir-fry the spinach and garlic in 1 tablespoon of the cooked oil until the spinach wilts, about 1 to 2 minutes. Turn off the heat and leave the spinach in the second wok to keep it warm.

Add scallions to the first wok; stir-fry a few seconds.

Add the chicken; mix a few seconds.

Add the 2 tablespoons Fermented Red Wine Rice.

Restir the binder and add it, stirring until the sauce coats the chicken.

PRESENTATION

Arrange the spinach as a border on a heated serving dish. Empty the contents of the wok inside the spinach border and garnish with pine nuts.

YIELD *3–8 servings*

NOTES

Substitution Three bunches of watercress, stems removed, may be substituted for the spinach.

SLIVERED CHICKEN AND PORK   Hunan

This is a popular dish in Changsha, the capital of Hunan. Chili peppers, grown there locally, are used frequently and in large quantities. The people of Hunan have such a high tolerance for spice that the seeds and membranes are invariably included in the dish. Variations of Slivered Chicken and Pork are frequently served in workmen's restaurants in Changsha, using only shredded pork or only shredded chicken, the chicken sometimes being combined with locally grown vegetables. The savory quality of this dish, however, is partially a result of the combination of shredded chicken and pork.

1/2 pound boneless, skinless chicken breasts
1/2 pound boneless pork

MARINADE
1 egg white
1 tablespoon sherry
1 tablespoon water chestnut powder
1 teaspoon salt
1/4 teaspoon white pepper

SEASONING SAUCE
2 teaspoons water chestnut powder
    dissolved in
1 tablespoon sherry
3 tablespoons sherry
2 tablespoons chicken stock

1 tablespoon sesame oil
1 tablespoon Chili Oil*

2 cups split and shredded leeks (white part only)
1 tablespoon minced garlic

2 cups cleaned, seeded, shredded fresh chili peppers
1/3 cup shredded sweet red peppers
1 teaspoon salt
1/2 teaspoon sugar

2 cups peanut oil

PREPARATION

Partially freeze the chicken and the pork; slice both thin, then shred.

Place the chicken, pork, and the ingredients for the marinade in a bowl and stir in one direction vigorously with chopsticks. Place the mixture in the refrigerator for at least 1 hour or up to 12 hours.

Combine the ingredients for the seasoning sauce.

Combine the sesame oil and Chili Oil.

COOKING PROCEDURE

Place the wok over high heat for about 1 minute. Pour in the peanut oil; turn the heat to medium until the oil reaches 325 degrees. Restir the chicken and the pork in the marinade; turn the heat to high and add the contents of the bowl to the wok all at once, stirring in a circular motion with a pair of chopsticks for about 1 minute until the chicken and pork turn white (opaque). Turn off the heat and pour the contents of the wok into a colander set over a bowl. Shake the colander gently to aid the draining, then place over a clean bowl.

Return the wok to medium heat. Add the leeks and garlic; stir-fry 1 minute.

Turn the heat to high and add the chili peppers, sweet peppers, salt, and sugar; continue to stir-fry for another minute.

Restir the seasoning sauce and add it all at once to the wok along with the chicken and pork. Stir-fry about 30 seconds, then turn off the heat.

Add the sesame oil and Chili Oil; mix briefly. Empty the contents of the wok onto a heated serving dish and serve immediately.

YIELD *3–8 servings*

NOTES

Substitution For a less spicy version of this dish, you can substitute 1 cup of icicle radish (Chinese turnip) for 1 cup of the chili peppers.

SLIPPERY CHICKEN

The name of this dish derives from the smooth, slippery texture the chicken acquires with the addition of egg white.

1 pound boneless, skinless chicken breasts

MARINADE
2 egg whites
1 tablespoon sherry
1 tablespoon water chestnut powder

SEASONING SAUCE
2 teaspoons water chestnut powder
    dissolved in
2 tablespoons sherry
2 tablespoons dark soy sauce
3 tablespoons sherry
1 teaspoon sugar
1 teaspoon Chinese red vinegar
2 teaspoons Hot Sauce*
1 teaspoon sesame oil

6 scallions (white part only), shredded

1 clove garlic, crushed

1 pound fresh spinach leaves

¹/₂ teaspoon salt

2 cups peanut oil

PREPARATION

Partially freeze the chicken, slice thin, then shred. Place the chicken and the ingredients for the marinade in a bowl and stir in one direction vigorously with chopsticks. Place the mixture in the refrigerator for at least 1 hour or up to 12 hours.

Combine the ingredients for the seasoning sauce.

COOKING PROCEDURE

Place the wok over high heat for about 1 minute. Pour in the oil; turn the heat to medium until the oil reaches 325 degrees.

Restir the chicken in the marinade. Turn the heat to high and add the contents of the bowl to the wok all at once, stirring with a pair of chopsticks in a circular motion for about 1 minute, until the chicken shreds have turned opaque. Turn off the heat and pour the oil and the chicken into a colander set over a bowl. Shake the colander gently to aid the draining, then place it over a clean bowl.

Return the wok to high heat. Add the scallions; stir-fry for 30 seconds.

Restir the seasoning sauce and add it all at once to the wok along with the chicken; stir-fry about 30 seconds. Empty the contents of the wok onto one side of a heated serving dish.

Using a second wok, heat 1¹/₂ tablespoons of cooked oil until hot but not smoking. Add the garlic and allow it to sizzle for a few seconds.

Add the spinach; stir-fry until it begins to wilt (1 to 2 minutes).

Add the salt; continue to stir-fry for another minute. Empty the spinach onto the other side of the serving dish. Remove the garlic clove. Serve immediately.

YIELD *3–8 servings*

STIR-FRIED CHICKEN WITH WALNUTS   Peking/Beijing

1 pound boneless, skinless chicken breasts

MARINADE
1 egg white
1 tablespoon water chestnut powder
1 tablespoon sherry

1/2 cup whole shallots, peeled
1 tablespoon sweet butter

1 cup walnut halves

SEASONING SAUCE
1/2 teaspoon water chestnut powder
    dissolved in
1 tablespoon sherry
1 tablespoon light soy sauce
1 tablespoon dark soy sauce
1/2 teaspoon sugar

2 cups peanut oil

1 teaspoon sesame oil

PREPARATION

Dice the chicken into ³/₄-inch pieces. Place the chicken and the ingredients for the marinade in a bowl and stir in one direction vigorously with chopsticks. Place the mixture in the refrigerator for at least 1 hour or up to 12 hours.

Sauté the shallots in 1 tablespoon of butter for 2 to 3 minutes. Reserve.

Heat the peanut oil in a wok over a medium heat until it reaches 325 degrees. Place the walnuts in a wire strainer and lower them into the oil. Fry until golden brown, about 30 seconds. Remove the nuts from the oil and drain on paper towels.

Combine the ingredients for the seasoning sauce.

COOKING PROCEDURE

Place the wok over high heat for about 1 minute. Pour in the peanut oil; turn the heat to medium until the oil reaches 325 degrees. Restir the chicken in the marinade, turn the heat to high, and add contents of the bowl to the wok all at once, stirring with a pair of chopsticks in a circular motion for about 1½ minutes, or until the chicken turns opaque. Turn off the heat and pour the contents of the wok into a colander set over a bowl. Shake the colander gently to aid the draining, then place it over a clean bowl.

Turn the heat to high. Return the chicken pieces and shallots to the wok; stir-fry for 1 minute.

Restir the seasoning sauce and add it all at once to the wok, continuing to stir-fry a few more seconds or until the sauce has evenly glazed the chicken.

Add the walnuts; mix briefly, then turn off the heat.

Add the sesame oil; mix again briefly. Empty the contents of the wok onto a heated serving dish and serve immediately.

YIELD *3–8 servings*

SHREDDED SMOKED CHICKEN Szechwan/Sichuan

Shredded Smoked Chicken is easily prepared, but it relies on a crucial ingredient—smoked chicken, which is a variation on smoked duck. Since that recipe (Tea Smoked Duck*) calls for a 5-pound duck (or chicken), it is very possible that a portion of the bird could be set aside for this outstanding dish.

1/2 pound boneless, skinless chicken breasts

MARINADE
1 egg white
1/2 tablespoon sherry
1/2 tablespoon water chestnut powder

SEASONING SAUCE
2 teaspoons water chestnut powder
    dissolved in
2 tablespoons sherry
*1 teaspoon Hot Sauce**
1 tablespoon bean sauce
1/2 teaspoon salt

1/4 cup cleaned, seeded, shredded sweet red
    peppers
3/4 cup cleaned, seeded, shredded fresh chili
    peppers
1 tablespoon minced garlic

3 tablespoons whole coriander leaves
    (no stems)
1/2 pound smoked chicken with the skin
    attached, shredded

1/2 cup salt-free smoked chicken stock

2 cups peanut oil

1 tablespoon sesame oil and
*1 teaspoon Chili Oil**

PREPARATION

Bone and skin the chicken breasts. Partially freeze the chicken; then slice thin and shred. Place the chicken and the ingredients for the marinade in a bowl and stir in one direction vigorously with chopsticks. Place the mixture in the refrigerator for at least 1 hour or up to 12 hours.

Combine the ingredients for the seasoning sauce.

COOKING PROCEDURE

Place the wok over high heat for about 1 minute. Add the peanut oil and heat over medium heat until it reaches 325 degrees. Turn the heat to high.

Restir the chicken in the marinade and add the contents of the bowl to the wok all at once, stirring in a circular motion with a pair of chopsticks for about 1 minute. Turn off the heat and pour out the oil and the chicken into a colander set over a bowl. Shake the colander gently to aid the draining, then place over a clean bowl.

Return the wok to high heat. Add the peppers and garlic; stir-fry for 1 minute.

Add the coriander and the smoked and the fresh chicken; stir-fry a few seconds.

Pour in the stock around the sides of the wok and bring it to a boil.

Restir the seasoning sauce and add it all at once to the wok; stir-fry until the sauce thickens.

Turn off the heat. Add the sesame oil and Chili Oil and mix briefly. Empty the contents of the wok into a heated serving dish and serve immediately.

YIELD *3–8 servings*

Three Thoughts Chicken is interesting not only because of the three different seasonings, which result in contrasting flavors, but also because of the three different cooking techniques, which bring about a contrast in texture. Because of the complicated cooking procedures involved, this recipe is for the advanced cook. Read over the recipe carefully and use an individual tray for each of the Three Thoughts.

1 whole 5-pound chicken, legs and wings removed

FIRST THOUGHT CHICKEN
MARINADE #1
1 tablespoon light soy sauce
1 tablespoon sherry
1 teaspoon sesame oil

1 egg white, slightly beaten
1/4 cup lumpy water chestnut powder

SECOND THOUGHT CHICKEN
MARINADE #2
1 egg white
2 teaspoons water chestnut powder
2 teaspoons sherry

BINDER
1/2 teaspoon water chestnut powder
*   dissolved in*
1 tablespoon sherry
2 tablespoons chicken stock

1/3 cup cleaned, seeded, triangle-cut sweet red
*   peppers*
1 cup snow peas, strung and slant-cut
1/2 teaspoon salt
1/4 teaspoon sugar

THIRD THOUGHT CHICKEN
MARINADE #3
1 egg white
2 teaspoons water chestnut powder
2 teaspoons sherry

SEASONING SAUCE
1/2 teaspoon water chestnut powder
*   dissolved in*
1 tablespoon sherry
1 tablespoon dark soy sauce
2 tablespoons reduced chicken stock**
2 teaspoons Chinese red vinegar
2 teaspoons sugar
1 teaspoon Hot Sauce*

1 teaspoon minced ginger root
1 teaspoon minced garlic
2 scallions (white and green parts), chopped

BINDER FOR GARNISH
1 teaspoon water chestnut powder
*   dissolved in*
1 tablespoon sherry

GARNISH
3 bunches watercress, stems removed
1/2 teaspoon salt
1/2 teaspoon sugar

1 teaspoon sesame oil

2 cups peanut oil

PREPARATION

Divide the chicken as follows:

First Thought Chicken
Bone and skin one side of the chicken breast, separating the fillet from the cutlet. Place the chicken and the ingredients for Marinade #1 in a bowl and toss to coat. Place the mixture in the refrigerator for at least 1 hour or up to 12 hours.

Second Thought Chicken
Bone and skin the other side of the chicken breast. Partially freeze, then slice thin. Place the chicken and the ingredients for Marinade #2 in a bowl and stir in one direction vigorously with chopsticks. Place the mixture in the refrigerator for at least 1 hour or up to 12 hours.

Mix the binder for the garnish.

Third Thought Chicken
Skin and bone the thighs; dice in ½-inch pieces. Place the chicken and the ingredients for Marinade #3 in a bowl and stir in one direction vigorously with chopsticks. Place the mixture in the refrigerator for at least 1 hour or up to 12 hours. Mix the seasoning sauce. Mix the binder.

COOKING PROCEDURE

First Thought Chicken
Allow the chicken to become room temperature. Place the wok over high heat for about 1 minute. Pour in the 2 cups of peanut oil; turn the heat to medium until the oil reaches 350 degrees. Dip the chicken in the beaten egg white, then coat in water chestnut powder. Lower the chicken pieces into the oil and fry for 3 minutes, turning once at midpoint. Using a wire strainer, remove the chicken from the wok. Drain well by placing the chicken in a single layer on several sheets of paper towels.

Second Thought Chicken
Reheat the oil to 325 degrees. Restir the chicken slices in the marinade and add the contents of the bowl all at once to the wok, stirring in a circular motion with a pair of chopsticks for about 1 minute, or until the chicken turns opaque. Remove the chicken slices from the oil with a wire strainer; place in a colander set over a bowl. Shake the colander a few times to remove the excess oil. Place the chicken on a separate plate.

Third Thought Chicken
Reheat the oil to 325 degrees. Restir the diced dark-meat chicken in the marinade and add the contents of the bowl all at once to the wok, stirring in a circular motion with a pair of chopsticks for about 2 minutes. Remove the diced chicken from the oil with a wire strainer and place it in a colander set over a bowl. Reheat the oil to 375 degrees. Return the diced chicken to the wok; fry for another 30 seconds. Remove the diced chicken from the oil; place it in a colander set over a bowl.

First Thought Chicken
Reheat the oil to 375 degrees. Return the chicken pieces to the oil; fry over high heat for another minute, turning once at midpoint. Using a wire strainer, remove the chicken pieces from the wok. Drain well by placing the chicken in a single layer on several sheets of paper towels. Remove the oil from the wok.

Second Thought Chicken
Turn the heat to high; stir-fry the red peppers, snow peas, salt, and sugar for 1 minute.

Return the chicken breast slices to the wok; stir-fry briefly.

Restir the binder and add it to the wok, stirring until the sauce thickens. Place the Second Thought Chicken on one third of a large serving dish.

Third Thought Chicken
Return the wok to high heat. Add 1 tablespoon of the cooked oil; stir-fry the ginger, garlic, and scallions for 30 seconds.

Return the diced chicken to the wok; stir-fry briefly.

Restir the seasoning sauce and add it to the wok all at once; stir-fry another 30 seconds. Turn off the heat.

Add the 1 teaspoon of sesame oil; mix briefly. Place the Third Thought Chicken on one third of the same serving dish, leaving space for garnish.

Garnish
Place a second wok over high heat for about 1 minute. Heat 1 tablespoon of cooked oil for a few seconds. Add salt and sugar.

Add the watercress and stir-fry for 30 seconds. Restir the binder and add it to the wok, continuing to stir-fry another few seconds.

First Thought Chicken
Slice in ½-inch crosswise pieces. Place the First Thought Chicken on the remaining third of the serving dish.

Use the watercress as garnish in between the Three Thoughts Chicken. Serve immediately.

YIELD *3–8 servings*

Romance and fantasy play an important role in the labeling of dishes among Chinese chefs. Frequently, dishes are given names based on their appearance rather than the ingredients of which they are composed. The mulberry tree was chosen because it is indigenous to China, and the paper made from the bark of the tree is used to wrap another classic dish, Salt Baked Chicken. The paper from the mulberry tree is not edible, unlike the leaves from the paper mulberry plant, which are eaten as a vegetable.

1/2 pound boneless, skinless chicken breasts (3 chicken cutlets)

2 1/2 tablespoons water chestnut powder

PORK MIXTURE
1/2 pound ground pork
1 tablespoon sherry
1/2 teaspoon sugar
1 teaspoon water chestnut powder

SEASONING SAUCE
3 tablespoons Fermented Red Wine Rice*
2 teaspoons dark soy sauce
2 teaspoons light soy sauce
1 tablespoon sherry
1 teaspoon sugar

SPINACH SEASONING SAUCE
1 tablespoon sherry
1/2 teaspoon water chestnut powder
1 teaspoon sugar
1 teaspoon salt
1 teaspoon sesame oil

1/4 cup salt-free chicken stock (or more)

1/2 pound spinach leaves

3 tablespoons peanut oil

1 hard-boiled egg, cut in half

PREPARATION

Sandwich the chicken cutlets between 2 layers of plastic wrap. Using a rubber mallet, pound them until they are slightly thinner. Remove the plastic wrap and sprinkle the chicken with 1 tablespoon water chestnut powder, pressing in with the palm of the hand.

Combine the ingredients for the pork mixture and spread it over the chicken cutlets. Sprinkle with the remaining 1 1/2 tablespoons water chestnut powder, pressing down slightly with the palm of the hand.

Combine the ingredients for the seasoning sauce.

Combine the ingredients for the spinach seasoning sauce.

COOKING PROCEDURE

Place a 12-inch iron skillet over high heat for about 1 minute. Add 2 tablespoons of the oil and heat until hot but not smoking. Lower the chicken cutlets, chicken side down, into the skillet and sauté over medium heat for 3 to 4 minutes. Turn the cutlets over; fry for another 3 to 4 minutes. Remove the cutlets from the skillet; pour out any excess oil.

Restir the seasoning sauce and add it all at once to the skillet, stirring over a medium heat for about 30 seconds. Pour in the chicken stock; continue to stir a few seconds. Return the cutlets to the skillet, pork side down; simmer uncovered over a low heat in the sauce for 15 minutes, basting frequently with a spoon. The finished dish should have no excess sauce. Remove skillet from heat source.

Place wok over high heat for 30 seconds. Add the remaining tablespoon of oil and heat until hot but not smoking. Add the spinach; stir-fry 1 minute.

Add the spinach seasoning sauce; stir-fry a few more seconds. Remove wok from heat.

PRESENTATION

Transfer the cutlets to a cutting board, pork side up. Cut into long strips, ½ inch wide. Arrange the spinach on a heated serving dish and place the chicken strips on top of the spinach, pork side up, along with the halved egg, to resemble a tree with a moon. Serve immediately.

YIELD *2–6 servings*

NOTES

Timing The entire preparation can be done 24 hours in advance and refrigerated. The sautéing of the chicken cutlets can be done several hours ahead, in which case some juices will be released while the chicken is cooling. When the cutlets are returned to the skillet, these juices should be included.

Tip If the sauce evaporates before the end of the 15-minute period, add more stock.

BEGGAR'S CHICKEN   **Shanghai**

When I first ate this dish as part of a twenty-three-course banquet in Hong Kong, the chicken was presented in the classical manner—in its own baked clay covering, which was cracked with a mallet at the dining table. One of the several stories as to the origin of its name is as follows: A beggar who was starving saw a chicken, wrung its neck, packed it in mud, and threw it in a fire. When it was cooked, he tore the mud away from the chicken, thereby removing the feathers. While he was eating, an emperor who was traveling passed by. Attracted by the delicious aroma, the emperor dined with the beggar. He loved the flavor so much that he asked the beggar to share his secret with him of how to cook the chicken. The beggar told him, and the emperor added it to the list of imperial court dishes.

The adaptation of this recipe calls for a clay pot rather than the six pounds of clay that would be required to wrap the chicken.

1 fresh-killed 5-pound chicken

MARINADE
2 tablespoons dark soy sauce
1 tablespoon sherry

STUFFING
1 cup shredded pork

1 tablespoon dark soy sauce
1 tablespoon sherry
1 teaspoon salt
1/2 teaspoon sugar

1 cup shredded bamboo shoots
1/2 cup Chinese mushrooms, soaked and shredded**
1/2 cup tiger lily buds, soaked, hard ends and knots removed**
1/2 cup preserved hot turnip

3 lotus leaves soaked in boiling water for 15 minutes

1 tablespoon peanut oil

1 tablespoon sesame oil

SPECIAL EQUIPMENT
1 clay pot with cover
Unwaxed dental floss
Thick sewing needle
Butcher's twine

PREPARATION

Rinse and dry the chicken well. Rub it with the marinade and allow to marinate for 2 hours.

To make the stuffing Having reconstituted the mushrooms and lily buds and done the necessary cutting, place the wok over high heat for about 1 minute. Add the peanut oil and heat until hot but not smoking. Add the pork; stir-fry for 2 to 3 minutes or until it turns white. Add the soy sauce, sherry, salt and sugar; mix well. Add the bamboo shoots, mushrooms, lily buds, and turnip; stir-fry 1 more minute. Empty the contents of the wok onto a plate and allow to cool.

Submerge the clay pot in cold water for 15 minutes.

Rub the skin of the chicken with the sesame oil.

Place the stuffing in the cavity of the chicken; sew up each end with dental floss. Wrap the chicken in 3 layers of soaked lotus leaves, then tie with butcher's twine. Place the chicken in the clay pot and cover.

COOKING PROCEDURE

Place the clay pot in the center of a cold oven. Turn the heat to 250 degrees, increasing the temperature every 5 minutes until it reaches 450 degrees. After 1 hour turn the heat to 400 degrees; continue to bake for another 1½ hours. Remove the clay pot from the oven, and place it on a terry-cloth towel. Remove the cover, and let stand for 5 minutes. Cut the lotus leaves open. Slip a wide metal spatula underneath the chicken and brace the other side with a wooden spatula (in order not to tear the skin). Carefully remove the chicken from the clay pot and place it on a heated platter. Pour around the chicken the juices that have accumulated in the bottom of the clay pot. Carve the chicken with chopsticks. Serve each person a piece of chicken, juices, and stuffing.

YIELD *5–10 servings*

NOTES

Timing The stuffing can be prepared, cooked, and refrigerated the day before. The chicken can marinate up to 24 hours ahead. Turn the chicken over in the marinade several times during this period.

Tips Clay pots are very fragile. Extreme temperature changes will make them crack. This is the reason for placing the pot in a cold oven and gradually increasing the oven temperature.

Clay pots are washed with a nylon sponge and hot water after the pot has thoroughly cooled. Never use soap.

The purpose of rubbing the skin of the chicken with sesame oil is to prevent the lotus leaves from sticking.

Chapter 13

DUCK
AND SQUAB

BARBECUED DUCK PORTIONS

In China the average family has no oven. It is possible to purchase barbecued poultry, meat, and innards at barbecue houses which have central ovens. These barbecued meats are purchased in quarter-, half-, or full-pound quantities. They are taken home and eaten as is, or they are used in a dish such as Roast Duck Lo Mein*. Although they are now found in other provinces, barbecued meats originated in Canton. I have created my own barbecue sauce for American kitchens.

MARINADE
3 tablespoons Tomato Sauce*
1 tablespoon sherry
1 teaspoon Hot Sauce*
1 tablespoon dark soy sauce
2 tablespoons dark brown sugar
2 teaspoons wine vinegar
1 clove garlic, minced
1/4 cup chopped scallions (white and green parts)
1 teaspoon minced ginger root

1 pound duck parts (legs and wings)

1 tablespoon honey

SPECIAL EQUIPMENT
Metal hooks (see Barbecued Roast Pork*)

PREPARATION

Combine the ingredients for the marinade.

Rinse the duck parts and dry thoroughly.

Place the duck parts in the marinade; massage them well with your hands and refrigerate for a minimum of 4 hours, or up to 24 hours. Turn the duck parts over in the marinade several times during this period.

COOKING PROCEDURE

Place an oven rack on the top level in the oven. Place a second rack on the floor of the oven. Preheat the oven to 350 degrees.

Remove the duck parts from the marinade and dribble honey over them with a pair of chopsticks.

Pierce each duck part with a metal hook and hang each hook over a rung of the top oven rack. To catch the drippings and keep the duck moist, place a roasting pan containing water to a depth of 1 inch on the second rack below the duck.

Roast for 45 minutes. Turn the heat to 450 degrees; roast for another 15 to 20 minutes.

Remove the duck parts from the oven. With a heavy cleaver and rubber mallet, chop them into bite-sized pieces. Place in a heated serving dish and serve immediately.

YIELD *2–6 servings*

NOTES

Tip Because Barbecued Duck Portions are equally good at room temperature, this dish is an excellent choice for picnics in the summertime.

Substitutions For the duck parts (legs and wings), you can use a whole duck or a whole chicken, cut as follows: Remove the legs and wings, split the duck or chicken in half, divide the breast into two parts lengthwise, cut each thigh in half through the bone. Alternatively, the duck or chicken parts can be cooked on an outdoor barbecue.

This is also an excellent marinade for steak or pork chops. Before placing in the marinade, lightly score the meat (make opposing diagonal cuts on both sides). If you have access to an outside barbecue, this is an excellent way to cook the meat.

If using flank steak, marinate for 8 hours to ensure its being tender.

Removing Fat from Duck

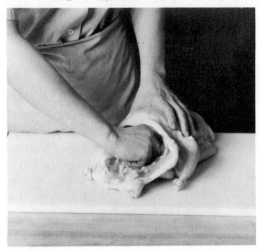

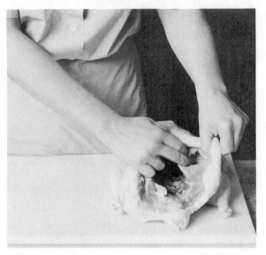

1. Using your fingers, remove the fat lodged between the thigh and the leg on both sides of the duck.

2. Create a hole that does not penetrate the skin.

This is a banquet dish because a whole roasted duck is considered extravagant and rare. Generally speaking, homes in China are not equipped with ovens, and since this dish requires an oven, it is only served in restaurants.

1 whole 5-pound duck

MARINADE
2 tablespoons dark soy sauce
1 tablespoon sherry
1 tablespoon sesame oil
2 teaspoons minced garlic
1 teaspoon Five Spice Powder*

2 slices ginger root
2 scallions (white and green parts), cut in
    2-inch pieces

BINDER
2 teaspoons water chestnut powder
    dissolved in
1 tablespoon sherry

1/4 cup sherry

SPECIAL EQUIPMENT
Butcher's twine

PREPARATION

Thaw the duck if frozen. Remove the pockets of fat lodged inside the cavity. Using your fingers, make a hole to remove the fat lodged between the thigh and the leg on the interior of both sides of the duck. Working with the duck breast side up, lift the piece of skin that extends over the neck and remove the excess fat, glands, and membranes with a sharp boning knife. Do not cut off this piece of skin, because when the duck is roasted the skin shrinks, and this piece is needed to cover the breast. Beginning at the neck end of the cavity, with the bird still lying breast side up carefully separate the skin from the meat, going down about 5 inches, by pulling the skin back with one hand and cutting with a boning knife through the fat and membranes with the other hand. Turn the duck breast side down, and do the same procedure along the top part of the back, separating

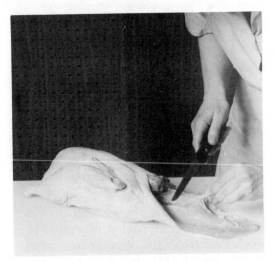

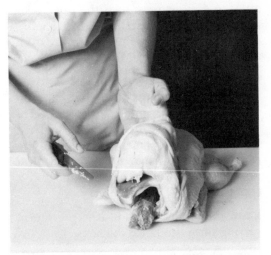

3. From the piece of skin extending from the neck, remove the glands that are in the shape of lima beans, the fat, and the membranes.

4. Starting at the neck, and using the tip of the boning knife, separate approximately 6 inches of the skin from the meat. Holding one hand under the skin, carefully shave off as much of the fat as possible without creating a hole in the skin. This procedure will allow whatever fat remains to drain during the cooking.

the skin from the meat for about 2 inches. Turn the duck breast side up. Put your hand underneath the outside of the skin and with the boning knife carefully shave off more excess fat from the inside of the skin. Do not make a hole in the skin.

Fill a roasting pan with water to a depth of 3 inches and bring it to a boil. Loop butcher's twine around the duck's wings. Holding the duck by the twine, submerge it in the boiling water for 2 minutes. Remove the duck and hang it in a cool place for 12 to 24 hours, or until the skin is dry.

Combine the ingredients for the marinade. Massage the duck with the marinade for several minutes, inside and out.

Place the ginger and scallions in the cavity of the duck.

Mix the binder.

COOKING PROCEDURE

Place an oven rack on the middle level in the oven. Place a second rack on the floor of the oven. Preheat oven to 325 degrees.

Fill a roasting pan with water to a depth of 1 inch. Place the pan on the lower oven rack. Place the duck directly on the middle-level rack, breast side up. Roast the duck for 1 hour. Insert a wooden spatula into the cavi-

(continued)

ty of the duck and remove it from the oven. (See Tips.) Turn the duck over and put it back in the oven, breast side down, to roast for 1 more hour. Increase the oven temperature to 450 degrees, turn the duck over again, and roast breast side up for 15 more minutes. Remove the duck from the oven and place on a rack to cool.

Remove the roasting pan from the oven and pour the contents of the pan (fat, water, and drippings) into a heatproof measuring cup. Remove the fat with the aid of a fat separator and return the liquid to the roasting pan. Stirring occasionally with a wooden spatula, reduce the liquid to ½ cup. Add the ¼ cup of sherry.

Restir the binder and add it to the sauce, stirring until the sauce thickens.

Using a heavy cleaver and a rubber mallet, chop the duck through the skin and bones into bite-size pieces; reshape the pieces on a serving platter to resemble a whole bird flattened out. Serve the sauce separately.

YIELD *4–8 servings*

NOTES

Timing For minimal loss of juices, it is best to defrost a duck in the refrigerator slowly for 1 or 2 days, so to prepare this dish you should plan at least three days ahead. Barbecued Duck, delicious at any temperature, is recommended for picnics, accompanied by Spicy Charcoal Peppers*.

Leftover duck can be used in Roast Duck Lo Mein* and in Gold and Silver Threads*.

Tips It is important to submerge the duck in boiling water, as it will remove some of the fat and will help the duck's skin dry out while hanging. If you have a terrace or a backyard, the ideal place to hang a duck is outside. There are other possibilities, such as in the shower (if your bathroom has a window), or anywhere inside near a window where the duck will be exposed to a draft. A fan will also work well. The duck, resting on a rack, can also be air-dried in the refrigerator. It is the air drying that will cause the duck's skin to dry out and will produce a very crisp skin when cooked. The skin will remain crisp even after the duck has completely cooled, in contrast to a duck roasted in the Western technique, whose skin shrivels when it begins to cool.

When turning the duck over, remove the duck as well as the roasting pan beneath it from the oven. Insert the wooden spoon into the cavity of the duck and tilt the duck so the fat and the juices are emptied into the roasting pan containing the water and the drippings. There are two reasons for this: to prevent the fat and drippings from dripping all over the oven (which will cause excessive smoke), and to save the juices the duck has released while roasting (which will add flavor to the sauce).

Substitution For the duck you can substitute a 5-pound fresh-killed chicken. The roasting time will be approximately the same.

SLICED DUCK WITH SPRING GINGER   Szechwan/Sichuan

Both extravagant and delicious, Sliced Duck with Spring Ginger is truly a banquet dish. Because it relies on the delicate flavor of the young ginger, which has a short season (August through October), it is a good idea to pickle several pounds of young ginger when it is in season.

1 whole 5-pound duck or 2 cups boneless, skinless duck meat

MARINADE
1 egg white
³/4 tablespoon water chestnut powder
³/4 tablespoon sherry

SEASONING SAUCE
1 teaspoon water chestnut powder dissolved in
2 tablesspoons sherry
1¹/2 tablespoons dark soy sauce
1 teaspoon Chinese red vinegar
1 teaspoon sugar
2 tablespoons chicken stock
1 teaspoon Hot Sauce*

5 tablespoons shredded ginger root, spring or Pickled Spring Ginger*
2 scallions (white and green parts), slant-cut
1 teaspoon minced garlic
¹/2 cup cleaned, seeded, triangle-cut sweet red peppers

¹/2 cup peeled and sliced water chestnuts
¹/2 cup snow peas, strung and slant-cut

2 cups peanut oil

2 teaspoons sesame oil

PREPARATION

Using the same boning technique as for chicken, bone the duck. Trim the fat from the meat and remove the tendons. Partially freeze the duck, then slice thin. Place the duck and the ingredients for the marinade in a bowl and stir in one direction vigorously with chopsticks. Place the mixture in the refrigerator for at least 4 hours or up to 12 hours.

Combine the ingredients for the seasoning sauce.

COOKING PROCEDURE

Place the wok over high heat for about 1 minute. Pour in the 2 cups of oil; turn the heat to medium until the oil reaches 325 degrees. Restir the duck in the marinade, turn the heat to high, and add the contents of the bowl to the wok all at once, stirring in a circular motion with a pair of chopsticks for about 1¹/2 minutes. Turn off the heat and pour the oil and the duck into a colander set over a bowl. Shake the colander gently to aid the draining, then place it over a clean bowl.

Return the wok to high heat. Stir-fry the ginger, scallions, garlic, and red peppers for 30 seconds.

Return the duck to the wok; stir-fry a few seconds.

Add the water chestnuts and snow peas and mix briefly.

Restir the seasoning sauce and add it all at once to the wok; stir-fry about 30 seconds.

Turn off the heat.

Add the sesame oil; mix a few seconds. Empty the contents of the wok onto a heated serving dish and serve immediately.

YIELD 2–6 servings

NOTES

Timing The boning of the duck can be done the day before.

Tips Use a fresh-killed duck, as refreezing is not advisable. Reserve the legs and wings for Barbecued Duck Portions*.

Substitutions For the boneless duck meat, you can substitute dark-meat chicken, pheasant, or any game bird large enough to bone.

SZECHWAN CRISPY DUCK Szechwan/Sichuan

Resourcefulness is one of the first qualities that come to mind when considering the Chinese. They have devised a method for cooking duck which is both ingenious and delicious. By marinating, steaming, and then deep-frying the duck, they are able to achieve a crisp skin with a moist, flavorful meat without the use of an oven. This method also eliminates the problem that occurs so often when roasting a duck according to Western techniques: the skin is crisp and the meat dry or the meat is tender and the skin not crisp enough.

1 whole 5–6-pound duck

2 sticks cinnamon, broken
2 whole star anise (16 pods)

1 tablespoon Szechwan Peppercorn Powder*
4 slices ginger root
1 whole scallion, cut in 2-inch pieces

1/4 cup (approximately) flour for coating

1 tablespoon dark soy sauce

BATTER
2 egg whites
3 tablespoons water chestnut powder
1 tablespoon sherry
1/2 teaspoon sugar
1/2 teaspoon salt

6 cups peanut oil

Watercress for garnish

2 tablespoons Szechwan Peppercorn Powder*
 for dipping (optional)

SPECIAL EQUIPMENT
Butcher's twine for turning duck

PREPARATION

Thaw the duck if frozen. Remove the pockets of fat lodged inside the cavity. Using your fingers, make a hole to remove the fat lodged between the thigh and the leg on the interior of both sides of the duck. Working with the duck breast side up, lift the piece of skin that extends over the neck and remove the excess fat, glands, and membranes with a sharp boning knife. Do not cut off this piece of skin, because when the duck is steamed the skin shrinks, and this piece is needed to cover the breast. Beginning at the neck end of the cavity, with the bird still lying breast side up carefully separate the skin from the meat, going down about 5 inches, by pulling the skin back with one hand and cutting with a boning knife through the fat and membranes with the other hand. Turn the duck breast side down, and do the same procedure along the top of the back, separating the skin from the meat for about 2 inches. Turn the duck breast side up. Put your hand underneath the outside of the skin and with the boning knife carefully shave off more excess fat from the inside of the skin. Do not make a hole in the skin.

Rinse the duck inside and out under cold running water, and dry well with paper towels.

Combine the cinnamon and star anise; roast them on a cookie sheet in an oven preheated to 325 degrees, or dry-roast them in a wok over a medium-low heat for 2 to 3 minutes.

Rub the 1 tablespoon of Szechwan Peppercorn Powder all over the inside and outside of the duck. Place the cinnamon, anise, the ginger slices, and the scallion in the cavity of the duck. Wrap the duck in a terry-cloth towel and place a heavy lid on top of the duck. Refrigerate at least 4 hours, up to 24 hours.

DUCK AND SQUAB

Rub flour all over the skin of the duck and place it breast side up in an oval-shaped dish with a high lip that will fit in a steamer. Steam for 1½ to 2 hours, or until the legs start to pull away from the duck. Remove the dish containing the duck from the steamer. Let the duck stand for 30 minutes. Slipping a spatula underneath the duck and inserting a wooden spoon into the cavity, carefully lift the duck out of the dish, tilting it slightly to let any remaining liquid in the cavity run out. Place the duck on a rack and allow it to stand. When it is thoroughly cool, rub it all over with the soy sauce. Wrap in foil and refrigerate for at least 2 hours or up to 24 hours.

Blend together the ingredients for the batter. Rub this batter all over the inside and outside of the duck. Let stand 30 minutes or longer, in which case refrigerate.

COOKING PROCEDURE

Tie butcher's twine around the wings to facilitate turning the duck when it is immersed in the oil.

Place the wok over high heat for about 1 minute. Pour in the oil and turn the heat to medium until it reaches 375 degrees. Turn the heat to high. Gently lower the duck into the oil, back side down. Cook, continuously spooning hot oil all over the exposed part of the duck. Continue to deep-fry, turning the duck occasionally with the help of the attached butcher's twine until it is crisp and golden brown (about 8 to 10 minutes).

Remove the duck from the oil and drain on several sheets of paper towels.

After placing watercress in the cavity of the duck, present the duck whole at the table. Return to the kitchen and, using a heavy cleaver and a rubber mallet, cut up the duck and reshape it on a serving platter to resemble a whole bird flattened out.

Serve with Szechwan Peppercorn Powder for dipping.

YIELD *4–8 servings*

CRISP BONELESS PRESSED DUCK   Canton/Guangzhou

This is a classic Cantonese way of preparing duck to which I have added one crucial step: the broiling of the duck, which eliminates the layer of fat that would otherwise exist between the skin and the meat. It is, at once, a variation and a refinement.

1 whole 5–6-pound duck

3 slices ginger root
*1 teaspoon Five Spice Powder**
3 tablespoons dark soy sauce
1/3 cup sherry

1 egg white, beaten until very frothy

1/3 cup water chestnut powder

SEASONING SAUCE
3/4 cup reduced duck stock, defatted
1/2 tablespoon hoisin sauce
1/2 tablespoon plum sauce

BINDER
1 tablespoon water chestnut powder
   dissolved in
2 tablespoons sherry

*1/3 cup almonds, roasted and crushed***

6 cups peanut oil

PREPARATION AND ADVANCE COOKING PROCEDURE

Thaw the duck if frozen. Wash and clean the duck and remove as much fat as possible. Cut off the piece of skin that extends over the neck. Remove all membranes. Using a heavy cleaver and rubber mallet, split the duck in half.

In a large pot combine 3 quarts of water, the ginger, the Five Spice Powder, soy sauce, and sherry and bring to a boil. Immerse the duck in this broth; cover and cook over medium-low heat for 1 1/4 hours, turning the duck occasionally. With a wire strainer, remove the duck from the broth and place on a rack resting on a plate. Allow to cool a few minutes.

Preheat the oven to 350 degrees.

While the duck is still warm, remove the back and the breastbone with your hands, leaving the legs and wings intact. Work gently so that the skin will not be torn. Place the duck in a roasting pan 5 inches from the heat; broil 20 minutes. Place the duck on a rack and cool. Brush lightly beaten egg white on the boned duck. Place the water chestnut powder in a strainer and, tapping the strainer with a knife, generously sprinkle the powder all over the duck.

Set up a steamer. On a plate resting on a rack, steam the duck for 20 minutes, or until the water chestnut powder is transparent. Remove the duck, still resting on the rack, to a clean plate, until dry and cool.

Reduce the stock in which the duck was cooked to 1 cup (see Tip). Remove the fat; the stock should now measure about 3/4 cup. Add hoisin and plum sauces. Stir and simmer a few minutes. Taste for seasoning. Reserve.

The entire preparation up to this point can be done 24 hours ahead.

Mix the binder.

FINAL COOKING PROCEDURE

Place the wok over high heat for about 1 minute. Pour in the oil and turn the heat to medium until the oil reaches 375 degrees. Turn the heat to high. Deep-fry the duck until both sides are golden brown (about 8 to 10 minutes). Drain on paper towels.

While the duck is frying, simmer the sauce. Restir the binder and add it to the sauce, stirring until the sauce thickens.

Chop the duck into bite-sized pieces. Arrange the pieces on a heated serving platter. Pour some of the sauce over the duck and sprinkle with the nuts. Serve the remaining sauce on the side. Serve immediately.

YIELD *4–8 servings*

NOTES

Tip For faster reduction of large quantities of stock, simmer the stock in a roasting pan, as the rate at which the liquid evaporates is more rapid due to the large surface of the pan.

GOLD AND SILVER THREADS

Canton/Guangzhou

As abalone and duck are delicacies to the Chinese, this is considered a banquet dish. The poetic name refers to the duck and abalone as the gold threads and to the bean sprouts as the silver. When I was in China, I dined at the Pan Hsi Restaurant in Canton, where Gold and Silver Threads is a specialty. I was also present at the dinner in New York City when six of the Pan Hsi chefs came to the United States to prepare some of the specialties of the restaurant. Gold and Silver Threads was one of the twenty-four courses served.

1/2 cup Chinese mushrooms, soaked and shredded**

1 cup leeks (white parts only), split and shredded

1/4 cup shredded bamboo shoots

1/4 teaspoon freshly ground white pepper

1/2 teaspoon salt

3/4 cup abalone

1/2 roast duck

2 tablespoons rendered duck fat**

2 cups bean sprouts

BINDER
2 teaspoons water chestnut powder dissolved in
2 tablespoons sherry

1/2 cup abalone, duck, and mushroom stock (see Tips)

PREPARATION

Having reconstituted the mushrooms and done the necessary cutting, place the two groups of ingredients in separate bowls.

Preheat the oven to 350 degrees. Slice, then shred the abalone, reserving the liquid from the can.

Remove the skin from the duck and shred; then remove the meat and shred. Place the duck skin in a single layer in a shallow roasting pan and roast for 20 to 30 minutes, or until crisp. Place the duck skin on paper towels to drain. Reserve the rendered duck fat for the cooking procedure.

Place the bean sprouts on several layers of paper towels 1 hour before stir-frying.

Mix the binder.

COOKING PROCEDURE

Place the wok over high heat for about 2 minutes. Add the bean sprouts; stir-fry without oil slowly, allowing the bean sprouts to become slightly scorched and attain a smoky flavor. Remove them from the wok.

Return the wok to medium heat. Add 2 tablespoons of the rendered duck fat and heat until hot but not smoking. Add the mushrooms and leeks and stir-fry for 2 minutes. Turn the heat to high.

Add the bamboo shoots, pepper, and salt together with the duck meat; stir-fry a few seconds.

Pour in the stock and bring to a boil.

Restir the binder and add it to the wok, stirring continuously for another few seconds.

Add the bean sprouts and abalone, continuing to stir-fry for a few seconds.

Empty the contents of the wok onto a heated serving dish, and garnish by surrounding with crisp duck skin. Serve immediately.

YIELD *3–6 servings*

NOTES

Tips The combined abalone, duck, and mushroom stock is derived from the liquid in the canned abalone, the reduced mushroom stock**, and the liquid that accompanies a Cantonese roast duck purchased at a Chinese barbecue house. If you are roasting your own, the duck stock is obtained from the deglazing of the roasting pan juices.

The remaining abalone and juice (from a 16-ounce can) can be used for Minced Chicken and Abalone Soup*.

You may buy or roast your own duck. It is preferable, but not crucial, that a Chinese roast duck be used for this recipe.

Although winter bamboo shoots are more difficult to shred than spring bamboo shoots, it is preferable to use them, as this is a banquet dish.

Storage Refrigerated, the abalone will last three days after the can has been opened.

ORANGE SPICED DUCK

This is a simple and excellent braised duck recipe, which I learned from Madame Chu. In contrast to many duck recipes, the aim of this dish is not a crisp skin, but rather the superb flavor of the leeks, sauce, and duck meat.

1 whole 5-pound duck

2 fresh navel oranges

2 cups leeks (white and green parts), split and cut in 2-inch pieces

2 cups salt-free duck stock (see Tips)

¼ cup dark soy sauce
½ cup sherry

2 tablespoons honey

1 teaspoon Five Spice Powder*

1 piece dried tangerine peel, 1 × 2 inches

1 piece fresh orange peel (zest only)

PREPARATION

Thaw the duck if frozen. Remove the giblets and the pockets of fat from the cavity. Cut all but approximately 3 inches of the skin extending from the neck. Lift the skin on the neck side and remove the excess fat, glands, and membranes. Rinse the duck under cold running water; drain, then wipe dry.

Peel the oranges and cut them in half, then cut each half into slices.

COOKING PROCEDURE

Preheat the oven to 375 degrees. Place the duck on a rack in a roasting pan and roast it in the oven for 1 hour (the rest of the cooking is done on top of the range). To help the fat drain, prick the duck with a trussing needle along the back and also between the thighs and legs. Do this after the first 30 minutes, then again after 45 minutes. Remove the duck from the oven.

Place the small round cake rack in the bottom of a wok or oval dutch oven. Distribute the leeks on the rack. Insert a wooden spoon into the cavity of the duck; carefully remove it from the roasting pan, keeping it level so as not to lose the juices that have accumulated during the roasting period. Place it on top of the leeks, breast side up. Pour out the fat from the roasting pan and reserve for another use.

Deglaze the roasting pan juices with duck stock.

Turn the heat to high under the duck; add the soy sauce and sherry directly over the duck. Bring to a boil.

Add the duck stock from the roasting pan around the sides of the wok and bring to a boil again. Cover, turn the heat to low, and simmer for 30 minutes.

Dribble 2 tablespoons of honey directly over the duck. Add Five Spice Powder, dried tangerine peel, and fresh orange peel to the sauce. Stir until the Five Spice Powder has dissolved. Baste the duck a few times. Continue to cook, covered, for 90 minutes or until the duck is very tender. Set the timer every 20 minutes to baste the duck and to check that the juices do not evaporate.

Slip a spatula underneath the rack and remove the duck (still resting on the rack). Place it on a large, heated serving platter. If necessary, reduce the remaining sauce and leeks to about ¾ cup. Pour the sauce over the duck, and place orange slices over and around it. Carve the duck with chopsticks.

YIELD *4–8 servings*

NOTES

Timing Up until the reducing of the sauce, the entire preparation and cooking procedure can be done a day in advance. Remove the duck, still resting on the rack, and the sauce to a covered plate or bowl, and refrigerate. Leaving the duck on the rack, place it in a covered wok and rewarm it in the sauce over a low heat for about 15 minutes. Then remove the duck, still resting on the rack, to a heated serving platter and slide it off the rack. Reduce the sauce in the wok, pour it over the duck, and garnish with orange slices.

Tips The duck stock can be made from the neck and giblets of the duck. For details on the preparation, see Poultry Stock*.

The purpose of keeping the duck on the rack during the entire cooking procedure is to prevent it from falling apart when transferring it from the wok to the serving dish. The duck must actually be overcooked, so the meat will easily fall off the bones when carved with chopsticks.

Substitution For the duck, you can substitute a 5-pound chicken. Reduce the cooking time in the wok to 1½ hours. It is not necessary to prick the chicken during the roasting time, as it is less fatty.

SLICED ROAST DUCK WITH SCALLIONS
Peking/Beijing

Sliced Roast Duck with Scallions is a variation on Peking Duck. It has the advantage of requiring only a few minutes of attention just before serving, whereas the difficult procedure of carving the hot Peking Duck is done at the table.

1 whole 5-pound duck
2 tablespoons honey
2 cups sherry

SEASONING SAUCE
1/4 cup hoisin sauce
1/4 cup reduced duck juices (see Cooking
   Procedure)
1 tablespoon sesame oil
2 teaspoons Hot Sauce*
2 tablespoons sherry
1 tablespoon dark soy sauce
1 teaspoon sugar

12 Peking Doilies*

1 tablespoon rendered duck fat**

1 tablespoon minced garlic
1 cup shredded scallions (white and green
   parts)

SPECIAL EQUIPMENT.
Butcher's twine for blanching duck

PREPARATION

Thaw the duck if frozen. Remove the pockets of fat lodged inside the cavity. Using your fingers, make a hole to remove the fat lodged between the thigh and the leg on the interior of both sides of the duck. Working with the duck breast side down, lift the piece of skin that extends over the neck and remove the excess fat, glands, and membranes with a sharp boning knife. Do not cut off this piece of skin, because when the duck is roasted the skin shrinks, and this piece is needed to cover the breast. Beginning at the neck end of the cavity with the bird lying breast side up, carefully separate the skin from the meat going down about 5 inches, by pulling the skin back with one hand and cutting with a boning knife through the fat and membranes with the other hand. Turn the duck breast side down, and do the same procedure along the top part of the back, separating the skin from the meat for about 2 inches. Turn the duck breast side up. Put your hand underneath the outside of the skin and with the boning knife carefully shave off more excess fat from the inside of the skin. Do not make a hole in the skin.

Fill a roasting pan with water to a depth of 3 inches and bring it to a boil. Add the honey and the sherry and stir a minute. Loop butcher's twine around the wings of the duck. Holding the duck by the butcher's twine, submerge it in the boiling water. With the other hand, ladle boiling water to baste the duck for about 2 minutes. Hang the duck in a cool place for at least 12 hours or until the skin has air-dried or is taut. Alternatively, place the duck on a high-legged rack resting on a plate and place it in the refrigerator for 24 to 36 hours, turning every 12 hours. This technique of air-drying will allow the skin to become crisp and remain crisp even after the duck has cooled.

Combine the ingredients for the seasoning sauce.

COOKING PROCEDURE

Place one oven rack on the middle level in the oven. Place the second rack on the floor of the oven. Preheat the oven to 375 degrees. Fill a shallow roasting pan with water to a depth of 1 inch and place it on top of the lower rack. Remove the duck, still resting on the high-legged rack, from the refrigerator. Place the duck, breast side up, directly on the middle-level rack and roast for 30 minutes. Check water level every 30 minutes during the entire roasting period to prevent the drippings from burning.

Remove the duck from the oven by inserting a wooden spoon into the cavity. Tip the duck and drain the juices from the cavity into a saucepan. Return the duck to the oven and roast breast side down for another hour at 300 degrees. Again, remove the duck from the oven by inserting a wooden spoon into the cavity. Drain the juices into the same saucepan.

Return the duck to the oven and roast breast side up for a final 30 minutes, at 375 degrees.

Remove the duck from the oven and drain any remaining juices from the cavity into the saucepan. Place the duck on a rack resting on a plate. Allow to cool.

Defat the duck juices, then reduce to ¼ cup and add to the seasoning sauce.

Remove the skin and then the meat from the carcass; slice it into 1 by 2-inch pieces, keeping the meat and the skin separate. (The dish can be prepared ahead through this step.)

Turn the oven to broil. Pour the liquid from the roasting pan into a heatproof cup. Remove 1 tablespoon of duck fat and reserve it for stir-frying.

Wrap the Peking Doilies in a dish towel and steam for 5 minutes.

Place the duck skin in a single layer on a metal platter and broil for 3 minutes.

Place the wok over high heat for about 1 minute. Add the 1 tablespoon of duck fat and heat until hot but not smoking. Add the garlic and scallions; stir-fry 1 minute.

Restir the seasoning sauce and add it to the wok all at once, stirring about 1 minute.

Add the duck meat and continue to stir-fry for another minute. Empty the contents of the wok onto a heated serving dish. Place the duck skin around the duck meat. Serve with Peking Doilies. Each person takes a doily and places a few pieces of duck skin and meat in the doily, which is then rolled and eaten.

YIELD *4–8 servings*

TEA SMOKED DUCK

This unique Chinese method of smoking poultry, which in no way resembles the Western procedure, imparts a mysterious and wonderful flavor. The Hunanese as well as the Szechwanese make use of this method. Because refrigeration is generally available in America as it is not in China, I have eliminated a preliminary step of soaking the duck in brine used as a preservative. The brine also produces a very strong-tasting bird, which is an acquired taste. Rice husks or peanut shells are sometimes used instead of the raw brown short-grain rice in this recipe. The type of tea may also vary. Any black tea will serve the purpose; however, Lapsang souchong is my first choice because it has an additional smoky flavor. Tea Smoked Duck requires from two to four days' advance planning, but the reaction from guests with sophisticated palates makes the effort worthwhile.

1 whole 5–6-pound duck

1 teaspoon salt
1 tablespoon Szechwan Peppercorn Powder*
4 slices ginger root
2 scallions (white and green parts), cut in 2-inch pieces

3 tablespoons sherry

1/2 cup brown sugar
1/2 cup Lapsang souchong tea leaves
1 cup raw brown short-grain rice

Water chestnut powder for dusting

6 cups peanut oil

SPECIAL EQUIPMENT
Butcher's twine for turning duck

PREPARATION

Thaw the duck if frozen. Remove the pockets of fat lodged inside the cavity. Using your fingers, make a hole to remove the fat lodged between the thigh and the leg on the interior of both sides of the duck. Working with the duck breast side up, lift the piece of skin that extends over the neck and remove the excess fat, glands, and membranes with a sharp boning knife. Do not cut off this piece of skin, because when the duck is steamed the skin shrinks, and this piece is needed to cover the breast. Beginning at the neck end of the cavity with the bird still lying breast side up, carefully separate the skin from the meat going down about 5 inches, by pulling the skin back with one hand and cutting with a boning knife through the fat and membranes with the other hand. Turn the duck breast side down, and do the same procedure along the top part of the back, separating the skin from the meat for about 2 inches. Turn the duck breast side up. Put your hand underneath the outside of the skin and with the boning knife carefully shave off more excess fat from the inside of the skin. Do not make a hole in the skin.

Rinse the duck under cold running water; drain, then wipe dry.

Place the wok over medium heat and add salt. Dry-roast the salt for a few minutes, then rub the salt and Szechwan Peppercorn Powder on the inside and outside of the duck.

Place the ginger slices and the scallions in the cavity of the duck. Tightly wrap the duck in a terry-cloth towel. Refrigerate for at least 6 hours, or up to 24 hours.

248   DUCK AND SQUAB

COOKING PROCEDURE

Remove the duck from the refrigerator and place it in an oval-shaped dish with a deep lip. Pour the sherry over the duck and set the dish on a rack at least 2½ inches tall inside a large (turkey) roasting pan with a tight-fitting, dome-shaped cover. Pour 3 to 4 inches of water into the roasting pan. Add more boiling water if necessary during the steaming process. Cover the pan and steam the duck for 1¼ to 1½ hours. The drumsticks will wiggle freely if the duck is done. Remove the duck and place it on a rack to cool. Reserve the duck stock for another recipe.

Line a wok with heavy-duty aluminum foil. Sprinkle the bottom with sugar, tea leaves, and uncooked rice. Arrange two chopsticks parallel to each other and about 2 inches apart on top of the combined sugar, tea, and rice; then place two more chopsticks on top of these in the opposite direction to form a tic-tac-toe pattern. Place the duck breast side up on the chopsticks. Line a wok cover with aluminum foil, extending the foil a few inches beyond the rim, and put the cover on the wok. It should fit tightly.

Turn the heat to medium; smoke the duck for 30 minutes without lifting the lid. Turn off the heat but do not remove the cover. Let the duck stand for 20 minutes longer.

Remove the duck from the wok (it should be well browned) and allow it to cool on a rack. The duck can be deep-fried (as described below) at this point or refrigerated for several days, if desired. Allow it to become room temperature before the final cooking procedure.

Using a small strainer filled with water chestnut powder, sprinkle the duck on all sides. Tie butcher's twine around the wings of the duck to facilitate turning it in the oil.

Place the wok over high heat for about 1 minute. Pour in the oil and turn the heat to medium until it reaches 375 degrees. Turn the heat to high. Lower the duck gently into the hot oil and deep-fry for 10 minutes, turning once at midpoint. Ladle oil over the duck continuously while it is frying. Remove the duck from the oil by holding onto the string; drain on several sheets of paper towels.

Using a heavy cleaver and a rubber mallet, chop the duck through skin and bone into bite-sized pieces; reassemble the pieces on a serving platter in the shape of a whole bird flattened out. Serve hot or at room temperature.

YIELD *4–8 servings*

NOTES

Tips If chicken is used instead of duck (see Substitution), leftover smoked chicken should be reserved for Shredded Smoked Chicken*.

Save the duck stock (or chicken stock) for Shredded Smoked Chicken* or Snow-White Cloud Soup*.

Substitution For the duck, you can substitute chicken, in which case the deep-fat frying procedure can be eliminated. If using chicken, steam for 1 hour (for a 5-pound chicken).

Storage Frozen stock will last one year.

SQUABS IN CASSEROLE

Squab is often eaten in Canton. It is also popular in northern China. In the South, when it is cooked whole it is deep-fried, braised (Squabs in Casserole), or roasted (Lemon Squab*). Squabs, since ancient times, have represented a certain harmony to the Chinese, who after attaching wooden pipes to the birds' feet, stood and looked at the sky, watching them fly through the air making their mystical music.

2 fresh squabs

MARINADE
12 to 14 shallots, peeled and left whole
4 cloves garlic, crushed
5 slices ginger root
2 tablespoons dark soy sauce
2 tablespoons oyster sauce
¼ teaspoon freshly ground black pepper
¼ cup sherry
2 teaspoons sugar
1 tablespoon sesame oil

2 tablespoons rendered chicken fat**
¼ cup salt-free chicken stock

PREPARATION

Wash and clean the squabs, removing head, feet, and innards. Pat dry with paper towels.

Place the squabs and the ingredients for the marinade in a bowl and toss to coat the squabs well. Marinate for 2 hours. Refrigeration is not required.

COOKING PROCEDURE

Place a heatproof casserole (3- or 4-quart or larger) over high heat. Add the chicken fat and heat until hot but not smoking. Remove the squabs from the marinade; place them breast side down in the casserole. Turn the heat to medium and cover; cook for 3 minutes. Turn the squabs over, cover again, and cook for another 3 minutes.

Pour in the marinade and the chicken stock. Simmer, covered, over a medium-low heat for 30 minutes, turning the squabs once after 15 minutes. Remove the squabs from the casserole and place them on a heated serving dish.

Remove the fat from the sauce. Return the sauce to the casserole and boil it down to a thick, syrupy glaze.

While the sauce is reducing, cut the squabs into serving pieces with poultry shears. Pour the sauce over the squabs and serve immediately.

YIELD *2–8 servings*

NOTES

Timing This dish can be prepared and cooked entirely the day ahead. After removing the fat from the sauce, pour it over the squabs and refrigerate. When ready to serve, reduce the sauce to a thick, syrupy glaze.

Substitutions For the squabs, you can substitute Rock Cornish hens or quail.

LEMON SQUAB

A banquet dish by Chinese standards, Lemon Squab is equally suitable to an American holiday menu. On such an occasion, each guest would dine on a whole bird.

2 squabs (1¹/₂–1³/₄ pounds total)

STUFFING
2 tablespoons minced lemon peel (zest only)
1 tablespoon lemon juice
1 scallion (white and green parts), chopped
2 tablespoons sweet bean paste
1 tablespoon sugar
¹/₄ teaspoon freshly ground black pepper
¹/₄ teaspoon Five Spice Powder*
2 tablespoons chicken stock
2 teaspoons dark soy sauce
1 tablespoon sesame oil

1 teaspoon honey
1 teaspoon water

SPECIAL EQUIPMENT
Butcher's twine for blanching squab
Unwaxed dental floss

PREPARATION

Clean the squabs; remove the head, feet, and innards.

Combine the ingredients for the stuffing. Place half of the stuffing in the cavity of each squab and sew up each end with unwaxed dental floss.

Bring 4 quarts of water to a rapid boil in a large saucepan. Tie butcher's twine around the neck of each squab and lower the squabs, one at a time, into the boiling water for 1 minute. Remove the squabs from the water; allow to drain for several minutes on a rack resting in a roasting pan. Hang the squabs in a cool place for several hours, preferably overnight. At this point the skin should be taut and dry.

Combine honey and water.

COOKING PROCEDURE

Preheat the oven to 400 degrees. Place the squabs, breast side up, on a rack resting in a roasting pan containing water to a depth of ¹/₂ inch. Roast the squabs for 15 minutes. Reduce the heat to 350 degrees and roast for another 45 minutes, turning once after 20 minutes.

Turn the heat to 450 degrees. Turn the squabs breast side up, brush with honey and water, and continue to roast for another 5 to 10 minutes.

Remove the squabs to a serving dish. Remove the dental floss and release the liquid contained within the cavity into the roasting pan. Reduce the liquid to a thick, syrupy glaze.

While the liquid is reducing, cut the squabs into quarters with poultry shears and discard the stuffing.

Pour the sauce over the squabs and serve immediately.

YIELD *2–6 servings*

NOTES

Timing After the squabs have hung and the skin has dried out, they can be placed on a rack resting in a shallow roasting pan and refrigerated for 1 day. Allow the squabs to become room temperature before roasting.

Tip The purpose of brushing the squabs with honey and water during the last 10 minutes of roasting is to aid the browning and to give the squabs a lacquered sheen.

Substitutions For the squabs, you can substitute quail, dove, or Rock Cornish hen.

Chapter 14

PORK

Recommended Cut of Pork

Boston butt is recommended for recipes in this book calling for boneless pork. It is located between the neck and the shoulder of the pig. There are two in each pig, one on either side. Boston butt weighs about 7 pounds, depending upon the size of the pig. There is a bladebone running through it, which is usually removed by the butcher before being sold. Many butchers divide the Boston butt into two pieces. The center portion is then called the CT butt; the other portion keeps the same name, Boston butt. The CT butt is a more desirable piece of meat. It is more fatty and as a result is juicier and has more flavor. The other portion is leaner and has quite a bit of gristle running through it. I never use this portion; I use only the CT butt. Within the CT butt there is a portion of meat which I refer to in this book as the "eye" or the "pork fillet." This piece can easily be removed from the CT butt.

The eye or fillet weighs about ¾ pound. It is ideal for Barbecued Roast Pork* as well as for any dish calling for shreds or slices of pork. Because there is no surrounding fat but only veins of fat running through it, it is possible to make symmetrical cuts of meat, whereas the remaining part of the CT butt has to be trimmed in between the slices when shredded or sliced, which will result in uneven pieces. Once the eye has been removed, the remaining portion of the CT butt can be used for Barbecued Roast Pork or for recipes requiring ground pork.

When shopping in a Chinese market, I have the butcher take out the eye of the CT butt and grind the rest. Ground pork for Chinese recipes should be ground once, not twice (the way Americans prefer for hamburger or other recipes requiring ground beef). Ground pork will keep for one month in the freezer. Freeze it in quarter- or half-pound packages.

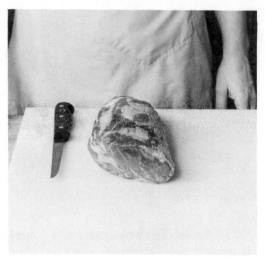

1. Boneless pork (CT butt), which is located between the neck and the shoulder of the pig.

2. Removing the eye (pork fillet).

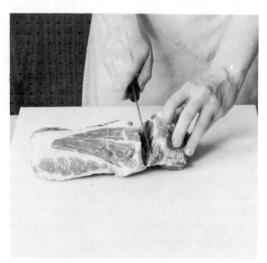

5. Cut the remaining portion of the CT butt into strips. To do this, cut off a 3-inch piece at the end.

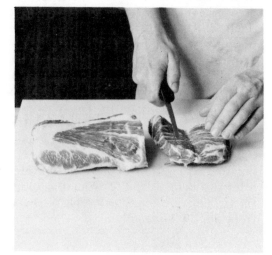

6. Butterfly this first cut end piece.

3. The eye of the CT butt is on the cutter's left.

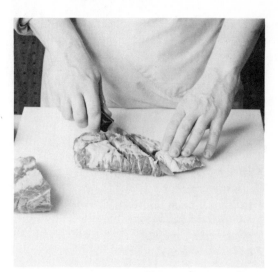

4. Cut the eye in half lengthwise; score each piece at intervals of about ½ inch.

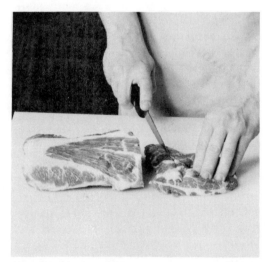

7. Score this piece at ½-inch intervals.

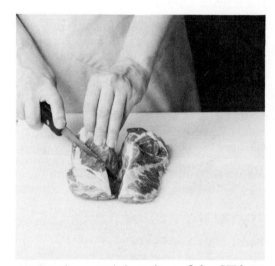

8. Cut the remaining piece of the CT butt in half and score.

BARBECUED ROAST PORK

Canton/Guangzhou

2 pounds boneless pork (CT butt)

MARINADE
4 slices ginger root
2 scallions (white and green parts), cut into
   2-inch lengths
2 tablespoons dark soy sauce
4 tablespoons hoisin sauce
2 tablespoons American chili sauce
$1/4$ teaspoon pepper
1 tablespoon plum sauce
1 tablespoon bean sauce
2 cloves garlic, crushed
3 tablespoons sherry

2 tablespoons honey

SPECIAL EQUIPMENT
Metal hooks

PREPARATION

Cut the pork into 5×3-inch strips, 1½ inches thick. Score each strip at intervals of about 1½ inches.

Combine the ingredients of the marinade. Place the pork in the marinade and refrigerate for 8 hours, turning once at midpoint. Reserve 2 to 3 tablespoons of the marinade to add to the sauce later on.

Allow the pork to reach room temperature. Dribble the honey over the pork.

COOKING PROCEDURE

Place one rack on the floor of the oven and one on the top level. Fill a shallow roasting pan with water to a depth of 1 inch and place it on the bottom rack to catch the drippings and to keep the pork moist.

Preheat the oven to 350 degrees.

Pierce each pork strip with a metal hook (see Tips), and hang each hook over a rung of the top oven rack. Roast for 40 minutes at 350 degrees and 15 minutes at 450 degrees. Remove the pork from the oven. Cool the pork for 5 minutes on a rack rest-

ing on a platter. Slice across the grain and serve.

YIELD 4–8 servings

NOTES

Timing Barbecued Roast Pork can be made a day or two in advance, then rewarmed before serving. When you plan to rewarm it, in order to prevent the pork from becoming overcooked and too dry reduce the original timing from 15 to 10 minutes at 450 degrees. When ready to serve, preheat the oven to 450 degrees. Put the pork on a rack, and place the rack in a shallow roasting pan; then roast for an additional 5 minutes.

Tips If a natural sauce is desired, remove the fat from the pork drippings and boil down to ¾ cup. Add 3 tablespoons marinade and boil again for 1 more minute. Serve on the side, or pour over Roast Pork. The sauce can be thickened, if necessary, with 2 teaspoons water chestnut powder dissolved in 1 tablespoon sherry. Add after the marinade has cooked for 1 minute in the sauce. If the sauce is not used or if there is any left over, it can be frozen and used instead of chicken stock for Roast Duck Lo Mein*.

Do not marinate pork longer than 8 hours, since it will toughen the meat.

Chili sauce is not a hot sauce; use an American brand such as Heinz or Del Monte.

The hooks used to hang the pork while roasting can be made by cutting wire coathangers into 3- or 4-inch pieces, bending them to form an S shape, boiling them in water for 10 minutes, scrubbing them with a steel wool pad until all the paint is removed, then filing the ends until they are smooth. If that sounds like a lot of work, it is. Other possibilities are drapery or shower curtain hooks, and poultry skewers, which can be bent into the appropriate shape.

Substitutions For the boneless pork, you can substitute spareribs. Leave the rack of spareribs whole, or cut in half if they are too long for the oven. Remove the skin from the concave side of the rack of spareribs, or have the butcher do this. On the thicker end of the rack, make shallow cuts between each rib, about 4 inches long. Marinate the ribs for 8 hours in the refrigerator, increasing the quantity of the marinade according to the weight of the ribs. Turn the ribs over in the marinade at midpoint. Allow them to reach room temperature before roasting.

Fill a shallow roasting pan with water to a depth of 1 inch and place it on the bottom oven rack. Preheat the oven to 350 degrees.

Pierce the rack of ribs with several metal hooks through the end of the ribs, and hang the hooks over the rungs of the top oven rack. Roast at 350 degrees for 50 minutes and then at 450 degrees for 10 minutes. Remove the ribs from the oven and allow to cool for 10 minutes. With a heavy cleaver, cut the ribs into single rib sections; leave these whole or cut into 2-inch segments, Chinese-style. Serve with Duck Sauce* or Chinese Mustard Sauce*.

The marinade in this recipe can be used for a variety of meats. Roast loin of pork or shoulder or loin of veal, when prepared with this marinade, makes a great family or company dinner. Place the meat in a plastic bag with the marinade in the refrigerator for 8 hours. (When using large cuts of meat, it is best to marinate them in a plastic bag because more of the marinade will adhere to the meat's surface.) Place a rack in a shallow roasting pan filled with 1 inch of water. The meat should be placed on top of the rack, above the water, with the fat side up. Roast at 325 degrees for 30 minutes to the pound, or until the meat reaches the internal temperature of 170 degrees.

This marinade is also excellent for making barbecued chicken. Quarter a 3½-pound chicken. Do not increase the marinade, or the chicken will be too salty. Marinate and roast the chicken for the same amount of time as the Barbecued Roast Pork.

Flank steak is another substitute. Score a flank steak lightly on both sides. Marinate for 4 to 8 hours in the refrigerator. Barbecue the flank steak on an outdoor grill or run it under the broiler for 3 to 4 minutes on each side. Slice against the grain. If a natural sauce is desired, place the flank steak on a rack resting on a metal steak platter. Pour in water to a depth of ¼ inch. When the steak is done, remove it and the rack. Deglaze the steak platter with ¼ cup sherry. Pour the sauce over the steak.

Lamb cut in chunks (from the leg) prepared in this marinade, as for shish kebab, is delicious. To the marinade, add 2 tablespoons of either chopped parsley or cilantro (fresh coriander) and 2 tablespoons lemon juice. Omit the 2 tablespoons of sherry. Barbecue the lamb chunks on an outdoor grill, or run them under the broiler for 3 to 4 minutes on one side and the same time on the opposite side. (Cut one chunk of meat to test for doneness: it should be pink inside.)

Storage Barbecued Roast Pork can be refrigerated for up to four days. It can be frozen for one month.

This is a typical Peking home-style dish, which is traditionally served as part of the meal. In America it is most frequently served as an appetizer. In either case, it is delicious and simple to prepare.

1/2 pound boneless pork

MARINADE
1/2 egg white
1 teaspoon water chestnut powder
1 teaspoon sherry

*1/4 cup Chinese mushrooms, soaked and shredded***
*12 dried tiger lily buds, soaked and knotted***
*2 tablespoons tree ears, soaked and shredded***
1/2 cup shredded bamboo shoots
2 cups split, shredded leeks (white parts only)

SEASONING SAUCE
1 teaspoon water chestnut powder dissolved in
1 tablespoon sherry
2 tablespoons dark soy sauce
1 tablespoon hoisin sauce
1/2 teaspoon sugar

8 Peking Doilies*

1 cup bean sprouts

1 cup shredded bok choy (white part only)

2 Egg Pancakes*, shredded

2 tablespoons peanut oil

PREPARATION

Partially freeze the pork; slice thin, then shred. Place the pork and the ingredients for the marinade in a bowl and stir in one direction vigorously with chopsticks. Place the mixture in the refrigerator for at least 1 hour or up to 12 hours.

Having reconstituted the mushrooms, lily buds, and tree ears and done the necessary cutting, place these and the bamboo shoots and leeks in a bowl.

Combine the ingredients for the seasoning sauce.

COOKING PROCEDURE

Wrap the Peking Doilies in a tea towel; steam for about 5 minutes while stir-frying the other ingredients.

Place the wok over high heat for about 2 minutes. Add bean sprouts; stir-fry without oil for 2 minutes. Remove them to a plate.

Add the oil and heat for 20 seconds, or until the oil is hot but not smoking. Add the pork shreds; stir-fry for about 2 minutes.

Add the mushrooms, lily buds, tree ears, bamboo shoots, and leeks; stir-fry another 2 minutes.

Add the bok choy; stir-fry for 30 seconds.

Restir the seasoning sauce and add it all at once to the wok; mix well.

Add the Egg Pancake shreds and the bean sprouts, distributing them within the mixture. Empty the contents of the wok onto a heated serving dish. Each person takes a doily, then places a few tablespoons of the filling on it, rolls it, and eats it.

YIELD *3–6 servings*

NOTES

Timing All the preparations can be done early in the day and the ingredients refrigerated.

(continued)

Tips Although this dish is traditionally served as the filling for Peking Doilies, consider it an excellent stir-fried pork and vegetable dish that can be served as part of a dinner, without the doilies.

Instead of making two separate Egg Pancakes, add 2 beaten eggs to a 12-inch iron skillet to make one large egg pancake.

Substitutions For the pork, you can substitute veal or boneless, skinless chicken; in the latter case, the chicken shreds should be stir-fried for 1 minute, removed from the wok, and then added at the very end with the eggs.

PORK IN PEKING SAUCE

Peking/Beijing

1 pound boneless pork (CT butt)

MARINADE
1 egg white
1 tablespoon water chestnut powder
1 tablespoon sherry

1/4 cup Chinese mushrooms, soaked and shredded**
1/2 cup shredded bamboo shoots
4 scallions (white and green parts), shredded

SEASONING SAUCE
1 teaspoon water chestnut powder dissolved in
2 tablespoons sherry
2 1/2 tablespoons hoisin sauce
1 tablespoon dark soy sauce

2 cups peanut oil

1 teaspoon sesame oil

PREPARATION

Partially freeze the pork; slice thin, then shred very fine. Place the pork and the ingredients for the marinade in a bowl and stir in one direction vigorously with chopsticks. Place the mixture in the refrigerator for at least 1 hour or up to 12 hours.

Having reconstituted the mushrooms and done the necessary cutting, place the vegetables in a bowl.

Combine the ingredients for the seasoning sauce.

COOKING PROCEDURE

Place the wok over high heat for about 1 minute. Pour in the 2 cups of peanut oil and turn the heat to medium until the oil reaches 325 degrees. Restir the pork in the marinade. Turn the heat to high and add the contents of the bowl all at once to the wok. Stir in a circular motion with a pair of chopsticks, separating the shreds, for 1 minute, or until the pork turns white. Turn off the heat and pour out the oil and the pork into a colander set over a bowl. Shake the colander gently to aid the draining, then place over a clean bowl.

Return the wok to high heat. In the oil that glazes the wok, stir-fry the mushrooms, bamboo shoots, and scallions for 1 minute.

Restir the seasoning sauce and add it all at once to the wok; stir-fry for about 30 seconds.

Add the pork again; stir-fry another 15 seconds, or until the sauce has evenly coated the pork shreds.

Add the sesame oil; turn off the heat. Mix for a few seconds. Empty the contents of the wok onto a heated serving dish and serve immediately.

YIELD *3–8 servings*

NOTES

Substitution For the pork, you can substitute flank steak.

DOUBLE-COOKED PORK

Szechwan/Sichuan

Double-Cooked Pork is a famous dish from Szechwan Province. It is traditionally made with fresh bacon, also referred to as pork belly. I prefer to use boneless pork fillet, which is a less fatty but very flavorful part of the pig, as it is more pleasing to the Western palate. The interesting texture of this dish is achieved by the "poaching" of the pork as a preliminary to stir-frying. The finished dish should have a sauce that simply glazes the meat.

3/4 pound boneless pork fillet (eye of CT butt)

SEASONING SAUCE
1 teaspoon Hot Sauce*
1 tablespoon hoisin sauce
1 tablespoon sweet soybean paste
1/2 tablespoon dark soy sauce
2 tablespoons sherry
1 tablespoon salt-free chicken stock
1 teaspoon sugar

2 fresh chili peppers, shredded
1 cup split, shredded leeks (white part only)

1 teaspoon minced garlic

1/4 cup chicken stock, for deglazing

3 1/2 tablespoons peanut oil

PREPARATION

Simmer the pork in boiling water to cover for 3 minutes. Drain and let cool. Slice the pork against the grain into 1/8-inch-thick slices.

Combine the ingredients for the seasoning sauce.

COOKING PROCEDURE

Place the wok over high heat for about 1 minute. Add 1 tablespoon of the oil and heat until hot but not smoking. Add the chili peppers and leeks. Turn the heat to medium; stir-fry for 2 minutes. Remove the vegetables from the wok.

Return the wok to high heat. Add 2 tablespoons of the oil and heat until hot but not smoking. Add all the pork slices; stir-fry for 2 minutes. Remove the pork slices from the wok.

Return the wok to medium heat. Add the remaining 1/2 tablespoon oil. Add the garlic; let it sizzle a few seconds.

Restir the seasoning sauce and add it all at once to the wok; stir-fry for about 30 seconds.

Return the pork and vegetables to the wok. Turn the heat to high; stir-fry until the sauce has evenly coated the pork and vegetables. Empty the contents of the wok onto a heated serving dish.

Return the wok to medium heat and add the 1/4 cup chicken stock, stirring constantly until the stock is reduced by half and forms a thick, syrupy glaze.

Turn the heat to high, then return the pork and vegetable mixture to the wok; mix briefly. Empty the contents of the wok onto the heated serving dish and serve immediately.

YIELD 2–6 servings

NOTES

Timing The entire preparation can be done a day in advance.

262

PORK

SHREDDED PORK WITH BLACK BEANS

Hunan

3/4 pound boneless pork

MARINADE
1 egg white
3/4 tablespoon water chestnut powder
3/4 tablespoon sherry

2 tablespoons fermented black beans

SEASONING SAUCE
1 teaspoon water chestnut powder
*   dissolved in*
2 tablespoons sherry
1 tablespoon dark soy sauce
1 teaspoon sugar

2 scallions (white and green parts), shredded
3 fresh chili peppers, seeded, cleaned, and
*   shredded*
2 teaspoons minced garlic
1 teaspoon minced ginger root

2 cups peanut oil

1 tablespoon sesame oil

PREPARATION

Partially freeze the pork; slice thin, then shred fine. Place the pork and the ingredients for the marinade in a bowl and stir in one direction vigorously with chopsticks. Place the mixture in the refrigerator for at least 1 hour or up to 12 hours.

Place the fermented black beans in a strainer and rinse under cold running water for 1 minute. Drain well.

Combine the ingredients for the seasoning sauce.

COOKING PROCEDURE

Place the wok over high heat for about 1 minute. Pour in the peanut oil; turn the heat to medium until the oil reaches 325 degrees. Restir the pork in the marinade. Turn the heat to high and add the contents of the bowl all at once to the wok, stirring in a circular motion with a pair of chopsticks for about 1 minute. Turn off the heat; pour out the oil and the pork into a colander set over a bowl. Shake the colander gently to aid the draining process, then place it over a clean bowl.

Return the wok to medium heat. In the oil that glazes the wok, stir-fry the black beans, scallions, chili peppers, garlic, and ginger for 1 minute.

Add the pork again; mix a few seconds.

Restir the seasoning sauce and add it all at once to the wok; stir-fry for about 30 seconds.

Turn off the heat; add the sesame oil and mix well. Empty the contents of the wok onto a heated serving dish and serve immediately.

YIELD *3–6 servings*

NOTES

Substitutions For the fresh chili peppers, you can substitute 1/2 cup shredded sweet pepper (in which case add 2 teaspoons Hot Sauce* to the seasoning sauce).

For the pork, you can substitute boneless, skinless poultry; flank or skirt steak; boneless leg of lamb; or boneless leg of veal.

RED-COOKED SHOULDER OF PORK   Peking/Beijing

Although the Chinese are not known for their casserole cooking, it exists, and Red-Cooked Shoulder of Pork is a typical Peking winter casserole dish. I have adapted it from *Madame Chu's Chinese Cooking School* cookbook. Although there are substitutions for the shoulder of pork called for in this recipe, the Chinese consider the shoulder of pork (in the United States also referred to as fresh cali or picnic roast) the preferred cut of meat because of its excellent flavor. The people of Peking are known for cooking large pieces of meat and poultry. The technique of red cooking in the Chinese cuisine means a dish slowly simmered for a long time with a large amount of soy sauce. The finished dish has a reddish brown cast and is called red-cooked because the Chinese consider red an auspicious color.

1 fresh shoulder of pork (5–6 pounds—cali, picnic)

1/2 cup Chinese mushrooms, soaked and left whole**
2 tablespoons tree ears, soaked**
30 tiger lily buds, soaked and knotted**

1/2 cup sherry
1/2 cup dark soy sauce

4 slices ginger root
4 scallions (white and green parts), cut into 1-inch pieces

1/2 cup mushroom stock**
4 cups water or vegetable stock or homemade salt-free chicken stock

2 tablespoons red rice (optional)

1/4 cup rock sugar

PREPARATION

Wash the pork shoulder in cold water.

Having reconstituted the mushrooms, tree ears, and lily buds, set aside.

COOKING PROCEDURE

Bring a large pot of water to a boil. Submerge the pork shoulder; bring the water to a boil again. Boil for 10 minutes. Wash and rinse the shoulder in cold water to remove the scum.

Place a rack in a large pot. Place the shoulder on top of the rack. Turn the heat to high. Pour the sherry and soy sauce directly over the pork. Place the ginger slices and scallion pieces on top of the pork. Add the mushroom stock and water around the sides of the pork. Add the red rice, if desired. Bring to a boil; cover and turn the heat to medium-low. Cook for 4 hours. Baste once every hour and occasionally check to see that it is simmering, not boiling.

After the shoulder has simmered for 4 hours, remove it from the pot by supporting one side of the pork with a wooden spoon and placing a spatula underneath the rack on which it is resting. Empty all the liquid into a 4-cup Pyrex measuring cup; remove the fat.

Place the rack and the shoulder back in the pot; add the defatted liquid. Turn the heat to high; bring to a boil. Add the mushrooms, tree ears, and tiger lily buds on top of the shoulder. Turn the heat to low; cook, covered, for another 1/2 hour.

Add the rock sugar to the liquid; cover again, and cook for another 1/2 hour.

Remove the cover; reduce the liquid until there is about 1 cup and it has a syrupy consistency.

Remove the shoulder from the pot again by supporting one side of the pork with a wooden spoon and placing a spatula underneath the rack. Place on a heated serving dish. Slip the shoulder off the rack. Pour the liquid over the shoulder. Serve immediately. Carve with chopsticks.

YIELD *6–12 servings*

PORK

NOTES

Timing The shoulder of pork can be cooked several days in advance and refrigerated. It can be rewarmed, covered, either on top of the stove over low heat or in a preheated 250-degree oven.

Tip It is important that this meat is actually overcooked so it will be soft enough to carve with chopsticks and will easily fall away from the center bone.

Substitutions For the shoulder of pork, you can substitute loin of pork or a whole, unboned Boston butt.

SHREDDED PORK WITH PRESERVED HOT TURNIP
Shanghai

1 1/2 cups split, shredded leeks (white part only)

1/4 cup Chinese mushrooms, soaked and shredded**

1/2 cup tiger lily buds, soaked and halved**

1/2 cup preserved hot turnip

1/2 cup shredded bamboo shoots

1 cake Spiced Pressed Bean Curd*, shredded

1/2 pound boneless pork

SEASONING SAUCE

1 1/2 teaspoons water chestnut powder dissolved in

1 tablespoon sherry

2 tablespoons dark soy sauce

2 tablespoons reduced mushroom stock**, cooled

1 teaspoon sugar

2 tablespoons peanut oil

PREPARATION

Having reconstituted the mushrooms and lily buds and done the necessary cutting, place the three groups of vegetables in separate bowls.

Partially freeze the pork; slice thin, then shred.

Combine the ingredients for the seasoning sauce.

COOKING PROCEDURE

Place the wok over high heat for about 1 minute. Add the oil and heat until hot but not smoking. Add the pork; stir-fry for 2 to 3 minutes, or until it turns white.

Add the leeks; stir-fry for 2 minutes.

Add the mushrooms, lily buds, preserved hot turnip, and bamboo shoots, continuing to stir-fry for 1 more minute.

Restir the seasoning sauce and add it all at once to the wok; stir-fry for about 30 seconds.

Add the bean curd; mix briefly. Empty the contents of the wok onto a heated serving dish and serve immediately.

YIELD *2–6 servings*

NOTES

Substitutions This dish can be adjusted to a vegetarian diet by substituting 1 cup bean sprouts and 1 additional cake of Spiced Pressed Bean Curd for the pork. Stir-fry the bean sprouts without oil in a very hot wok for 1 minute. Remove them from the wok before adding the oil and stir-frying the leeks. Return the bean sprouts to the wok along with the bean curd at the end of the recipe.

SHREDDED PORK WITH GARLIC SAUCE

Szechwan/Sichuan

³/4 pound boneless pork

MARINADE
1 egg white
1 tablespoon water chestnut powder
2 teaspoons sherry

SEASONING SAUCE
1 teaspoon water chestnut powder
  dissolved in
2 tablespoons sherry
1 tablespoon dark soy sauce
1 tablespoon light soy sauce
2 teaspoons wine vinegar
2 teaspoons sugar
*2 teaspoons Hot Sauce**
2 tablespoons chicken stock

1 tablespoon minced garlic
2 teaspoons minced ginger root
2 scallions (white and green parts), shredded

*³/4 cup fresh water chestnuts, peeled, washed
  and shredded*

2 cups peanut oil

1 tablespoon sesame oil

PREPARATION

Partially freeze the pork; slice it thin, then shred very fine. Place the pork shreds and the ingredients for the marinade in a bowl and stir in one direction vigorously with chopsticks. Place the mixture in the refrigerator for at least 1 hour or up to 12 hours.

Combine the ingredients for the seasoning sauce.

COOKING PROCEDURE

Place the wok over high heat for about 1 minute. Pour in the peanut oil; turn the heat to medium until the oil reaches 325 degrees. Restir the pork in the marinade, turn the heat to high, and add the contents of the bowl all at once to the wok, stirring in a circular motion with a pair of chopsticks, separating the shreds, for about 1 minute, or until the pork turns white. Turn off the heat and pour out the oil and the pork into a colander set over a bowl. Shake the colander gently to aid the draining, then place over a clean bowl.

Return the wok to high heat. In the oil that glazes the wok, stir-fry the garlic, ginger, and scallions for 30 seconds. Add the water chestnuts.

Restir the seasoning sauce and add it all at once to the wok; stir-fry for about 5 seconds.

Add the pork again; stir-fry another 15 seconds, or until the sauce has evenly coated the pork shreds.

Add the sesame oil; turn off the heat. Mix a few seconds. Empty the contents of the wok onto a heated serving dish and serve immediately.

YIELD *2–6 servings*

NOTES

Substitutions For the water chestnuts, you can substitute jicama or icicle radish (Chinese turnip). If using Chinese turnip, add it to the wok along with the garlic, ginger, and scallions.

For the pork, you can substitute boneless, skinless poultry; flank or skirt steak; boneless leg of lamb; or boneless leg of veal.

SLICED PORK WITH CHILI PEPPERS   Szechwan/Sichuan

³/4 pound fillet of pork (eye of CT butt)

MARINADE
1 egg white
³/4 tablespoon water chestnut powder
³/4 tablespoon sherry

SEASONING SAUCE
1 teaspoon water chestnut powder
  dissolved in
2 tablespoons sherry
2 tablespoons dark soy sauce
2 teaspoons Chinese red vinegar

12 dried chili peppers, left whole
2 teaspoons minced ginger root
2 cloves garlic, minced
3 scallions (white and green parts), slant-cut

2 cups peanut oil

1 tablespoon sesame oil

PREPARATION

Partially freeze the pork; slice thin. Place the pork and the ingredients for the marinade in a bowl and stir in one direction vigorously with chopsticks. Place the mixture in the refrigerator for at least 1 hour or up to 12 hours.

Combine the ingredients for the seasoning sauce.

COOKING PROCEDURE

Place the wok over high heat for about 1 minute. Pour in the peanut oil. Turn the heat to medium until the oil reaches 325 degrees. Turn the heat to high. Restir the pork in the marinade and add the contents of the bowl all at once to the wok, stirring in a circular motion with a pair of chopsticks for 1 minute, or until the pork turns white. Turn off the heat; pour out the oil and the pork into a colander set over a bowl. Shake the colander gently to aid the draining, then place it over a clean bowl.

Return the wok to high heat; in the oil that glazes the wok, stir-fry the chili peppers, ginger, garlic, and scallions for 1 minute.

Return the cooked pork to the wok; continue to stir-fry for another minute.

Restir the seasoning sauce and add it all at once to the wok; stir-fry for 30 seconds.

Turn off the heat; add the sesame oil and mix briefly. Empty the contents of the wok onto a heated serving dish and serve immediately.

YIELD *3–6 servings*

NOTES

Substitutions For the pork, you can substitute boneless, skinless poultry; flank or skirt steak; boneless leg of lamb; or boneless leg of veal.

FUKIENESE FRIED PORK CHOPS

Fukien/Fujian

8 pork chops, center-cut, weighing 4 ounces
   each

MARINADE
3 tablespoons Fermented Red Wine Rice*
1/2 tablespoon sugar
1 1/2 tablespoons water chestnut powder
1 egg white, beaten slightly
1 teaspoon salt
1/4 teaspoon freshly ground black pepper

1/4 cup chicken stock
1 tablespoon dark soy sauce

1/2 cup chopped scallions (white and green
   parts)
1/2 cup cleaned, seeded, and diced sweet red
   peppers
3 cloves garlic, minced

4 cups peanut oil

PREPARATION

Trim the fat from the pork chops.

Combine the ingredients for the marinade
in a bowl; add the pork chops and toss well.
Refrigerate for at least 6 hours or up to 12
hours.

COOKING PROCEDURE

Place the wok over high heat for about 1
minute. Pour in the oil; turn the heat to
medium until the oil reaches 375 degrees.
Turn the heat to high. Deep-fry four pork
chops for 3 to 4 minutes, turning once at
midpoint. Using a wire strainer, remove
the pork chops from the wok. Drain well by
placing them in a single layer on several
sheets of paper towels. Repeat the procedure with the four remaining pork chops.
Remove the oil from the wok.

Add the chicken stock and soy sauce to the
marinade remaining in the bowl in which
the pork chops were marinated. Stir well.

Return the wok to high heat. In the oil that
glazes the wok, stir-fry the scallions, red
pepper, and garlic for 1 minute.

Add the chicken stock and soy sauce mixture around the sides of the wok, continuing to stir another 30 seconds. Turn off the
heat.

Arrange the pork chops in an overlapping
pattern on a heated serving dish. Pour the
sauce over the pork chops and serve immediately.

YIELD 3–8 servings

CRISPY SPARERIBS IN SWEET SOYBEAN SAUCE
Peking/Beijing

1 1/2 *pounds spareribs*

MARINADE
1/2 *tablespoon sweet soybean paste*
1 *tablespoon sherry*
1 *tablespoon light soy sauce*

SEASONING SAUCE
1 1/2 *tablespoons sweet soybean paste*
1/2 *tablespoon light soy sauce*
1 *tablespoon sherry*
3 *tablespoons brown sugar*
3 *tablespoons Chinese red vinegar*
1/2 *teaspoon Five Spice Powder**
3 *tablespoons salt-free chicken stock*

BINDER
1 *teaspoon water chestnut powder*
    dissolved in
1 *tablespoon salt-free chicken stock*
1 *teaspoon sesame oil*

1/2 *cup lumpy water chestnut powder*

1 *teaspoon minced garlic*
2 *scallions (white and green parts), shredded*

2 *cups peanut oil*

PREPARATION

Have the butcher cut the spareribs into 1-inch pieces. Remove any excess fat. With your hands, toss the spareribs in the marinade. Place them in the refrigerator for 4 to 12 hours.

Combine the ingredients for the seasoning sauce in a small saucepan. Bring the sauce to a simmer, stirring occasionally. Remove it from the heat and reserve.

Mix the binder.

Drain the spareribs, reserving the marinade. Add the marinade to the seasoning sauce. Coat the spareribs with the lumpy water chestnut powder.

COOKING PROCEDURE

Place the wok over high heat for about 1 minute. Pour in the peanut oil; turn the heat to medium until the oil reaches 350 degrees; then turn the heat to high. Add half the spareribs and fry for 5 minutes, turning occasionally. The oil should maintain a temperature of 325 degrees. Using a wire strainer, remove the spareribs from the wok. Drain well by placing the spareribs on several sheets of paper towels. Repeat the frying process with the remaining spareribs. Allow the spareribs to cool for at least 30 minutes.

Over high heat, bring the oil to 375 degrees. Add half the spareribs and fry this time at 375 degrees for about 1 minute, or until they are brown and crisp. Repeat with the remaining spareribs. Drain the spareribs again on fresh paper towels.

Remove the oil from the wok. In the oil that glazes the wok, stir-fry the garlic and scallions over low heat for 30 seconds.

Restir the seasoning sauce and add it all at once to the wok; bring it to a boil over high heat.

Restir the binder and add it to the wok, stirring until the sauce thickens.

Add the spareribs; stir-fry quickly to coat the spareribs evenly with the sauce, for about 1 minute. Empty the contents of the wok onto a heated serving dish and serve immediately.

YIELD *2–6 servings*

NOTES

Timing The entire preparation and first frying of the spareribs can be done early in the day. After the spareribs have completely cooled, refrigerate. Allow the spareribs to come to room temperature before the second frying.

STEAMED SPARERIBS
WITH FERMENTED BLACK BEANS   Szechwan/Sichuan

2 pounds spareribs, trimmed, cut into 1-inch
   pieces

2 tablespoons fermented black beans
2 tablespoons minced garlic

2 tablespoons sherry
2 teaspoons sugar
2 tablespoons light soy sauce
1 teaspoon Hot Sauce*

2 tablespoons water chestnut powder

1/4 cup cleaned, seeded, and minced fresh red
   chili peppers

2 tablespoons peanut oil

COOKING PROCEDURE

Place the wok over high heat for 30 seconds. Add the oil and heat until hot but not
smoking. Add 1 pound of the spareribs,
letting them brown, while stir-frying slowly.
When brown, remove them from the wok
with a wire strainer, allowing the excess fat
to drip back into the wok. Add the remaining pound of spareribs and repeat the
browning procedure.

Return the first pound of spareribs to the
wok along with the fermented black beans
and garlic; stir-fry for 1 minute.

Add the sherry, sugar, light soy sauce, and
Hot Sauce; mix for a few seconds. Empty
the contents of the wok onto a serving platter that will fit into a steamer, and allow to
cool for at least 1 hour.

Sprinkle the water chestnut powder over
the spareribs and toss with your hands to
mix until it is dissolved. Sprinkle with the
minced chili peppers. Place the spareribs in
the steamer. Cover and steam over high
heat for 30 minutes.

Remove the spareribs from the steamer
and pour off the liquid into a heatproof
cup. Remove the fat and pour the de-
greased juices over the spareribs. Serve immediately.

YIELD *4–8 servings*

NOTES

Timing Up to the steaming, the entire recipe can be prepared the day ahead and refrigerated.

Tip Leftover spareribs may be reheated as
follows: Preheat the oven to broil; place the
spareribs on a broiling pan and broil for 4
minutes, turning once at midpoint. Spareribs will be brown and crisp when reheated
in this manner and can be served as an appetizer.

Substitution For the red chili peppers, you
can substitute fresh green chili peppers.

CURED PORK BELLY WITH CHILI PEPPERS   Hunan

I discovered this dish while eating in a workmen's restaurant in Changsha, the capital of Hunan. The curing and smoking of pork and poultry is a specialty of this region. This dish is particularly unusual because of the smoky flavor permeating the sauce, achieved by the cured pork and the caramelizing of sugar.

1 piece cured pork belly weighing ¹/₄ pound

1 cup cleaned, seeded, and triangle-cut fresh chili peppers

1 tablespoon sugar

¹/₄ cup chicken stock

PREPARATION

Rinse the pork belly under cold running water. Trim the rind. Place it on a plate that will fit into a steamer and steam it for 10 minutes. Remove the pork from the steamer and allow it to cool, reserving any juice that was released during the steaming procedure to add to the chicken stock. Slice the pork belly thin.

COOKING PROCEDURE

Place the wok over high heat for about 1 minute. Add the sliced pork belly and stir-fry for 2 minutes. Remove the pork from the wok, allowing any fat that has been rendered during the stir-frying process to remain in the wok.

Return the wok to high heat and stir-fry the chili peppers for 1 minute. Remove the chili peppers, allowing any fat to remain in the wok.

Turn the heat to low. Add the sugar and stir with a wooden spoon until it caramelizes. Slowly add the chicken stock and pork juices, stirring until well blended.

Return the wok to high heat; add the pork and chili peppers, continuing to stir-fry another minute. Empty the contents of the wok onto a heated serving dish and serve immediately.

YIELD *2–6 servings*

NOTES

Timing The entire preparation can be done a day in advance and the pork refrigerated.

Substitutions Smithfield ham** or baked, smoked domestic ham can be substituted for the cured pork belly.

POOR MAN'S PEKING DUCK

Peking/Beijing

The title for this dish is self-explanatory, as pork is far less expensive than duck. When eating Poor Man's Peking Duck you will be thinking, not of economy, but rather of a superb, crisp, flavorful dish, reminiscent of the most desirable part of the skin of Peking Duck.

1¹/₂ pounds fatty, boneless pork (CT butt)

MARINADE
2 tablespoons sherry
1 tablespoon dark miso
1 tablespoon dark soy sauce
1 tablespoon hoisin sauce
1¹/₂ tablespoons sugar
1 tablespoon minced garlic
1 tablespoon shredded ginger root
3 scallions (white and green parts), shredded
1 teaspoon Five Spice Powder*

BATTER
3 tablespoons flour
3 tablespoons cornstarch
1 egg, beaten
¹/₄ cup cold, flat beer

PEKING DUCK SAUCE
¹/₄ cup hoisin sauce
2 tablespoons sherry
2 teaspoons sesame oil

12 Peking Doilies*

3 scallions (white and green parts), shredded

2 cups peanut oil

PREPARATION

Partially freeze the pork; then cut it into thick strips ¹/₄ inch by 3 inches.

Combine the ingredients for the marinade in a bowl; then add the pork strips, massaging them well with the marinade. Refrigerate for at least 12 hours or up to 24 hours.

To make the batter Combine the flour and cornstarch. Stir in the egg until the mixture is smooth. Pour in the beer and continue to stir until well combined. Refrigerate, uncovered, for at least 4 hours or up to 24 hours.

Combine the ingredients for the Peking Duck Sauce.

COOKING PROCEDURE

Preheat the oven to 375 degrees. Spread the marinated pork strips in a shallow roasting pan and bake for 1 hour. Using chopsticks, separate the pork strips every 20 minutes. Take the roasting pan out of the oven and remove the pork strips with a wire strainer; drain on several layers of paper towels. Allow to cool.

Place the wok over high heat for about 1 minute. Pour in the peanut oil, turn the heat to medium, and heat until the oil reaches 375 degrees.

Add the pork strips to the bowl containing the batter. Stir them until they are well coated.

Turn the heat to high and add one quarter of the pork mixture to the wok. With a pair of chopsticks in each hand, separate the pork strips while frying for 30 seconds. Using a wire strainer, remove the pork from the wok. Drain well by placing the pork shreds in a single layer on several sheets of paper towels. Repeat the frying procedure until all the pork has been fried. The entire preparation can be done several hours in advance up to this point.

Wrap the Peking Doilies in a dish towel and steam in a bamboo steamer for 5 minutes.

Reheat the oil to 375 degrees. Refry the pork strips in two batches for 30 seconds each. Drain well on paper towels.

Presentation Place the fried pork strips on a plate. Each person takes a doily, spreads it with about 1 teaspoon Peking Duck Sauce, adds a few shreds of scallion, then places a few tablespoons of the pork strips in the doily. The doily is then rolled and eaten.

YIELD *3–6 servings*

NOTES

Timing The Peking Doilies, whether homemade or purchased, can be frozen several months in advance.

The pork can be marinated 24 hours in advance. The batter can be made early in the day and refrigerated.

The Peking Duck Sauce can be prepared several days in advance.

The scallions can be shredded early in the day and refrigerated.

The pork can be baked early in the day and, when thoroughly cooled, refrigerated. Allow the pork strips to return to room temperature before deep-fat frying. The first frying of the pork can be done several hours in advance.

Tip This dish can be served as an appetizer or as part of a multi-course Chinese dinner.

Chapter 15

BEEF

BEEF WITH BABY GINGER

1 pound flank steak, trimmed

MARINADE
1 tablespoon dark soy sauce
1 tablespoon sugar
1 teaspoon water chestnut powder

SEASONING SAUCE
1 teaspoon water chestnut powder
    dissolved in
2 tablespoons sherry
1 tablespoon dark soy sauce

1/2 cup paper-thin-sliced baby (spring) ginger
1/2 cup shredded scallions (white and green
    parts)

3 tablespoons peanut oil

PREPARATION

Partially freeze the steak. Cut it in half with the grain, then slice it against the grain into 1/4-inch-thick pieces.

Place the beef and the ingredients for the marinade in a bowl and stir in one direction vigorously with chopsticks. Place the mixture in the refrigerator for at least 1 hour or up to 12 hours.

Combine the ingredients for the seasoning sauce.

COOKING PROCEDURE

Place the wok over high heat for about 1 minute. Add the oil and heat until hot but not smoking. Restir the beef in the marinade and add half the quantity to the wok; stir-fry for about 1 minute, or until the beef is seared on both sides. Remove the beef from the wok with a spatula and wire strainer, allowing the fat to drain back into the wok. Repeat the frying procedure with the remaining beef; remove it from the wok.

Remove all but approximately 1 tablespoon oil from the wok and stir-fry the ginger and scallions for 1 minute over high heat.

Restir the seasoning sauce and add it to the wok all at once along with the beef; stir-fry for about 30 seconds. Empty the contents of the wok onto a heated serving dish and serve immediately.

YIELD *3–8 servings*

NOTES

Substitution For the spring ginger, you can substitute Pickled Spring Ginger.*

1 pound flank steak, trimmed

MARINADE
1 tablespoon oyster sauce
1/2 egg white
1 teaspoon sherry
1 teaspoon water chestnut powder

SEASONING SAUCE
1 1/2 tablespoons oyster sauce
1 tablespoon dark soy sauce
2 tablespoons sherry
1 teaspoon sugar

BINDER
1 teaspoon water chestnut powder
    dissolved in
1/4 cup chicken stock

1 1/2 cups Spanish onions, thinly sliced in
    half-moon shapes

1 cup broccoli florets, blanched

2 teaspoons minced ginger root

3 (or more) tablespoons peanut oil

1. Cut a whole flank steak in half with the grain. This is done so that the slices will not be too long.

PREPARATION

Partially freeze the steak. Cut it in half with the grain, then slice against the grain into 1/4-inch-thick pieces. Place the beef and the ingredients for the marinade in a bowl and stir in one direction vigorously with chopsticks. Place the mixture in the refrigerator for at least 1 hour or up to 12 hours.

Combine the ingredients for the seasoning sauce.

Mix the binder.

COOKING PROCEDURE

Place the wok over high heat for about 1 minute. Add 1 tablespoon peanut oil and heat until hot but not smoking. Add the onion slices; stir-fry for 2 minutes. The onions should be slightly scorched.

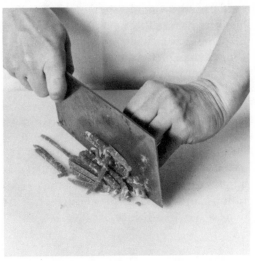

2. Partially freeze the flank steak to facilitate the slicing.

3. To shred, stack three or four slices of flank steak and make thin shreds.

Add the broccoli and stir-fry for 30 seconds. Remove the vegetables from the wok.

Return the wok to high heat; add the remaining 2 tablespoons oil. Restir the beef in the marinade and add half the quantity to the wok. Stir-fry for about 1 minute, or until the beef is seared on both sides. Remove the beef from the wok with a spatula and a wire strainer, allowing the fat to drain back into the wok. If necessary, add an additional tablespoon of oil before stir-frying the second batch of beef. Return the first

batch of beef to the wok along with the minced ginger root; continue to stir-fry for a few seconds.

Restir the seasoning sauce and add it all at once to the wok along with the onions and broccoli.

Restir the binder and add it to the wok, stirring until the sauce thickens. Empty the contents of the wok onto a heated serving dish and serve immediately.

YIELD *3–8 servings*

FIVE STAR SPICY BEEF

Cold sliced aromatic shin of beef is frequently included as part of a cold platter that comes as a first course in a traditional Chinese banquet. Other meats included in this platter would be roast pork, roast duck, abalone, and shrimp, with various vegetables for garnish. A more elaborate version would be shaped in the form of an animal, such as a peacock. Although this dish is traditionally served as a first course, I suggest including it as part of a cold buffet, as it holds up well for hours and all the preparations and cooking procedures can be done a day in advance.

1 piece shin of beef (round part—about
  1 1/2 pounds)
1 large Spanish onion, quartered
2 slices ginger root
4 whole black peppercorns

1 package unflavored gelatin

S A U C E
1 tablespoon minced garlic
2 fresh chili peppers, cleaned, seeded, and
  finely chopped
1/4 cup cleaned, seeded, and finely chopped
  sweet red peppers
3 tablespoons sesame oil
3 tablespoons light soy sauce
2 teaspoons sugar
3 tablespoons red wine vinegar
1/4 cup finely chopped scallions (white and
  green parts)
2 teaspoons Hot Sauce*

PREPARATION AND COOKING PROCEDURE

Place 3 quarts water in a large, heavy pot and bring it to a boil. Add the shin of beef and return the water to a boil. Remove the scum as it surfaces. This procedure will take 2 to 3 minutes. Add the onion, ginger slices, and peppercorns. Cover, turn the heat to low, and simmer for 1 1/2 hours. Remove the cover, turn the heat to medium-low, and simmer until the beef is tender. (Use a cake tester or poultry skewer to determine the tenderness of the meat.) This should take about another hour. Remove the beef from the pot with a wire strainer and let it cool on a rack resting on a plate. Wrap the beef well and refrigerate.

Turn the heat to medium and reduce the liquid remaining in the pot to a full 1 1/4 cups. Strain the beef stock into a measuring cup. Refrigerate until the fat solidifies, then remove the fat.

Heat the beef stock in a small saucepan to return it to a liquid state. Dissolve the gelatin in 1/4 cup of the stock and let it stand for 5 minutes. Keep a low heat under the remaining stock, add the gelatin, and heat until the gelatin is no longer visible (about 2 minutes).

Pour approximately 1 cup of stock into a 1-cup custard ramekin and place it in the refrigerator. This entire procedure can be done early in the day or several days ahead.

Combine the ingredients for the sauce.

One half hour before serving Slice the meat paper thin and arrange it in overlapping slices on a serving platter.

Restir the sauce and spoon it over the beef. Baste the meat with the sauce three to four times before serving.

When ready to serve Remove the jellied stock from the ramekin; slice horizontally into five circles about 3/8 inch thick. Cut each circle into a star shape with a cookie cutter and place the stars around the beef on the serving platter.

Serve at room temperature.

YIELD *4–8 servings*

NOTES

Tip This sauce is excellent served over blanched, cold string beans or asparagus. These can be served as an appetizer, as you would serve asparagus vinaigrette before a Western meal, or as part of the main course of a Chinese meal.

Substitution For the shin of beef, you can substitute the center cut of a filet mignon (toward the tail). The filet should weigh 1½ pounds after it is trimmed.

Bring a large pot of water to a boil and add the filet. Cover and let the filet boil 15 minutes over medium heat. Remove it from the pot with a wire strainer and let it drain on a rack resting on a plate. Refrigerate it until cold. Discard the water.

Slice the meat very thin (it should be blood rare). Spoon the sauce over the filet ½ hour before serving. Baste the filet with the sauce a few times before serving.

1 pound filet mignon tail, trimmed

MARINADE
1 egg white
1 tablespoon water chestnut powder
1 tablespoon sherry

¹/₂ pound lotus root (weighed before peeling)

SEASONING SAUCE
1¹/₂ tablespoons dark miso
1 tablespoon dark soy sauce
1 tablespoon hoisin sauce
2 tablespoons sherry
2 teaspoons Hot Sauce*
1 teaspoon red wine vinegar

1 cup leeks, split and cut into 1-inch pieces
  (white parts only)

2 teaspoons minced ginger root
2 cloves garlic, minced

4¹/₂ tablespoons peanut oil

PREPARATION

Cut the beef into 1¹/₂-inch cubes. Place the beef and the ingredients for the marinade in a bowl and stir in one direction vigorously with chopsticks. Place the mixture in the refrigerator for at least 1 hour or up to 12 hours.

Peel the lotus root, then slice it into ¹/₈-inch rounds. Blanch the lotus root for 1 minute; drain, then place it in a bowl.

Combine the ingredients for the seasoning sauce.

COOKING PROCEDURE

Place the beef cubes on several layers of paper towels to drain.

Place the wok over high heat for about 1 minute. Add 1¹/₂ tablespoons of the oil and heat until hot but not smoking. Turn the heat to medium. Add the leeks; stir-fry for 1 minute.

Add the lotus root; continue to stir-fry for another minute. Remove the vegetables from the wok.

Place the wok over high heat. Add the remaining 3 tablespoons of oil to the wok and heat until the oil is very hot. Add ¹/₂ pound of the beef; stir-fry slowly to allow the beef cubes to brown. This should take about 2 minutes. Remove the beef from the wok. Repeat the procedure with the remaining beef. Remove the beef cubes from the wok. Pour out the remaining oil.

Return the wok to medium heat. In the oil that glazes the wok, stir-fry the ginger and garlic for 30 seconds.

Restir the seasoning sauce and add it all at once to the wok. Stir-fry for about 30 seconds.

Return the beef cubes to the wok; stir-fry for about 30 seconds, or until the seasoning sauce has evenly coated the beef cubes.

Return the leeks and lotus root to the wok; stir-fry for another minute. Empty the contents of the wok onto a heated serving dish and serve immediately.

YIELD *3–8 servings*

NOTES

Substitutions For the beef, you can substitute flank steak. Cut the entire flank steak in half with the grain. Freeze, then cut it against the grain into ¹/₄-inch-thick slices.

  Although the visual effect will not be the same, you can substitute snow peas (strung and left whole) or asparagus (roll-oblique-cut then blanched) for the lotus root. Add the snow peas at the same time that you would add the lotus root but stir-fry for only 30 seconds.

DRY SAUTÉED SHREDDED BEEF   Szechwan/Sichuan

The Chinese give equal priority to texture and to taste. For that reason this famous dish of Szechwan Province contains meat cooked until it becomes crisp and chewy.

1/2 pound flank steak, trimmed
1/2 teaspoon salt

SEASONING SAUCE
1 teaspoon dark soy sauce
2 teaspoons light soy sauce
1 teaspoon black rice vinegar
1 teaspoon Fermented Wine Rice* liquid
1 teaspoon sugar
1 teaspoon Hot Sauce*

1/2 cup split, shredded leeks (white part only)
1/2 cup shredded carrots

1 cup strung, shredded snow peas

1 teaspoon minced garlic

3 tablespoons peanut oil

PREPARATION

Slice, then cut the flank steak into *thick* shreds. Sprinkle with the salt.

Combine the ingredients for the seasoning sauce.

COOKING PROCEDURE

Place the wok over high heat for about 1 minute. Add the oil and heat until it smokes. Add the beef and stir-fry for 4 minutes, separating the shreds of beef during the cooking process. Pour the beef and the oil into a strainer set over a bowl. Do not wash the wok. All of the above can be prepared up to 4 hours ahead.

Return the wok to medium heat. Add 1 tablespoon of the cooked oil. Stir-fry the leeks and carrots for 2 minutes.

Add the snow peas; stir-fry for 1 more minute. Remove the vegetables from the wok to a separate dish.

Turn the heat to high. Add the beef again, with the oil in which it was cooked; stir-fry for 1 to 2 more minutes, or until the beef is dry and very crisp.

Add the garlic; stir-fry for a few seconds.

Restir the seasoning sauce and add it all at once to the wok, stir-frying for a few more seconds.

Return the vegetables to the wok and stir-fry until well combined. Empty the contents of the wok onto a heated serving dish and serve immediately.

YIELD *2–6 servings*

This recipe is my adaptation of the classic orange or sesame seed beef. It would be a rare event for a cut of meat such as filet mignon to reach even a banquet table in China, simply because it is so scarce. A more authentic cut of meat to use for this dish would be shin of beef or flank steak. The reason I have chosen filet mignon for this recipe is because it is the most tender cut of meat from the steer, and if it is cut in large cubes, it is possible to produce a crisp outside texture with a rare inside. When you use flank steak, the meat must be thinly cut to become tender. It therefore cooks so quickly it can be served only well done. I use filet mignon instead of shell steak or sirloin because at the high temperatures to which the beef is subjected, it will still remain tender.

1 pound filet mignon tail, trimmed

MARINADE
1 egg white
1 tablespoon water chestnut powder
1 tablespoon sherry

3 pieces dried orange peel, about 1 × 2 inches

SEASONING SAUCE
1 teaspoon water chestnut powder dissolved in
2 tablespoons sherry
2 tablespoons Kikkoman soy sauce
2 tablespoons sugar
2 tablespoons salt-free chicken stock
1 teaspoon Hot Sauce*
1/2 teaspoon wine vinegar
1 teaspoon sesame oil

GARNISH
1/2 cup snow peas, strung and left whole
1 teaspoon butter

2 scallions (white and green parts), chopped
2 teaspoons minced ginger root
1 clove garlic, minced
1 fresh red chili pepper, cleaned, seeded, and chopped

3 cups peanut oil

PREPARATION

Cut the beef into 1 1/2-inch cubes. Place the beef cubes and the ingredients for the marinade in a bowl and stir in one direction vigorously with chopsticks. Place the mixture in the refrigerator for at least 1 hour or up to 12 hours.

Place the wok over high heat for about 1 minute. Pour in the peanut oil; turn the heat to medium until the oil reaches 350 degrees. Add the orange peel and fry for about 15 seconds, or until it turns a darker brown. Drain it on a paper towel. Once it is cool, break the orange peel into smaller pieces, then pulverize it in an electric coffee mill. Reserve the oil for frying the beef.

Combine the ingredients for the seasoning sauce.

COOKING PROCEDURE

Heat the oil in which the orange peel was fried over medium heat until it reaches 375 degrees. Turn the heat to high. Add the beef, one third at a time, cooking each portion about 30 seconds. Bring the oil temperature back to 375 degrees each time before adding more beef. Using a wire strainer, remove the beef cubes from the wok. Drain them well by placing them on several sheets of paper towels. (All the above procedures can be done ahead. It is not necessary, however, for the beef to cool before continuing the recipe.)

Reheat the oil over high heat to 375 degrees and fry the beef a second time, a third at a time, for about 15 seconds each. Drain the beef cubes again on several layers of paper towels. Remove the oil from the wok.

In a second wok, stir-fry the snow peas in the butter for 1 minute over medium-low heat. Set aside.

Place the first wok over high heat and add the scallions, ginger, garlic, and chili pepper; stir-fry for about 30 seconds.

Restir the seasoning sauce and add it all at once to the wok; stir-fry for about 30 seconds, or until the sauce thickens.

Return the beef to the wok along with the crushed orange peel; stir-fry rapidly in order to coat the meat evenly with the sauce. This will take about 30 seconds.

Place the contents of the wok in the center of a flat, round serving platter. Arrange the snow peas around the beef, radiating out all around like the spokes of a wheel. Serve immediately.

YIELD *3–8 servings*

NOTES

Tips The finished dish should have no excess sauce and the meat should be evenly glazed. This dish demands an adept stir-fryer to achieve these effects.

Substitution For the fresh chili pepper, you can substitute ¼ cup chopped sweet red pepper, in which case add an additional ½ teaspoon Hot Sauce* to the seasoning sauce.

¹/₂ pound bay scallops

MARINADE
¹/₂ egg white
1 teaspoon water chestnut powder
1 teaspoon sherry

*¹/₄ cup Chinese mushrooms, soaked and
  diced***

³/₄ pound shell steak, trimmed

¹/₄ teaspoon freshly ground black pepper
1 clove garlic, crushed

SEASONING SAUCE
1 tablespoon oyster sauce
1 tablespoon dark soy sauce
¹/₂ cup chicken stock

BINDER
*2 teaspoons water chestnut powder
    dissolved in*
1 tablespoon sherry

1 teaspoon minced garlic
2 scallions (white and green parts), chopped
1 teaspoon minced ginger root

¹/₂ cup peeled, sliced fresh water chestnuts
1 cup strung, slant-cut snow peas

2¹/₂ tablespoons peanut oil

PREPARATION

Wash, drain, and dry the scallops. Spread the scallops on several layers of paper towels for 10 minutes. Place the scallops and the ingredients for the marinade in a bowl and stir in one direction vigorously with chopsticks. Place the mixture in the refrigerator for at least 1 hour or up to 12 hours.

Having reconstituted the mushrooms, set them aside.

Rub the steak with the black pepper and crushed garlic. Wrap it, and freeze for 1 hour.

Combine the ingredients for the seasoning sauce.

Mix the binder.

COOKING PROCEDURE

Preheat the broiler for 20 minutes. Place the steak on a rack that will fit into a steak platter. Add ¹/₃ cup water to the bottom of the platter. Broil the steak as close to the heat source as possible for 20 minutes, turning once at midpoint.

During the last 8 minutes of broiling, place the wok over high heat for about 1 minute. Add the oil and heat until hot but not smoking. Add the garlic, scallions, and ginger; stir-fry for 30 seconds.

Restir the scallops in the marinade and add the contents of the bowl all at once to the wok, continuing to stir-fry for 1 minute.

Add the mushrooms; stir-fry for 1 minute.

Restir the seasoning sauce and add it all at once to the wok. Bring it to a boil.

Add the water chestnuts and snow peas.

Restir the binder and add it to the wok, continuing to stir-fry until the sauce thickens. Turn off the heat.

Remove the steak from the broiler, leaving the platter containing the accumulated juices in the oven to keep it hot. Slice the steak across the grain in ½-inch-thick pieces. Return the steak to the platter. Reheat the scallop mixture in the wok over high heat for 30 seconds. For presentation purposes and sizzling effect, both the steak platter and the scallop mixture must be hot. Pour the scallops and the sauce over the steak slices at the table in front of the guests.

NOTES

Tips The purpose of partially freezing the steak before broiling it is to produce a crusty exterior. If you have access to a barbecue or to a professional broiling system, this step can be omitted.

The purpose of adding water to the bottom of the steak platter is to prevent the juices from burning during broiling. When turning the steak after ten minutes, check to see if more water is necessary. When the steak is removed from the oven, the juices in the bottom of the platter should be reduced to a few tablespoons. If the liquid is too plentiful, place the platter over direct heat until the juices have formed a thick syrupy glaze. This will add an extra-rich flavor to the sauce.

Substitutions For the shell steak, you can substitute filet mignon.

For the bay scallops, you can substitute sea scallops, slicing them into ¼-inch circles before marinating.

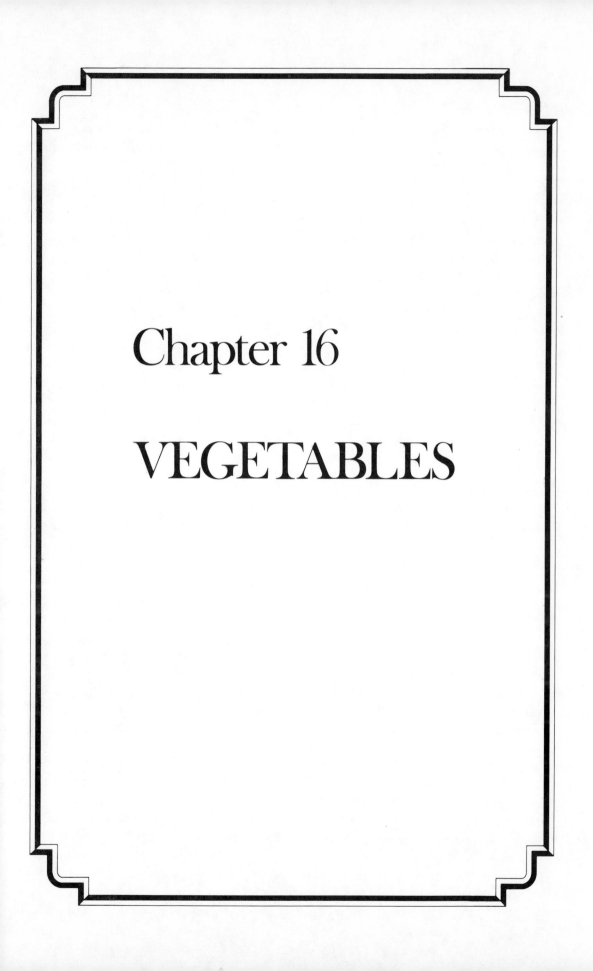

Chapter 16

VEGETABLES

Chinese Vegetables

Fresh vegetables play an extremely important role in the Chinese cuisine. The ratio of vegetables to meat is higher in Chinese cooking, which results in fewer calories and less cholesterol. The Chinese are masters at cooking vegetables because of the stir-fry technique, which preserves the maximum amount of flavor, color, crunch, and vitamins. When stir-frying vegetables, you can use either peanut oil or rendered poultry fat. Although stir-frying is the most commonly employed method, other techniques are used as well, examples of which are dry-frying, deep-fat frying, blanching, and braising.

It is always possible to substitute fresh American vegetables when Oriental ones are not available. Never use canned or frozen vegetables when preparing Chinese food. As a general rule, always use vegetables within the shortest time possible after purchasing, as the flavor and vitamin content deteriorate fast. Ideally, vegetables should be picked, cooked, and eaten within a few hours. Wash all leafy vegetables in a large basin of cold water to which a few tablespoons of white vinegar have been added. This procedure removes soil and preservatives. Drain and dry all vegetables well before adding them to the wok. This can be done in a salad spin-dry. Vegetables must be completely dry for stir-frying.

Vegetables that require blanching before stir-frying should be prepared in the following manner: First cut them, then bring a large kettle of water to a rapid boil, submerge the vegetables for thirty to sixty seconds, remove them with a wire strainer and plunge them into ice water for about one minute, then drain and dry. This procedure can be done a day in advance and the vegetables refrigerated. All vegetables, whether they require blanching or not, can be cut and refrigerated a day in advance as a time-saving device; however, there will be a further vitamin loss.

Bean Curd

The Chinese rely heavily on bean curd for a protein substitute. In China, it is referred to as "meat without bones." The following six recipes for fresh bean curd are economical, low in calories, highly nutritious, and simple to prepare.

STEAMED BEAN CURD

Canton/Guangzhou

2 cakes Japanese bean curd
1 tablespoon dark soy sauce
1 teaspoon sugar

1 teaspoon sesame oil

GARNISH
1 scallion (white and green parts), minced
1 teaspoon minced Smithfield ham**

PREPARATION

Slice each bean curd cake in half horizontally, retaining its square shape. Place the bean curd halves on a plate that will fit into a steamer with 1 inch clearance. Pour the soy sauce and sugar over the bean curd.

COOKING PROCEDURE

Steam the bean curd for 5 minutes.

Remove the bean curd from the steamer; dribble sesame oil over it. Sprinkle with the scallion and ham; serve immediately.

YIELD *4 servings*

SPICED PRESSED BEAN CURD

4 cakes fresh Chinese bean curd

MASTER SAUCE
2 cups water
¹/₃ cup dark soy sauce
1 teaspoon Five Spice Powder*
2 teaspoons sugar

PREPARATION

Wrap the bean curd cakes in a single layer in a terry-cloth towel. Place a heavy, flat weight, such as a chopping block, on top of the towel. Allow the cakes to stand for 4 hours. During this period, change their position on the towel once.

COOKING PROCEDURE

Bring the master sauce to a simmer in a saucepan. Cook for 5 minutes over the lowest heat possible. Add the bean curd cakes; simmer for 10 minutes, turning once at midpoint. The sauce should completely cover the bean curd. Remove the bean curd from the sauce and place in a glass container. Pour the sauce over the bean curd and allow it to cool overnight in the refrigerator. Remove the bean curd from the master sauce the next day.

NOTES

Storage Refrigerated, Spiced Pressed Bean Curd will keep for one week. The master sauce can be refrigerated for up to two months and used again.

DEEP-FRIED BEAN CURD WITH OYSTER SAUCE
Canton/Guangzhou

4 cakes fresh Chinese bean curd

SEASONING SAUCE
2/3 cup chicken stock
2 tablespoons oyster sauce

BINDER
1 teaspoon water chestnut powder
    dissolved in
1 tablespoon sherry

2 cups roll-oblique-cut asparagus

2 scallions (white and green parts), slant-cut

2 cups peanut oil

PREPARATION

Wrap the bean curd cakes in a single layer in a terry-cloth towel. Place a heavy, flat weight, such as a chopping block, on top of the towel. Allow to stand for 2 hours. During this period, change the position of the cakes on the towel once. Cut each cake into triangles, 4 per cake.

Combine the ingredients for the seasoning sauce.

Mix the binder.

COOKING PROCEDURE

Place the wok over high heat for about 1 minute. Pour in the oil; turn the heat to medium until the oil reaches 375 degrees. Turn the heat to high. Fry half the bean curd triangles for 1½ minutes, or until they are golden brown, turning once at midpoint. Using a wire strainer, remove the bean curd from the wok. Drain well by placing the bean curd triangles in a single layer on several sheets of paper towels. Repeat with remaining batch of bean curd.

Remove all but 1 tablespoon of the oil from the wok. Turn the heat to medium. Stir-fry the asparagus for 2 minutes.

Turn the heat to high. Add the scallions; stir-fry for 30 seconds.

Restir the seasoning sauce and add it all at once to the wok; bring to a boil.

Restir the binder and add it to the wok, stirring until the sauce thickens.

Arrange the bean curd triangles in upright positions on a flat, heated serving dish. Pour the sauce over the bean curd and serve immediately.

YIELD *4–8 servings*

NOTES

Tip To determine the tender portion of the asparagus, hold the bottom of each individual stalk in one hand, in a gently closed fist. With the other hand, palm open, slap the green stalk so it breaks cleanly. Discard the bottom portion.

SAUTÉED BEAN CURD WITH SHRIMP SAUCE

Canton/Guangzhou

4 cakes fresh Chinese bean curd
1/3 cup flour
1 egg, beaten

SEASONING SAUCE
*2 ounces shrimp, shelled, washed, drained,
    dried, and minced*
1 tablespoon sherry
1 tablespoon dark soy sauce
1 teaspoon sugar
1/2 cup chicken stock

BINDER
*2 teaspoons water chestnut powder
    dissolved in*
2 tablespoons sherry

1 teaspoon minced ginger root
1 scallion (white and green parts), chopped

3 tablespoons peanut oil

1/2 tablespoon sesame oil

PREPARATION

Wrap the bean curd cakes in a single layer in a terry-cloth towel. Place a heavy, flat weight, such as a chopping block, on top of the towel. Allow to stand for 2 hours. During this period, change the position of the cakes on the towel once. Cut each cake into 6 slices. Dredge them in the flour, then soak them in the beaten egg.

Combine the ingredients for the seasoning sauce.

Mix the binder.

COOKING PROCEDURE

Place the wok over high heat for about 1 minute. Add the peanut oil and heat until hot but not smoking. Turn the heat to medium. Arrange the bean curd in the wok in a single layer; sauté for 2 minutes on each side. Remove the bean curd from the wok; drain on paper towels.

Return the wok to high heat. In the oil that remains in the wok, stir-fry the ginger and scallion for 30 seconds.

Restir the seasoning sauce and add it all at once to the wok; stir-fry for about 30 seconds.

Restir the binder and add it to the wok, stirring until the sauce thickens.

Turn off the heat. Add the sesame oil; mix briefly. Place the sautéed bean curd on a flat, heated serving dish; pour the sauce over the bean curd and serve immediately.

YIELD *4–8 servings*

SZECHWAN VEGETARIAN'S BEAN CURD

Szechwan/Sichuan

1 clove garlic, minced
$^1/_2$ cup chopped scallions (white and green parts)
1 teaspoon minced ginger root

$^1/_3$ cup Chinese mushrooms, soaked and diced**
$^1/_4$ cup diced winter bamboo shoots

SEASONING SAUCE
1 tablespoon dark soy sauce
1 tablespoon sherry
$^1/_2$ teaspoon sugar
2 teaspoons Hot Sauce*
1 tablespoon bean sauce

4 pieces fresh Chinese bean curd

BINDER
2 teaspoons water chestnut powder dissolved in
1 tablespoon sherry

2 tablespoons chicken stock
2 tablespoons reduced mushroom stock**

2 tablespoons peanut oil

1 teaspoon sesame oil

1 teaspoon Szechwan Peppercorn Powder*

PREPARATION

Having reconstituted the mushrooms and done the necessary cutting, place the two groups of vegetables in separate bowls.

Combine the ingredients for the seasoning sauce.

Cut each bean curd cake into 16 pieces.

Mix the binder.

COOKING PROCEDURE

Place the wok over high heat for about 1 minute. Add the peanut oil and heat until hot but not smoking. Add the garlic, scallions, and ginger; stir-fry for 30 seconds.

Add the mushrooms and bamboo shoots; stir-fry for 1 minute. Empty the contents of the wok onto a heated serving dish.

Restir the seasoning sauce and add it all at once to the wok; stir-fry for about 30 seconds.

Return the vegetable mixture to the wok along with the bean curd pieces; stir-fry briefly.

Pour in the stock around the sides of the wok; bring it to a boil.

Restir the binder and add it to the wok, stirring until the sauce thickens.

Turn off the heat; add the sesame oil. Mix briefly. Empty the contents of the wok onto a heated serving dish. Sprinkle with Szechwan Peppercorn Powder and serve immediately.

YIELD *4–8 servings*

MA PO TOU FU

Ma Po Tou Fu is a flavorful classic Szechwan dish favored throughout China. This spicy, aromatic bean curd, redolent with chili oil, chili paste, and Szechwan Peppercorn Powder, is a dish named after the wife of a famous chef in Ch'eng-tu, the capital of Szechwan Province (often called the second Peking). The name translates as "bean curd of the pockmarked wife," a fanciful title that in this case reflected reality. The dish dates back to the Manchu Dynasty, during the reign of Emperor T'ung Chih (1862–75).

2 pieces fresh, large (Japanese) bean curd, if available, or substitute 4 pieces fresh, small Chinese bean curd

SEASONING SAUCE
1 tablespoon dark soy sauce
1 tablespoon sherry
1 tablespoon dark miso
1/2 teaspoon sugar
2 teaspoons Hot Sauce*

BINDER
2 teaspoons water chestnut powder dissolved in
1 tablespoon sherry

1/4 pound ground pork

2 teaspoons minced ginger root
1 teaspoon minced garlic
1/3 cup chopped scallions (white and green parts)

1/4 cup salt-free chicken stock

2 tablespoons peanut oil

1 teaspoon sesame oil

1/2 teaspoon Szechwan Peppercorn Powder*

PREPARATION

Wrap the bean curd pieces in a single layer in a terry-cloth towel. Place a heavy, flat weight, such as a chopping block, on top of the towel. Allow to stand for 2 hours. During this period, change the position of the pieces on the towel once. Cut the bean curd into 1/2-inch pieces.

Combine the ingredients for the seasoning sauce.

Mix the binder.

COOKING PROCEDURE

Place the wok over high heat for about 1 minute. Add the peanut oil and heat until hot but not smoking. Add the pork; stir-fry for 2 to 3 minutes, or until it turns white, breaking it into small pieces. Remove the pork from the wok with a spatula and wire strainer, allowing the fat to remain in the wok.

Add the ginger, garlic, and scallions; stir-fry for 30 seconds.

Restir the seasoning sauce and add it all at once to the wok; stir-fry for about 30 seconds.

Pour in the stock; bring to a boil.

Add the bean curd; toss briefly.

Restir the binder and add it to the wok, stirring until the sauce thickens.

Turn off the heat and add the sesame oil; mix well. Empty the contents of the wok onto a heated serving dish. Sprinkle with Szechwan Peppercorn Powder. Serve immediately.

YIELD 4–8 servings

STIR-FRIED FAVA BEANS

Canton/Guangzhou

2 pounds fresh fava beans

2 cloves garlic, minced
1/2 cup chopped scallions (white and green parts)

1/2 cup chicken stock

2 teaspoons sugar
2 tablespoons dark soy sauce

1/2 cup sliced water chestnuts

2 tablespoons peanut oil

PREPARATION

Shell the fava beans, then remove the outer casing surrounding each bean.

COOKING PROCEDURE

Place the wok over medium heat for about 1 minute. Add the oil, then the fava beans; stir-fry for 1 minute.

Add the garlic and scallions; stir-fry for 15 seconds.

Pour in the chicken stock; continue to stir-fry until almost all the chicken stock has evaporated.

Add the sugar and soy sauce; stir-fry 1 minute.

Add the water chestnuts; stir-fry another minute. Empty the contents of the wok onto a heated serving dish and serve immediately.

YIELD *3–6 servings*

SZECHWAN SWEET AND SOUR CABBAGE

Szechwan/Sichuan

1 1/2 pounds Shantung cabbage
1 tablespoon salt
2 tablespoons finely shredded ginger root

1/4 cup Japanese rice vinegar
1/4 cup sugar
1 tablespoon Chili Oil*
2 dried chili peppers, seeded and shredded

1 1/2 tablespoons peanut oil

PREPARATION

Remove the core from the cabbage and discard. Cut the cabbage into 2-inch pieces. Place the cabbage on a large plate, toss with the salt, and cover with paper towels. Place a heavy, flat weight over the paper towels and let stand for about 6 hours. Squeeze the liquid from the cabbage with your hands. Toss the cabbage with the ginger shreds.

COOKING PROCEDURE

Place the wok over medium heat for about 30 seconds. Add the peanut oil, then the vinegar, sugar, Chili Oil, and chili peppers. Turn the heat to low; stir with chopsticks for a few seconds, or until the sugar is dissolved. Pour the sauce over the cabbage and toss well. Place the cabbage in a covered serving dish. Refrigerate for 24 hours. Serve cold or at room temperature.

YIELD *4–8 servings*

NOTES

Storage Refrigerated, Szechwan Sweet and Sour Cabbage will keep for one week.

SAUTÉED DUCK POTATOES Canton/Guangzhou

*¹/₂ pound duck potatoes***

¹/₂ cup split, chopped leeks (white part only)
¹/₂ teaspoon salt
¹/₄ teaspoon freshly ground white pepper

*2 tablespoons rendered poultry fat***

PREPARATION

Peel, wash, then slice the duck potatoes into ¹/₄-inch rounds.

COOKING PROCEDURE

Place a 12-inch iron skillet over medium heat for about 1 minute. Add the poultry fat; heat for 1 more minute. Place the sliced duck potatoes in a single layer in the skillet. Sprinkle the leeks on top of the duck potatoes. Add the salt and pepper. Sauté, shaking the skillet occasionally, for 3 to 4 minutes. Turn the duck potatoes over and sauté for another 3 to 4 minutes. Empty the contents of the skillet onto a heated serving dish and serve immediately.

YIELD *3–6 servings*

SPICY BRAISED EGGPLANT

The following two recipes for eggplant are excellent served hot or cold. These are dishes to remember when you're planning a Chinese buffet or a multi-course Chinese dinner. If you are serving the eggplant cold, it can be made several days in advance; however, you if you are serving it hot, it should not be rewarmed. Since eggplant absorbs an excessive amount of oil when stir-fried, I have borrowed from the French technique of salting and weighting the eggplant first, which extracts the moisture, removes the bitterness, and aids in the browning. If this precaution is not taken, then three times the amount of oil or poultry fat is required.

1 medium eggplant (about 1–1¹/₄ pounds)
¹/₂ cup cleaned, seeded, and triangle-cut sweet red pepper
1 teaspoon salt

SEASONING SAUCE
1 tablespoon Tientsin preserved vegetable**, minced
1 tablespoon hot bean sauce
1¹/₂ tablespoons dark soy sauce
2 tablespoons chicken stock
1 teaspoon honey
1 teaspoon Hot Sauce*

¹/₃ cup ground pork

¹/₂ tablespoon minced ginger root

1 tablespoon minced garlic

2 scallions (white and green part) chopped
¹/₂ tablespoon Chinese red vinegar

2¹/₂ tablespoon rendered poultry fat**

¹/₂ tablespoon sesame oil

PREPARATION

Cut the eggplant (do not peel) first into circles ¹/₂ inch thick, then into strips 2 to 3 inches long and ³/₈ inch wide. Toss the eggplant and red pepper with the salt and spread on a cookie sheet. Put paper towels over the eggplant and red pepper, then place a chopping block or some other flat, heavy object over the paper towels. Let stand for at least ¹/₂ hour. Rinse the eggplant and pepper very well under cold running water. Drain dry with a towel or in a salad spin-dry; place in a bowl.

Combine the ingredients for the seasoning sauce.

COOKING PROCEDURE

Place the wok over high heat for about 1 minute. Add 1 tablespoon of the poultry fat; heat until hot but not smoking. Add the ground pork; stir-fry until it turns white. Remove the pork from the wok, leaving any excess fat in the wok.

Add the remaining 1¹/₂ tablespoons of poultry fat to the wok. When it is hot, add the ginger and garlic; let sizzle a few seconds.

Add the eggplant and red pepper; stir-fry for about 3 to 4 minutes, pressing down with a spatula to aid in browning.

Add the cooked pork along with the seasoning sauce; continue to stir-fry over high heat for 1 more minute.

Add the scallions and vinegar; stir-fry for a few more seconds.

Turn off the heat and add the sesame oil. Stir to mix. Empty the contents of the wok onto a serving dish. Serve the eggplant hot, at room temperture, or cold as an appetizer.

YIELD *3–6 servings*

NOTES

Tip If you wish to omit the pork and make this a vegetarian dish, double the amount of sweet red pepper.

Either Szechwan or Tientsin preserved vegetable** can be used.

Storage Refrigerated, Spicy Braised Eggplant keeps for up to one week.

See introduction to previous recipe.

1 medium eggplant (about 1 pound)
1 teaspoon salt

SEASONING SAUCE
1 1/2 tablespoons dark soy sauce
2 teaspoons Hot Sauce*
2 tablespoons chicken stock
2 teaspoons sugar
2 teaspoons black rice vinegar
1 tablespoon sherry

1 tablespoon minced garlic

1 sweet red pepper, cleaned, seeded, and cut
into 1/2-inch strips
2 scallions (white and green parts), chopped
2 teaspoons minced ginger root

3 tablespoons rendered poultry fat**

1 tablespoon sesame oil

PREPARATION

Cut the eggplant (do not peel) first into circles 1/2 inch thick, then into strips 2 to 3 inches long and 3/8 inch wide. Toss the eggplant with the salt and spread on a cookie sheet. Put paper towels over the eggplant,

then place a chopping block or some other flat, heavy object over the paper towels. Let stand for at least 1/2 hour. Rinse the eggplant very well under cold running water. Drain and dry with a towel or in a salad spin-dry; place in a bowl.

Combine the ingredients for the seasoning sauce.

COOKING PROCEDURE

Place the wok over high heat for about 1 minute. Add the poultry fat and heat until hot but not smoking. Add the eggplant; stir-fry for 3 minutes, pressing down on the strips with a spatula to aid the browning.

Add the garlic; stir-fry for 1 minute.

Add the red pepper, scallions, and ginger; stir-fry for 1 more minute.

Restir the seasoning sauce and add it all at once to the wok; stir-fry for 30 seconds.

Turn off the heat, add the sesame oil, and mix briefly. Empty the contents of the wok onto a heated serving dish. Serve immediately or at room temperature.

YIELD 3–6 servings

BARBECUED EGGPLANT

1 medium eggplant (about 1 1/4 pounds)

SEASONING SAUCE
3 tablespoons hoisin sauce
1 tablespoon dark miso
1 tablespoon light soy sauce
1 tablespoon sherry
1 teaspoon sugar

1 tablespoon unhulled sesame seeds

1 scallion (white and green part), chopped

1/4 cup chicken stock

1 tablespoon peanut oil

PREPARATION

Slant-cut the eggplant (unpeeled) into 1/2-inch-thick slices.

Combine the ingredients for the seasoning sauce.

Place the wok over low heat. Add the sesame seeds; stir until they turn brown. Remove them from the wok and allow to cool.

COOKING PROCEDURE

Preheat the oven to broil.

Steam the eggplant slices over high heat for 5 minutes. Remove them from the steamer; allow to cool. Arrange the eggplant slices in a single layer on a rack resting in a shallow roasting pan; broil for 5 minutes on each side. Transfer the eggplant to a preheated flat serving dish and arrange the slices in an overlapping pattern.

Place the wok over high heat for about 1 minute. Add the oil and heat until hot but not smoking. Add the scallion; stir-fry for a few seconds.

Restir the seasoning sauce and add it all at once to the wok; stir-fry for about 30 seconds.

Pour in the stock; stir another 15 seconds.

Pour the sauce over the eggplant slices; sprinkle with the sesame seeds. Serve immediately.

YIELD *3–6 servings*

NOTES

Timing The eggplant can be steamed and allowed to cool several hours before broiling.

Tip If an outdoor barbecue is available, the eggplant will have a superior flavor.

DEEP-FRIED STUFFED EGGPLANT   Szechwan/Sichuan

BATTER
1/3 cup flour
1 cup cornstarch
2 eggs
2/3 cup cold, flat beer
3 tablespoons sesame oil

1 medium eggplant (about 1 1/4 pounds)
2 teaspoons salt

FILLING
1 teaspoon dried shrimp
1/2 pound ground pork
2 scallions (white and green parts), chopped
1 teaspoon minced ginger root
1 teaspoon dark soy sauce
1 tablespoon sesame oil

SEASONING SAUCE
1 tablespoon dark miso
1 tablespoon dark soy sauce
1 tablespoon sugar
1 tablespoon Chinese red vinegar

BINDER
2 teaspoons water chestnut powder
    dissolved in
1 tablespoon sherry
1/2 cup salt-free chicken stock

1 clove garlic, minced
1 scallion (white and green parts), chopped
1 teaspoon minced ginger root

4 cups peanut oil

1 teaspoon sesame oil

PREPARATION

Combine the ingredients for the batter. Refrigerate, uncovered, for at least 4 hours or up to 24 hours.

Peel, then slant-cut the eggplant into 1/4-inch slices. Place the slices on a large plate and sprinkle them with the salt. Cover with paper towels weighted with a chopping block and let stand for 1 hour. Rinse the eggplant slices very well under cold running water. Drain and dry well.

Cover the shrimp with boiling water for 15 minutes. Drain and mince.

Combine the ingredients for the filling.

Combine the ingredients for the seasoning sauce.

Mix the binder.

Spread 1 full tablespoon of the filling on one side of each eggplant slice, then fold in half and press to seal.

COOKING PROCEDURE

Place the wok over high heat for about 1 minute. Pour in the peanut oil; turn the heat to medium until the oil reaches 375 degrees. Turn the heat to high. Divide the eggplant into two batches. Dip each slice of the first batch of eggplant in the batter, then place these slices in the oil and fry for 3 minutes, turning once at midpoint. Using a wire strainer, remove the eggplant from the wok. Drain well by placing the fried pieces in a single layer on several sheets of paper towels. Repeat with the remaining half of the eggplant.

Fry each batch of eggplant a second time for 1 minute. Drain again on paper towels. Remove the oil from the wok.

Return the wok to medium heat. In the oil that glazes the wok, stir-fry the garlic, scallion, and ginger for 1 minute.

Restir the seasoning sauce and add it all at once to the wok; stir-fry for about 30 seconds.

Restir the binder and add it to the wok, stirring until the sauce thickens.

(continued)

Turn off the heat. Add the 1 teaspoon sesame oil.

Place the eggplant slices on a heated serving dish. Pour the sauce over the eggplant and serve immediately.

YIELD *3–6 servings*

NOTES

Timing The entire recipe can be prepared early in the day through the first frying of the eggplant.

Tip In order to decrease the beer's carbonization, pour it from glass to glass a few times, then refrigerate; or pour it into a glass filled with ice cubes for a few seconds.

PICKLED SPRING GINGER

¹/₂ pound spring ginger

BRINE SOLUTION
¹/₄ cup sugar
¹/₂ cup Japanese rice vinegar
¹/₂ cup water

PREPARATION

Peel the ginger, then slice it paper thin. Blanch the ginger for 1 minute, then drain. Combine the brine solution, stirring until the sugar dissolves. Place the ginger slices and the brine solution in a glass jar with a tight-fitting cover.

NOTES

Timing Refrigerated, Pickled Spring Ginger will last at least 2 years.

Tip When recipes in this book call for fresh spring ginger and it is not in season, use the Pickled Spring Ginger.

STIR-FRIED YOUNG MUSTARD GREENS

Canton/Guangzhou

1 1/2 pounds young mustard greens

SEASONING SAUCE
1 teaspoon water chestnut powder
dissolved in
2 tablespoons sherry
1 tablespoon oyster sauce
1 tablespoon dark soy sauce

1 teaspoon minced ginger root
1 teaspoon minced garlic
2 scallions (white and green parts), chopped
1 teaspoon sugar
1/4 teaspoon freshly ground black pepper

1 1/2 tablespoons peanut oil

PREPARATION

Leaving the mustard greens tied in a bunch, remove 1/2 inch of the stems with one stroke of the cleaver and discard. Cut the mustard greens into 3-inch lengths, separating the stems from the leafy parts. Wash, drain, and dry.

Combine the ingredients for the seasoning sauce.

COOKING PROCEDURE

Place the wok over high heat for about 1 minute. Add the oil and heat until hot but not smoking. Add the ginger, garlic, scallions, sugar, and pepper; stir-fry for 30 seconds.

Add the stems of the mustard greens and stir-fry for 1 minute.

Add the leafy parts and stir-fry for another minute, or until wilted.

Restir the seasoning sauce and add it all at once to the wok; stir-fry for about 30 seconds. Continue to stir-fry another few seconds until the mustard greens and the seasoning sauce are well combined. Empty the contents of the wok onto a heated serving dish and serve immediately.

YIELD *3–6 servings*

NOTES

Substitutions For the mustard greens, you can substitute yu choy, bok choy, or Shantung cabbage; Chinese or American broccoli can also be used, but after the broccoli is cut, 1 minute of blanching is required before stir-frying.

¹/₄ cup dried straw mushrooms
1 cup Chinese mushrooms
1 can (10 ounces) abalone mushrooms,
   drained
1 can (15 ounces) peeled straw mushrooms,
   drained

SEASONING SAUCE
¹/₃ cup chicken stock
1 tablespoon oyster sauce
2 teaspoons dark soy sauce
¹/₂ teaspoon sugar
2 tablespoons reduced Chinese mushroom
   stock**

BINDER
1 teaspoon water chestnut powder
   dissolved in
1 tablespoon sherry

1 cup strung, slant-cut snow peas

1¹/₂ tablespoons peanut oil

PREPARATION

Dried straw mushrooms: Rinse under cold running water, then soak in cold water to cover for 2 hours, or until soft. Discard the liquid. Remove the outside skin and discard. Leave the mushrooms whole.

Chinese mushrooms: Soak and cut into 1-inch pieces.**

Abalone mushrooms: Remove 1 inch of the stems and discard; cut into quarters.

Canned straw mushrooms: Leave whole.

Combine the ingredients for the seasoning sauce.

Mix the binder.

COOKING PROCEDURE

Place the wok over high heat for about 1 minute. Add the oil and heat until hot but not smoking. Add all the mushrooms; stir-fry for 1 minute.

Add the snow peas; stir-fry for 30 seconds.

Add the seasoning sauce and bring it to a boil.

Restir the binder and add it to the wok, stirring until the sauce thickens. Empty the contents of the wok onto a heated serving dish and serve immediately.

YIELD *4–8 servings*

STIR-FRIED VEGETABLES
WITH BRAISED MUSHROOMS
Canton/Guangzhou

1 pound string beans

3/4 cup shallots, peeled and left whole

2 cleaned, seeded, and triangle-cut sweet red
   peppers

2 ears of corn (kernels)

BINDER

1/2 teaspoon water chestnut powder
   dissolved in

1 tablespoon sherry

1 teaspoon Hot Sauce*

1 cup Braised Mushrooms*, measured with
   liquid (see following recipe)

2 tablespoons liquid from Braised
   Mushrooms*

1 tablespoon butter

1 tablespoon peanut oil

PREPARATION

Trim only the stem end of the string beans.
Wash, drain, and steam or blanch the string
beans for 2 to 3 minutes. Put them in a
large bowl of ice water to stop the cooking
and retain the color. Drain and dry them
well.

Sauté the shallots over low heat in the butter for 2 to 3 minutes. Reserve.

Mix the binder.

COOKING PROCEDURE

Place the wok over high heat for about 1
minute. Add the oil. When the oil is hot but
not smoking, add the shallots, peppers, and
corn. Stir-fry for 1 minute.

Add the string beans and stir-fry for 1
more minute.

Add the Braised Mushrooms and the
mushroom liquid; mix well.

Restir the binder and add it to the wok,
stirring until the sauce thickens. Empty the
contents of the wok onto a serving dish.
Serve hot or at room temperature.

YIELD 4–8 servings

NOTES

Tip This dish can be prepared a day in advance and served as an appetizer, salad, or
vegetable course.

BRAISED MUSHROOMS

Although this dish is delicious eaten on its own, it is primarily used as a seasoning for other vegetable dishes, such as Stir-Fried Vegetables with Braised Mushrooms*.

1 pound fresh American cultivated mushrooms

1¹/₂ tablespoons dark soy sauce

2 tablespoons peanut oil
2 tablespoons butter

PREPARATION

Wash the mushrooms under running water. Cut off and discard a portion of the brown end of each stem. Slice lengthwise ¹/₄ inch thick through the stem and into the cap, keeping each slice in the shape of a mushroom. One pound should yield about 6 cups.

COOKING PROCEDURE

Place the wok over high heat for about 1 minute. Add the oil and butter; heat until the butter melts and the foam starts to subside, but before it turns brown. Add the mushrooms; lower the heat to medium. Sauté the mushrooms for 10 minutes, stirring from time to time.

Add the soy sauce; sauté for 1 more minute. Empty the contents of the wok onto a dish. Serve hot or at room temperature.

NOTES

Tip To use this recipe as part of another dish (as an enhancing ingredient), stir well and use the mushroom liquid as well as the mushrooms. Add just before the binder in any vegetable recipe.

Storage When cool, place the mushrooms with their liquid in a glass jar and cover; refrigerate. The cooked mushrooms will keep in the refrigerator for 2 to 3 days.

SPICY CHARCOAL PEPPERS   Hunan

Spicy Charcoal Peppers is a typical dish of Hunan, where fresh chili peppers are locally grown in abundance. It is a popular dish among all my students because it is simple and tasty and can be prepared several days in advance. It can be served as an appetizer or as part of a multi-course Chinese dinner. These peppers are also an excellent accompaniment to a Western meal, such as roast chicken or leg of lamb. This dish is particularly appealing because of the bright red and green color combination and the attractive triangle cut.

The peppers may be served hot, cold, or at room temperature but should not be reheated.

1¹/2 pounds cleaned, seeded, and triangle-cut fresh peppers (any combination of sweet red, bell, and chili; cut pieces should yield 4 full cups)
1 teaspoon salt

SEASONING SAUCE
1 tablespoon light soy sauce
1 teaspoon Hot Sauce*
2 teaspoons wine vinegar
¹/2 teaspoon sugar

1¹/2 tablespoons rendered poultry fat**

PREPARATION

Place the peppers on a cookie sheet and sprinkle them with the salt. Cover them with paper towels, then put a weight over the towels. Let them stand at least 2 hours. Drain and dry the peppers well.

Combine the ingredients for the seasoning sauce.

COOKING PROCEDURE

Place the wok over high heat for about 1 minute. Add the poultry fat; heat until hot but not smoking. Add the peppers; stir-fry for 4 to 5 minutes, pressing down on them with a spatula to aid the scorching. The peppers should be visibly charred. (It is the scorched skin of the peppers that gives them the charcoal flavor.)

Add the seasoning sauce all at once to the wok; continue to stir-fry until all the liquid is absorbed. Empty the contents of the wok onto a serving dish and serve hot or cold.

YIELD *3–6 servings*

NOTES

Tip This dish can be as spicy or as mild as your personal taste requires. The more chili peppers used, the hotter it will be. When cutting the chili peppers, make smaller triangle cuts than for the sweet peppers in order to distribute the spice more evenly.

SEASONAL STIR-FRIED VEGETABLES

SEASONING SAUCE

1 teaspoon water chestnut powder
    dissolved in
1 tablespoon sherry
1 tablespoon dark miso
1 tablespoon dark soy sauce
2 tablespoons chicken stock

1/2 cup shallots, peeled and left whole

1 sweet red pepper, cleaned, seeded, and
    triangle-cut

1/2 cup peeled, sliced fresh water chestnuts
3 cups strung whole snow peas

1 tablespoon sweet butter

1 tablespoon peanut oil

PREPARATION

Combine the ingredients for the seasoning
sauce.

COOKING PROCEDURE

Place the wok over high heat for about 1
minute. Add the butter. Reduce the heat to
low and heat until the butter has melted
and the foam subsides. Add the shallots
and sauté for 2 to 3 minutes.

Turn the heat to high and add the peanut
oil. Add the red pepper and stir-fry for 1
minute.

Add the water chestnuts and snow peas and
stir-fry for about 30 seconds.

Restir the seasoning sauce and add it all at
once to the wok, continuing to stir-fry another minute. Empty the contents of the
wok onto a heated serving dish and serve
immediately.

YIELD *3–6 servings*

SHREDDED VEGETABLES HUNAN STYLE Hunan

Because the Chinese eat and enjoy vegetables all year long, they consider a meal without rice and vegetables a welcome departure from their everyday pattern. Banquets are planned without rice or vegetables, and the emphasis is placed on meat, poultry, and fish. It is for this reason I should not have been surprised that, after almost a week in China, there had been a total absence of vegetables in my diet (except for chili peppers, leeks, and chives). As requests for vegetables were ignored in our preordered banquets, I decided to try a different tactic: I took my laundry bag in hand and headed for the market to buy my own.

In the lowlands around Changsha, Hunan, an impressive variety of vegetables is grown. They are readily available in the marketplace in an array of colors: winter melon, sponge melon, pumpkin (similar to our own pumpkin, but deeper orange, and with a taste like acorn squash), Hunan cabbage, many varieties of leafy green vegetables, very young watercress, jicama, turnip, lotus root, sword beans, purple string beans, long beans (Chinese string beans), garlic, chives, crimson chili peppers, and sweet bell peppers both red and green.

The market was quite busy by the time I arrived a few minutes before 6 A.M. By resorting to the age-old technique of pointing, I soon filled my laundry bag at a cost of about one yuan, or seventy-five cents. (When I handed one man a yuan, he couldn't change it, and I had to give him a chiao, which is one tenth of a yuan, or one tenth of seventy-five cents.)

Upon returning to the hotel, I asked the chef there if he could cook the vegetables for our group, and he did that very day. They were simply stir-fried and superb! My favorite dish was shredded sword beans with chili peppers. Sword beans are a broad flat bean not grown in America, but snow peas substitute very well.

By Chinese standards, Shredded Vegetables Hunan Style would be a home-style dish, but it could be included in a banquet, served to guests as a separate course, the way we would eat a salad. It is simple, beautiful, and refreshing.

BINDER
1/2 teaspoon water chestnut powder dissolved in
1 tablespoon sherry
2 tablespoons chicken stock
1 teaspoon Hot Sauce*

1 cup split, shredded leeks (white part only)
1 cup cleaned, seeded, and shredded fresh chili peppers
1 teaspoon salt
1/2 teaspoon sugar

2 cups shredded snow peas

2 tablespoons rendered poultry fat**

2 teaspoons sesame oil

PREPARATION
Mix the binder.

COOKING PROCEDURE
Place the wok over high heat for about 1 minute. Add the poultry fat and heat until hot but not smoking. Add the leeks, chili peppers, salt, and sugar. Turn the heat to medium and stir-fry for 2 minutes.

Turn the heat to high. Add the snow peas; continue to stir-fry for 1 minute.

Restir the binder and add it to the wok, stirring another 30 seconds.

Turn off the heat. Add the sesame oil. Empty the contents of the wok onto a heated serving dish and serve immediately.

YIELD *3–6 servings*

STIR-FRIED WATERCRESS WITH FERMENTED BEAN CURD

BINDER

*1 teaspoon water chestnut powder
    dissolved in*
2 tablespoons sherry
1 cube fermented bean curd, mashed

1 clove garlic, minced
1/2 teaspoon salt
1/2 teaspoon sugar

*3 bunches watercress, stems removed, washed,
    drained, and dried*

1 1/2 tablespoons peanut oil

PREPARATION

Mix the binder.

COOKING PROCEDURE

Place the wok over high heat for 30 seconds. Add the oil; heat until hot but not smoking. Add the garlic, salt, and sugar; stir for a few seconds.

Add the watercress; stir-fry for 1 minute.

Restir the binder and add it to the wok, stirring until the sauce thickens. Empty the contents of the wok onto a heated serving dish and serve immediately.

YIELD *3–8 servings*

NOTES

Tips Stir-fried watercress with or without the addition of fermented bean curd makes an excellent edible garnish to many fish, poultry, and beef dishes.

As bean curd contains fewer calories than cottage cheese, this dish makes a delicious, satisfying, nutritious low-calorie lunch.

Substitutions For the watercress, you can substitute 1 pound of spinach, stems removed, or the leafy green parts of bok choy. Frequently only the white part of bok choy will be called for in a recipe. This recipe is an excellent way to utilize the leafy green parts.

Chapter 17

EGGS, RICE, AND STARCHY PREPARATIONS

EGG PANCAKE

1 egg, beaten
1 tablespoon peanut oil

COOKING PROCEDURE

Place a 10-inch iron skillet over high heat for about 1 minute. Add the oil. While the oil is heating, rotate the skillet above the heat so the oil is evenly distributed. Pour off the excess oil. Add the egg, all at once. Rotate the skillet so that a large, thin pancake is formed.

Remove the egg pancake by inverting the skillet on a flat surface. Allow the pancake to cool before handling.

Egg pancakes are used for a variety of recipes in this book.

YIELD 1 pancake

NOTES

Tip A wok can be used instead of the skillet.

1. Pour the egg into the center of the skillet.

2. Rotate the skillet.

3. Invert the skillet to remove the pancake.

CHINESE OMELET I

FILLING

1 small chicken breast, boned, skinned, and diced (about 6 ounces boneless chicken meat)

2 duck livers, diced

2 ounces ($^1/_3$ cup) shrimp, shelled, washed, drained, dried, and diced
$^1/_2$ teaspoon salt
$^1/_4$ teaspoon ground white pepper
$^1/_3$ cup diced Westphalian ham

3 ounces ($^1/_2$ cup) fresh mushrooms, diced
$^1/_4$ cup diced bamboo shoots
$^1/_2$ cup chopped Chinese chives

BINDER

2 teaspoons water chestnut powder dissolved in
1 tablespoon sherry

9 large eggs
1 tablespoon flour
$^1/_2$ teaspoon salt
$^1/_4$ teaspoon freshly ground white pepper

3 tablespoons peanut oil
$2^1/_2$ tablespoons sweet butter

SPECIAL EQUIPMENT
Cheesecloth, washed and squeezed dry

PREPARATION

Place the bamboo shoots in the cheesecloth, then squeeze until all the water is extracted.

To cook the filling Place the wok over medium-high heat for about 1 minute. Add 1 tablespoon of the oil and 1 tablespoon of the butter and heat for about 30 seconds. Add the diced chicken and cook, stirring constantly for 1 minute.

Add the livers and mix briefly.

Add the shrimp, $^1/_2$ teaspoon salt, $^1/_4$ teaspoon pepper, and ham; cook for 1 more minute. Empty the contents of the wok into a bowl. Do not wash the wok.

Heat $^1/_2$ tablespoon of the oil in the same wok over medium-high heat. When it is hot, add the mushrooms, bamboo shoots, and chives. Cook for 1 minute. Mix well.

Return the chicken mixture to the wok along with the binder; mix well for a few seconds. Empty the contents of the wok into the same bowl.

To prepare the eggs Separate the egg yolks from the whites and allow the eggs to reach room temperature. Beat the egg whites until stiff with a wire whisk or electric beater. Beat the yolks for 30 seconds. Add the flour, $^1/_2$ teaspoon salt, $^1/_4$ teaspoon pepper, and egg yolks to the egg whites. Mix well.

COOKING PROCEDURE

To make an omelet Place an 8-inch omelet pan over medium-high heat for 30 seconds. Add $^1/_2$ tablespoon of the oil and $^1/_2$ tablespoon of the butter. When the foam subsides (this should happen *before* the butter turns brown), pour in one third of the egg mixture. Turn the heat to medium, and cook 1 minute.

Sprinkle one third of the filling mixture over the omelet and continue cooking until the omelet is firm enough to turn over (about 2 minutes). Shake the pan to avoid the omelet's sticking.

To flip the omelet Slide a spatula under it, tilt the pan to one side, ease almost the entire omelet out of the pan, and then turn it over. Cook for another minute. Slide the first omelet into a heated round serving dish and repeat the procedure twice. If possible, use two omelet pans. Serve immediately.

YIELD *3 omelets*

NOTES

Timing The filling can be cooked a day in advance and refrigerated. Allow it to reach room temperature before making the omelet.

Tip As this recipe makes three omelets, the ingredients can be divided into thirds.

Substitution For the duck livers, you can substitute chicken livers.

CHINESE OMELET II

Flip the omelet by sliding it almost out of the tilted pan.

FILLING

4 medium-sized Chinese mushrooms, soaked
    and minced**
$^1/_4$ pound shrimp
1 bunch watercress (about 4 ounces)
6 ounces ground pork
$^1/_4$ cup minced fresh water chestnuts
2 scallions (white and green parts), chopped
$^1/_2$ teaspoon minced ginger root
2 tablespoons light soy sauce
1 tablespoon sherry
1 teaspoon sesame oil
$^1/_2$ teaspoon sugar
$^1/_4$ teaspoon freshly ground white pepper

9 eggs

3 tablespoons clarified sweet butter
3 tablespoons peanut oil

PREPARATION

To make the filling Having reconstituted the mushrooms, set them aside. Shell, wash, drain, dry, and coarsely mince the shrimp. Blanch the watercress for 30 seconds. Drain and squeeze it to remove the excess moisture; then chop fine. Combine the ingredients for the filling. Stir well in one direction with several chopsticks.

Divide the filling into three equal parts.

Beat 3 eggs together in a bowl with one third of the filling. Premix the other two thirds in two separate bowls.

COOKING PROCEDURE

To make an omelet Place an 8-inch omelet pan over medium-high heat for 30 seconds. Add 1 tablespoon of the butter and 1 tablespoon of the oil, and heat until the foam subsides but before the butter turns brown.

Add the egg mixture all at once. After a few seconds, shake the pan several times. Cover, turn the heat to low, and cook for 5 minutes. Uncover and shake the pan again. Cover and cook another 4 or 5 minutes, or until the eggs have set.

To flip the omelet Slide a spatula under the omelet, tilt the pan to one side, ease the omelet out of the pan by a few inches, and then turn it over (see photograph above). Cook for another minute. Slide the first omelet into a heated round serving dish and repeat the procedure twice. If possible, use two omelet pans. Cut into wedges and serve immediately.

YIELD *3 omelets*

NOTES

Tips The leftover portion can be sliced and served cold the following day.

    A single-portion omelet can use 2 eggs with $^1/_2$ cup filling.

    Do not flip the omelet until it is set.

CHINESE OMELET III

FILLING

¹/₃ cup diced cooked lobster, crab, or shrimp
¹/₄ cup minced water chestnuts
¹/₄ cup chopped scallions (white and green parts)
2 tablespoons minced Smithfield ham**
1 tablespoon cleaned, seeded, and minced sweet red pepper
Freshly ground white pepper to taste

3 eggs, beaten

¹/₂ tablespoon sweet butter

1 tablespoon peanut oil

PREPARATION

Combine the ingredients for the filling.

COOKING PROCEDURE

Place an 8-inch omelet pan over medium-high heat for 30 seconds and add the butter and oil. When the foam subsides (this should happen before the butter turns brown), add the filling.

Turn the heat to low and stir for about 30 seconds with a wooden spatula, then turn the heat to medium, and add the eggs. Cover and cook for about 5 minutes, or until the eggs are set.

To flip the omelet Slide a spatula under it, tilt the pan to one side, ease the omelet out of the pan a few inches, and turn it over. Cook for another few seconds. Slide the omelet onto a heated serving dish; cut into wedges and serve.

YIELD *1 omelet*

NOTES

Tip Do not flip the omelet until it is set.

STEAMED EGG CUSTARD

1/2 pound shrimp (or fresh crab meat or
    lobster)
1 1/2 cups chicken stock
4 large eggs, beaten
1/2 teaspoon salt
2 teaspoons dark soy sauce
1/4 teaspoon freshly ground white pepper
1 scallion (white and green parts), chopped
1 tablespoon sweet butter, melted
1 tablespoon minced Smithfield ham**

PREPARATION

Shell the shrimp, then wash, drain, dry, and dice them into 1/2-inch pieces.

Bring the chicken stock almost to the boiling point. While beating the eggs in a bowl, very gradually pour in the heated chicken stock in a thin stream so that the eggs are slowly warmed. Add the salt, soy sauce, and pepper; continue to beat until well combined. Add the shrimp, scallion, butter, and ham to the egg mixture; combine well.

COOKING PROCEDURE

Pour the egg mixture into a soufflé dish, or any serving dish that is oval or round and a few inches deep. Put the dish in a steamer. Steam the custard for 8 minutes over low heat, or until set. (This timing is based on the custard's measuring 1 1/2 inches deep in its container; if the depth varies, adjust the timing accordingly.) Serve immediately.

YIELD *2–6 servings*

BOILED WHITE RICE

1 1/2 cups water
1 cup long-grain rice

COOKING PROCEDURE

Bring the water to a rapid boil over high heat in a heavy 1 1/2-quart enamel saucepan with a tight-fitting cover. Add the rice. When the water returns to a rapid boil, stir with chopsticks in a figure-8 motion. Cover, turn the heat to low, and simmer the rice for 15 minutes. Turn off the heat and let the rice relax for 20 minutes. Do not remove the saucepan from the burner unless you are cooking on an electric range. Remove the cover and stir with chopsticks. Serve immediately.

NOTES

Timing The rice will stay warm up to 30 minutes after the relaxing period if kept on the same burner.

If you wish to make the rice in advance, it can be rewarmed in a water bath either on top of the range or in a preheated 350-degree oven.

Tips Perfectly cooked rice has "fish eyes," or little holes that form on the top.

Leftover cooked rice can be used for fried rice or rice pudding.

YIELD *3 servings*

1 1/2 cups flour
2/3 cup (scant) boiling water
Sesame oil

PREPARATION

Pour the flour in a mixing bowl. Do not sift.

Gradually add the boiling water until the flour is well mixed and the batter is slightly sticky. Cover the dough with a damp paper towel or dish towel and let stand for 10 minutes.

Knead the dough for 5 minutes, then cover it again and let stand for 30 minutes.

Roll out the dough 1/8 inch thick. Using a round cookie cutter 4 inches in diameter or the top of a jar, cut the dough into circles.

Brush lightly with sesame oil and stack 2 circles together with the oiled sides facing each other.

Roll out the dough until the circles are 5 to 6 inches in diameter. Continue until all the circles are cut, stacked, and rolled.

COOKING PROCEDURE

In an ungreased heavy flat pan or wok, dry-cook each circle over low heat until it bubbles slightly. Turn it over and dry-cook the other side.

Remove it from the pan and pull the 2 pieces apart.

Wrap the doilies in a dish towel and steam before serving, for about 5 minutes.

YIELD *10 doilies*

NOTES

Tips You can make your own doilies from flour and boiling water or, if you prefer, you can buy them. Many different brands are available in Chinese communities. They should be wrapped in a dish towel and steamed for five minutes.

Another short cut to making Peking Doilies is to order them from a restaurant; they are usually listed on Chinese menus as pancakes to accompany Mo Shu Ro (pork). When ordering them, specify that you are planning to steam them yourself and you therefore want them flat, not folded, as the folds create cracks in the dough.

Storage Peking Doilies can be frozen for several months after they have been dry-cooked and pulled apart. Double-wrap the doilies in aluminum foil and then in a plastic bag. Allow them to defrost before steaming.

¹/₄ cup Chinese mushrooms, soaked and diced**

¹/₂ cup crab meat

¹/₄ cup chopped chives

4 egg whites

BINDER

¹/₄ cup milk

1¹/₂ tablespoons water chestnut powder

¹/₂ cup milk

¹/₄ teaspoon freshly ground white pepper

1 teaspoon salt

1 teaspoon sugar

¹/₃ cup diced shrimp

1 duck liver, diced

1 teaspoon water chestnut powder

5 tablespoons peanut oil

¹/₃ cup pine nuts, roasted**

PREPARATION

Having reconstituted the mushrooms, set aside.

Beat the egg whites slightly, until foamy.

Mix the binder.

Combine the egg whites, binder, and the ¹/₂ cup milk in a bowl, along with the pepper, salt, and sugar.

Mix the diced shrimp and duck liver with the 1 teaspoon water chestnut powder.

Add the mushrooms, crab meat, and chives to the milk mixture.

COOKING PROCEDURE

Place the wok over high heat for about 1 minute. Add 1 tablespoon of the oil and heat until hot but not smoking. Add the shrimp and duck liver; stir-fry for 30 seconds. Remove the contents from the wok.

Return the wok to high heat and add the remaining oil. Heat until hot but not smoking. Turn the heat to low. Stir the milk mixture very well to redistribute the binder, then pour the mixture into the wok.

Return the duck liver and shrimp to the wok; stir until set. Empty the contents of the wok onto a heated serving dish.

Sprinkle with pine nuts. Serve immediately.

YIELD *2–6 servings*

ROAST DUCK LO MEIN Canton/Guangzhou

Noodles are traditionally served on birth-days because the length of the noodles sym-bolizes longevity. However, noodle dishes are common fare among the Chinese and therefore are rarely included as part of a banquet. Because my recipe for Roast Duck Lo Mein contains many more vegetables and duck in relation to noodles than the typical lo mein, it is a frequent part of the banquets that I cater. Both beautiful and delectable, it also makes a great one-dish meal as it contains protein, starch, and car-bohydrates. Because noodles, the principal ingredient in this recipe, are long and thin, for eye appeal the subordinate ingredients are shredded. The preparation is time-con-suming because of this shredding of the meat and vegetables.

1/2 cup Chinese mushrooms, soaked, stemmed, and shredded**
1 1/2 cups split, shredded leeks (white part only)

1 whole Cantonese roast duck (see Tip)

1/4 cup reduced mushroom stock**
3/4 cup duck and chicken stock

1/4 cup dark soy sauce
2 tablespoons oyster sauce

BINDER
2 tablespoons water chestnut powder dissolved in
3 tablespoons sherry

3/4 pound fresh egg noodles (lo mein)
1 tablespoon peanut oil

1 cup bean sprouts

2 cloves garlic, minced
1 tablespoon minced ginger root

1 cup shredded bok choy (white part only)
1 cup shredded hairy melon
1 cup shredded snow peas
1/2 cup shredded sweet red pepper

1 cup shredded bok choy (green part only)

6 1/2 tablespoons rendered duck fat**

PREPARATION

Having reconstituted the mushrooms, set aside.

Drain all the liquid from inside the cavity of the duck and add it to the mushroom stock. Add enough chicken stock to make 1 cup stock.

Using a heavy cleaver and a rubber mallet, split the duck in half. Remove the skin from the duck and shred it. Remove the meat and shred it.

Preheat the oven to 350 degrees. Place the duck skin in a single layer on a shallow roasting pan and roast in the oven for 20 to 30 minutes, or until crisp. Reserve the ren-dered duck fat for cooking. Place the duck skin on paper towels to drain.

Combine the soy sauce, oyster sauce, and 1 cup duck-mushroom-chicken stock.

Mix the binder.

To prepare the noodles Bring to a boil 4 quarts water and the oil. Add the noodles and boil for about 3 minutes. While the noodles are cooking, lift them with a pair of chopsticks to prevent them from sticking together. Pour the noodles into a colander to drain; rinse with cold water and drain again.

(continued)

COOKING PROCEDURE

Preheat the oven to 250 degrees. Place the wok over high heat for about 2 minutes. Add the bean sprouts and stir-fry for about 2 minutes without oil. Remove them from the wok. Return the wok to high heat. Add 1½ tablespoons duck fat and heat until hot but not smoking. Spread one third of the noodles in the bottom of the wok so they form a flat, round shape. To prevent the noodles from sticking, shake the wok about every 10 seconds. Cook the noodles until they are very brown (about 2 minutes), then flip the noodle pancake and allow the other side to brown (another 2 minutes), continuing to shake the wok every 10 seconds. Remove the noodle pancake from the wok onto a flat heatproof dish. Repeat twice with the remaining noodles, frying one third at a time. Place the three noodle pancakes on the serving dish so they form a border around it. Do not cover. Place the serving dish in the preheated oven, *uncovered,* while you are stir-frying the duck and vegetable mixture.

In a saucepan, bring the soy sauce, oyster sauce, and stock to a simmer.

In the same wok, heat the remaining 2 tablespoons duck fat over medium heat. Add the garlic and ginger; stir-fry for a few seconds.

Add the mushrooms and leeks; stir-fry for 2 minutes.

Turn the heat to high, add the white part of the bok choy, hairy melon, snow peas, and red pepper; stir-fry for 1 minute.

Add the simmering stock mixture around the sides of the wok and let it come to a boil.

Restir the binder and add it to the vegetable mixture along with the green part of the bok choy and the roast duck. Mix well.

Return the bean sprouts to the wok. Mix briefly.

1. To flip the noodle pancake, hold the wok handle with both hands, then thrust the wok forward and upward.

2. The wok leaves the heat source to retrieve the flipped pancake.

Put the vegetable-duck mixture in the center of the dish so the noodles will form a border. Garnish with the crisp shredded duck skin and serve immediately.

YIELD *4–8 servings*

NOTES

Timing The entire preparation can be done early in the day. Do not refrigerate the duck skin after roasting, as it will lose its crispness.

Tip Cantonese roast duck can be purchased in a Chinese barbecue house if you live near a Chinese community (a second choice is Barbecued Whole Duck*). Remove the liquid from the cavity of the Cantonese roast duck, then the skin, then the meat from the carcass. The carcass can be saved to add to the stockpot.

Substitutions The total amount of vegetables called for is 7 full cups, and there are as many substitutions for vegetables as there are fresh vegetables in season. If Oriental vegetables are not available, substitute zucchini, yellow squash, carrots, broccoli, or kohlrabi. Any type of fresh pasta can be substituted for the lo mein. For the roast duck, you can substitute 2 cups Barbecued Roast Pork*.

Seafood lo mein is also another delicious possibility:
1. Substitute 1 pound lobster and/or crab, both of which must be steamed first, shredded, then added to the wok when the recipe calls for duck.

2. Substitute 1 pound scallops and/or shrimp, marinated in egg white, water chestnut powder, and sherry, passed through, then removed from the wok. This step is considered part of the preparation and therefore can be done early in the day and the seafood refrigerated. Bring it to room temperature; add to the wok when the recipe calls for the duck to be added.

3. Substitute any combination of lobster, crab, scallops, or shrimp.

Beef lo mein is also an appealing choice. Substitute 1 pound flank steak. Partially freeze the meat; then slice it in half with the grain. Take one of the halves and slice it thinly against the grain. Place several of these slices on top of one another and shred lengthwise until you have 1 pound shredded meat. Follow the instructions for the scallops and/or shrimp.

Vegetable lo mein makes another excellent alternative. Increase the vegetables in the recipe to 9 cups. Eliminate the duck.

Storage The duck skin, liquid, and meat can be refrigerated for 3 days or frozen for 1 month.

CURRIED BEEF NOODLES

Canton/Guangzhou

3/4 pound flank steak

MARINADE
2 teaspoons dark soy sauce
1 teaspoon sherry
1 teaspoon sugar
1/2 teaspoon salt
1 teaspoon minced garlic

SEASONING SAUCE
2 tablespoons curry sauce
2 teaspoons Hot Sauce*
1 tablespoon American chili sauce
1 1/2 tablespoons dark soy sauce

BINDER
2 teaspoons water chestnut powder
  dissolved in
1 tablespoon sherry

1/2 pound fresh egg noodles (lo mein)
2 teaspoons salt

2 1/2 teaspoons sesame oil

2 cups sliced onions

1 1/2 cups diced ripe tomatoes

1 cup shredded snow peas

8 tablespoons peanut oil

PREPARATION

Partially freeze the flank steak; slice, then shred. Mix the steak well in the marinade ingredients. Allow the meat to marinate at least 1/2 hour or up to 24 hours.

Combine the ingredients for the seasoning sauce.

Mix the binder.

Bring 4 quarts water to a rapid boil. Lower the noodles into the water. Add 1 teaspoon of the salt and 1 tablespoon of the peanut oil to the water. Cook the noodles over high heat for 2 to 3 minutes, stirring constantly and lifting the noodles out of the water with a pair of chopsticks to prevent them from sticking together. Drain the noodles in a colander. Rinse under cold running water and drain again. Toss with 1 1/2 teaspoons of the sesame oil.

COOKING PROCEDURE

Place the wok over high heat for about 1 minute. Add 4 tablespoons of the peanut oil and heat until the oil is hot but not smoking. Distribute the noodles in the wok to form a round pancake. Sprinkle with 1 teaspoon salt. Cook the noodles for 2 to 3 minutes on one side. To prevent the noodles sticking, shake the wok occasionally. When the noodles are brown on one side and slightly scorched, flip them over to brown the other side.

Preheat the oven to 250 degrees. Slide the noodles onto a flat, heated serving dish. Do not cover. Place in the preheated oven.

Return the wok to high heat. Add 1 tablespoon of the peanut oil, then add the onions; stir-fry for 1 to 2 minutes, or until they have wilted and begun to scorch.

Add the tomatoes, stir-frying for 1 more minute.

Add the snow peas; stir-fry for 30 seconds. Remove the contents of the wok to a plate.

(continued)

Return the wok to high heat. Add the remaining 2 tablespoons peanut oil. Restir the beef in the marinade and add the contents of the bowl to the wok all at once, stir-frying until the meat loses its redness.

Restir the seasoning sauce and add it to the wok, continuing to stir-fry for another 30 seconds.

Return the vegetables to the wok and mix briefly.

Restir the binder and add it to the wok, stirring until the mixture thickens.

Turn off the heat. Add the remaining 1 teaspoon sesame oil. Mix well.

Place the contents of the wok in the center of the noodles, leaving a border of noodles surrounding the beef and vegetable mixture. Serve immediately.

YIELD *3–8 servings*

COLD NOODLES WITH SPICY SESAME SAUCE
Szechwan/Sichuan

1 recipe Spicy Sesame Sauce*

$^1/_3$ pound fresh egg noodles (lo mein)

$^1/_3$ cup shredded cucumber

1 tablespoon peanut oil
1 tablespoon sesame oil

PREPARATION

Make the Spicy Sesame Sauce.

COOKING PROCEDURE

In a 6-quart saucepan, bring 5 quarts water to a rapid boil. Add the noodles and peanut oil. Boil the noodles for 2 minutes. To avoid excessive sticking, constantly stir and lift the noodles out of the water with a pair of chopsticks. Drain the noodles in a colander, rinse with cold water, and drain again.

Mix the noodles with the sesame oil. Allow the noodles to cool completely.

Stir the Spicy Sesame Sauce and pour over the noodles, tossing until they are well coated with the sauce. Add the shredded cucumber and toss again. Serve immediately.

YIELD *3–6 servings*

NOTES

Timing Both the noodles and the sauce can be prepared the day ahead and refrigerated. Toss the noodles and the sauce together before serving.

DEEP-FRIED SHANGHAI NOODLES

Shanghai

¹/₃ pound fresh Shanghai noodles
4 cups peanut oil

PREPARATION

Spread the noodles on a working surface and cut into quarters.

COOKING PROCEDURE

Place the wok over high heat for about 1 minute. Pour in the oil; turn the heat to medium until the oil reaches 350 degrees, then turn the heat to high. Fry a handful of noodles at a time over high heat until they turn light brown, about 1¹/₂ minutes.

Using a wire strainer, remove the noodles from the wok. Drain them well by placing them in a single layer on several sheets of paper towels.

Reheat the oil to 350 degrees and repeat the procedure until all the noodles have been fried. Allow them to cool for 30 minutes.

Reheat the oil to 375 degrees. Refry the noodles a handful at a time for a few seconds, or until they turn golden brown. Using a wire strainer, remove the noodles from the wok. Drain them well by placing them in a single layer on several sheets of paper towels. Allow to cool.

YIELD *20 servings*

NOTES

Tips Divide the fresh noodles (sold by the pound) into three portions. Freeze two thirds. Frozen, they will last two months.

Serve as a snack or appetizer with any or all of the following: Duck Sauce*, Chinese Mustard Sauce*, Spicy Dipping Sauce*, and Spicy Sesame Sauce*. Serve as a dessert sprinkled with confectioners' sugar.

BEEF CHOW FUN

Canton/Guangzhou

1/2 pound trimmed flank steak

MARINADE
1/2 egg white
1 teaspoon sherry
1 teaspoon water chestnut powder

1 pound fresh chow fun (rice noodles)

SEASONING SAUCE
1 teaspoon water chestnut powder
   dissolved in
2 tablespoons sherry
1 1/2 tablespoons dark soy sauce
1 tablespoon oyster sauce

1/4 pound mung bean sprouts

2 scallions (white and green parts), chopped
1 1/2 cups shredded snow peas

5 tablespoons peanut oil

PREPARATION

Partially freeze the flank steak. Slice, then shred. Mix the beef in the marinade and refrigerate for at least 1 hour or up to 12 hours. Cut the chow fun in noodle shapes the size of fettucine (1/2 inch wide, 5 inches long).

Combine the ingredients for the seasoning sauce.

COOKING PROCEDURE

Place the wok over high heat for about 2 minutes. Add the bean sprouts and stir-fry for about 2 minutes without oil. Remove them from the wok.

Return the wok to high heat. Add 3 tablespoons of the oil and heat until hot but not smoking. Add the chow fun and stir-fry for 2 to 3 minutes. Remove the noodles to a heatproof flat serving dish. Do not cover. Place in a preheated 250-degree oven.

Return the wok to high heat and add 1 more tablespoon oil. Add the scallions and snow peas; stir-fry for 30 seconds. Remove the vegetables from the wok to the same serving dish as the noodles.

Return the wok to high heat and add the remaining 1 tablespoon oil. Stir the beef in the marinade again and add it to the wok. Stir-fry for 2 minutes, or until the beef loses its redness.

Restir the seasoning sauce and add it to the wok, stirring for a few seconds to mix it well with the beef.

Return the vegetables, including the bean sprouts, and the noodles to the wok and mix until all the ingredients are well combined. Empty the contents of the wok onto the same heatproof dish and serve immediately.

YIELD *3–8 servings*

NOTES

Tip Stir-fry the noodles in constant motion to prevent them sticking together. If the heat is high enough, the noodles will scorch, which is a desired effect.

CURRIED RICE VERMICELLI — Canton/Guangzhou

7 ounces dried rice vermicelli, weighed dry

1/2 pound shrimp

MARINADE
1/2 egg white
1 teaspoon water chestnut powder
1/2 tablespoon sherry
1/2 teaspoon salt

SEASONING SAUCE
3 tablespoons curry sauce
2 tablespoons dark soy sauce
2 tablespoons sherry

1/4 pound bean sprouts

1/4 cup minced shallots
1 cup split, shredded leeks (white part only)

1 teaspoon salt
1/2 teaspoon sugar

1 cup shredded snow peas
1 cup shredded hairy melon
*1/2 cup cleaned, seeded, and shredded sweet
    red pepper*

1/4 pound Barbecued Roast Pork*, shredded

1 Egg Pancake*, shredded

5 tablespoons peanut oil

PREPARATION

Soak the rice vermicelli in warm water to cover for 20 minutes. Drain.

Shell the shrimp, split in half lengthwise, wash, drain, and dry well. Place the shrimp and the ingredients for the marinade in a bowl and stir in one direction vigorously with chopsticks. Place the mixture in the refrigerator for at least 1 hour or up to 12 hours.

Combine the ingredients for the seasoning sauce.

COOKING PROCEDURE

Place the wok over high heat for about 2 minutes. Add the bean sprouts and stir-fry without oil for 2 minutes. Remove them from the wok.

Return the wok to high heat. Add 1 table-spoon of the oil and heat until hot but not smoking. Restir the shrimp in the marinade and add all at once to the wok. Stir-fry the shrimp until they are almost pink (about 1 minute). Remove the shrimp from the wok.

Return the wok to high heat and add 3 tablespoons of the oil. Add the vermicelli and stir-fry for 2 minutes, pressing down on them with the side of the spatula to aid the browning. Remove the vermicelli to a heatproof dish. Do not cover. Place it in a preheated 225-degree oven for no longer than 10 minutes.

Return the wok to medium heat and add the remaining 1 tablespoon oil. Add the minced shallots and shredded leeks; stir-fry for 2 minutes.

Add the salt and sugar.

Turn the heat to high and add the snow peas, hairy melon, and red pepper; stir-fry for 1 more minute.

Add the Barbecued Roast Pork and mix briefly.

Add the shredded egg and mix briefly.

Remove the heatproof dish from the oven and place the vegetable mixture on top of the noodles.

Return the wok to high heat. Restir the seasoning sauce and add to the wok. Stir-fry for about 30 seconds.

Return the noodles, the vegetable mixture, along with the bean sprouts, and the shrimp to the wok; stir-fry for another minute, evenly distributing the entire mixture. Empty the contents of the wok onto the same heatproof dish and serve immediately.

YIELD *3–6 servings*

NOTES

Substitutions For the rice vermicelli, you can substitute rice sticks; increase the soaking time to 1 hour.

For the hairy melon, you can substitute zucchini.

SZECHWAN RICE STICK NOODLES

Szechwan/Sichuan

6 ounces rice stick noodles, weighed dry

1/2 pound shrimp

MARINADE
1/2 egg white
1 teaspoon water chestnut powder
1/2 tablespoon sherry
1/2 teaspoon salt

1/3 cup raw peanuts

1/4 pound mung bean sprouts

1 tablespoon dried shrimp
1 tablespoon Tientsin preserved vegetable**,
    minced
2 scallions (white and green parts), shredded
2 teaspoons salt
2 teaspoons sugar

1 cake Spiced Pressed Bean Curd*, shredded
2 Egg Pancakes*, shredded
1 tablespoon dark soy sauce
2 teaspoons Hot Sauce*

5 tablespoons peanut oil

1 tablespoon sesame oil

PREPARATION

Soak the rice stick noodles in warm water to cover for 1 hour. Drain.

Shell the shrimp, split in half lengthwise, wash, drain, and dry well. Place the shrimp and the ingredients for the marinade in a bowl and stir in one direction vigorously with chopsticks. Place the mixture in the refrigerator for at least 1 hour or up to 12 hours.

Cover the dried shrimp with boiling water for 15 minutes; drain, then mince.

Roast the peanuts on a cookie sheet in a preheated 325-degree oven until golden brown (about 15 minutes). Allow the peanuts to cool, then grind in an electric coffee mill or food processor.

COOKING PROCEDURE

Place the wok over high heat for about 2 minutes. Add the bean sprouts and stir-fry without oil for 2 minutes. Remove them from the wok.

Return the wok to high heat. Add 3 tablespoons of the peanut oil. Add the rice stick noodles; stir-fry for 2 minutes. Remove them to a heatproof dish. Do not cover. Place them in a preheated 225-degree oven for no longer than 10 minutes.

Return the wok to high heat. Add 1 tablespoon of the peanut oil. Restir the shrimp in the marinade and add them all at once to the wok. Stir-fry the shrimp until they are almost pink (about 1 minute). Remove the shrimp from the wok.

Return the wok to medium heat and add the remaining 1 tablespoon peanut oil. Add the dried shrimp, preserved vegetable, scallions, salt, and sugar; stir-fry for 15 seconds.

Turn the heat to high. Add the Spiced Pressed Bean Curd, egg shreds, soy sauce, and Hot Sauce; stir-fry for 30 seconds.

Return the shrimp to the wok along with the rice sticks and bean sprouts; stir-fry for 30 seconds, or until all the ingredients are well combined.

Turn off the heat. Add the sesame oil and peanuts. Mix well.

Empty the contents of the wok onto the same heatproof dish and serve immediately.

YIELD *2–6 servings*

NOTES

Substitution For the rice sticks, you can substitute rice vermicelli, in which case the soaking time is decreased to 20 minutes.

Chapter 18

DIPS
AND SAUCES

SPICY DIPPING SAUCE

Spicy Dipping Sauce goes well not only with most Chinese appetizers, but also with lightly blanched vegetables or steamed shellfish.

1 tablespoon light soy sauce
1 tablespoon dark soy sauce
1 tablespoon Japanese rice vinegar
1 tablespoon wine vinegar
1 tablespoon Chinese red vinegar
1/2 teaspoon sesame oil
1/2 teaspoon sugar
2 teaspoons minced ginger root
1 teaspoon minced garlic
1/2 teaspoon Hot Sauce*

PREPARATION

Combine the ingredients in a mixing bowl and blend thoroughly.

YIELD *approximately 1/2 cup*

NOTES

Storage Stored in a covered glass jar in the refrigerator, Spicy Dipping Sauce will keep for one month.

DUCK SAUCE

This is a sauce that I originally learned from Madame Chu. It is traditionally eaten in China with roast goose or roast duck; however, many Americans enjoy it as an accompaniment to various appetizers, such as spareribs, spring rolls, and butterfly shrimp.

1 cup Chinese plum sauce
1 cup peach preserves
1 cup apricot preserves
1 1/2 cups unsweetened applesauce
2 tablespoons hoisin sauce
1 tablespoon prepared Chinese Mustard Sauce*
1 tablespoon cognac

PREPARATION

Combine the ingredients in a food processor or by hand.

YIELD *approximately 5 cups*

NOTES

Tips If you wish to keep the sauce for longer than six months, omit the applesauce when combining the other ingredients and add it when you are ready to serve the sauce.

A jar of homemade Duck Sauce would make a well-received gift.

Storage Refrigerated in a covered jar, the sauce will keep for six months.

Hot Sauce (or Chili Paste) plays an important role in Szechwan cooking. Most restaurants and cooks buy a commercially made product, from which there are many to choose. For several years I used a commercially made chili paste, until one day Madame Chu encouraged me to try a homemade hot sauce that was being made and sold by Madame Koo, who owned a small Chinese takeout restaurant in New York City. I tried it and loved it, then passed the word on to all my students. The aroma, the taste—everything was superior to what I was accustomed to buying. When Madame Koo closed her restaurant I decided to develop my own Hot Sauce. I held on to my last bottle of Madame Koo's sauce for comparative sniffing and tasting. With the help of students in various classes, I created a Hot Sauce that was perfected after much experimenting over a period of years. This sauce can be applied to all cuisines: a Mexican chili, an Italian red tomato fra diavolo sauce for shrimp or lobster, an Indian curry. It can also be added to dips, soups, omelets, and melted cheese sandwiches.

1 1/2 cups cleaned, seeded, and minced sweet
    red peppers
1/2 cup cleaned, seeded, and minced sweet
    green pepper

12 cloves garlic, minced

2 teaspoons sugar

1 4-ounce jar whole roasted pimientos, pureed

12 tablespoons Chili Oil, measured with
    crushed chili
1 tablespoon wine vinegar
1 tablespoon sesame oil

1/4 cup peanut oil

PREPARATION AND COOKING PROCEDURE

Place the minced red and green peppers in a strainer over a bowl and allow them to drain for several minutes, pushing down with the back of a large spoon to extract as much moisture as possible. Reserve the juice.

Place a 12-inch wok or an iron skillet over high heat for about 1 minute. Add the peanut oil. Turn the heat to medium, and heat the oil until it is hot but not smoking. Add the minced garlic and stir until it has browned lightly.

Turn the heat to high. Add the drained peppers; stir-fry for 2 minutes.

Add the sugar and reserved pepper juice, bring to a boil, then turn the heat to medium. Simmer the mixture until all the liquid has evaporated.

Turn the heat to low, and simmer for another 5 minutes (about 10 to 12 minutes in all), stirring occasionally. During the last minute of cooking, add the pureed pimientos and stir well.

Turn the flame off and add the Chili Oil, wine vinegar, and sesame oil. Allow the sauce to cool; then place it in small glass jars and refrigerate.

YIELD *approximately 2 cups*

NOTES

Timing The first step in preparing Hot Sauce is to make the Chili Oil.

Tips Always stir Hot Sauce before measuring, as the oil separates. Generally, 1 to 2 teaspoons will make a dish pleasantly spicy; more or less can be added according to the individual's taste.

(continued)

Mincing the peppers in a food processor will speed up the preparation. Before placing them in the processor, they must be cleaned, seeded, and diced. If you use a processor, a great deal of juice will be extracted from the peppers while they are being minced. This liquid should be drained, reserved, and added to the sauce when the recipe indicates.

In order to avoid washing the processor container, first mince the garlic, then the peppers, and finally the pimientos.

Storage Once made and cooled, the Hot Sauce can be stored in small covered glass jars. Refrigerated, it will keep for six months.

CHILI OIL

Szechwan/Sichuan and Hunan

1 cup peanut oil
6 tablespoons chili powder

PREPARATION AND COOKING PROCEDURE

Place a 12-inch wok over high heat for about 1 minute. Pour in the oil and heat over a medium flame until it reaches 375 degrees. Remove the wok from the heat and let it stand 1 minute. Add the chili powder all at once. Allow the chili oil to cool in the wok, then place it in a covered glass jar and refrigerate.

YIELD *1 1/4 cups*

NOTES

When you are making Hot Sauce*, the chili oil is measured with chili powder. For all other purposes, Chili Oil should be strained once it has cooled, and the chili powder discarded.

It is very important that the temperature of the oil be accurate. If the oil is too hot, the chili powder will burn. If the oil is not hot enough, it will not take on the roasted aroma that gives the oil and the sauce its wonderful flavor. A solution to this problem is to cook the chili powder over a low flame in the oil for about 1 minute, or until the chili powder darkens. When the temperature of the oil is right, the aroma is similar to that of roasted peanuts.

Storage Store the chili powder in a covered jar in the refrigerator.

Store the Chili Oil in a covered glass jar and refrigerate. It will keep for one year.

CHINESE MUSTARD SAUCE

This is an excellent mustard sauce that can be used in salad dressings, on sandwiches, and in sauces for Western dishes.

1/2 cup dry mustard
1/4 cup boiling water (approximately)
1/4 cup medium-dry sherry
1/2 cup Pommery mustard

PREPARATION

Put the dry mustard in a bowl. While stirring with a wooden spoon, add boiling water until the mustard reaches the consistency of thick pancake batter.

Add the sherry and stir until smooth.

Stir in the Pommery mustard.

YIELD *1 1/2 cups*

NOTES

Tips If you wish to make the Mustard Sauce thinner, add more sherry.

Mustard Sauce can be made in a food processor if desired.

Storage Mustard Sauce will keep for one year in a covered glass jar in the refrigerator.

FIVE SPICE POWDER

2 tablespoons ground fennel seeds

1 tablespoon ground star anise

2 tablespoons Szechwan Peppercorn Powder*
2 tablespoons ground cinnamon
1 tablespoon ground cloves

PREPARATION

Grind the fennel seeds in an electric coffee mill and remove.

Grind the star anise in the coffee mill.

Combine the fennel seeds and star anise with the remaining ground spices. Place the powder in a covered glass jar.

YIELD *1/2 cup*

NOTES

Tip Five Spice Powder can be purchased in Chinese markets.

Storage Five Spice Powder can be kept in the refrigerator for one year.

SZECHWAN PEPPERCORN POWDER   Szechwan/Sichuan

Szechwan Peppercorn Powder is used as a seasoning as well as a dry dip for appetizers.

1/2 cup Szechwan peppercorns

COOKING PROCEDURE

Place a wok or heavy skillet over medium heat for about 30 seconds. Do not add oil. Add the Szechwan peppercorns. Dry-cook them for 3 minutes, stirring slowly but constantly, or until they turn dark brown. (The peppercorns will start to smoke before they turn brown.) Remove them from the wok and allow them to cool.

Place the peppercorns in a blender, food processor, or electric coffee mill; blend until they become a powder. Place the powder in a strainer and tap it through until only the husks remain. Discard the husks. (There will be no husks if you use a coffee mill.) Place the powder in a covered glass jar.

NOTES

Storage Stored in a covered glass jar in the refrigerator, Szechwan Peppercorn Powder will keep for several months.

OPTIONAL VARIATION

Place a wok or heavy skillet over medium heat for about 30 seconds. Add 2 teaspoons coarse salt; dry-cook for 2 to 3 minutes, or until the salt begins to darken. After it cools, add it to the Szechwan Peppercorn Powder.

SESAME SEED BUTTER

Szechwan/Sichuan

1/2 pound unhulled sesame seeds
1/4 cup sweet butter, at room temperature
1/4 cup sesame oil

PREPARATION AND COOKING PROCEDURE

Preheat the oven to 325 degrees. Place the sesame seeds in a shallow roasting pan and bake for 20 to 30 minutes, or until golden brown. Allow them to cool.

Place the sesame seeds in a food processor or blender along with the butter and sesame oil. Process or blend the mixture until it has the consistency of peanut butter. If you use a blender, add the butter and oil first. Place in covered glass jars.

YIELD 2 cups

NOTES

Tips Sesame Seed Butter (or paste) can also be purchased in health food stores and Chinese markets.

Substitutions For the Sesame Seed Butter, you can substitute peanut butter or tahini, which is available at health food stores.

Storage Refrigerated in covered glass jars, Sesame Seed Butter will keep for several weeks. Frozen, it will keep for six months.

SPICY SESAME SAUCE

Szechwan/Sichuan

Spicy Sesame Sauce is traditionally tossed with fresh egg noodles, resulting in the classic Szechwan dish known as Cold Noodles with Spicy Sesame Sauce*.

*1/4 cup Sesame Seed Butter**
1 scallion (white and green parts), chopped
1 teaspoon minced garlic
5 tablespoons brewed black tea
1 tablespoon plus 2 teaspoons dark soy sauce
*1 1/2 teaspoons strained Chili Oil**
2 teaspoons sesame oil
2 teaspoons sugar
2 teaspoons wine vinegar

PREPARATION

Combine all of the ingredients and mix well.

YIELD 3/4 cup

NOTES

Timing If you wish to make this sauce several days in advance, do not chop or add the scallions until the day before.

Tips This sauce is an excellent accompaniment to boiled or fried wontons. It also makes a delicious dip for raw or lightly blanched vegetables.

TOMATO SAUCE

This basic tomato sauce, used in various recipes in this book, has a consistency between tomato sauce and paste. By adding the appropriate seasoning when needed, you can adapt it to many different cuisines.

*1 large can (35 ounces) tomatoes or
    3 pounds fresh, well-ripened tomatoes*

1 cup split, minced leeks (green part only)
1 tablespoon minced garlic

1 teaspoon sugar
1 teaspoon freshly ground black pepper

2 tablespoons sweet butter
1 tablespoon peanut oil

PREPARATION

Pass the tomatoes through a food mill or puree them in a food processor.

COOKING PROCEDURE

Sauté the leeks and garlic in the butter and oil for 5 minutes over medium-low heat.

Add the pureed tomatoes, sugar, and pepper; bring to a simmer, stirring well to combine all the seasonings.

Simmer over low heat for 1 hour, or until thick.

Pass the sauce through a food mill again or return it to the food processor and blend until the sauce is smooth. Allow to cool.

YIELD *approximately 2 cups*

NOTES

Tip Choose a brand of canned tomatoes without basil. If you use fresh tomatoes, buy them several days or even a week in advance so they can ripen properly. I have found that—except for a few months in the summer—a good quality of canned tomatoes produces a better sauce.

Storage Refrigerated in covered glass jars, the sauce will keep for one week. For long-term storage (up to six months), freeze the sauce in small containers.

FERMENTED WINE RICE

2 cups sweet rice

*1¹/2 teaspoons wine yeast, crushed to a fine
   powder*
1 teaspoon flour

SPECIAL EQUIPMENT
Cheesecloth

PREPARATION

Soak the rice in water to cover for 4 hours.
Drain.

COOKING PROCEDURE

Place the rice in a steamer over a piece of
cheesecloth that has been rinsed and
wrung out; steam for ¹/2 hour. Empty the
rice into a colander; peel off the cheesecloth. Rinse the rice in warm water for
about 1 minute. Drain it for a few seconds.
The rice should still be warm.

Sprinkle the wine yeast and the flour over
the rice and mix well with a pair of chopsticks. Place the rice in a casserole measuring 8 × 8 inches. Using your index finger,
make a well in the center of the rice right
through to the bottom of the casserole.
Cover the casserole with aluminum foil,
then wrap it in a terry-cloth towel. Place
the wrapped casserole in a warm place,
such as a linen closet, for 3 days, or until
the well has filled with liquid.

Place the rice and all the liquid from the
casserole in a covered glass jar.

YIELD *approximately 4 cups*

NOTES

Tips Wine yeast comes in the form of a
round ball, about the size of a mothball. It
can be stored for several months in a covered jar in the refrigerator.

You can crush wine yeast in an electric
coffee mill or with a rolling pin, placing it
between layers of waxed paper.

Once you have made a jar of wine rice, it
is necessary to open the jar once a week to
release any gas. When you make a new
batch, save about ¹/2 cup of the old and add
it to each quart of the fresh wine rice after
the new batch has fermented. This will
give it a stronger fermented taste.

Storage Refrigerated, the fermented wine
rice will keep at least four months.

FERMENTED RED WINE RICE

1/4 cup red rice

1 cup Fermented Wine Rice* (measured with the liquid)

PREPARATION

Place the red rice in a strainer and rinse it well. Drain.

COOKING PROCEDURE

Place the red rice and 1 1/2 cups water in a heavy saucepan with a tight-fitting cover. Bring it to a boil, uncovered, stirring with chopsticks in a figure-8 motion. Cover, turn the heat to very low, and simmer the rice for 1 1/2 hours, or until all the water has evaporated. Turn off the heat; let the rice relax in the covered saucepan for 20 minutes.

Remove the cover and stir with chopsticks. Mix in the Fermented Wine Rice.

Place the combined mixture in a food processor or blender, and blend for 2 or 3 seconds. Place the Fermented Red Wine Rice in a covered glass jar and refrigerate.

YIELD *1 1/2 cups*

NOTES

Tip Once you have made a jar of Fermented Red Wine Rice, it is necessary to open the jar once a week to release any gas.

Storage Refrigerated, it will keep for about four months.

Chapter 19

DESSERTS

The Chinese cuisine is not known for its desserts, as many of the great desserts of the world are dairy-based, and dairy products have always been scarce in China. Working within these limitations, the Chinese commonly use lard instead of butter, and imported evaporated milk instead of fresh milk. In the desserts in this book I have called for butter, which may seem odd to those who have read other Chinese recipes calling for lard, but it has been recorded that the Chinese used butter over four thousand years ago.

Cookies and cakes are eaten as snacks and never at the conclusion of a meal; however, curiously enough, when my group arrived in Peking around 9:00 P.M. (after traveling from New York to Chicago to Los Angeles to Japan), we were asked at the hotel if we would like a light or heavy meal. We responded, "Light." We were then served bread, butter, milk, coffee, and pound cake. Expect the unexpected.

PINEAPPLE BANANA SHERBET

4 cups (approximately) diced well-ripened
  fresh pineapple
1 well-ripened banana, diced
3 egg whites, at room temperature
1/2 cup sugar
3 tablespoons fresh lemon juice

PREPARATION

Put the pineapple and banana through a food mill or puree them in a food processor.

Beat the egg whites until soft peaks form; reserve.

Beat the sugar and the lemon juice into the pineapple-banana puree until the sugar dissolves (about 3 to 4 minutes). Add the reserved beaten egg whites and continue to beat for another 2 minutes.

Cover the bowl containing the sherbet with aluminum foil and place it in the freezer.

Freeze for 2 to 3 hours, or until the sherbet begins to set. The time will depend on the temperature of the freezer, which should ideally be at 0 degrees or below.

When the sherbet is partially set, beat it again for 2 to 3 minutes. If the sherbet has become too solid, let it soften at room temperature. Cover and freeze the sherbet for another hour, beat again, and serve in sherbet glasses or wine goblets.

YIELD *6 servings*

NOTES

Tip Perfectly ripened fruit that smells and tastes sweet is crucial to the success of this dessert.

Substitutions Pureed mangoes, peaches, strawberries, or raspberries (berries have to be passed through a food mill to remove the seeds) can be substituted for the pineapple.

ALMOND FLOAT

Almond Float is a light and refreshing dessert traditionally served in China between courses at a banquet to refresh the palate, the way the French would serve a sorbet. A banquet I attended in Changsha, Hunan, served three different sweetened soups, each followed by many more courses. This dessert is most commonly made with evaporated milk and water. I have specified fresh whole milk because I prefer the taste. Although it may seem unusual to include fresh berries in a Chinese recipe, I have done so here because they add color and because wild strawberries were eaten in ancient China.

1 1/2 cups milk, less 2 tablespoons
2 tablespoons sugar
1 envelope plain gelatin
2 tablespoons water
2 teaspoons almond extract
4 tablespoons almond liqueur
1 can (20 ounces) lichees
1 can (11 ounces) mandarin oranges
1 can (16 ounces) loquats
1 cup fresh berries or fruits in season (strawberries, raspberries, cherries, or blueberries)
1/2 cup white grape juice or white wine

PREPARATION AND COOKING PROCEDURE

Heat the milk and sugar in a saucepan over medium heat until the milk is very hot but not boiling, stirring occasionally with a wooden spoon or chopsticks. While the milk is heating, in a bowl dissolve the gelatin in the water. Add the gelatin to the milk; lower the heat, and stir the mixture until the gelatin is thoroughly dissolved (about 1 minute). Turn off the heat and add 1 teaspoon of the almond extract and 2 tablespoons of the almond liqueur. Stir the mixture to blend, then pour it into a buttered 8 × 8-inch Pyrex dish. Place the dish in the refrigerator until the Almond Float sets (2 to 3 hours).

In a large glass bowl place all the fruits with the canned juices, grape juice or wine, and the remaining 2 tablespoons almond liqueur and 1 teaspoon almond extract. Stir the mixture with chopsticks in a figure-8 motion. Refrigerate until ready to serve.

All of the above procedures can be done a day ahead.

PRESENTATION

Slant-cut the set Almond Float (solidified milk) into diamond shapes by first making straight vertical cuts slightly more than 1 inch apart, then making diagonal cuts, also about 1 inch apart. Slide them into the fruit mixture with a blunt knife or metal spatula. Serve immediately, or refrigerate for several hours until ready to serve.

YIELD *8 servings*

ALMOND MILK

1 1/4 cups raw blanched almonds
4 cups milk
1/2 cup sugar
1/4 cup water chestnut powder
4 tablespoons almond liqueur
2 cups fresh berries (such as strawberries,
*   raspberries, or blueberries)*

PREPARATION AND COOKING PROCEDURE

Preheat the oven to 325 degrees. Place the almonds in a shallow roasting pan and roast them for about 15 minutes, or until they turn light brown. Remove them from the oven and let them cool.

Put the roasted almonds in a food processor and, using the on and off technique, grind them finely. If you do not have a food processor, use a blender.

In a 2- to 3-quart saucepan, combine 3 1/2 cups of the milk with 1 cup of the ground almonds and the sugar. Bring the mixture to a simmer over medium-low heat, stirring occasionally with chopsticks in a figure-8 motion. Remove the pan from the heat; cover, and let the almonds steep for 1 hour.

Strain the mixture through a sieve set over a bowl, pressing down hard on the almonds with the back of a wooden spoon to extract their moisture before discarding them.

Return the almond-flavored liquid to the saucepan and bring it to a simmer over low heat.

Dissolve the water chestnut powder in the remaining 1/2 cup milk; stir it into the liquid. Stirring constantly, simmer the custard for about 2 to 3 minutes, or until it thickens.

Add 2 tablespoons of the almond liqueur and stir to blend.

Strain the custard through a sieve into a bowl. To prevent a skin forming, place a sheet of cellophane in direct contact with the custard. Refrigerate at least 6 hours or overnight.

Two hours or more before serving, wash and dry the berries. If using strawberries, hull them but leave them whole. Toss and marinate the berries in the remaining 2 tablespoons almond liqueur.

Before serving, remove the custard from the refrigerator and beat it well with a wire whisk. Pour the custard into a glass bowl; place the marinated berries in the center, and sprinkle with the remaining 1/4 cup ground almonds.

YIELD *6 servings*

STEAMED CHINESE FRUIT CAKE

Steamed Chinese Fruit Cake, also known as Sticky Cake because the glutinous rice flour gives the cake a sticky consistency, is traditionally served on New Year's Eve. Sticky Cake is made in honor of the God of the Kitchen, who reports to heaven on the family's behavior for the previous year. As the Chinese believe that a good report to heaven from the Kitchen God brings a New Year of fulfilled wishes, they traditionally leave him a cake sticky enough to keep him from talking too much as his mouth will be stuck shut.

1 tablespoon flour (approximately)
2 eggs, separated
1/4 cup sweet butter
1/2 cup sugar
1 1/4 cups glutinous rice flour
1/3 cup milk
1 cup Chinese dried fruits, pitted (if necessary) and diced, such as preserved seedless plums, preserved pears, or dates
1 piece crystallized ginger, diced (optional)
1/2 cup broken walnuts

PREPARATION

Fill with water to a depth of 4 inches an aluminum or enamel roasting pan with a dome-shaped cover. In the center of the pan, place a can from which the bottom and top have been removed; put a rack on top of the can.

Grease a small loaf pan (approximately 4 × 8 inches) with butter, then dust lightly with flour, tapping out the excess.

Beat the egg whites with an electric beater or wire whisk until they form stiff peaks. Do not wash the beater.

Cream the butter and sugar with the beater for about 2 to 3 minutes, or by hand until they are light and fluffy.

Add the egg yolks and beat for 1 more minute.

Add a third of the rice flour and mix with the electric beater at a low setting or with a wooden spoon. Mix in half the milk and continue to mix in the rice flour and milk alternately.

Stir in the dried fruits, crystallized ginger, and walnuts.

Fold in the egg whites.

Pour the whole mixture into the prepared loaf pan; place it on the rack in the steamer (roasting pan) and cover the pan.

COOKING PROCEDURE

Place the steamer over medium-high heat and steam for 1 hour. Remove the loaf pan from the steamer.

Cool the cake in the loaf pan, then remove it and slice it thin. Arrange the slices on a plate.

YIELD *8 servings*

NOTES

Timing Steamed Chinese Fruit Cake can be made several days in advance and served at any temperature.

Tip Leftover slices can be toasted and eaten for breakfast.

ALMOND COOKIES

The reason these Almond Cookies are superior to the classic ones found in Chinese bakeries is that I use almonds in the cookie dough, whereas the Chinese use almond extract only. I also use eggs instead of yellow food coloring and butter instead of lard.

2 cups plus 40 whole raw blanched almonds
1¹/2 cups flour, sifted
¹/8 teaspoon salt
¹/2 cup white sugar
¹/4 cup brown sugar
³/4 cup sweet butter, chilled
2 egg yolks, slightly beaten
2 tablespoons almond liqueur
1 teaspoon almond extract

PREPARATION

Preheat the oven to 325 degrees. Spread all the almonds in a single layer on a cookie sheet and roast them until they turn light brown, about 12 to 15 minutes. Let the almonds cool. Reserve 40 whole almonds for garnish. Pulverize the remaining almonds in a food processor or blender.

Sift the flour, salt, and sugars into a bowl.

Work in the butter with a pastry blender, or use a food processor fitted with a steel blade by placing the sifted flour, salt, and sugars in the container, turning the machine on, and adding the chilled butter quickly, a tablespoon at a time, until blended.

Mix in the pulverized almonds.

Add the beaten egg yolks, almond liqueur, and almond extract. Continue to blend with either the pastry blender or the food processor. If using a food processor, blend only a few more seconds, using the on and off technique.

Refrigerate the cookie dough for at least 6 hours or overnight.

COOKING PROCEDURE

Preheat the oven to 375 degrees. Break off tablespoon-sized pieces of dough and shape them into balls. Flatten each ball into a ¹/4-inch-thick round with the side of a cleaver that has been dipped in flour (to prevent the dough from sticking). Slide them off the cleaver with the aid of an icing spatula dipped in flour.

Place the cookies on greased cookie sheets, at least 1 inch apart.

Place an almond in the center of each cookie and press it down slightly, to secure it.

Bake the cookies for 7 minutes, then reduce the oven temperature to 325 degrees. Continue to bake for another 5 to 7 minutes, or until they become golden brown. Remove the cookies from the oven, then, using a spatula, place the cookies on racks to cool.

YIELD *40 cookies*

SESAME SEED COOKIES

¹/₂ cup hulled sesame seeds
¹/₄ cup white sugar
¹/₄ cup brown sugar
7 tablespoons sweet butter
1 tablespoon sesame oil
1 egg
1 cup flour, sifted

Sesame oil for greasing

TOPPING
¹/₄ cup hulled sesame seeds
¹/₃ cup white sugar

PREPARATION

Place the ³/₄ cup total of sesame seeds in a dry wok and stir them over low heat for a few minutes, or until they are light golden. Cool and reserve.

Cream the sugars, butter, and the 1 tablespoon sesame oil together with an electric mixer or in the bowl of a food processor fitted with a steel blade. Add the egg and continue to mix until well combined. If using a food processor, remove the mixture from the container. With as few strokes as possible, use a wooden spoon to stir the flour and ¹/₂ cup sesame seeds into the mixture.

Refrigerate the dough at least 6 hours or overnight.

To prepare the topping Place the ¹/₄ cup cooled sesame seeds in a food processor, coffee mill, or blender and grind to a fine powder. Add the sugar and process 1 or 2 more seconds.

COOKING PROCEDURE

Preheat the oven to 375 degrees. Grease cookie sheets with sesame oil.

Break off tablespoon-sized pieces of dough and shape them into balls. Flatten each ball into a ¹/₄-inch-thick round with the side of a cleaver that has been dipped in flour (to prevent the dough from sticking). Slide them off the cleaver with the aid of an icing spatula dipped in flour.

Sprinkle each cookie with some of the topping, then place the cookies on the cookie sheets, at least 1 inch apart.

Bake the cookies for 10 to 12 minutes, or until they become lightly browned. Remove the cookies from the oven. Using a spatula, place the cookies on racks to cool.

YIELD *36 cookies*

SESAME SLICES

¹/₄ cup hulled sesame seeds
¹/₃ cup sugar
1 cup evaporated milk
2 eggs
2 tablespoons sugar
²/₃ cup flour
1 teaspoon lemon peel (zest only)
Sesame oil for greasing
Water chestnut powder

4 cups peanut oil

PREPARATION AND COOKING PROCEDURE

Place the sesame seeds in a dry wok and stir them over low heat for a few minutes, or until they are light golden. Cool and crush them to a fine powder in a food processor fitted with a steel blade (or in a blender or electric coffee mill). Mix them with the ¹/₃ cup sugar; set aside.

Heat the evaporated milk in a saucepan over low heat; bring it to a simmer.

Place the eggs in a bowl and beat well; then beat in the 2 tablespoons sugar. Slowly add the hot milk to the eggs. Beat in the flour until the batter is smooth.

Pour the contents of the bowl into the saucepan and add the lemon zest. Cook in a water bath over low heat, stirring constantly with a wooden spoon until the mixture becomes a very stiff paste. Grease an 8-inch-square pan with sesame oil and spread out the batter evenly. Chill the batter in the refrigerator for 6 hours or overnight.

Either slice the batter into 1¹/₂-inch squares and dust on both sides generously with water chestnut powder, or roll the refrigerated batter into small balls (smaller than walnut size), dusting them generously with water chestnut powder.

Place the wok over high heat for about 1 minute. Pour in the peanut oil; turn the heat to medium until the oil reaches 375 degrees. Turn the heat to high. Deep-fry the slices or balls a few at a time for 3 to 4 minutes, or until they become crisp and golden brown. Using a wire strainer, remove the slices or balls from the wok and drain them well in a single layer on several sheets of paper towels.

Sprinkle half of the sesame-sugar mixture on a serving platter. Arrange the fried slices or balls on top and spinkle them with the remaining sesame-sugar mixture. Serve immediately.

YIELD *6 servings*

SNOWBALLS   (Chinese Doughnuts)

2 tablespoons sweet butter
1 cup boiling water
1 cup flour
4 eggs

½ cup granulated sugar

4 cups peanut oil

PREPARATION AND COOKING PROCEDURE

Place the butter in a saucepan over medium heat. Add the boiling water to the saucepan, and stir until the butter dissolves and the mixture comes to a boil. Turn the heat down to very low.

Put the flour into a sifter and sift it directly into the boiling water; stir well. Add 1 egg and mix well; when the mixture is blended, add the remaining 3 eggs, one at a time, mixing well after each addition. The dough should be very soft, moist, and sticky.

Place the wok over high heat for about 1 minute. Pour in the oil and turn the heat to medium until the oil reaches 325 degrees. Wet one hand and take up a lump of dough in that hand. Close your fist tightly so that a round ball of dough about the size of a golf ball is squeezed out between the thumb and index finger. Cut the ball off with a table-spoon and drop it into the hot fat. Repeat the procedure with the remaining dough, frying seven balls at a time in a 14-inch wok. Fry for about 10 minutes. The dough-nut should puff up to three times the size of the dough and should be hollow in the center. Using a wire strainer, remove the doughnuts from the wok. Drain well by placing them in a single layer on several sheets of paper towels. Repeat the proce-dure with the remaining seven doughnuts.

Place the sugar on a flat plate and roll each doughnut in the sugar. Sprinkle sugar on top of each. Serve the doughnuts hot or at room temperature.

YIELD *14 doughnuts*

CANDIED WALNUTS

¹/₂ pound shelled walnuts

6 tablespoons sugar

2 cups peanut oil

COOKING PROCEDURE

In a saucepan, bring 1 quart water to a rapid boil over high heat. Add the walnuts and boil over medium heat for 5 minutes. Turn off the heat. Drain the nuts and return them to the saucepan on the burner. Leave the heat off; add the sugar and mix well. To allow the sugar to melt, leave the saucepan covered for 1 minute.

Place the walnuts on a plate in a single layer and allow them to dry for 10 minutes.

Place a 12-inch wok over high heat for about 1 minute. Pour in the oil; turn the heat to medium until the oil reaches 350 degrees. Using a wire strainer, lower the walnuts into the oil and deep-fry them for about 2 minutes, or until the sugar coating has caramelized. In order to achieve an even brown color, stir the walnuts constantly while they are frying. Remove the walnuts with a wire strainer and place them in a single layer on a brown paper bag to drain. Allow them to cool before serving.

NOTES

Tip It is very important that the sugar has melted before the nuts are allowed to cool, otherwise they will not caramelize when fried.

Substitution For the walnuts, you can substitute pecans.

Storage Refrigerated and covered in a glass jar, they will last 1 month.

WATER CHESTNUT PUDDING

¹/₂ cup jujube (Chinese red dates)
¹/₄ cup sweet rice
¹/₂ cup walnuts
1 cup fresh water chestnuts, peeled
¹/₄ cup brown sugar
3 egg whites, at room temperature
Brown sugar for sprinkling

PREPARATION AND COOKING PROCEDURE

Rinse and then soak the jujube in 1 cup warm water for 6 hours. Drain them, reserve the liquid, and remove the pits. Place the pitted jujube and the water in which they were soaking in a saucepan and simmer for 20 minutes.

Rinse the sweet rice, cover with cold water, and soak for 4 hours. Drain. Bring 1 cup cold water to a boil in a saucepan. Add the sweet rice, bringing it to a rapid boil; stir with chopsticks, and cover. Turn the heat to low and steam the rice for 30 minutes. Turn off the heat and allow the rice to relax for 20 minutes. Remove the cover, stir, and set the rice aside.

Soak the walnuts in ¹/₂ cup cold water for 1 hour.

Mince the water chestnuts with two cleavers, or place the water chestnuts in a food processor fitted with a steel blade and, using the on and off technique, mince them. Remove the water chestnuts from the processor.

To the same container of the food processor (a blender may also be used), add the jujube and the water in which they were simmered, and the walnuts and the water in which they were soaked, along with the cooked rice and the ¹/₄ cup brown sugar. Using the on and off technique, process the mixture until it is well blended.

Return the minced water chestnuts to the blended mixture and process for a few more seconds.

Empty the contents of the container into a saucepan. Place the saucepan in a water bath over medium heat.

In a second large saucepan, bring 2 quarts of water to a simmer.

Place the egg whites in a bowl and beat them until stiff peaks form.

Transfer the egg whites to the simmering water and poach them gently for about 1 minute, or until the egg whites have set.

PRESENTATION

Divide the pudding between six sherbet glasses, place one sixth of the egg white mixture on top, sprinkle lightly with additional brown sugar, and serve immediately.

YIELD *6 servings*

NOTES

Timing The entire preparation and cooking procedure of the pudding can be done the day ahead, in which case the pudding must be refrigerated. When ready to serve, place the saucepan containing the pudding in a water bath and heat until warmed.

The egg whites must be beaten and poached immediately before serving.

Bibliography

The primary sources for the historical and regional information in this book were the following:

Lee, Calvin B. T., and Lee, Audrey Evans. *The Gourmet Chinese Regional Cookbook.* New York: G. P. Putnam's Sons, 1976.

Lo, Kenneth. *Chinese Regional Cooking.* New York: Pantheon Books, 1979.

Chang, K. C., ed. *Food in Chinese Culture.* New Haven: Yale University Press, 1977.

Lin, Hsiang-ju, and Lin, Tsuifeng. *Chinese Gastronomy.* New York: Hastings House, 1969; reprinted 1977 by Harcourt Brace Jovanovich (a Harvest/HBJ Book).

Other informative sources included:

Simonds, Nina. "Chinese Cuisine." *Gourmet,* 1979, 1980.

Chu, Grace Zia. *Madame Chu's Chinese Cooking School.* New York: Simon & Schuster, 1975.

Lin, Florence. *Florence Lin's Chinese Regional Cookbook.* New York: Hawthorn Books, 1975.

Claiborne, Craig, and Lee, Virginia. *The Chinese Cookbook.* Philadelphia and New York: J. B. Lippincott Company, 1972.

Chang, Wonona W. and Irving B.; Kutscher, Helene W. and Austin H. *An Encyclopedia of Chinese Food and Cooking.* New York: Crown Publishers, 1970.

Schrecker, Ellen, with Schrecker, John. *Mrs. Chiang's Szechwan Cookbook.* New York: Harper and Row, Publishers, 1976.

Mail Order Sources

The Chinese Kitchen
P.O. Box 218
Stirling, N.J. 07980
(201) 464-2859

(Best results with this company. Free catalog upon request. No shipping charge anywhere in the U.S.A. All ingredients called for in this book are available.)

Star Market
3349 North Clark Street
Chicago, Ill. 60657
(312) 472-0599

Shing Chong & Company
800 Grand Avenue
San Francisco, Calif. 94108
(415) 982-0949

Index

Abalone, 74
  and chicken soup, 138
  with duck (Gold and Silver Threads),
    242–43
Almond
  Cookies, 351
  Float, 348
  Milk, 349
Amaranth, 59
Anise, star, 74
Appetizers and dim sum
  Curried Chicken Filling, 111
  Diced Spicy Chicken in Lettuce Leaves,
    92
  dumplings, fried (Jao-Tze), 102–4
  Fish Fillets, Smoked, 120
  Fish Rolls, Crispy, 118
  Ham and Fish Slices, 119
  Icicle Radish Balls, 96
  Pearl Balls, 97
  Peking Rolls, 126–27
  Phoenix and Dragon Legs, 114–15
  Pork Buns, Baked Roast, 106–7
  Pork Buns, Steamed Roast, 108–10
  Sesame Seed Beef, 131–32
  Shrimp, Deep-Fried Butterfly, 121–22
  Shrimp and Minced Meat Filling, 112
  Shrimp Balls in Rice Paper, 98–99
  Shrimp Cutlets, 123
  Shrimp in Laver Rolls, Minced, 124
  Shrimp Roll, Tricolor, 116–17
  Shrimp Stuffed Mushrooms, 113

  Snow Crab Claws, Stuffed, 105
  Steamed Dumplings in Wonton Skin
    (Shao Mai), 100–1
  Stuffed Shrimp in Bean Curd Sheets,125
  Turtle Chicken, Tangy, 95
  Vegetable Package, 93
  Vegetable Rolls with Sesame Seed
    Sauce, 128–30
  Walnut Chicken, Deep-Fried, 94
Asparagus, for bean curd with oyster
    sauce, 293

Bamboo shoots, 74
Bamboo steamer, wet-steaming in, 46
Banana and pineapple sherbet, 347
Banana peppers, 66
Banquets, 31–32
Barbecue(d)
  Duck, Whole, 234–36
  Duck Portions, 233
  Eggplant, 301
  Roast Pork, 258–59
  sauce, for charred shrimp, 180
  Tilefish, 157
Bass
  Crispy Hunan Style, 155
  Fillet of, with Wine Sauce, 159
  Sea, Sweet and Pungent, 156–57
  Steamed, with Fermented Black Beans,
    149
  See also Fish

Bean(s)
  fava, 61
    stir-fried, 297
  long, 64
  See also Black beans
Bean curd, 75–76
  Deep-Fried, with Oyster Sauce, 293
  Fermented, Stir-Fried Watercress with,
    311
  Ma Po Tou Fu, 296
  Sautéed, with Shrimp Sauce, 294
  sheets, for stuffed shrimp, 125
  Spiced Pressed, 292
  Steamed, 291
  Szechwan, Vegetarian's, 295
Bean sauce, fermented, 76
Bean sprouts
  for Gold and Silver Threads, 242–43
  for Mo Shu Ro, 260
  mung, 59
Beef
  with Baby Ginger, 277
  Chow Fun, 329
  Curried, Noodles, 326–27
  Dry Sautéed Shredded, 283
  Five Star Spicy, 280–81
  Lotus, 282
  Orange, 284–85
  in Oyster Sauce, 278–79
  sesame seed, 131–32
  Sizzling, with Scallops, 286–87
Beggar's Chicken, 228–29
Beijing cooking. *See* Peking cooking
Beverages, 32
Black beans, 75
  braised, with chicken, 206–7
  fermented, for steamed sea bass, 149
  fermented, for steamed spareribs, 270
  shredded pork with, 263
Black bean sauce
  for clams, 173
  for soft-shell crabs, 166
Black rice vinegar, 87
Blanching, 49
Blue crabs, fried, 162
Bok choy, 59
  for Mo Shu Ro, 260
  for Steamed Dumplings in Wonton
    Skin, 100–1
Boning chicken, 193–97

Braising, 48
Broad bean paste, Peking, 77
Broccoli, Chinese, 60
Broth, Stuffed Clams in, 139
Buns
  Baked Roast Pork, 106–7
  Steamed Roast Pork, 108–10
Butter, Sesame Seed, 340
Butterfly Shrimp, Deep-Fried, 121

Cabbage
  celery, 84
  pickled, Szechwan pork soup with, 141
  Shantung, 60
  Sweet and Sour, Szechwan, 297
Cake, Fruit, Steamed Chinese, 350
Candied Walnuts, 355
Cantonese cooking, 14–16, 28, 98, 100,
    105, 106, 108, 111, 112, 114, 119,
    121, 149, 165, 166, 167, 169, 170,
    171, 172, 173, 176, 178, 184, 187,
    202, 203, 204, 207, 234, 240, 242,
    244, 250, 251, 258–59, 278, 282,
    286, 291, 293, 294, 297, 298, 304,
    305, 306, 307, 322, 323, 326, 329,
    330
Carp, Steamed, with Purple Basil, 152–53
Celery cabbage, 84
Chicken
  and abalone soup, 138
  Beggar's, 228–29
  boning, 193–97
  Braised, with Black Beans, 206–7
  Chengdu Style, 208
  Chinaman's Hat, 210–11
  Chunked, Hunan Style, 209
  Chun-Pi, 212
    cutting and reassembling, 200–2
  Diced Spicy, in Lettuce Leaves, 92
  dicing, 198–99
  with Fermented Red Wine Rice, 219
  filling, curried, 111
  Five Flavors, 203
    fried, with scallion sauce, 204
    gingered, braised, 205
  Moon over Mulberry Tree, 226–27
  Orange, 216–17
  for Peking Rolls, 126–28
  for Phoenix and Dragon Legs, 114–15

Chicken (*continued*)
    Pon Pon, 218
    Shredded, with Garlic Sauce, 214
    slicing and shredding, 198–99
    Slippery, 221
    Slivered, and Pork, 220
    Smoked, Shredded, 223
    Soy-Braised, 207
    Stir-Fried, with Walnuts, 222
    Szechwan Diced, 213
    Tangy Turtle, 95
    Three Thoughts, 224–25
    Velvet, 215
    Velvet Soup with Shrimp Balls, 137
    Walnut, Deep-Fried, 94
    Wings with Oyster Sauce, 202
Chili Crabs, 163
Chili Oil, 337
Chili paste, 78, 336–37
Chili peppers, 66
    cured pork belly with, 271
    dried, 77
    sliced pork with, 267
    See also Pepper(s)
Chinaman's Hat, 210–11
Chinese Fruit Cake, Steamed, 350
Chi-tzu, 77
Chives, 60
Chopping block, 56
Chow Fun, 82
    Beef, 329
Chun-Pi chicken, 212
Clams
    in Black Bean Sauce, 173
    stuffed, in broth, 139
Cloud ears, 87
Communal dining, 25
Cookies
    Almond, 351
    Sesame Seed, 352
Cooking
    Eastern regional, 16–18
    Northern regional, 11–14
    Southern regional, 14–16
    Western regional, 18–21
Cornstarch, 87
Crab
    blue, fried, 162
    chili, 163
    and shrimp, Szechwan style, 164

snow, stuffed claws, 105
soft-shell, with black bean sauce, 166
soft-shell, with ginger sauce, 165
Crab meat sauce, for spinach, 167
Crispy Fish Rolls, 118
Crispy Spareribs in Sweet Soybean Sauce, 269
Cucumber, sweetened white, 77
Curried Beef Noodles, 326–27
Curried Chicken Filling, 111
Curried Rice Vermicelli, 330–31
Curry sauce or paste, 77
Custard, Steamed Egg, 320

Dates
    Chinese (jujube), 77
    without stone, 77
Deep-fat frying, 42–43
    vs. passing through, 44
Defatting, 49
Deglazing, 48
Dessert
    Almond Cookies, 351
    Almond Float, 348
    Almond Milk, 349
    Fruit Cake, Steamed Chinese, 350
    Pineapple Banana Sherbet, 347
    Sesame Seed Cookies, 352
    Sesame Slices, 353
    Snowballs (Chinese Doughnuts), 354
    Walnuts, Candied, 355
    Water Chestnut Pudding, 356
Diced Spicy Chicken in Lettuce Leaves, 92
Diet, people's, 31
Dim sum, basics, 91
    See also Appetizers and dim sum
Dining
    communal, 25
        hotel, 26–27
        restaurant, 27–28
    from street vendors, 25
        waterborne, 25–26
    in workmen's restaurants, 26
Dipping sauce
    for Chinaman's Hat, 210
    spicy, 335
Doilies, Peking, 321
Double-cooked pork, 262

Doubling recipes, and passing through, 42
Dough
  for Baked Roast Pork Buns, 106
  for fried dumplings (Jao-Tze), 102
  for Steamed Roast Pork Buns, 108
Doughnuts, Chinese (Snowballs), 354
Duck
  with abalone (Gold and Silver Threads), 242–43
  barbecued portions, 233
  barbecued whole, 234–36
  crispy, Szechwan, 238–39
  Orange Spiced, 244–45
  Pressed, Crisp Boneless, 240–41
  removing fat from, 234–35
  Roast, Lo Mein, 323–25
  roasting whole, 47–48
  Sliced Roast, with Scallions, 246–47
  Sliced, with Spring Ginger, 237
  Tea Smoked, 248–49
Duck potatoes, 60
  sautéed, 298
Duck sauce, 335
  Peking, 272
Dumplings
  fried (Jao-Tze), 102–4
    in Wonton Skin, Steamed (Shao Mai), 100–1

Eastern regional cooking, 16–18
Egg(s)
  Chinese Omelet I, 316–17
  Chinese Omelet II, 318
  Chinese Omelet III, 319
  Custard, Steamed, 320
  Pancake, 315; for Peking Rolls, 126
Egg noodles, 81–82
Eggplant, 60–61
  Barbecued, 301
  Deep-Fried, Stuffed, 302–3
  in Garlic Sauce, 300
  Spicy Braised, 299
Equipment, 53–54
  and maintenance, 54–56

Fava beans, 61
  stir-fried, 297

Fermented Red Wine Rice, 343
Fermented Wine Rice, 342
Filling
  for Baked Roast Pork Buns, 106
  for Chinese Omelet I, 316
  for Chinese Omelet II, 318
  for Chinese Omelet III, 319
  for Crispy Fish Rolls, 118
  Curried Chicken, 111
  for Deep-Fried Stuffed Eggplant, 302
  for fried dumplings (Jao-Tze), 102–4
  for Minced Shrimp in Laver Rolls, 124
  for Peking Rolls, 126
  Shrimp and Minced Meat, 112
  for Shrimp Balls in Rice Paper, 98
  for Steamed Dumplings in Wonton Skin (Shao Mai), 100
  for Steamed Roast Pork Buns, 108
  for Stuffed Clams in Broth, 139
  for Vegetable Rolls with Sesame Seed Sauce, 128
Fish
  Carp, Steamed, with Purple Basil, 152–53
  Fillet of Bass with Wine Sauce, 159
  Flatfish, Fukienese, 158
  Pinecone, 160
  Rolls, Crispy, 118
  Slices, with Ham, 119
  Smoked, 161
  Smoked Fillets, 120
  Snapper, Steamed Whole, with Fermented Wine Rice, 154
  Szechwan Steamed Whole, 150–51
  Tilefish, Barbecued, 157
  See also Bass
Five Flavors Chicken, 203
Five-spice powder, 78, 338
Five Star Spicy Beef, 280–81
Flatfish, Fukienese, 158
Flour
  light measurement, 50
  rice, 84
Four-Style Mushrooms, 305
Fried Milk, 322
Fruit Cake, Steamed Chinese, 350
Frying, deep-fat, 42–44
Fukien cooking, 21–22, 118, 125, 139, 158, 219, 226, 268, 343

Fujian cooking. *See* Fukien cooking
Fukienese Flatfish, 158

Garlic sauce
    eggplant in, 300
    for lobster, 168
    for scallops, 174
        for shredded chicken, 214
        for shredded pork, 266
    See also Sauce; Seasoning sauce
Ginger
    baby, beef with, 277
    crystallized, 78
    root, 61–62
    sauce for soft-shell crabs, 165
    See also Spring ginger
Gingered Chicken, Braised, 205
Glutinous rice, 84–85
Gold and Silver Threads, 242–43
Golden needles, 79
Green sauce, for Tangy Turtle Chicken,
    95

Hairy melon, 67–68
Ham
    and Fish Slices, 119
    Smithfield, 78
Hoisin sauce, 76
Hotel dining, 26–27
Hot and Spicy Scallops, 175
Hot sauce, 78, 336–37
Hunan cooking, 18, 19, 21, 26, 27, 92,
    93, 96, 97, 140, 143, 152–53, 155,
    175, 182, 209, 220, 263, 271, 308,
    310
Hunan Home-Style Soup, 140
Husks, rice, 84

Icicle radish (Chinese turnip), 64
    balls, 96
Italian (banana) peppers, 66

Jao-Tze (fried dumplings), 102–4
Japanese rice vinegar, 87
Jicama, 69
Jujube, 77

Kohlrabi, 84
Kung Pao Shrimp, 181

Lake Tungting Shrimp, 182
Lard, leaf, 78
Laver Rolls, Minced Shrimp in, 124
Laver sheets, dried, 78
Leeks, 64
    for Dry Sautéed Shredded Beef, 283
    for Lotus Beef, 282
        for Sautéed Duck Potatoes, 298
    for Stir-Fried Lobster, 172
Lemon Squab, 251
Lettuce Leaves, Diced Spicy Chicken in,
    92
Lichee, 78
Lily buds, tiger, 79
Liquor, rice, 84
Lobster
    Cantonese, 170
    Cantonese, Steamed, 171
    in Garlic Sauce, 168
        Sautéed with Soybean Paste, 169
    for Snow-White Cloud Soup, 143
        Stir-Fried with Shredded Leeks, 172
    for Taro Seafood Nest, 189
Lo Mein, Roast Duck, 323–25
Longan, 78
Long beans, 64
Loquat, 78
Lotus, 79–80
Lotus Beef, 282

Ma Po Tou Fu, 296
Master sauce, for spiced pressed bean
    curd, 292
Meal planning, 32–35
Meat
    minced, and shrimp filling, 112
    roasting large pieces, 46–47
Melon, hairy, 67–68
Menus, 34–35
Milk
    Almond, 349
    Fried, 322
Minced Chicken and Abalone Soup, 138
Minced Meat and Shrimp Filling, 112
Miso, 77

Mixing, 50
Moon over Mulberry Tree, 226–27
Mo Shu Ro, 260–61
Mung bean sprouts, 59
Mushrooms, 80–81
  braised, 307
  braised, for stir-fried vegetables, 306
  dried, 80–81
  Four-Style, 305
  Shrimp Stuffed, 113
Mustard Greens, 64
  Stir-Fried Young, 304
Mustard Sauce, Chinese, 338

Noodle(s)
  Beef Chow Fun, 329
  Cold, with Spicy Sesame Sauce, 327
  Curried Beef, 326–27
  Curried Rice Vermicelli, 330–31
  Egg, 81–82
  Roast Duck Lo Mein, 323–25
  Shanghai, Deep-Fried, 328
  Soup, Pork Chop, 142
  Szechwan Rice Stick, 332
Northern regional cooking, 11–14
Nuts, 82

Oil, 82–83
  chili, 337
Orange Beef, 284–85
Orange Chicken, 216–17
Orange peel, dried, 83
Orange Spiced Duck, 244–45
Oyster sauce, 83
  beef in, 278–79
  for chicken wings, 202
  for deep-fried bean curd, 293

Pancake
  egg, 315
  egg, for Peking Rolls, 126
  Peking Doilies, 321
Parsley, Chinese, 64
Passing through, 41–42
  vs. deep-fat frying, 44
Pearl Balls, 97
Peas, 65

Peking (Beijing) cooking, 11–14, 94, 102,
    116, 123, 126–27, 137, 138, 156,
    159, 180, 205, 206, 210, 215, 222,
    246, 260, 264, 269, 272, 321
Peking Doilies, 321
Peking Rolls, 126–27
Peking sauce, for pork, 261
People's diet, 31
Peppercorn, 83
Peppercorn Powder, Szechwan, 339
Pepper(s), 66
  banana, 66
  Spicy Charcoal, 308
  See also Chili peppers
Phoenix and Dragon Legs, 114–15
Pineapple Banana Sherbet, 347
Pinecone Fish, 160
Piquant Sauce, Shrimp with, 177
Plum sauce, 83
Pon Pon Chicken, 218
Poor Man's Peking Duck, 272–73
Pork
  Barbecued Roast, 258–59
  Belly, Cured, with Chili Peppers, 271
  Buns, Baked Roast, 106–7
  Buns, Steamed Roast, 108–10
  and chicken, slivered, 220
  Chop Noodle Soup, 142
  Chops, Fukienese Fried, 268
  Double-Cooked, 262
  for fried dumplings, 102–3
  Icicle Radish Balls, 96
  for Moon over Mulberry Tree, 226
  Mo Shu Ro, 260–61
  Pearl Balls, 97
  in Peking Sauce, 261
  Poor Man's Peking Duck, 272–73
  preparing CT butt for barbecuing,
    256–57
  recommended cut, 255
  Red-Cooked Shoulder of, 264–65
  Shredded, with Black Beans, 263
  Shredded, with Garlic Sauce, 266
  Shredded, with Preserved Hot Turnip,
    265
  Sliced, with Chili Peppers, 267
  Spareribs, Crispy, in Sweet Soybean
    Sauce, 269
  Spareribs, Steamed, with Fermented
    Black Beans, 270

Pork (*continued*)
  for Steamed Dumplings in Wonton
    Skin, 100–1
  Szechwan, and Pickled Cabbage Soup,
    141
  tenderloin, stir-fried scallops with,
    176–77
Potatoes
  duck, 60
  for Taro Nest, 190
Poultry
  fat, rendered, 83–84
  roasting whole, 46–47
  stock, 135–36
  See also Chicken; Duck
Powder
  Five-Spice, 78, 338
  rice, 84
  Szechwan Peppercorn, 339
Prawns, Stuffed, 178–79
Preserved hot turnip, 84
  shredded pork with, 265
Preserved vegetable, 84
Pressed Duck, Crisp Boneless, 240–41
Pudding, Water Chestnut, 356

Red-Cooked Shoulder of Pork, 264–65
Red-cook simmering, 48
Red rice, 85
Reducing, 49
Red vinegar, 87
Red wine rice, fermented, with chicken,
  219
Red wine vinegar, 87
Restaurant dining, 27–28
Rewarming, 40–41
Rice, 84–85
  fermented red wine, with chicken, 219
  Patties, 145
  Pearl Balls, 97
  Soup, Sizzling, 144
  White, Boiled, 320
Rice flour, 84
Rice noodles, 82
  for Taro Nest, 190
Rice Patties, 145
Rice powder, 84
Rice Stick Noodles, Szechwan, 332
Rice sticks, 82

Rice vermicelli, 82
  curried, 330–31
Rice vinegar
  black, 87
  Japanese, 87
Roasting, 46–48

Sauce
  barbecue, for charred shrimp, 180
  black bean, for clams, 173
  black bean, for soft-shell crabs, 166
  crab meat, for spinach, 167
  curry, 77
  dipping, for Chinaman's Hat, 210
  Dipping, Spicy, 335
  Duck, 335
  for Five Star Spicy Beef, 280
  ginger, for soft-shell crabs, 165
  green, for Tangy Turtle Chicken, 95
  hoisin, 76
  hot, 78, 336–37
  for Lake Tungting Shrimp, 182
  master, for spiced pressed bean curd,
    292
  mustard, Chinese, 338
  Peking, for pork, 261
  Peking Duck, 272
  piquant, for shrimp, 177
  plum, 83
  red wine rice, fermented, 343
  scallion, for fried chicken, 204
  sesame, spicy, 340
  sesame seed, for vegetable rolls, 128–
    30
  shrimp, for bean curd, sautéed, 294
  for Shrimp Stuffed Mushrooms, 113
  and stir-frying, 40
  sweet and pungent, for sea bass, 156
  sweet and sour, for pinecone fish, 160
  sweet soybean, for crispy spareribs, 269
  tomato, 341
  wine, for fillet of bass, 159
  wine rice, fermented, 342
  See also Garlic sauce; Oyster sauce;
    Seasoning sauce
Sautéing, 46
Scallions, 66
  Sliced Roast Duck with, 246–47
Scallion sauce, for fried chicken, 204

Scallops
  in Garlic Sauce, 174
  Hot and Spicy, 175
  Sizzling Beef with, 286–87
  Stir-Fried, with Pork Tenderloin, 176–
    77
  for Taro Seafood Nest, 189
Sea bass. *See* Bass
Seafood. *See* Fish; Shellfish
Seasonal Stir-Fried Vegetables, 309
Seasoning sauce, 50
  See also Garlic sauce; Oyster sauce;
    Sauce; individual recipes
Sesame oil, 83
Sesame sauce, spicy, 340
  for cold noodles, 327
Sesame seed
  beef, 131–32
  butter, 340
  cookies, 352
  sauce, for vegetable rolls, 128–30
Sesame Slices, 353
Shallots, 66–67
Shao Mai (Steamed Dumplings in
    Wonton Skin), 100–1
Shellfish
  abalone and chicken soup, 138
  Clams in Black Bean Sauce, 173
  Stuffed Clams in Broth, 139
  Taro Seafood Nest, 189
  See also Crab; Lobster; Scallops;
    Shrimp
Sherbet, Pineapple Banana, 347
Sherry, 85
Shredded Vegetables Hunan Style, 310
Shrimp
  balls, for Chicken Velvet Soup, 137
  Balls in Rice Paper, 98–99
  Butterfly, Deep-Fried, 121–22
  butterflying, 179
  Charred, in Barbecue Sauce, 180
  and Crab Meat Szechwan-style, 164
  cutlets, 123
  dried, 85
  for fried dumplings, 102–3
  for Icicle Radish Balls, 96
  Kung Pao, 181
  Lake Tungting, 182–83
  Minced, in Laver Rolls, 124
  and Minced Meat Filling, 112

mushrooms stuffed with, 113
  for Phoenix and Dragon Legs, 114–15
  with Piquant Sauce, 177
  Prawns, Stuffed, 178
  Roll, Tricolor, 116–17
  Salt and Peppery, 184
  for sautéed bean curd, 294
  with Snow Peas, 185
  spicy, with pork flavor, 188
  splitting, 183
  steamed, 187
  for Steamed Dumplings in Wonton
    Skin, 100–1
  Stuffed, in Bean Curd Sheets, 125
  for Taro Seafood Nest, 189
  with Two Flavors, 186–87
Shrimp paste
  for stuffed mushrooms, 113
  for tricolor roll, 116
Sichuan cooking. *See* Szechwan cooking
Sing qua, 68
Sizzling Rice Soup, 144
Slippery Chicken, 221
Smoked duck, tea, 248–49
Smoked fish, 161
Smoked Fish Fillets, 120
Smoked shredded chicken, 223
Snapper, steamed whole, with fermented
    wine rice, 154
Snowballs (Chinese Doughnuts), 354
Snow Crab Claws, Stuffed, 105
Snow peas, 65
  for Beef Chow Fun, 329
  for Curried Beef Noodles, 326
  for Dry Sautéed Shredded Beef, 283
  for Four-Style Mushrooms, 305
  Shrimp with, 185
  for Sizzling Beef with Scallops, 286
Snow-White Cloud Soup, 143
Soft-Shell Crabs with Black Bean Sauce,
    166
Soft-Shell Crabs with Ginger Sauce, 165
Soup
  Chicken Velvet with Shrimp Balls, 137
  Hunan Home-Style, 140
  Minced Chicken and Abalone, 138
  Pork Chop Noodle, 142
  Sizzling Rice, 144
  Snow-White Cloud, 143
  Stuffed Clams in Broth, 139

Soup *(continued)*
  Szechwan Pork and Pickled Cabbage,
    141
Southern regional cooking, 14–16
Soybean paste
  fermented, 77
  for lobster, 169
  sweet, 76
Soybean sauce, sweet, for crispy
    spareribs, 269
Soy-braised chicken, 207
Soy sauce, 85
Spareribs
  steamed, with fermented black beans,
    270
  in sweet soybean sauce, 269
Spicy Charcoal Peppers, 308
Spinach
  with Crab Meat Sauce, 167
    for Moon over Mulberry Tree, 226
Sponge melon, 68
Spring ginger, 62–63
  pickled, 303
  for sliced duck, 237
  See also Ginger
Squab
  in Casserole, 250
  Lemon, 251
Squash, 67–68
Staples, 73–74
Star anise, 74
Starch, tapioca, 87
Steamed Dumplings in Wonton Skin
    (Shao Mai), 100–1
Sticky rice, 84–85
Stir-frying, 39–40
Stirring, 50
Stock
  adding, and stir-frying, 40
  emergency, 50
  poultry, 135–36
Straw mushrooms, 81
Street vendors, 25
Stuffed Clams in Broth, 139
Stuffing
  for Beggar's Chicken, 228
  for lemon squab, 251
  for shrimp in bean curd sheets, 125
  for snow crab claws, 105
Sugar snap peas, 65

Sweet and pungent sea bass, 156–57
Sweet and Sour Cabbage, Szechwan, 297
Sweet red peppers, 66
Sweet rice, 84–85
Szechwan cooking, 18–21, 95, 128–30,
    131–32, 141, 142, 150, 154, 161,
    163, 164, 168, 174, 177, 181, 186,
    188, 208, 212, 213, 214, 218, 221,
    223, 224–25, 237, 238–39, 248,
    262, 266, 267, 270, 280, 283, 284,
    295, 296, 297, 298, 299, 302, 327,
    332, 336, 337, 339, 340
Szechwan Crispy Duck, 238–39
Szechwan Pork and Pickled Cabbage
    Soup, 141
Szechwan Steamed Whole Fish, 150
Szechwan Sweet and Sour Cabbage, 297

Tangy Turtle Chicken, 95
Tapioca starch, 87
Taro, 68
  Nest, 190
  Seafood Nest, 189
Tea, 85–86
Tea Smoked Duck, 248–49
Thickening agents, 86–87
Three Thoughts Chicken, 224–25
Tiger lily buds, 79
Tilefish, barbecued, 157
Tomato Sauce, 341
Tree ears, 87
Tricolor Shrimp Roll, 116
Turkey roaster, dome-shaped, wet-
    steaming in, 45–46
Turnip, Chinese (icicle radish), 64, 96
Turnip, preserved hot, 84
  shredded pork with, 265
Twice-frying, 43

Vegetable(s)
  description and cutting technique for,
    59–70
  package, 93
  preserved, 84
    Rolls with Sesame Seed Sauce, 128–30
  Seasonal, Stir-Fried, 309
  Shredded, Hunan Style, 310
  Stir-Fried, with Braised Mushrooms, 306

Velvet chicken, 215
Vermicelli, curried rice, 330–31
Vinegar, 87

Walnut(s)
    Candied, 355
    Chicken, Deep-Fried, 94
        chicken with, stir-fried, 222
Waterborne dining, 25–26
Water chestnut(s), 69
    for beef with scallops, 286
    for fried dumplings, 102–4
    pudding, 356
Water chestnut powder, 86
Watercress
    for fried dumplings, 102–3
    for shrimp with two flavors, 186

Stir-Fried, with Fermented Bean Curd,
    311
Western regional cooking, 18–21
Wet-steaming, 44–46
Wine rice, fermented, 342
    red, 343
    steamed whole snapper with, 154
Wine sauce, for fillet of bass, 159
Wine yeast, 87
Winter melon, 68
Wok, maintenance, 55
Wonton skin, steamed dumplings in,
    100–1
Wood ears, 87
Workmen's restaurants, dining in, 26

Yu choy, 60

KAREN LEE, author of *Chinese Cooking for the American Kitchen,* has taught Chinese cooking in New York City since 1972, where she also supervises a highly successful catering business. Her cooking school has been recommended by the New York *Times, Bon Appétit, Cuisine, Better Homes & Gardens, Town & Country, House & Garden* and *Travel & Leisure*. She has made numerous appearances on radio and television throughout the country, and has lectured for retailers, cooking schools, and charitable organizations. She is currently a food consultant to a major corporation. New York *Times* food critic Patricia Wells says, "Karen Lee's food is as extraordinary as her classes . . . She sacrifices nothing to taste, while paying close attention to nutrition and economy."

Once apprenticed to the renowned Mme. Grace Chu, Karen Lee went on to develop her own remarkable style. Influenced by French cooking methods such as the reducing, deglazing, and defatting of sauces, she incorporated these techniques into Chinese cooking, thereby combining the most healthful and sophisticated methods of the world's two master cuisines.

Many of the recipes in this book were built upon concepts discovered during a recent trip to the People's Republic of China with the Newspaper Food Editors and Writers Association, and have never before been published. Karen Lee lives in New York City with her son, Todd.

ALAXANDRA BRANYON, author of three Off-Broadway plays, is the playwright/lyricist half of Branyon/Kitchings, a song-writing team which has written numerous pop songs and two musical comedies, the latter of which received an award from the American Society of Composers, Authors and Publishers.

KEN KORSH is an internationally recognized photographer who maintains a studio in New York City. His clients include *Ladies' Home Journal, Redbook, Kodak,* and *Burger King*.